# HITLER'S V-WEAPONS

## THE BATTLE AGAINST THE V1 AND V2 IN WWII

# V HITLER'S
# V-WEAPONS

## THE BATTLE AGAINST THE V1 AND V2 IN WWII

### AN OFFICIAL HISTORY

COMPILED BY
**JOHN GREHAN**

Frontline Books

## HITLER'S V-WEAPONS
## The Battle Against the V1 and V2 in WWII

This edition published in 2020 by Frontline Books,
an imprint of Pen & Sword Books Ltd,
47 Church Street, Barnsley, S. Yorkshire, S70 2AS.

This book is based on file reference AIR 41/72, from a series of records from the
Air Ministry, which is held at The National Archives, Kew, and is licensed under
the Open Government Licence v3.0. Appendix xviii is based on file reference
AIR 16/577, which is also which is held at The National Archives, Kew.

Preface Copyright © John Grehan
Text alterations and additions © Frontline Books

The right of John Grehan to be identified as the author of the preface has been
asserted by him in accordance with the Copyright, Designs and Patents Act 1988.

ISBN: 978-1-52677-005-9

Pen & Sword Books Ltd incorporates the imprints of Air World Books, Pen &
Sword Archaeology, Atlas, Aviation, Battleground, Discovery, Family History,
History, Maritime, Military, Naval, Politics, Social History, Transport, True Crime,
Claymore Press, Frontline Books, Praetorian Press, Seaforth Publishing and
White Owl.

For a complete list of Pen & Sword titles please contact:

PEN & SWORD BOOKS LTD
47 Church Street, Barnsley, South Yorkshire, S70 2AS, UK.
E-mail: enquiries@pen-and-sword.co.uk
Website: www.pen-and-sword.co.uk

Or

PEN AND SWORD BOOKS,
1950 Lawrence Road, Havertown, PA 19083, USA
E-mail: Uspen-and-sword@casematepublishers.com
Website: www.penandswordbooks.com

Printed and bound by TJ International Ltd, Padstow, Cornwall

# Contents

### Part VII
### Rocket and Flying Bomb Attacks on the United Kingdom,
### 25 November 1944 – 29 March 1945

### APPENDICES

# Preface

The UK, and London in particular, had endured and survived the Blitz. The threat of invasion had long since passed and despite the so-called 'Baby Blitz' mounted by the Luftwaffe throughout the early months of 1944, Londoners had shown that, in Winston Churchill's memorable words, they could 'take it'. But then, on the night of 12/13 June 1944, death came from the skies in a new and terrifying form.

That night, local farmer Edwin Woods of the Royal Observer Corps, was on duty at his post, designated Mike 3, high on the Kent Downs at Lyminge. Just after 04.00 hours he received a message from Maidstone ROC Centre telling him there was something happening near Boulogne. Mr Wood, through his binoculars, saw a 'fighter on fire' but it was just outside his sector. He gave a reading to Maidstone and handed over to his colleagues at Observer post Mike 2 at Dymchurch. Mike 2, located at the top of a Martello tower on the seafront, was manned by Mr E.E. Woodland and Mr A.M. Wraight. At 04.08 hours they spotted the approach of an object spurting red flames from its rear end and making a noise like 'a Model-T-Ford going up a hill.' What they saw was the first Fieseler Fi 103 flying bomb – the first of Hitler's vengeance weapons, the *Vergeltungswaffe 1*.

The men and women of the Royal Observer Corps had been anticipating this moment for months and the two spotters on top of the tower knew exactly what they had to do: The men followed the strange object in the sky with their binoculars. When it had approached to within five miles of Mike 2, Mr Woodland seized the telephone and passed the warning to Maidstone ROC Centre. 'Mike 2, Diver, Diver, Diver – on four, north-west one-o-one.'[1]

The atmosphere in the underground bunker at Air Defence of Great Britain (ADGB) HQ at Bentley Priory was relaxed that early summer's morning. Suddenly one of the WAAF tellers sat up as if given an electric shock. She hesitated for a second, as though disbelieving what she had heard in her headphones. Then she called 'Diver, Diver' and the whole Operations Room was galvanised into a frenzy of activity: 'A dozen hands reached for telephones, the main table plotters suddenly forgot their fatigue and the controller watched in amazement as an extraordinary track progressed at great speed across the table towards London.'[2]

The missile continued over the North Downs before it fell to earth with a loud explosion at Swanscombe, near Gravesend, at 04.18 hours. Before there had been time to take stock of the situation, another 'Diver' track had appeared, turned westward, and exploded just north of Cuckfield in Sussex. Two more quickly followed, with one dropping in Bethnal Green and the other close to Sevenoaks in Kent. It was the Bethnal Green bomb which caused the first V1 casualties in the UK.

It was not until three days later that the British public was officially told about the new weapons, following two further nights of attacks, when Herbert Morrison, the Home Secretary revealed all to the House of Commons on 16 June: 'It has been known for some time that the enemy was making preparations for the use of pilotless aircraft against this country, and he has now started to use this much-vaunted new weapon. A small number of these missiles were used in the raids of Tuesday morning, and their fall was scattered over a wide area; a larger number was used last night and this morning. On the first occasion, they caused a few casualties, but the attack was light, and the damage, on the whole, was inconsiderable. Last night's attack was more serious, and I have not as yet full particulars of the casualties and damage, nor of the numbers 2302 of pilotless aircraft destroyed before they could explode. The enemy's preparations have not, of course, passed unnoticed, and counter-measures have already been, and will continue to be, applied with full vigour. It is, however, probable that the attacks will continue and that, subject to experience, the usual siren warning will be given for such attacks.'[3] Mr Morrison was, of course entirely correct. The attacks were certainly to continue.

The V1 flying bombs initially proved difficult for the fighters and anti-aircraft guns of the Air Defence of Great Britain to counter, but with a move of the gun belt away from the London area to the south coast and improved tactics by the RAF, a large proportion of the V1 were destroyed long before they could reach the capital. Eventually, with the heavy bombing of the launch sites and then the advances of the Allied ground forces across northern France, the V1 menace was all but eliminated. Indeed, at a Press conference on 8 September 1944 Duncan Sandys, chairman of what was called the Flying Bomb Counter-

Measures Committee, gave an account of the defeat of Hitler's terror weapon. 'Except possibly for a few last shots,' the Member of Parliament for Norwood, declared triumphantly, 'the Battle of London is over.'

It was at 18.43 hours that very same day, that Londoners, so familiar with the sound of detonating bombs and mines, heard an explosion unlike any they had experienced previously. It was a sound described as 'like a clap of thunder'. People were puzzled. There had been no air raid siren and no enemy aircraft seen in the sky, and neither had there been heard the instantly recognisable spluttering of a V1, and anyway, Duncan Sandys had said that the danger to London had passed. The *Daily Express* echoed the bewilderment of its readers: 'What happened on 8 September?' The paper asked. 'It was early evening when the whole of London was startled by two terrific explosions. In Staveley Road, Chiswick, the men were taking an evening stroll to the local. Someone was practising scales on the piano in the front room. The women were gossiping at the garden gates. Some others were listening to the radio ... "We heard no sound before the explosion rocked the ground", said the bewildered people in the district. "There was absolutely no warning like the whistle of a bomb or the chug of a flying bomb engine. We did not see anything either." ... A yawning crater 15 feet deep and 30 feet wide opened where a man had been about to cross the road ... Eight houses on either side were completely wrecked and many more were severely damaged.'

The Government, anxious to prevent alarm and panic among Londoners and the explosions and others that followed were put down to being 'exploding gas-mains'. There were soon so many 'flying' gas-mains that it became a joke among Londoners whenever they heard a bang. Of course, the explosions were the detonations of V2 rockets, which flew at such speeds and altitudes that interception by guns or aircraft was impossible. The British public were only officially notified of this by the Prime Minister on 10 November. Fortunately, the war was reaching its conclusion and little more than 1,400 V2s were launched against the UK, almost all of which were directed at London.

This official history of the fight against Hitler's Vengeance Weapons produced by the Air Ministry's Air Historical Branch, deals with the UK's response to the V1 and V2 campaigns, and how knowledge of the German's long-range weapons programme was gradually accumulated before the first V1s struck that night in June 1944. It's factual and detailed approach enables the reader to experience the problems faced by the RAF's Air Chief Marshal Sir Roderic Hill, General Sir Frederick Pile the General Officer Commanding Anti-Aircraft Command and,

interestingly, Air Vice-Marshal William Gell of Balloon Command, in
dealing with this unprecedented challenge.

Their efforts were, by their nature, defensive, and with the V
Weapons being so difficult to counter in the air the best form of defence
against them was attack, and much space is given in the book to the
'Crossbow' operations undertaken by Bomber Command supported by
the USAAF Eighth Air Force. Crossbow – the attack upon the V
Weapons production, storage and launch facilities – was considered so
important that on 18 June 1944 it was given precedence over any other
air force operations.

With a large number of supplementary appendices to add to its
informative text, which includes highly detailed plans for the
evacuation of London by the government and measures to deal with
those people rendered homeless by the flying bombs as well as listing
the location of every V2 strike in the country, this official history is the
most comprehensive record of the UK's successful measures in
combating an aerial threat, the like of which had never been
encountered before.

*John Grehan*
*Storrington, June 2019*

[1] Bob Ogley, *Doodlebugs and Rockets* (Froglets Publications, Brasted Chart, 1992), p.28.
[2] Derek Wood, *Attack Warning Red, The Royal Observer Corps and the Defence of Britain 1925 to 1992* (Carmichael & Sweet, Portsmouth, 1992), p.7.
[3] Historic Hansard, House of Common Debates, 16 June 1944 vol 400 cc2301-3.

# Publisher's Note

This 'official history' is reproduced in the form that it was originally written. Aside from correcting obvious spelling mistakes or typographical errors, we have strived to keep the edits and alterations to the absolute minimum.

# Part I

# Spring 1943 – August 1943

**1. Introduction.**

*a. The Decline of the German Air Force.*

The decline in the fortunes of Germany which set in during the last months of 1942 was nowhere more clearly displayed than in the air. In the three years prior to the war the German Air Force had been perhaps the most important single military factor in Europe. Instructed and uninstructed were alike impressed by its potential striking power which to no small extent explained the success of German policy. Nor did war deflate its reputation. The first two years demonstrated that the force was well trained and well equipped. It was certainly checked in the August and September of 1940; but during the following winter and spring the night attack of Britain continued; and in the Mediterranean the same efficiency as had marked the earlier campaigns in Poland, Scandinavia and Western Europe was displayed in the Balkans and Crete.

However, this turn on the part of Germany first to the south-east and then to Russia eased the pressure of the air offensive against the United Kingdom. Thenceforwards, the German Air Force was at worst a nuisance, and chiefly a mere threat. Moreover, from the end of 1942 the offensive strength of the force so far declined or was so much needed for other tasks that a repetition of attacks on the scale of 1940/1 became practically impossible. Thus, throughout the period preparatory to the Allied invasion of France it was unlikely that the economy of this country and the forces assembling here would be subjected to a scale of attack so heavy that it might jeopardise the plans that had been laid.

*b. The Role of Long-Range Weapons.*

But by means of flying bombs and rockets the bombardment of London was made possible at a time when more orthodox methods were almost

1

out of the question. This does not mean that the Germans had this object clearly in mind throughout the phase in which the weapons were developed. It is certainly untrue for the A.4 rocket; for experiments directly linked with this weapon were taking place in Germany before war broke out. It may be true in the case of the flying bomb, the development of which does not appear to have begun until the first half of 1942.[1] However, intensive development of both weapons dates from the middle of 1942 when the Germans may well have realised that they were committed to the Russian campaign for much longer than they had visualised and that, in consequence, heavy bomber attacks on the United Kingdom, in reply to those which were beginning to be made on Germany, were problematical.

## 2. Early Intelligence.

The first serious evidence to fall into British hands that the Germans were developing rockets for military purposes came as early as November 1939 in the form of information which became known in this country as the "Oslo" Report. Later events proved this to be an especially reliable document on prospective German weapons some of which were in the very early stages of development. For example, the Hs.293 glider bomb, which the report mentioned, did not come into use until the summer of 1943.[2]

It was not until the end of 1942 that fresh information was received. Then, on 18th December 1942, a hitherto untested source of intelligence sent in the first of three reports which together indicated that on the last day of November 1942 and the first two in December trials of a long-range rocket had been carried out near Swinemünde on the Baltic coast. At least four more reports were received in the first quarter of 1943 linking similar trials more precisely with Peenemünde. This place was known to be important as a research centre and three photographic reconnaissances had been flown over it between May 1942 and March 1943. The whole story was given added credibility through the unwitting indiscretions of two high ranking German prisoners.

What was the size and performance of the rocket that was being tested was doubtful. Most reports indicated that it had a range of some one hundred and thirty kilometres; a war head containing five tons of explosive had also been mentioned. The latter was thought at first to be an exaggeration. According to Dr. A.D. Crow, Director of Projectile Development of the Ministry of Supply, the weight of the warhead was more likely to be about one ton.[3]

But by April 1943 there appeared to Military Intelligence at the War Office to be sufficient evidence to justify informing the Vice-Chief of the

Imperial General Staff,[4] Lieutenant General A.E. Nye, who after consultation with Professor C.D. Ellis, the Scientific Adviser to the Army Council, and Dr. Crow, brought the matter before the other Vice-Chiefs of Staff on 12th April 1943. This would have been a serious step to take on any matter where only preliminary and imprecise intelligence was available. It was especially grave when the threat that was apprehended had such extensive implications both for the defence of the country and for the security of the projected invasion. For in effect it asked that special notice should be taken of the threat, commensurate with the dangers that might rise from it.

**3. The Sandys Investigation.**
It is not surprising, therefore, that the main result of the meeting of the Vice-Chiefs was that a special investigation was set in train. Its direction, however, was put in the hands, not of a serving officer, but of a member of the government, Mr. Duncan Sandys, Joint Parliamentary Secretary to the Ministry of Supply. His appointment dated from 19th April 1943.[5] To begin with, he was required to answer a number of specific questions: whether a rocket of the dimensions and performance indicated by V.C.I.G.S. was technically possible; what stage of development the Germans had reached; what counter-measures were possible and how they could be improved.[6] He was instructed to report back to the Chiefs of Staff; and it was with the authority of the latter that he could call upon scientists in other departments besides his own, for advice and help. It soon became clear, however, that the process of obtaining conclusive answers to the various questions that Mr. Sandys had been asked was likely to take a long time. Consequently, the various individuals and branches of departments which Mr. Sandys relied upon for assistance were embraced during May and June 1943 in an extraordinary organisation which overrode the usual divisions of responsibility, the whole being under the direction of Mr. Sandys. This organisation lasted until November 1943. Through its various parts practically all the work of investigation during this period was carried out.

**4. The Problem of Identifying the Rocket.**
That work was chiefly of two sorts: first, the establishing of the character of the threat; second, the planning of counter-measures. Ideally, of course, the second task was best attempted when the first had been settled. But this was never possible during these first six months of investigation, and the two activities had perforce to go on concurrently.

*a. The Nature of the Evidence: Estimations of the Size and Effect of the Weapon.*

As was to be expected, the most difficult problem facing the investigators was to discover exactly what sort of weapon the Germans were developing. Their approach took a dual form: first, to collect, collate and analyse all the relevant intelligence that was obtained from our sources in Germany and elsewhere and from photographic reconnaissances; second, to reconstruct the sort of weapon which the Germans might well have developed in the existing state of scientific knowledge and technical skill.

The first of these tasks was principally in the sphere of existing agencies of intelligence. Mr. Sandys could and did, request photographic reconnaissances and the special interrogation of prisoners of war. He also arranged that all intelligence information should be transmitted to him and to the scientists and technicians whom he consulted, although some of them were Intelligence officers. He thus overlapped the service branches in this type of work. But the collection of intelligence was entirely the work of those sources and contacts which supplied us with information from Europe; and the role of photographic reconnaissance was chiefly to follow up lines of investigation which came first from agents on the ground.

For four months, from April to July 1943, nothing came from this sort of source which made it possible to establish beyond doubt what size of weapon the Germans were developing. A general picture emerged, however, the main features of which were that a rocket was certainly being developed and that Peenemünde was undoubtedly the main experimental station and possibly also a centre of production. A photographic reconnaissance on 22nd April 1943 gave the information necessary for a comprehensive report tracing the structural developments that had taken place at Peenemünde during the previous year. It told us nothing about long range weapons, but at least it showed that a great deal of heavy construction had already taken place and that more was in progress. We were to discover during the next few weeks that large numbers of foreign workers were employed there, most of whom had been recruited in Belgium and Luxembourg.[7] Two more reconnaissances on 12th and 23rd June supplied photographs showing two large objects which appeared to be rockets, some forty feet long and seven feet wide. One of them surprisingly called attention to itself by its light colour; but both were sufficiently unobtrusive as only to be recognised on photographs of excellent quality. Photographic reconnaissance also confirmed reports of heavy constructions in Northern France. As early as July 1943 suspicious and large excavations were detected at Watton, near Calais, at Wizernes and at Bruneval. But there was nothing to connect them for certain with what was taking place at Peenemünde. In sum – and apart from the fact that Peenemünde was important – the evidence that had accumulated by the beginning of August would bear no positive conclusions about the rocket, save that it was being developed. Certainly, there was nothing definite about the size and performance of the weapon. Looking back, it is now possible to select accurate details from the reports that were coming in; but usually these were associated with other details that were clearly false; nor was there any single report sufficiently accurate and comprehensive to furnish intelligence with a clear line to follow up.

During the same four months the approach of Mr. Sandys' scientific advisers also yielded no results. Early in the investigation it was calculated that the very approximate characteristics of the rocket might include a length of twenty feet, a diameter of ten feet, and a total weight of seventy tons with a warhead of up to ten tons. This implied a much more destructive projectile than that postulated in the initial report of the V.C.I.G.S.; but quite apart from the scientific factors involved the estimate was in fact more in line with such vague information as had been obtained up to that time from agents. Nor was it much amended when the rockets photographed at Peenemünde were examined; for these were reckoned to be nearly forty feet long, seven feet wide, sixty to one hundred tons in weight and containing two to eight tons of explosive. The main difficulty in estimating the weight of the warhead and the performance of the weapon was that almost nothing was known of the propellant that the Germans had developed. It was suspected that they had evolved an entirely new fuel; and the calculations mentioned above were based on the assumption of a propellant with twice the calorific content of cordite. Yet it was known that no variant of cordite could possibly have been produced to give such results. The probability was, therefore, that some form of liquid fuel had been developed; and one of Mr. Sandys' committees sat under Sir Frank Smith to investigate the possibilities.

If the Germans had indeed succeeded in producing a rocket of these dimensions the implications were truly terrible. Early in June the Ministry of Home Security estimated that a rocket containing ten tons of explosive might cause complete or partial demolition over an area of radius of 850 feet and might kill six hundred people. Two months later Mr. Herbert Morrison informed the Prime Minister that if one such rocket fell in the London area every hour for thirty days the cumulative casualties might be 108,000 killed and as many seriously injured. The figures made no allowance for overlap of craters not for the large-scale evacuation, official and unofficial, that would take place. But even if they were discounted by as much as a half or even three quarters the results might well be such that it would be impossible to maintain London as a centre of government and an area of production.[8]

*b. Criticisms by Lord Cherwell.*
And as the implications were so grave, yet nothing positive was known about the weapon which might bring about this disastrous situation, it is not surprising that a determined effort was made between June and September 1943, chiefly by Lord Cherwell, to shake the foundations of the case in favour of the rocket. Lord Cherwell's arguments were partly scientific. He fastened on what was a weak point in the case as presented up to that date, namely that the Peenemünde rockets were clearly single stage, which meant, according to the best-informed opinion in this country, that its maximum range would only be forty miles. He also pointed out that most of the agents' reports mentioned that the rockets would be steered by radio. This seemed to him practically impossible as the projectile would be rotating so rapidly. There was also the point that the only conceivable fuel for so large a body was one that was unknown to scientists in this country.

But his arguments were partly based on the grounds of common sense. He could not believe that the Germans would develop a weapon of sixty tons or more that would require huge launching installations which would be impossible to conceal and would therefore be heavily attacked. Then the firing trials of such a missile would surely be accompanied by terrific flashes of light; yet there had been no such reports from the Baltic area. [9] Finally, his suspicions that the whole story was a hoax were heightened by what appeared to be remarkable negligence on the German's part: that they had failed to camouflage the rocket-like objects that had been photographed at Peenemünde. If the Germans were attempting a hoax, he thought it probable that they hoped thereby to conceal some other project, possibly, he suggested, the development of pilotless aircraft.

Events were to show, of course, that there was no hoax. The rocket was certainly being developed; and those who believed this were not convinced by Lord Cherwell's arguments. In fairness to him, however, it should not be forgotten that some of his objections were quite valid, not for the rocket that the Germans actually developed and used, but for the hypothetical rocket of far greater dimensions with which Mr. Sandys and his advisers were, so to speak, threatening the country at this time.

## 5. The Beginning of Counter-Measures.

It was in this atmosphere of belief in the rocket as a threat, yet without any certain knowledge of the nature of the rocket or the organisation of supply and production that must undoubtedly have been behind it, that the first counter-measures were planned and carried out. As far as civil defence and radar were concerned, the work of planning and establishing what would be required went on chiefly through two committees, one presided over by Sir Findlater Stewart of the Home Defence Committee and the other, the Interdepartmental Radio Committee, by Sir Robert Watson-Watt. P.R.U. activities were also a vital part of counter-measures; and some indication has been given of the work that was done in photographing Peenemünde and Watten. But a beginning was also made in formulating a policy of counter-bombing.

*a. Selection of Targets for Attack.*

It had been obvious from the moment that the investigation began that the only means lying readily to hand by which the German preparations might be interfered with was the bombing of all relevant targets. So much was clear: but with the exception of Peenemünde itself next to nothing was known in the spring and summer of 1943 of any other experimental stations, centres of production, or launching sites. The Ministry of Economic Warfare thought that certain extensions to the I.G. Farben factories at Leuna, Ludwigshafen, and Oppau might be connected with the fuel of the rocket: Friedrichshafen was also suspected of being a centre for the manufacture of electrical components. These factories were down for attack as part of the main bomber offensive against German industry (Operation "Pointblank"). Watten and the other new constructions in northern France were also thought to be possible targets. Otherwise little was known of the best places to attack.

The question of an attack on Peenemünde was first seriously considered towards the end of June, when it was decided to despatch a strong Bomber Command force as soon as there were sufficient hours of darkness, which would not be until early August. A directive to this effect, in which the Leuna and Ludwigshafen factories were also specified for attack, was issued to Bomber Command early in July. General Eaker, who was commanding the 8th U.S.A.A.F. at this time, was also consulted; and he agreed to supplement, if necessary, Bomber Command attacks on these targets by attacks in daylight carried out as soon as possible afterwards. Also, early in July the preparation of the special charts required for the "Oboe" technique of radio-aided bombing was put in hand against the possibility that attacks would be called for against launching sites in northern France. This was entirely a preliminary measure. So little was known of the purpose of the suspicious works in that region or of the details of their construction that no decision to attack them was made until early August. In any case, it seemed likely that the best method of attack would be to employ Lancasters using "Oboe" and dropping 12,000 lb. or 20,000 lb. earth displacement ("Tallboy") bombs, neither of which was expected to be available before September at the earliest. Meanwhile, Flying Fortresses of the 8th Air Force, attacking in daylight and dropping 2,000 lb. demolition bombs, would be the most suitable aircraft; and it was this type that was actually used for the first attacks against Watten.

*b. Attacks on Suspected Production Centres, Watten and Peenemünde, June-August 1943.*
Friedrichshafen, Ludwigshafen and Oppau were all attacked during this period. Little damage was thought to have been caused to the suspicious extensions at the I.G. Farben factories; but reports filtered through in August that the attack on Friedrichshafen, which had been carried out by sixty Lancasters on the night of 20th June, had affected the production of radio and electrical components of the rocket. The Askania electrical plant in Berlin, which may have been engaged on the same sort of work, was also heavily damaged in an attack on the city in July.

Watten was not attacked until 27th August when 185 Fortresses dropped 326 tons of bombs. Nineteen direct hits were observed. A further attack was made by 58 Fortresses on 7th September but the weather was poor and only five direct hits were obtained. Nevertheless, work on the site was practically suspended for over two months; and not until December did the Germans once more make big efforts to complete it. In the interval Watten was not further attacked.

The heaviest blow at the German preparations was rightly reserved for Peenemünde. The night of 17th August was the first one that was suitable and 597 aircraft were despatched by Bomber Command. 1,937 tons of bombs were dropped and forty aircraft were lost. Photographic reconnaissance after the attack and such information as came out of Germany showed that very heavy damage was caused, especially in one of the two works areas, in the camps for workers and technicians and to the railway system. Numerous technical and administrative officers were believed to have been killed. Two large production sheds and a number of suspected firing points were undamaged; but as otherwise the damage was so heavy and as the sheds presented a difficult target it was decided not to repeat the attack until more was

8

known of what the Germans would continue to do there. As to this it is known that the place remained in use, though it is unlikely that it functioned with the same efficiency; and there is good reason to believe that the considerable dispersal of research and development which subsequently occurred was at least partly due to the bombing. In any case the attack was well conceived if only from the psychological point of view in that it represented the first direct attack on the enemy's preparations after four months of indecisive analysis and conjecture.

## Part II

# September 1943 – December 1943

### 6. Introduction.

To begin with, it was the long-range rocket which almost entirely exercised all those connected with Mr. Sandys' investigation. Originally their attention had been directed specifically to the rocket; and as there was indeed evidence of its development it had remained to their minds the prime threat to the country. But during the summer of 1943 reports were received which indicated another type of weapon. Its precise form was not known. As early as June there was a report of an "air mine with wings, long distance steering and a rocket drive" which would be launched against London by catapult. Other reports received during July and early August also suggested the use of pilotless aircraft; while one of late July stated that there were two long range weapons under development, a rocket and something akin to the Queen Bee (the radio-controlled light aircraft that had been developed by the Royal Air Force). Not until the end of August, however, were reports received of such circumstance and authority as to make it fairly clear that some form of pilotless aircraft was just as real and immediate a threat as the rocket. Up to that time the study of this sort of weapon and even of glider bombs and jet-propelled aircraft, although these were clearly within the sphere of the Air Ministry and the Ministry of Aircraft Production, had also come into Mr. Sandys' orbit. But on 6th September he pointed out to the C.A.S. that his responsibilities were becoming so wide that some rationalisation was necessary; and at his request the Air Ministry formally took over responsibility for investigating German jet propulsion, in which pilotless aircraft were included. Thus, within a short time of our first knowledge of the new weapon the Air Ministry were responsible for obtaining further information about it and devising counter-measures against it; though all the intelligence data on flying bombs continued to be examined by Mr. Sandys and his staff, as well as by the Intelligence staffs at the Air Ministry and War Office, for some months to come. Any differentiation on the basis of the two sorts of weapon would in fact have been impossible, so confused, and confusing, were the reports.

**7. Early Intelligence of the Flying Bombs.**

A report dated 12th August 1943 from a particularly reliable source and one unusually well placed to learn of new weapons developed by the German Army reinforced all that had been suspected of the rocket and at the same time corroborated the reports that had been received of pilotless aircraft. The source mentioned two weapons: a rocket officially called "A.4", and a pilotless aircraft, "PH17". He claimed to know very little about the latter as it was not being developed by the Army, and the designation he gave it turned out later to be false. Moreover, he misled us by attributing to the rocket the launching procedure of the flying bomb. Even so, coming from him the report was of great value, the more so as it reached London shortly before another report which embodied a hurried sketch made of a pilotless aircraft which had landed on the Danish island of Bornholm in the Baltic. From this it appeared that the aircraft contained an explosive charge, probably of the order of 1,000 lbs., and that it had some form of rocket propulsion. Much about the weapon remained conjectural, notably the form of propulsion and the method of steering; but by the end of September 1943 it was fairly certain that a flying bomb[10] was being developed and had reached an advanced stage. There were strong indications that the German Air Force were responsible for it, probably in rivalry with the German Army and the A.4 rocket.

**8. Confusion between the Rocket and the Flying Bomb: Further Attempts to Establish the Nature of the Rocket.**

As between the two weapons, however, there was still some confusion; and insofar as within a few weeks more certain information had been obtained about the flying bomb than of the rocket over a much longer period there was still a tendency to disbelieve the latter. The position was not made any clearer by a detailed report received in late September of information obtained in July and August. It purported to refer exclusively to the long range rocket; mentioned Peenemünde and the neighbouring village at Zempin where an experimental unit, led by a Colonel Wachtel, was carrying out firing trials; and said that this unit would form the basis of a unit known as 'Flak Regiment 155W' which was expected to move to northern France in late October or early November. Regimental headquarters would be at Amiens and it would operate 108 "catapults" sited in a belt Amiens – Abbeville – Dunkirk.

The report thus forecast with considerable accuracy the organisation that was eventually to launch flying bombs; but the connection that was erroneously traced between Colonel Wachtel and the rocket was not finally cleared up until the end of November.

In the meantime, a determined effort was made through an examination of such concrete evidence as there was, related to the scientific and technical problems involved, to establish the nature of the rocket. During the late summer of 1943 a British fuel expert – Mr. I. Lubbock of the Asiatic Petroleum Company – had visited the United States and examined a liquid fuel which was being produced there and which was suitable for rocket propulsion. The main constituents were aniline and nitric acid. Using a fuel of this sort it was possible to build a single-stage rocket, such as those which had been photographed at Peenemünde, with sufficient range to attack the United Kingdom from north-west Europe. The dimensions of such a weapon which were advanced as a possibility by a committee of eminent British scientists included a warhead of 5 to 15 tons if the maximum range was 130 miles, and of 1 to 5 tons if it was 200 miles. If extra thrust was given to the fuel (and a 15% increase was possible judging from laboratory tests in the United States) a warhead of ten to twenty tons at the shorter range and of five to twelve tons at the longer might be achieved. The overall weight of the projectile would be over fifty tons. As to its accuracy, the scientists reported that half the rounds fired might fall within a circle of about five miles radius round the mean point of impact at a range of 150 miles. The estimates, it should be noted, were the work of eleven men whose claim to eminence in this particular field of science was uncontested in this country. There was one dissenter – Dr. A.D. Crow of the Ministry of Supply. Unfortunately, there was little reliable evidence from the usual intelligence sources with which the hypothetical estimate could be compared. One detailed report had arrived late in August from the source who had first brought the terms 'A.4' and "PH17" to our notice. According to him, the Peenemünde rocket was 16 metres long and 4.5 wide (this was obviously an error). He did not know its weight but the explosive charge was equivalent in effect to a British four-ton bomb. Its range was about two hundred kilometres and it reached an altitude of some 35,000 metres. This indicated a less destructive weapon than that visualised by the scientists; but in the circumstances confirmatory reports were needed.

The contradiction between the two sorts of estimate had not been resolved when, towards the end of October, Mr. Sandys reported the possibility of an attack at an earlier date than had been estimated previously. During September and October evidence of production had been accumulating and there was some reason to believe that up to five hundred rockets had been manufactured. In Consequence, Mr. Sandys advised the Chiefs of Staff on 24th October that there was a possibility of an attack on London with the equivalent of some 2,500 to 10,000 tons of bombs during any single week in November or December; while by the early months of 1944, by which time the rocket might be in full production, heavier and sustained attacks might be possible.

On the evidence that was available at the time this was undoubtedly the worst case form the British point of view. Not surprisingly it caused no little concern. A special meeting of the Defence Committee was held on the following day: The Prime Minister presided, and Field Marshal Smuts was present. In many respects the meeting traversed the same ground as the last conference on rockets held by the Prime Minister in June. There were still three sorts of opinion. There were those who disbelieved in the rocket, or at any rate in a rocket of the specifications suggested by the scientific committees, those who held by the latter, and those who said that intelligence pointed unmistakably to a rocket but that its nature was not yet clear. Field Marshal Smuts, bringing a fresh mind to the subject, thought that something was certainly being developed; while the Prime Minister himself was so far convinced that he decided to make a statement in a secret session of the House of Commons. It was also decided that some of the scientists previously consulted should examine with Lord Cherwell the scientific factors available. On the operational side, attacks were to be made on the suspicious constructions in northern France and on factories believed to be involved in rocket production. Photographic reconnaissance of northern France was to be given priority.

The results of a series of meetings of scientists held during the last week in October were summarised in a report compiled by Sir Stafford Cripps. As far as the hypothetical rocket of some sixty tons was concerned, the conclusion was that it was theoretically possible and capable of construction. As for the objects photographed at Peenemünde there were certain objections to accepting them as rockets. For one thing they were fitted with fins which would add greatly to the difficulty of firing them if, as had been assumed so far, some form of mortar was necessary. Furthermore, the objects had hemispherical heads which would seriously reduce their range; though they might be simply practice warheads. On the other hand, the Germans appeared to be making some kind of preparations for attack from northern France; and, therefore, they had confidence either in a weapon already developed or in their ability to overcome any practical difficulties that might arise. Consequently, the rocket could not be discounted.

## 9. Transfer of Full Responsibility to the Air Ministry.

This was judicious enough; and on the available evidence little more could have been said. But it was not satisfactory from the point of view of those who were responsible for operations. Already in October the Chiefs of Staff had instructed their Joint Intelligence Sub-Committee to examine all relevant intelligence; which made a second authority – the other being Mr. Sandys – examining the same body of evidence and reporting to the Chiefs of Staff. On this account Mr. Sandys himself suggested to the Chiefs of Staff that the machinery of investigation should be rationalised, either by the Joint Intelligence Sub-Committee being placed under him for this particular question or by himself dropping out of the investigation all together. As the Chiefs of Staff were by this time anxious to pursue intensive operational counter-measures they preferred the second course; and on 11th November they recommended to the Prime Minister that all Mr. Sandys' responsibilities should be transferred to the Air Ministry in the person of the Deputy Chief of Air Staff. Nominally the Air Ministry had been responsible for the study of flying bombs since early September; but as the two types of weapon were part of our intelligence problem Mr. Sandys had continued to play an important part in respect of each. Moreover, by the middle of November, although the rocket was still unsubstantial enough for its very existence to be doubted by some exceptionally experienced and capable officers, the flying bomb and the organisation behind it was being identified rapidly and a programme of counter-measures against it was taking shape. It was, therefore, proper that a service department should be responsible for counter-measures and for further investigation. And as there was a close connection between the two sorts of weapon, especially in intelligence work, so it was best to make the same authority responsible for both. The transfer of responsibilities from Mr. Sandys to the Deputy Chief of Air Staff, Air Marshal Bottomley, was effected by 18th November.

## 10. The Emergence of the Flying Bomb and the Identification of Launching Sites.

To understand how it was that the flying bomb, having, so to speak, started later than the rocket had yet overhauled and passed it, it is necessary to take up the intelligence story in early October of 1943. At that date Colonel Wachtel's projected organisation in northern France had not been connected with flying bombs. But reports were coming in of numerous unexplained emplacements in the Pas de Calais and Cherbourg areas. Some of these referred to what became known eventually as "large sites", of which Watten and Wizernes had been the first to come under suspicion; and large sites at Siracourt and Marquise-Mimoyecques in the Pas de Calais and at Martinvast in the Cherbourg penuinsula, in addition to Watten and Wizernes, were all under observation by the end of October 1943. But there were still others about whose purpose little was known. Agents were being briefed as thoroughly as available information would permit; but their task was complicated by the enormous amount of defence construction being carried out in northern France. Not until 28th October was a really useful report obtained. It referred to work going on at Bois Carré, ten miles north-east of Abbeville, and described a rough plan made by a workman showing "a concrete platform with a centre axis pointing directly to London". Photographs were obtained from a reconnaissance flown on 3rd November. They showed a concrete platform some thirty feet long and twelve feet wide with its axis aligned on London, two rectangular buildings and one square one, and three buildings shaped like skis. From this last characteristic the term "ski site" arose. There were no defences at Bois Carré and nothing to connect the site either with rockets or flying bombs. Nevertheless, previous photographs were scrutinised and further reconnaissances flown; and in less than a fortnight twenty-nine ski sites had been identified, while agents' reports gave the approximate location of seventy to eighty more. The great majority were disposed in a band of country between Dieppe and Calais. They bore no discernible relation to the coastline or to any orthodox scheme of defence but they were all between 130 and 140 miles from London. There was also a group of a maximum of ten sites within two miles of the north coast of the Cherbourg peninsula. What was obviously required at this juncture was a firm link between this large programme of construction and what was happening at Peenemünde. One was not long in being established. Typically, enough it came only after many months of careful work in Germany. Early in 1943 it had been appreciated that if the Germans were developing long range projectiles, they would want to track them in flight beyond visual range, for which radar would be necessary. For the skill and experience required they would almost certainly call upon the 14th Company of the Air Experimental Signals Regiment, which specialised in radar. The regiment was well known to Air Intelligence for the part it had played in developing and operating radio beams during the night attack of this country; and a watch had been maintained on its later activities. Until October, however, all that could be discovered was that the 14th Company was deployed round the shores of the Baltic on the Islands of Rügen and Bornholm and as far east as Stolpmünde. Then one of our sources succeeded in transmitting a detailed report from which it was clear that the company was plotting flying bombs launched from Peenemünde and also from Zempin, a few miles along the coast from Peenemünde.

During October a small aircraft with a wing span of about twenty feet had been photographed at Peenemünde. Previous cover was re-examined, and a similar aircraft was identified on photographs taken on 22nd July and 30th September. In view of the other reports that were being received it was fairly certain that this was a flying bomb; but this was not finally confirmed, nor was a connection established with the ski sites in northern France, until the activities of the 14th Company had been followed up by photographic reconnaissance. Unfortunately, the weather during most of November was unsuitable and it was not until the 28th that photographs could be obtained. But they were worth waiting for. The sortie was so timed as to stand a good chance of catching an aircraft on a launching ramp; and one was in fact identified in this position at Peenemünde. At Zempin there were buildings closely resembling the characteristic structures associated with the ski sites; and there were also ramps elevated at about 10° and pointing in the direction along which the German trials were known to have been carried out. Altogether, after these photographs had been interpreted there was no longer much doubt that the ski sites in northern France were intended for the launching of flying bombs. On 4th December photographic reconnaissance of the whole of northern France within 140 miles of London and Portsmouth was ordered. The range of this reconnaissance was later extended to 150 miles. By the end of 1943, however, the enormous task was three-quarters finished. 88 ski sites had been identified, and at least fifty more were suspected.

By the same date other details of the general picture had been filled in. Chiefly on the basis of the trials plotted by the 14th Company and of photographs an estimate of the performance and dimensions of the flying bomb was prepared which in most particulars proved accurate.[11] The only point on which there was some doubt was the size of the warhead. This was due to lack of evidence concerning the engine. The three most likely methods of propulsion were considered to be, (a) a continuously burning rocket using liquid fuel, (b) a turbo-jet, (c) the propulsive duct or "athodyd" system. The last finally proved correct; but it was not until a flying bomb crashed in Sweden in May 1944 that this was definitely established.

As for production, a number of factories connected with rockets and flying bombs had been correctly identified, but on the whole very little was known. This is not surprising. In the first place, output may well have been kept low throughout 1943 in case technical modifications were required. Secondly, the Germans went to extreme lengths to disperse the manufacture of components through the engineering and electrical industries. Lastly, it is now known that final assembly was not carried out by industrial concerns but by a number of German Air Force munitions depots.

One feature was fairly clear, however, and that was the unit that would be responsible for the actual launchings. This was quite definitely Flakregiment 155(W) under the command of Colonel Wachtel. It was known that besides a headquarters at Zempin there were four Abteilungen either at full strength or in cadre form. It was known also that Colonel Wachtel with elements of the unit had arrived in France about the middle of November 1943. On the other hand, Air Intelligence had been led to believe that the regiment would operate 108 "catapults", which seemed too many even for a regiment containing four Abteilungen (three was more usual); and the discrepancy led to a mistaken search for a larger organisation than in fact existed. As the Germans actually built approximately that number of ski sites the explanation may be that a number of reserve sites were constructed as an insurance against bombing, though there is also the possibility, for which evidence only became available late in 1944, that a further firing regiment was planned.

But in sum, as far as Air Intelligence was concerned, real progress had been made by the end of 1943 in identifying the nature of the weapon and the organisation that would operate it: enough was known, at any rate, for a big programme of counter-measures to be embarked upon. Moreover, the last three months of the year had seen the flying bomb replace the rocket as the more immediate menace; not until the summer of 1944 was there to be quite the same concern about the rocket as had been shown between April and November 1943. There was more willingness to leave the service departments, the Air Ministry in particular, to continue their study of rocket development without undue interference either from the Chiefs of Staff or the War Cabinet. Partly this signified a somewhat belated recognition of the ability of the normal agencies of intelligence to discover what sort of rocket the Germans were developing; but partly it reflected the extent to which the flying bomb had ousted the rocket as the main threat. For, as we shall now see, it was against flying bombs, and in particular, the flying bomb launching sites that counter-measures were principally directed.

## 11. The Organisation of Counter-Measures.
From the middle of November 1943, the Air Ministry was responsible for the study of long-range weapons, the planning of counter-measures

and, through the Deputy Chief of Air Staff, for the co-ordination of the work that was going on in civil as well as service departments. Until the end of the year this responsibility was expressed in a somewhat unorthodox form. A new directorate – the Directorate of Operations (Special Operations) was set up in the Air Ministry to co-ordinate all intelligence work on 'Crossbow' (the code name now in use to describe all German long-range weapons) and to plan operations. The Director was responsible to the Deputy Chief of Air Staff. But he was also responsible to a body outside the Air Ministry the Joint Intelligence Sub-Committee of the Chiefs of Staff, in his capacity as chairman of a specially created offshoot of the Chiefs of Staff, the 'Crossbow' Sub-Committee. This was an inter-departmental intelligence committee which analysed all relevant intelligence data. Certain practical difficulties arose in the daily working of this committee and it was abolished early in January 1944. Its functions were then transferred to the Director of Operations (S.O.) who remained responsible both for co-ordinating intelligence and formulating counter-measures. Thus, except for the closing months of 1943, it was this Directorate which was responsible, through the Deputy Chief of Air Staff to the Chiefs of Staff and the Defence Committee, for most of the detailed planning and intelligence of 'Crossbow'. On the civil side, the Deputy Chief of Air Staff exercised his general responsibility through an inter-departmental co-ordinating committee. This tended to be a body that simply reviewed progress: the details of civil defence, evacuation and security schemes being in the hands of the Ministry of Home Security and the Home Defence Executive.

## 12. Bombing Policy and Operations, October – December 1943.

*a. Attack of Large Sites.*

In addition to the large sites at Watten, Wizernes, Marquise-Mimoyecques, and Martinvast which had been located before the end of August, three more suspicious constructions were discovered in the next two months and were put in the same category. They were at Sottevast in the Cherbourg peninsula and Siracourt and Lottinghem in the Pas de Calais. Watten had been badly damaged by the 8th Air Force in August and early September. It was decided, however, as there was so great a demand for Fortress attacks against Germany and as, in any case, the most economical attacks against this sort of target would only be possible when the 12,000 lb. bomb had been produced, that an attempt should be made to interfere with the work at the sites by fighter-bombers of Fighter Command and Marauders of the 9th Air Force. Their attention was confined to Mimoyecques and Martinvast and, when intense activity recommenced there in December, to Watten. Construction at the other sites was not sufficiently advanced to warrant attack. In addition, the village of Audinghem, which had been taken over by the Todt organisation, was heavily attacked. By the middle of December, 2060 tons of bombs had been dropped on these four targets; and the damage at each was so great that attacks were temporarily suspended. A close watch was maintained on all sites, however; for although their purpose was not yet known they could not be connected with orthodox means or requirements of warfare.

### b. Attack of Production Centres.

The attack of the production centres of long-range weapons was largely a matter of reliable and precise intelligence. Throughout the last months of 1943 agents were reporting many firms that were manufacturing rocket components; which might have meant that production was planned on a large scale, that it was widely dispersed or that false information was being put out in Germany. In September the Ministry of Economic Warfare compiled a list of seven firms that might be building rocket casings and four that might be making electrical and other components. Seven of these were damaged, four of them severely, in Bomber Command attacks of September and early October. Three factories in Schweinfurt which were also thought to be involved in rocket production were heavily damaged in an attack by the 8th Air Force on 15th October. But in each case the damage was a subsidiary effect of attacks that were primarily designed to injure German industry in general and the aircraft industry in particular. As late as the end of October neither Bomber Command nor the 8th Air Force had clear instructions on the place which attacks on rocket production should occupy in their respective offensives.

At the meeting of the Defence Committee on 25th October on the subject of rockets the Chief of the Air Staff agreed to arrange for all suspected factories to be included "on a high priority" in the targets attacked by the British and American heavy bombers. Yet when he had examined the matter further, he felt bound to conclude that it was practically impossible at this stage to brief the bombers to attack specific factories and he informed the Prime Minister to this effect on 4th November. There were a number of reasons. In the first place, there was not enough evidence to show that the destruction of any one of the factories so far named would affect rocket production. Secondly, the navigational equipment of Bomber Command, while it was accurate enough to put a force over an urban area, would not permit the bombing of specific factories. As for the American heavy bombers, their primary task was to destroy the industry behind the German fighter force; and unless there was definite knowledge of some particular focus of rocket production which if damaged would severely limit output, he considered it unjustifiable to divert the American effort. He suggested that the Ministry of Economic Warfare and the Joint Intelligence Sub-Committee should re-examine the question of rocket production and produce a short list of relevant factories. These would be allotted the same degree of importance as targets in the German aircraft industry and would be attacked as conditions allowed. The Chief of the Air Staff pointed out, however, that Bomber Command would probably be able to attack only those factories located within an industrial area.

The suggested inquiry was put in hand and was completed by the middle of November. By that time the flying bomb had assumed far greater importance than before; and the search for factories connected with 'Crossbow' was, therefore, not confined to those thought to be providing rocket components. Five factories were advanced as profitable targets, though simply on the grounds that they were the most frequently referred to of the many factories that had been mentioned in intelligence reports. Each was thought to be making either A.4 rockets or flying bombs. They were the Maybach works and the Zeppelin works at Friedrichshafen, Julius Pintsch at Fürstenwalde, near Berlin, Klein Schanzlin Becker at Frankenthal, near Mannheim, and the Henschel works at Wiener Neustadt. Work was also thought to be going on at the Opel works at Rüsselsheim and the Volkswagen works at Fallersleben, both in the Mainz area, and at the Hanomag works, Hanover. Eleven other factories were added to this list of secondary targets.

The first four of the primary targets were passed to Bomber Command with instructions that they were to be attacked in the course of their current operations against German industry. The new significance of the fifth factory at Wiener Neustedt was brought to the notice of the Mediterranean Air Command. No attacks were carried out, however, during the rest of 1943. Sufficient damage had already been caused at Friedrichshafen and Wiener Neustadt to justify delay. But the factories at Fürstenwalde and Frankenthal were unsuitable targets for Bomber Command. Both were in isolated positions and to attack them was only practicable when special navigational equipment (3 cm. H2S) was available. Even then a large force would be necessary; and as the rate of fitment of the new equipment was expected to be only three a week the prospects of heavy attack were not favourable.

This unsatisfactory situation caused little concern, which would be remarkable except that the 'Crossbow' situation had changed so much since October with the positive identification of the flying bomb and the extensive programme of ski sites. From November 1943 attention was concentrated far more on northern France, where there appeared to be targets of undeniable validity, than on the production centres in Germany, on which information was fragmentary and imprecise.

### c. Attack of Ski Sites.

The identification of the ski sites and their connection with flying bombs marked the biggest advance in our knowledge of German preparations since the threat had first been realised. But before any bombers were diverted to their attack a survey of the construction of the sites and the degree of completion in each case was carried out in order to determine what was the most economical weight of attack and in what order the sites were best attacked. A report was rendered to the Chiefs of Staff on 2nd December. All available information went to show that the degree of reinforcement of the various ski site buildings was very light; and judging by the accuracy achieved in attacks on large sites it was estimated that the following scales of effort would be necessary before a site was so badly damaged that it required almost complete reconstruction:

| Bomb Tonnage for One Site | | Number of Sorties | |
| --- | --- | --- | --- |
| | | a. For One Site. | b. For 100 Sites |
| Heavy Bombers | | | |
| Fortress (by day) | 90 tons | 25 | 2,500 |
| Lancasters (by night | | | |
| Using "Oboe")[12] | 125 tons | 28 | 2,800 |
| Light and Medium Bombers | | | |
| Mitchell | 390 tons | 215 | 21,500 |
| Marauders | 170 tons | 95 | 9,500 |

At the same date some thirty of the sixty sites so far identified were estimated to be half complete for civil engineering but no military engineering appeared to have been started at any of them. Initial attacks were to be carried out by the 2nd Tactical Air Force and the American 9th Bomber Command[13] against sites at least half completed in order to discover what were the best methods of attack to employ: thereafter all sites were to be bombed as they reached this stage of completion. A few attacks of an experimental kind were also to be carried out by heavy bombers; but unless the medium and fighter-bomber attacks proved insufficient it was not intended to divert heavy bombers to this type of target. The training of the two forces would be interfered with by this programme but was expected to be offset by the increase in battle experience. Moreover, it was hoped that the attacks would provoke the German fighters in northern France to battle and thus give escorting British and American fighters the opportunity of destroying the defensive power of the German Air Force in the west.

When 2nd Tactical Air Force and 9th Bomber Command began their attacks, which was 5th December, the expectation was that twenty-five ski sites would have been neutralised by the end of 1943. But the expectation was soon belied. The very first operation – in which 198 Marauders were despatched against three sites – demonstrated how difficult it would be for medium bombers to find and attack their targets in winter weather and with the bomb sites available at this time;[14] for only 52 Marauders dropped their bombs, and these without success. Bad ground haze persisted during the next seven days and at least seven operations had to be cancelled or were abortive. Three sites which had been allotted to Bomber Command for attack by night were also left alone because of the weather. In view of the delay General Eaker was asked to consent to a heavy attack on as many sites as possible by the heavy bombers of the 8th Air Force; and this was agreed to. For the moment, however, all that was contemplated was an isolated operation. There was no question of interfering with the attack of the German aircraft industry.

The weather improved a little during the third week in December and more attacks were made by medium and fighter-bombers and one by Bomber Command. On 20th and 21st December a total of about two hundred German fighters came up to meet our attacks and twelve were believed to have been destroyed. Thereafter there was rarely any attempt on the part of the enemy fighter force to oppose attacks on ski sites. Not until 24th December was the weather suitable for the 8th Air Force; but on that day 672 Fortresses attacked twenty-four sites, dropping nearly fourteen hundred tons of bombs. Serious damage was believed to have been caused at thirteen sites.

No more attacks were carried out by the 8th Air Force during the last week of the year. 2nd Tactical Air Force and 9th Bomber Command were active, however, and attacked twenty-five sites with over five hundred tons of bombs: in addition, Bomber Command attacked four sites at night. Altogether, between 5th December, when the attacks began, and the end of the year the following tonnages were dropped on ski sites:

| | No. of Sites Attacked. | Bomb Tonnage. |
|---|---|---|
| Tactical Air Forces } | 47 | 1398 |
| 8th Air Force        } | | 1472 |
| Bomber Command | 5 | 346 |

Twelve sites were thought to have been neutralised in these attacks and nine more seriously damaged:[15] fifteen others had been affected, six were untouched, and ten had not been photographed.

## 13. Conclusion.

These were the beginnings of a bombing campaign that was eventually to bring about the abandonment of the ski sites. But the policy governing the bombing of ski sites had not been properly defined by the end of 1943. There was still doubt concerning the role of the heavy bombers, both American and British; or, to make the same point in a different way, it was still not clear what proportion of bombing effort was to be allocated between 'Crossbow' and German industry. Nor was it clear how the invasion expedition (Operation 'Overlord') might be affected. It was in fact to be an influence on bombing policy and even more on air defence; for the areas from which the invasion of France were to be launched were not those which were principally threatened by 'Crossbow'; and the question of allocating the resources of air defence was thereby complicated. What was eventually decided belongs chiefly to an account of what took place in 1944, though some preliminary steps had been taken during December 1943.

This lack of clarity about operational plans at the end of 1943 is only to be expected. Up to that date 'Crossbow' had been primarily an intelligence problem. Only in the last few weeks of the year, by the identifying of one of the new weapons and the means whereby it was intended to launch it, had the problem so far been solved that it could be passed on to the operational staffs. Thereafter the main interest lies in the offensive counter-measures that were executed and the defensive ones that were planned; and intelligence then played its more usual role of handmaid to operations.

# Part III

# January 1944 – 12th June 1944

## 14. First Plans for Defence Against 'Crossbow'.

*a. Civil Defence and Security Precautions.*

One result of the first vague rumours of long-range rockets had been the formation of a special committee of the Home Defence Executive under Sir Findlater Stewart to consider various questions of civil defence: e.g., a system of public warning, the deception and confusion of the enemy, control of the press, evacuation from London, transfer of Government departments, provision of additional shelters and the reinforcement of existing casualty and rescue services. Numerous plans were made and embodied in a report that was approved by the Defence Committee on 30th June 1943. A warning system had been devised which was to be ready by 15th October; a plan had been prepared to confuse the enemy by the extensive use of smoke and flash simulators, but as it entailed a good deal of labour and material it remained a paper scheme; plans were also ready for the evacuation of 100,000 of London's priority classes and 20,000 were also to be evacuated from Portsmouth and Southampton; accommodation in the London area had been earmarked for half a million homeless people; and reserves of Morrison shelters were being concentrated near London and in the Solent area.

This sort of problem, however, could only be tackled satisfactorily if there was fairly definite information, first, of the likely scale of attack, second of the date at which it could be expected to begin. Nothing certain was known on either of these points during 1943. But on the whole as the year went by the civil departments became less disposed to commit themselves to big preparations for meeting a threat which might not materialise, and which, if it did, might not be so terrible as had at first been thought. By November 1943 the original estimates of casualties had been scaled down to between ten and twenty killed by each rocket that fell in London; and there was general agreement that the very earliest date at which attack might begin was January 1944. Consequently, at a meeting of the Defence Committee on 18th November, it was decided that all plans covering the security of the population in general and the government in particular should be completed on paper but should remain at that stage. The decision was the more willingly made in view of the C.A.S.'s advice that if heavy attacks began the whole weight of the British and American bomber forces would be diverted to the bombing of the firing points.

Up to the date of this meeting the main danger appeared to be the rocket, which with its short time of flight and invulnerability to the usual means of air defence created a special and difficult problem. It is significant at once of the lessening apprehension of rocket attack and of the increasing concern with flying bombs that between November 1943 and June 1944 little was added to the policy laid down by the Defence Committee at the earlier date. Only when flying bomb attacks began did questions of civil security become once more a major concern of government.

*b. Radar, Sound Ranging and other Prospective Counter-Measures.*
A number of counter-measures other than bombing and orthodox air defence were also considered. In the months when the only threat appeared to be rockets it was appreciated that the only way in which it might be possible to diminish the enemy's rate of fire would be to bomb the centres of production, the lines of communication between Germany and the areas from which the projectiles were being launched and the firing points or launching sites themselves. Very little was known, as we have already noted, about the first of these three types of target. Nor had the firing points themselves been identified. Something could be done, however, for it seemed practically certain that the attack would come from northern France; and counter-measures would be greatly simplified if equipment was prepared that would locate firing points within that area.

The obvious means that lay at hand was radar. Consequently, one of Mr. Sandys' earliest measures was to set up a committee under Sir Robert Watson-Watt to see whether existing radar equipment could track rockets and plot the positions from which they had been fired. It appeared that the requirements of long range and a wide field of view were best met by the existing Chain Home Stations round the south and south-east coasts. However, except in rare cases and with highly skilled operators, they could not be expected to identify rocket tracks unless special apparatus was installed. Fortunately, such was due to come into service in the summer of 1943 in the form of Cathode Ray Direction

Finding (C.R.D.F.) equipment. This had been developed to improve the location of aircraft and displayed instantaneously, and in a form suitable for automatic photography, the range and bearing of all targets within a field of view of 120° in front of the C.H. station. Early in July 1943 the first of these sets was installed at Rye; and by August five C.H. stations between Ventnor and Dover had been fitted. From July onwards operators were trained to identify the characteristic trace that was to be expected from a rocket. A continuous watch was also maintained at these stations which, with three more to the west of the Isle of Wight, were the basis of the public warning system that had been devised. In December, however, the watch was abandoned subject to reinstitution at eight hours' notice.

Flying bombs were not thought to demand special radar measures to the same extent as rockets. If they flew at three to four thousand feet, as the majority were expected to do, and on a straight and steady course, the radar equipment in service on the south and south-east coasts for normal aircraft tracking was expected to suffice. A procedure for identifying flying bombs and transmitting data was laid down early in 1944 and operators were trained in it.

Preliminary measures were taken in the summer of 1943 to locate rocket firing points by means of flash spotting and sound ranging. Coastal artillery units between Folkestone and Dover were responsible for the first. For sound ranging, four troops of the 11th Royal Artillery Survey Regiment were allotted two deployment areas in Kent from which they could cover the area Calais – Boulogne and, less efficiently, Abbeville – Fécamp. Like most early measures against rockets there was a period between the end of 1943 and the summer of 1944 in which little was done in this field.

Two other sorts of proposed counter-measures are also worth noting, although little came of them. The background to their consideration was the lack of intelligence about what the Germans were preparing in northern France. It was therefore suggested as early as July 1943 that a Commando raid might be launched against the suspected firing points in the Pas de Calais. The operation would have been extremely hazardous; there was a likelihood that information obtained would be delayed in reaching England; and so, little was known about the sites or likely launching technique that it would have been difficult to give our men the precise briefing that is a necessary preliminary to this sort of venture. Consequently, nothing was arranged. However, when the ski sites had been identified and connected with flying bombs the Air Ministry again suggested that a Commando raid might bring back some valuable information. On this occasion Major-General Laycock, the

Chief of Combined Operations, reported that simultaneous raids by parties of four or five men on eight to twelve sites might have some chance of success; but he considered such an operation justified only if intelligence could be obtained in no other way. There the proposal was dropped. It came up again towards the end of June 1944 but it was still considered impracticable. In any case the Commandos were fully committed at that time.

The second type of operation that was proposed was not dissimilar. It was to obtain information from a captured German technician about the purpose of the large sites in northern France. This was a task that came within the sphere of the Special Operations Executive. It involved even more than the usual difficulties. Not only had an S.O.E. agent to be dropped in one of the most heavily guarded areas of occupied Europe and picked up again, he had to capture a suitable technician and bring him back to this country for interrogation; for an agent suitable for the job of kidnapping would not be the man to ask the right technical questions and ensure that the answers he received were reliable and accurate. S.O.E. reported unfavourably on the project; but such importance was attached to it that a suitable individual was selected for capture. It turned out, however, that he and others like him were so closely guarded that the enterprise would have been too hazardous even for the determined and resourceful men upon whom S.O.E. could call.

*c. The Place of A.D.G.B.*

All these plans and proposals for defence both on the civil and military side, were necessary. But it was on the air defences already in being that the security of the country chiefly depended. This was not actually the case to begin with. Fighters (at any rate in a defensive role), guns and balloons were helpless against rockets; and only the radar stations, of the various components of the air defence of Great Britain, appeared to have any value, and that entirely passive. The position was altered, however, when the threat took the form of a pilotless aircraft. Against this sort of attack the existing defences could expect some success. Indeed, it is worth remarking that no other defence was possible. The indications were that the new weapon would not be directed by radio, so jamming by radio counter-measures was out of the question. The possibility of diverting the missiles by setting up a powerful magnetic field near London was also considered; but the amount of copper and electric power that would have been required was so great that the scheme was pronounced quite impracticable. Thus, within a fortnight of the purpose of the ski sites becoming known the Deputy Chief of Air

Staff reported to the Chiefs of Staff that "an appreciation of the threat from pilotless aircraft has been forwarded to the Air Commander-in-Chief, A.E.A.F., with instructions to consider in consultation with G.O.C.-in-C., Anti-Aircraft Command[16] counter-measures possible with the resources at his disposal and to prepare plans accordingly." By the end of December 1943 Air Marshal Hill, Air Marshal Commanding A.D.G.B., had prepared an outline plan which was approved by Air Chief Marshal Leigh-Mallory and submitted to the Chiefs of Staff. Fighters, guns and balloons were to be deployed in three separate areas on the approaches to London and deployments were also proposed to cover Bristol and Southampton. No important changes in the disposition of searchlights, which already covered London and the other threatened areas, were visualised. In the London defence scheme the fighter area was nearest to the South coast. By day, standing patrols were to be maintained over the coast and inland. By night, similar patrols would be organised and intruder aircraft would be employed to intercept the flying bombs near the point of launching. On the North Downs all available A.A. guns – some five hundred heavy and seven hundred light – would be deployed. Immediately behind the guns would be a balloon belt where as many balloons as possible would be kept permanently at a suitable operational height.

The scheme at once raised the problem of providing the necessary guns and balloons without seriously weakening defences already in being or budgeted for the future. In the case of balloons, the Chiefs of Staff were at the time considering the reduction of the balloon defences of the United Kingdom; and if the saving proposed was devoted to defence against flying bombs the problem could be solved. The question of guns was more difficult. The most convenient sources of supply were 21st Army Group and the anti-aircraft training and firing camps. 21st Army Group was part of the forces required for the invasion of France and most of its guns would only be available until D-day at the latest. Consequently, the plan for defence against flying bombs had to be so arranged that as few guns as possible were taken from this source, which made it necessary to find the majority from formations of Anti-Aircraft Command remote from the areas threatened by flying bombs. In all, 264 heavy guns were to be provided in this way. But to this the Chiefs of Staff objected; and in February the plan was abandoned.

## 15. The Relation Between 'Overlord' and 'Crossbow'.[17]
*a. Estimates of the Direct Effect of Flying Bomb Attack.*
To understand why this was done it must be appreciated to what extent the requirements of the invasion of France were dictating military plans

during the closing months of 1943 and early 1944. Invasion was a project long and carefully prepared. The Atlantic powers were committed to it; for, despite the hazards, it offered the one means of early victory. And not only were they committed to the project in general, they were committed by the end of 1943 to a particular plan which was inflexible in most of its essential parts if the invasion was to take place at the appointed date. For most of 1943 the obstacles to its success were appreciated and had been discounted as far as possible. As far as the preparatory period and the actual seaborne expedition were concerned the most obvious threat was air attack. But the position in the air was such that it could be faced with confidence; although an attack as heavy and sustained as the Luftwaffe in the west could launch might well cause serious damage at the invasion ports and the shipping concentrated there.

The new German weapons, however, created an unforeseen, and largely unforeseeable, problem. Not much could be done about it until something was known of the likely form and direction of attack. But as soon as the ski sites had been identified and it was known that the immediate threat was attack by flying bombs the possible effect on 'Overlord' was examined.

A first report was produced by Lieut.-General F. E. Morgan, Chief of Staff to the Supreme Commander, on 20th December 1943.[18] It was based on a number of assumptions, two of which reflected the inadequate intelligence of the scale and direction of the German attack. These were first, that one hundred launching sites would be used against the 'Overlord' ports and assembly areas, second, that the maximum German effort would be equivalent to 2,000 tons of bombs each 24 hours sustained throughout the 24 hours. This was quite the worst case from the defenders' point of view. At the time only ten per cent of the identified ski sites were aligned on Bristol. One third of the remainder were in range of Southampton. The rest were aimed at London and at London not so much as an 'Overlord' port but as a centre of population and government.

However, the conclusions were that the present invasion plan was impossible unless it was carried out from the South coast; that movement of the assault force westwards from Southampton, where it would be in less danger of attack, would require transport and supply re-arrangements that could hardly be completed if the expedition was to be launched punctually; that the existing plan should stand and the risk of casualties be accepted; but that if it was decided to amend it the decision must be taken immediately to allow as much time as possible for new arrangements to be made.

No major changes were in fact made; and with the mounting success of the attack on ski sites during the first three months of 1944 the danger of attack appeared to recede. The final verdict came at the end of March from General Eisenhower, who stated, "a. 'Crossbow' attack will not preclude the launching of the assault from the South coast ports and the probable incidence of casualties does not make it necessary to attempt to move assault forces west of Southampton. b. Though some interference with the loading of shipping and aircraft in the Thames and Southampton areas must be expected, it is not sufficient to justify plans for displacement of shipping and craft from these areas." This remained the authoritative statement of the effect to be expected from flying bombs. No attempt was in fact made to attack the invasion fleet by these means; and altogether the direct effect of 'Crossbow' on the expedition was negligible.

*b. Effect on 'Overlord' On Defence Against 'Crossbow'.*
But there were a number of less direct ways in which the two projects were related; for although invasion might not itself be seriously threatened it made such demands upon the forces, both American and British, in the United Kingdom, that both defensive and offensive counter-measures against 'Crossbow' were inevitably affected. It was on this account that the original defensive plan against flying bombs was modified. This as it stood could only be have been carried out at the expense of the defences of numerous towns in southern and south-west England and of the training of anti-aircraft units of 21st Army Group. Moreover, when the question of special defences against flying bombs was being considered early in 1944, the disposition of the air defences on the 'Overlord' ports had already been agreed upon, leaving what was regarded as the minimum number of fighters and ancillary defences for the rest of the United Kingdom. Consequently, if flying bomb attacks began when the 'Overlord' defences were required, as might well happen, either these would have to be reduced, which was hardly to be accepted when so much depended on the expedition, or the defences of the rest of the country, already reduced, would have to be reduced still further.

It was in an attempt to overcome this difficulty that on the instructions of the Chiefs of Staff what was known as the Concurrent 'Overlord' and 'Diver' Plan was prepared during February 1944 to take the place of the original plan for defence against flying bombs prepared two months earlier. It was designed to make the most of the available air defences in a situation where defences were required at the same time both for the invasion expedition and against flying bombs, with the former receiving prior attention. In other words, it met a situation where flying bomb attacks coincided with the final preparations for invasion or with invasion itself.

*c. The Concurrent 'Overlord' and 'Diver' Plan of Air Defence.*
The plan, which was prepared at Headquarters, A.D.G.B., adhered to the same disposition of the various components of air defence as the original, discarded plan. That is to say that fighters were to be the first line of defence against flying bombs and would man patrol lines by day and night over the coast and inland as far as the gun belt. This, for the defence of London, would be on the North Downs; for the defence of Bristol, in the Yeovil – Shaftesbury area. London was also to be protected by a belt of balloons on the high ground between Caterham in the west and Cobham in the east. Additional searchlights were to be placed forward of the gun belt south of London to assist the gunners at night. In the Solent area the defences allotted for the protection of the invasion expeditions were, with the addition of two searchlights batteries (48 lights), reckoned sufficient to deal with flying bombs as well as piloted aircraft.

The plan involved allotting eight-day fighter squadrons specially to flying bomb patrols. Six would be drawn from No. 11 Group and would man the patrol lines forward of the gun belt on the North Downs. Two others from No. 10 Group would defend the Bristol area, using normal methods of interception, i.e. standing patrols would not be flown. As for fighter patrols at night, it was hoped that five squadrons would be available in the south-east and three further west.

Similarly, the balloons and searchlights that the plan earmarked for 'Diver' involved little or no reduction in the defences of 'Overlord'. The London balloon belt was to contain 480 balloons, most of which were available by the end of March 1944 as a result of reductions in the static balloon barrages of the United Kingdom. The only balloons still in operation that would be required were those in the barrages at Swansea, Cardiff and Newport. These were to be withdrawn for the belt only when flying bomb attacks began. The eleven batteries of searchlights, additional to those already deployed in the south, that the plan entailed could be found without much difficulty from existing defences in South Wales and north-east England.

Altogether, as far as it allotted fighters, balloons and searchlights to flying bomb defence, the Concurrent Plan was little more than a restatement of the original plan and involved no special problems. The disposition of the gun defences, however, was another matter. Three situations had to be considered. The first – Case A – was that which would apply prior to 1st April 1944, the date at which the defences of

31

the 'Overlord' bases were to be at full strength. The guns that it was planned to allot to flying bomb defence under Case A included 128 American heavy guns; and Case B covered the situation that would arise if for some reason these guns were not available. Case C could not be expressed precisely in terms of guns, for it denoted the situation which might apply after April 1st when there was some likelihood that more American guns could be utilised.

In each of these three situations there were three main requirements for anti-aircraft guns in the United Kingdom. First and foremost, the defence of the 'Overlord' bases; second, defence against flying bombs, and in particular the defence of London; third, the defence of the rest of the country, including London, against attacks by piloted aircraft. That the latter was necessary the night attacks of January to March 1944 were a sufficient reminder.

Under Case A, i.e. before 1st April, the complete anti-aircraft defences of the 'Overlord' bases were not required; for not until that date would the last and most important stages of assembly be reached. When they were, some six hundred heavy anti-aircraft guns and eight hundred light were to reinforce the defences already in position giving a total of no less than 1442 heavy and 1122 light guns. Thus, between the date by which the Concurrent Plan had been prepared, 4th March 1944, and the beginning of April, a large number of guns was available to be called upon if flying bomb attacks began. Nevertheless, the allotment of guns for the latter purpose under Case A was numerically the same as in Case B, partly because the time in which Case A would apply was so short, partly because the Chiefs of Staff were determined to let nothing interfere with what they regarded as an adequate defence for the invasion expedition; and if once a large number of guns went into action against flying bombs before the 'Overlord' preparations reached their peak it might have been difficult to redeploy any of them for the defence of the 'Overlord' bases.

With insignificant exceptions the total gun resources before and after 1st April but prior to D-Day were the same. They amounted to 2735 heavy guns and 1870 light guns. 21st Army Group and 1st U.S. Army Group accounted for 432 heavy and 670 light guns. The rest were in Anti-Aircraft Command and Home Forces. Under Case B, which was the worst in that it envisaged separate deployments both for 'Overlord' and 'Diver' and also the absence of 128 American guns, the 'Overlord' defences and the guns in anti-aircraft regiments detailed to move on or shortly after D-Day, embraced 1258 heavy and 950 light guns, leaving some fourteen hundred heavy guns and nine hundred light for defence against flying bombs and the rest of the country. The needs of the latter dictated the scale of the former. Thirty-two gun defended areas in Anti-Aircraft Command at which 910 heavy guns were deployed were selected as suitable areas from which withdrawals could be made for the needs of invasion as well as 'Diver'. Not all these guns could be withdrawn while the threat of normal air attack remained; and the minimum security was estimated to be some 546 guns. A more drastic reduction was planned in the defences of vital points protected by light guns. Forty-two were to be stripped of all protection, thus making available some two hundred guns. Out of these resources of Anti-Aircraft Command, 192 heavy and 138 light guns were held in readiness to man the 'Diver' gun belt defending London. If American heavy guns could be called upon (and by 15th April it appeared that 96 might be available) they would replace a similar number of Anti-Aircraft Command guns, not be additional to them. All told, the gun belt was planned to contain these 192 heavy guns and 246 light guns,[19] 108 of the latter being provided by 21st Army Group. The Bristol gun belt was to be manned until D-Day by 96 heavy and 36 light guns of 21st Army Group. As Bristol was only menaced by the flying bomb sites on the Cherbourg peninsula, which it was hoped would be neutralised shortly after the landing in France, no arrangements were made for maintaining the Bristol defences after D-Day.

This allotment compared unfavourably with that which had been recommended in the original plan of defence against flying bombs. As against the 528 heavy guns and 804 light guns which the original plan envisaged only 288 heavy and 282 light guns were to be deployed under the Concurrent Plan. It was hoped that the American guns might prove more efficient than the British; but even so, so big a reduction needs explaining.

In the first place it should not be forgotten that the original plan was prepared on the assumption that flying bomb attacks would begin before the preparations for invasion were completed. Thus, a greater proportion of the reduction in the defences of the rest of the country could be devoted to 'Diver' than in a situation where additional defences were also needed for the invasion bases. Secondly, the policy of the Chiefs of Staff was to ensure the fullest possible protection for the invasion expedition from normal air attack which, as has been seen, was reckoned a greater danger than attack by flying bombs. Consequently, the scale of defences available for other purposes was dictated by that required for 'Overlord'. It was, however, anticipated that the position would be easier after D-Day; and in fact, more guns were deployed in the London gun belt within a fortnight after flying bomb attacks began than were allowed for in the Concurrent Plan. Finally, the original plan was drafted in December 1943, i.e. before the attacks on ski sites were properly under way. The Concurrent Plan, however, was prepared in February 1944 and approved by the end of the month[20] when the attacks on sites had been going on for over two months with such success that there was good reason to believe that the potential scale of flying bombs attack had been seriously affected. In short, there did not at the later date appear to be the same urgent need for a powerful defensive system as in the last weeks of 1943; and in any case 'Crossbow' had to take second place to 'Overlord'. It is the bombing operations, and in particular the attacks on ski sites, that brought about this happier state of affairs that must now be considered.

## 16. Bombing Counter-Measures.
*a. General Considerations.*
The review of counter-bombing was left at the stage reached by the end of 1943, when no comprehensive policy had been formulated but when such of the Allied bombing effort as was being brought to bear on German preparations was being applied almost entirely against the ski sites in northern France. The large sites were also receiving some attention, although their purpose was not yet known, and certain suspected centres of rocket and flying bomb production had been attacked, but only insofar as they were centres of piloted aircraft production. Little was known of this aspect of German preparations.

What forces ought to be employed against 'Crossbow', what sort of attacks should be carried out, what size of effort would be required, were not easy questions to answer at the beginning of 1944. It had first been thought that the best instruments would be the American 9th Air Force and the British 2nd Tactical Air Force, (including No. 2 Group of Bomber Command), which were the offensive components of the Allied Expeditionary Air Forces. If these formations had been capable of neutralising the sites in northern France the main obstacle to the efficient distribution of the Allied bomber resources in the United Kingdom would have been overcome. Not that this would have been easy; for the two forces had an essential part to play in the bombing preparatory to invasion, and even more in the invasion itself and the subsequent battles. Moreover, their tactical role demanded a high and peculiar standard of training to fit them for the task of co-operating with ground forces; and their own commanders, not to speak of the army commanders, were loath to allow their training schedules to be interfered with. Against this, however, could be set the experience that would be gained, and was gained, in actual operations.

But the first attacks by the medium bombers and fighter-bombers of A.E.A.F. were disappointing. Their performance could be expected to improve with practice, especially that of the 9th Air Force which was a new and inexperienced formation. Nevertheless, it was calculated early in January 1944 that A.E.A.F. squadrons were not likely to destroy more than fourteen ski sites a month; and as the existence of ninety-three sites had already been confirmed this meant that A.E.A.F. would be forced to maintain a heavy scale of attack well into the summer, which would seriously affect its role in invasion. Consequently, it was impossible to escape the conclusion that regular attacks would have to be carried out by heavy bombers if the German preparations were to be restrained. The main body of the heavy bomber forces of Bomber Command was hardly a suitable instrument for the attack of sites, though good results could be expected from some of the specially trained squadrons of the Command. On the other hand, the Fortresses of the 8th Air Force, were admirably suited; and it was estimated that in any one major attack by this force six sites could be expected to be destroyed.

However, this force, like Bomber Command, was committed to the attack of German industry. It was not, it is true, irrevocably committed; but Lieut. General Doolittle, its commander,[21] no less than Air Chief Marshal Harris of Bomber Command, regarded the offensive against German industry as vital to the success of the invasion of France and the defeat of Germany; and both men were loath to direct their forces to any other task. Nor was the Chief of Air Staff, who exercised a responsibility for the strategic air offensive to the Combined Chiefs of Staff, himself convinced that 'Crossbow' was such a threat that it warranted any major change in bombing policy. Yet the fact remained that the American heavy bombers would have to be employed if the Germans were not to have a good proportion of sites ready for use by the time that the invasion of France would be launched, if not earlier. The principle was therefore agreed upon between the British Chiefs of Staff, and Lieut. General Spaatz, Commanding General of the U.S. Strategical Air Forces, that the sites in northern France should only be attacked by the 8th Air Force "whenever weather conditions over Germany do not allow of major attacks there but permit precision bombing over northern France". In addition, Air Chief Marshal Harris was instructed to regard the destruction of eight selected ski sites as the primary task of his Stirling squadrons whenever these were not operating against targets in Germany. The principle, as we shall see, was only departed from in exceptional circumstances; and only a little more than one tenth of the effort of the 8th Air Force between December 1943 and June 1944 was devoted to 'Crossbow' targets. But it is abundantly clear that Lieut.-General Doolittle and, later, when Bomber Command were required to attack sites in strength, Air Chief Marshal Harris were antagonistic to what they regarded as a commitment of far less importance than either the offensive against Germany or against the enemy forces in the west.

But there was at least one type of target that they were allowed to ignore: namely, suspected centres of flying bomb and rocket production. Our intelligence on this subject remained weak throughout the period under review, January – June 1944. Consequently, the Chiefs of Staff agreed on 1st February that production centres should not be attacked until more definite evidence was available. Where, however, a suspected factory was also a part of the German aircraft industry, attacks were made on it in virtue of its latter function. Thus, on 24th April the Dornier assembly works at Löwenthal was attacked by 98 Fortresses. On the night of 27th April, 291 Lancasters attacked Friedrichshafen. Similarly, hydrogen peroxide plants were attacked more by virtue of their importance to the German production of jet-propelled piloted aircraft than to that of flying bombs and rockets. And as at the time of writing little is known of the effect of our bombing upon the production of the latter, and as such as it was, was largely a secondary result of attacks on the German aircraft industry and on the German economy in general, no attempt will be made here to trace a relation between the two. That there was a relation is hardly to be doubted; but what was its significance can only emerge when the bombing offensive against Germany as a whole is analysed.

In sum, the background to the bombing of the German preparations for attack is as follows. The obvious target, and one well within range of every type of bomber in the United Kingdom was the complex system of sites that the Germans were preparing in northern France. It was this type of target upon which attack was concentrated to the virtual exclusion of other targets that were suspected of being connected with flying bombs and rockets. But as the sites presented a difficult target their attack could not be left to the light and medium bombers and fighter-bombers of the 9th Air Force and the 2nd Tactical Air Force; in addition, the heavy bombers of the 8th Air Force, and a few of Bomber Command, had to be employed. However, both the tactical and strategical bomber forces had other tasks to perform. The first had an important programme of training to carry out which, so it was believed, could only be neglected at the expense of its efficiency as the chief air arm supporting the troops who would land in France. Moreover, from March onwards it was needed for bombing attacks directly related to the plan of invasion. Similarly, in the weeks immediately preceding invasion the heavy bombers were required to assist the expedition as well as to continue the offensive against German industry which they had been pursuing for so long. It happened, therefore, that although there were very large forces of bombers in the United Kingdom during 1944 and although the total number of identified sites in northern France was little more than one hundred, the scale of attack against 'Crossbow' targets was never, to say the least, an over-insurance against the completion of the German preparations.

*b. Intelligence on the German Site Programme, January – April 1944.*
By the beginning of January 1944 ninety-six ski sites had been identified in northern France. There was some evidence from ground sources that the Germans would build as many as one hundred and fifty; but the additions were never constructed. That the ski sites were intended for the launching of flying bombs was beyond doubt: indeed this, and the performance of the weapon itself, were the only points on which there was real assurance.

By the same date seven large sites had been found. They were at Watten, Wizernes, Mimoyecques, Siracourt, Lottinghem, Sottevast and Martinvast, of which the last two were on the Cherbourg peninsula. At all of them much labour and material was being expended; all were within one hundred and fifty miles of London on which all seemed to be orientated with the exception of Martinvast which was aligned on Bristol; and none of them could be connected with any ordinary military or industrial purpose. And as our agents' reports almost invariable connected them to rockets it was assumed that they were intended to play some important part in the German attack. An eighth site at Hidrequent, near Calais, had also come under suspicion; but even less could be deduced from the construction there than at the other large sites.

There was also a third category of site. The fact that none of the ski sites were served by railways of normal gauge had early suggested that the Germans probably intended to deliver supplies to them by road from supply depots which would be linked with railway communications with Germany. Ground sources offered no relevant information but towards the end of 1943 evidence of what came to be called "supply sites" began to accumulate from successive photographic reconnaissances. It was not until February 1944, however, that the evidence was sufficiently conclusive for a report on the subject to be passed to the Chiefs of Staff. This specified seven places where supply sites appeared to be under construction. One of them was on the Cherbourg peninsula. The others extended in an arc just inland from the belt covered by the ski sites, and with one exception were evenly spaced at intervals of twenty miles. All were served by rail and had good road communications; work on them had started about the same time as on ski sites; certain standardised buildings were common to them; and all were heavily defended by anti-aircraft guns.

If supply was their purpose, they would obviously be a profitable target at the right time. A close photographic watch was accordingly maintained on them; and by the end of April another site had been identified and a ninth (making the second in the Cherbourg peninsula) was suspected. By the same date three were considered to be complete; three more were expected to be complete within a fortnight; the others would not be ready for about a month. But there had been no activity at any which indicated that supplies were moving in; and attacks upon them had been withheld for this reason.

### c. The Problems of Attacking Sites.
Thus, the first half of 1944 saw attacks confined to ski sites and large sites. Neither presented easy targets. Each type was contained within a square of three hundred to four hundred yards and only a small proportion of this area was occupied by essential constructions. Accurate visual attack therefore depended to a great extent on good visibility. For example, the bomb aimer in the Marauder, which was the most up-to-date of the medium bombers, had to identify his target at a range of at least six miles if he was to bomb accurately. Blind bombing with the aid of radio navigational devices had to be no less accurate; and only "Oboe" of the various aids in service at the time was sufficiently precise for the task.

Low-level and dive bombing had their advocates; and both methods were comparatively successful, especially the former. But the success was at the cost of higher casualties than those suffered by the medium and heavy bombers. For although it was only on rare occasions that the German fighter reaction to our attacks was at all spirited, anti-aircraft defences were increased to the point at which the Pas de Calais and the Cherbourg peninsula were amongst the most heavily defended areas in Europe. In the ski site belt between Dieppe and St. Omer there were only some sixty heavy and sixty light anti-aircraft guns in December 1943; but by the end of the following May there were about five hundred and twenty and seven hundred and thirty of the respective types. The sites in the Cherbourg peninsula were already covered by strong anti-aircraft defences. These were further increased, however, until there were at least two hundred guns in the area. Moreover, in the case of the large sites the problem of how to attack successfully and economically was made especially difficult by the strength of the main constructions. Few attacks with 12,000 lb. bombs were carried out until after 6th June; until then 2,000 lb. bombs were normally used, more to smash rail and road communications at the sites and to interfere with work than to destroy the massive concrete buildings. The ski sites were not so robustly constructed. 500 lb. and even 250 lb. bombs were sufficient to cause serious damage.[22]

*d. Progress of the Attacks, January – March 1944.*
During the first half of January seventy-nine ski sites, but no large sites, were attacked (some more than once), the bulk of the effort being made by the squadrons of A.E.A.F. Bomber Command carried out eight attacks and the 8th Air Force operated on 14th January only. Results were not very good. Only eight sites were certainly made Category A, four by the 8th Air Force in their single operation and four by A.E.A.F. squadrons. As it was our policy, so the Chief of Air Staff stated, to neutralise the German building programme completely, the rate of neutralisation would have to be increased, otherwise the Germans would have as many as sixty sites ready by the end of February. This was the more certain in that there was evidence that the repair of damaged sites had begun. Moreover, there were good reasons for using some of the heavy bomber resources against the large sites, four of which – Siracourt, Watten, Sottevast and Lottinghem – had reached, or would reach within a month, a state of development where they could well be attacked again.

All this meant that an increased scale of effort, or alternatively a more accurate one, was required. For a whole week, however, further operations were held up by bad weather and it was not until 21st January that attacks recommenced, both the 8th Air Force and, at night, Bomber Command taking part. Forty-five sites were attacked but first reconnaissances showed that only four had been made Category A, all as the result of attacks by the 8th Air Force. Six Fortresses, two Mosquitos and two fighters were lost; but there was some compensation as out of approximately sixty German fighters that came up to meet our aircraft eighteen were claimed as destroyed.

Yet despite the fact that Fortresses had so far been the most successful aircraft employed the Chief of Air Staff was still loath to divert heavy bombers from their other tasks. Indeed, the Stirling squadrons of Bomber Command, which had met with little success in their night attacks, were diverted from sites at the end of January in order to drop arms to French resistance groups in Haute-Savoie. It was held that while the attack on sites had not come up to expectations nearly one-third had been neutralised since 5th December and another third damaged less severely, and more accurate bombing by A.E.A.F. could be expected as experience accumulated and the weather improved. The performance of the A.E.A.F. squadrons did in fact improve during the last week in January, even though the weather over northern France was still poor. At least six sites were made Category A in attacks in which only nine hundred tons of bombs were dropped and only four aircraft were lost. Unfortunately, during the week 30th January – 5th February the weather was bad. Only a very small effort – 248 tons – entirely by A.E.A.F. squadrons, was possible and no sites were vitally damaged.

By this time a good deal of data had been accumulated on the damage that had been caused to sites and on the rate of repair of damaged sites. It was not as comprehensive as was wished but it allowed a prediction of the progress that could be expected under varying conditions.[23] On the assumption that the Germans were working to a programme of one hundred and twenty sites[24] it was calculated that if attacks were carried out by A.E.A.F. only on all suitable days, and if the Germans maintained the existing rate of repair, no less than eighty-nine sites would probably be complete at the end of March. If double sorties were carried out, as would be possible with the longer days, the number completed would be about seventy-two. If the 8th Air Force participated on all days that were suitable for visual bombing over northern France but not over Germany sixty-two sites would be ready. If they participated on all suitable days irrespective of the conditions over Germany the figure would fall still further to twenty-eight. In the two latter cases, if A.E.A.F. made double sorties between 15th February and the end of March, the number of sites that would be completed would be forty-six and twelve respectively.

The implications of this prediction were obvious enough: they were that A.E.A.F. must continue, and if possible, increase their effort and that the 8th Air Force must operate more frequently than hitherto. However, no new instructions were issued to either force that would have ensured a heavier scale of attack. In February the total weight of bombs dropped on sites was 5527 tons, which was less by twelve hundred tons than that dropped in January. In the same month sixty-seven per cent of A.E.A.F. bomber sorties were against sites compared to nearly ninety-four per cent in the previous month. The 8th Air Force effort fell by comparatively little in terms of sorties and bombs but it was only thirteen per cent of its total effort as compared with twenty-three per cent in January. In March the effort of the two forces against sites fell still more. The heavy bombers of 8th Air Force made altogether eleven thousand sorties of which only nine hundred and seventy were against sites. The comparable figures during the same month for the bombers of A.E.A.F. were six thousand one hundred and two thousand three hundred.

The weather during the two months was often a hindrance to operations over northern France but there were other factors that helped to account for the fall in the scale of attack. The 8th Air Force had first claim on the fighters of the 9th Air Force whenever targets in Germany were to be attacked; which meant that on those days there were fewer fighters left for covering operations by 9th Air Force bombers. The operations against Berlin early in March, for example, employed practically all the 9th Air Force fighters; and there was a period during the same month when a complete group of medium bombers (54 aircraft) was only allowed a fighter escort of one squadron. Secondly, with the increase in the anti-aircraft defences of the ski site area, and in particular round Abbeville and St. Pol, medium altitude and low-level attacks became increasingly hazardous, which led to representations by Air Chief Marshal Leigh-Mallory that certain heavily defended sites, including most of the large sites, should be attacked only by heavy bombers. But it was not until the middle of March that the 8th Air Force took over this responsibility: in the meantime, the scale of effort by A.E.A.F. against such sites was low. Thirdly, as the time for invading France drew nearer, more of the Marauders of the 9th Air Force were required for preliminary bombardment, especially of railways; and while from the beginning of March a minimum of seventy Marauders was allotted to the attack of sites the A.E.A.F. effort against sites inevitably dropped.

However, an improvement in bombing accuracy during February and March compensated for the somewhat lower effort compared to that of the preceding two months. "Oboe"-equipped Mosquitoes were used to lead formations of medium bombers; and good results continued to be obtained by Fortresses, and by Mosquitoes and Bostons of No. 2 Group in low-level attacks. Mitchells also began to improve. Altogether, by the end of March sixty-five sites were Category A and another twenty Category B. A number of sites had been repaired by the Germans but there was good reason to believe that although our scale of attack had not been as heavy as it might have been it was still heavier than the Germans had budgeted for. Labour appeared to have been seriously disorganised to the point at which repair work was chiefly carried out by pioneer companies of the German Army and at only about one half of the original ninety-six sites, though as we shall shortly see, not without some success. In sum, therefore, the position was fairly satisfactory; and on 4th April the Chief of Air Staff said at a Chiefs of Staff meeting that providing the number of completed sites could be kept down to ten to twenty a concentrated bombing attack should see the whole of the ski site programme neutralised.

But this applied only to ski sites. The situation in respect of large sites was not considered to be as satisfactory. Attacks on these had been carried out since the end of January chiefly by the 8th and 9th Air Forces. Thirty-nine attacks were made and nearly four thousand tons had been dropped. At Martinvast the damage was such that the site could be ignored for three months even if vigorous repairs were undertaken. Lottingham and Wizernes had also been seriously damaged and were reckoned to be out of action for at least six weeks. At the four others, however, only slight damage appeared to have been inflicted. It was true, of course, that as far as was known, these sites were connected with rockets, not flying bombs, and that the former was not believed to be as immediate a threat as the latter. But as construction went ahead at the large sites the massive main buildings became progressively less vulnerable to attack. Consequently, from the end of March a heavier weight of attack was brought to bear upon them.

*e. Progress of the Attacks, April – 12th June 1944.*

How quickly the rate of neutralisation could be altered became evident during the second week in April. The reduced effort of March had been more successful proportionately in neutralising sites than any previous month; but it seems to have given the Germans an opportunity to improve the rate of repair.[25] And whereas in the middle of March it had been estimated that there would only be the equivalent of ten sites ready for action by 15th April, by that date it seemed that as many as twenty-five might be completed. The Chiefs of Staff felt compelled to take action; and in late March and April they addressed a number of communications to the chief air force commanders which were designed to bring down a bigger weight of attack on flying bomb sites. After their meeting on 21st March both Air Chief Marshal Leigh-Mallory and Lieutenant General Spaatz were requested to intensify the attacks of their forces; to which they responded that bad weather continued to hinder operations. After their meeting a fortnight later the Deputy Chief of Air Staff again wrote to Air Chief Marshal Leigh-Mallory and emphasised the importance of maintaining attack on the sites. Again, Air Chief Marshal Leigh-Mallory pointed out on 11th April that on nearly half the days of the previous month operations had been impossible owing to the weather. In addition, targets other than ski sites had been given priority of attack; while most of the ski sites still intact were in heavily defended areas where tactical bombers were liable to heavy losses. Air Chief Marshal Leigh-Mallory asked, therefore, that the 8th Air Force should make at least one full-scale effort each week against ski sites in order to ensure that the menace was kept under control.

A week later the Chiefs of Staff pursued the matter further in a letter addressed still higher in the chain of command, to General Eisenhower himself. The Supreme Allied Commander had by this time taken over the direction of the operations of the strategical and tactical air forces in the United Kingdom but responsibility to the War Cabinet for action effecting the security of the United Kingdom still remained with the British Chiefs of Staff. Accordingly, on 18th April 1944 a letter was sent to him in which the Chiefs of Staff expressed the War Cabinets concern – and their own – at the deterioration of the ski site position.[26] The Supreme Commander was told that unless action was taken immediately to bring to bear a heavy scale of attack the enemy might be able to recover from previous bombing and build up a threat which would divert strong Allied air forces, perhaps at a time when the invasion of France called for our greatest effort in the air. He was also made aware of the dissatisfaction of the Chiefs of Staff at the failure to damage seriously the majority of the large sites. But still the Chiefs of Staff fought shy of demanding a reduction of the effort against German industry, which was the biggest obstacle to increasing the weight of attack on 'Crossbow'. Their requirement was phrased thus: "(The Chiefs of Staff) request that you give attacks on 'Crossbow' objectives priority over all other operations except 'Pointblank' until such time as the threat is overcome and that both the 8th Air Force and the Tactical Air Forces be instructed to take fullest advantage of any opportunities to attack both large sites and ski sites form now onwards."

The close relationship between the two operations was certainly appreciated by the Supreme Commander and his deputy, Air Chief Marshal Tedder. On 19th April the latter wrote to Air Chief Marshal Leigh-Mallory, with reference to the Chiefs of Staffs request to General Eisenhower, and agreed that both the ski sites and large sites could not be allowed to develop at their present rate. But he did not indicate any interference with the heavy bomber offensive; he laid down simply that "attacks on 'Crossbow' objectives by the Tactical Air Forces should be given priority over all other air operations."

This limited concentration of the available bombing forces against 'Crossbow' fell short of what Air Chief Marshal Leigh-Mallory wanted. Nor was it what the Chief of Air Staff understood as Air Chief Marshal Tedder's policy; for at a meeting of the Chiefs of Staff on 20th April he reported that at an earlier meeting of the War Cabinet Defence Committee, Air Chief Marshal Tedder had said that a satisfactory degree of effort against 'Crossbow' targets would only be forthcoming if they were given priority for attack over 'Pointblank'; and the Chief of Air Staff understood that Air Chief Marshal Tedder had already arranged this. In the light of the latter's letter of the 19th to Air Chief Marshal Leigh-Mallory it appears that the Chief of Air Staff had misunderstood him.[27] What is important, however, is that while the 8th Air Force was not, apparently, given a fresh instruction covering the proportionate effort to be devoted to 'Pointblank' and 'Crossbow' the tonnage dropped on the latter notably increased from the middle of April. Over four thousand tons of bombs were dropped on ski sites by the 8th Air Force and A.E.A.F. during the second half of the month compared with only as much for the whole of March. Sixteen hundred tons of bombs were also dropped on large sites during the same period. Results were good in the case of the ski site attacks: seventy-five sites were Category A and seventeen Category B at the end of April compared to sixty-one and twenty-four in the respective categories on 16th April. At the large sites, however, no fresh major damage could be discerned. Accordingly, on 2nd May the Chiefs of Staff agreed that attacks on large sites should be carried out in preference to those on ski sites. It is not untypical that far from this resulting in a larger effort only eleven hundred tons were dropped on large sites during the first half of May, which was only two-thirds the tonnage dropped during the second half of April. A similar weight of bombs was dropped in the second half of May.

During May and early June attacks on ski sites continued to be as successful as those on large sites were not. The number of ski sites reckoned Category A was eighty-six, eight were Category B and only two were undamaged. Considering that the relative effort of the 8th Air Force was only a little more than five per cent and that of A.E.A.F. twenty-five per cent for the first half of the month and only ten per cent during the second half, this was very satisfactory. The fall in the second half of the month itself reflected the success of previous attacks and was the response of A.E.A.F. to a request form the Chiefs of Staff that more effort should be put into preparations for 'Overlord'. There were, however, still four large sites which were reckoned virtually undamaged; but after 30th May no further attacks were made upon them until after flying bomb attacks had begun. In sum, with the exception of two attacks against a selected supply site (made for reasons which will shortly be apparent), the attack of sites practically came to an end at the end of May. By then the needs of invasion, which had been increasingly clamant as D-Day approached, were demanding all the Allied bomber resources.

## 17. The Situation Prior to the Commencement of Flying Bomb Attacks.

*a. Comparative Danger of Flying Bomb and Rocket Attack.*

Of the two types of 'Crossbow' target that were attacked in 1944 prior to D-Day one, the ski sites, was known to be for the launching of flying bombs, the other, the large sites, was only thought to be connected with rockets. Our definite information of the first compared to our lack of certainty concerning the second only reflected the state of intelligence on all aspects of the two weapons. Investigation into rockets had gone on during the winter of 1943 and in the following spring. New and important information had been coming in, fresh evidence of development had been found and new channels of intelligence had been opened. But the main problems had yet to be solved: i.e. the weight of the rocket, and in particular that of the warhead, the propellant fuel or fuels and the method of launching. Consequently, the few targets that were known or suspected remained an objective subsidiary to the flying bomb sites. Large sites, as we have seen, were attacked, but rather as an insurance against a possible failure on the part of intelligence and in order to delay the time when successful attack upon them would be exceptionally difficult than because rockets were deemed as immediate a menace as flying bombs.

*b. Estimates of the Scale and Time of Flying Bomb Attack: Gaps in our Intelligence.*

It is significant that in all the estimates made during the first months of 1944 of the possible scale of attack against the United Kingdom rockets were not taken into account: the calculations were worked out in terms of flying bombs only; some allowance being made for attacks by piloted aircraft. The possibility of dependable assessments was largely determined by what was known of the characteristics of flying bombs, what stage their development had reached, how many had been produced and what was the rate of fire at the launching sites. But on most of these points there were gaps in our intelligence; on some little or nothing was known.

Thanks to the information that had been coming through since the autumn of 1943 on the trials that the Germans were conducting on the Baltic coast most of the details of the performance of the weapon had been established, and, as it turned out, with fair accuracy. The height 3,000 feet, at which flew the majority of the flying bombs that were launched against London was lower by two to three thousand feet than had been anticipated. Otherwise there were no serious discrepancies between estimated and actual performance. The method of propulsion remained uncertain until late in May 1944, when officers of Air Intelligence were able to examine a flying bomb that came down in Sweden; and for this reason, it was not possible to be precise about the size of the warhead until a short time before the attacks begun. However, a warhead weighing approximately one ton was usually assumed, which was not far removed from its size in fact.

Intelligence sources on the Baltic coast continued to transmit details of successive trials, from which it followed that development work was still taking place, and from which A.D.I. (Science) and his staff were able to work out the factor of accuracy for the weapon. Stated in terms of bombs launched that would reach the London area, this changed from 30 per cent in January to nearly 60 per cent in April, reflecting improved performance in the German trials.

But the fact that trials were still going on during the early part of 1944, presumably in order to improve the accuracy of the weapon and perfect the technique of launching, did not mean – nor was it taken to mean – that flying bombs were not already being produced. How many had been produced and what was the rate of production was simply not known;[28] and in the absence of this information estimates of the likely scale of attack were little more than guesses. However, some sort of estimate was called for and one was proffered by the Joint Intelligence Committee through the Chiefs of Staff on 2nd February 1944.

It was as follows, mid-March being the date by which it might become operative.

"1. An initial 'blitz' equivalent to 400 tons of bombs spread over a period of 10 hours.

2. Two repeats of (1) at 48-hour intervals.

3. Thereafter, 600 tons a month of which 400 at most can be in one 'blitz' of 10 hours. If sustained attack is adopted, 20 tons a day."

With the advance in knowledge of the extent of the ski site programme and as the bombing of sites achieved notable results a further estimate was advanced in the middle of March, though once more there was no evidence of the scale of German production. However, assuming that two thousand flying bombs had been produced and that monthly production was in the region of a thousand, it was calculated that the Germans would have so few completed ski sites (probably about ten) by the middle of April that they would be capable of mounting only the following scale of attack.

"i. 5 'blitz' attacks in the first 15 days, each being equivalent to 160 tons of blast bombs over a period of 10-12 hours at intervals of 48 hours.

ii. Subsequently, 5 attacks in the next 15 days, each equivalent to 80 tons of blast bombs over periods of 10-12 hours at intervals of 48 hours."

The Air Staff, for it was they who were responsible for the estimate, pointed out that on the night of 18th/19th February German bombers had dropped 135 tons of bombs on London, the implication presumably being that prospective attacks by flying bombs would be no worse than the raids that London had been suffering.

And indeed, as April and May went by and the number of ski sites capable of firing remained at less than ten there is no reason to doubt that the scale of attack from this sort of site would have been negligible. This is, of course, an index of the success that had attended the Allied bombing; for while counter-measures had not gone as smoothly as might have been wished it is beyond dispute that they had neutralised almost completely the machinery of ski sites from which the Germans had originally planned to launch their attack.

*c. Appearance of the Modified Sites.*
But it is equally clear that long before the Allied attacks had begun to show such splendid dividends the Germans had decided on an amended policy of site construction.[29] Air Intelligence, however, knew nothing of this until the end of April 1944. Then on 27th April scrutiny of the results of a photographic reconnaissance of the Cherbourg peninsula revealed what was suspected to be a new type of site near the village of Belhalmelin. During the next fortnight the examination of previous photographs and fresh reconnaissances showed that an extensive programme of new sites was indeed being carried out, having been started, so it was thought, early in April. On 13th May A.C.A.S. (I) reported that twenty of the new sites had already been identified, nine in the Pas de Calais and eleven in the Cherbourg peninsula. They were termed "modified sites" by Air Intelligence for a good reason, that while they included certain essential features of the ski sites, they had none of the ski-shaped buildings that had been such a distinguishing feature of the latter. Apart from the launching ramp and square non-magnetic building, in which the gyro compass of the flying bomb was adjusted, the other buildings of the modified site were not standardised as they were at ski sites; and further to confuse reconnaissance and hinder identification, many of the sites embodied innocuous seeming farm buildings.

During the next three weeks intense photographic reconnaissance revealed many more sites. By 12th June, the day before the first flying bombs were launched against London, sixty-six modified sites had been identified; forty-two were in the area Somme – Pas de Calais, all aligned on London, and twenty-four in the Cherbourg peninsula and the Calvados department, all aligned on South coast ports and Bristol. This implied a far swifter rate of construction than at ski sites; and the explanation was, so Air Intelligence reported on 9th June, that prefabricated units were used for the square building and the foundations of the launching ramp – the two essential components of the site. Once these structures had been placed in position the whole site could be completed within a fortnight.

The threat was obvious enough and was appreciated the more clearly coming as it did at a time when the ski sites were being dealt with effectively. But modified sites were an even more difficult target than ski sites. An experimental attack was carried out by Typhoon bombers of the 2nd Tactical Air Force on a site in the Cherbourg peninsula on 27th May, but met with little success, the pilots reporting that it had been extremely difficult to find. However, there was some doubt whether the new launching system was best attacked at the sites themselves. The size and construction of a typical modified site included no facilities, so far as could be seen, for storing and assembling flying bombs. Therefore, the rate of fire might be most affected if the sources from which missiles and fuel were transported to the sites were identified and attacked. Here the eight so-called supply sites came into the picture once more. Up to the middle of May these had remained inactive; nor was there any correlation between their location and that of the modified sites, some being as close as three miles, others as far away as twenty-five. But presumably they had been erected for a purpose, which seemed to be that of supply, and presumably the Germans intended to use them, for all were well defended. Thus on 16th May the Chiefs of Staff "invited the Air Ministry to examine and report on the desirability of attacking supply sites rather than the new type of pilotless aircraft sites." Ten days elapsed before a report was rendered. In it, it was admitted that no relationship between the two types of site could be established; but as photographic reconnaissance alone could not settle what was the purpose of the supply sites it was recommended that an attack by heavy day bombers be made against a selected site. This would at least display the enemy's reaction and, if it was followed closely by photographic reconnaissance, might indicate the contents of the various buildings. The Chiefs of Staff agreed.

The first attack was made against the site at Beauvoir on 29th May by sixty-four Marauders of the 8th Air Force; a second attack by Liberators of the 8th Air Force was made a few days later. In all, 293 tons of bombs were dropped. Results were not considered satisfactory but there was this that was thought to be significant: that up to 10th June the Germans had made no attempt to repair a number of breaches that had been made in the railway line that led to the site. Nor had there been any indications at other supply sites that the Germans were moving in supplies. 12th June arrived, therefore, with the supply sites still an unknown quantity and with no connection established between them and the modified sites.

*d. Final Reports on the Prospects of Flying Bomb Attack.*
It had always been appreciated that an indication that attack was imminent would be obtained partly from the state of preparedness at the launching sites, partly, and more particularly, from reports of the movement of supplies towards the sites. Up to and including 11th June there was no evidence that supplies were on their way; and on 11th June the Deputy Chief of Air Staff reported that the general position was as follows.

"It is estimated that the fire power which might be developed from those ski sites aligned on London is equivalent to that of approximately 8 completed sites. This is on the assumption that all the necessary technical equipment and weapons are available at sites; there is as yet no confirmation of this. On this basis it is estimated that the scale of attack on Greater London by pilotless aircraft does not amount to more than the equivalent of 90 tons of bombs in a period of ten hours. The number of times it will be possible for the enemy to repeat such a scale of attack will depend upon the reserve of weapons he is able to accumulate in firing areas. It is likely that the damage caused to his communications and the fact that other transport commitments have overriding priority will so affect the delivery of pilotless aircraft from Germany that, for the time being, he will not be able to sustain more than minor harassing attacks.

The above estimate of the scale of attack does not take into account the modified sites. From an examination of the evidence received to date, it does not appear probable that these sites will be completed and capable of operating pilotless aircraft on any appreciable scale within the next three or four weeks."

Fortunately for the credit of Air Intelligence this was not the last forecast before the attack opened. On the same day as the report was rendered, photographic reconnaissances were flown over a number of modified sites in the Pas de Calais. They were the first since 4th June, the weather having been bad during the intervening week. Photographs of nine sites were immediately examined by the Central Interpretation Unit, and the resulting interpretation was embodied in a report that was made to the Chiefs of Staff by A.C.A.S. (I) on the morning of 12th June.

It appeared that there was much activity at six out of the nine sites; rails had been laid on the launching ramps at four sites; and at six sites the square non-magnetic building had been completed. A report had also been received on the 11th from a usually reliable source that on the 9th/10th a train of thirty-three wagons, each nearly sixty feet long, and each loaded with three "rockets" had passed through Ghent for Tourcoing. According to our agent, further trains were expected. In the view of Air Intelligence, the objects were more likely to be the fuselages of flying bombs rather than A-4 rockets. A.C.A.S. (I) summed up the situation thus.

"Without further evidence no definite conclusion can be arrived at in regard to the intended scale and timing of an attack on this country, but the indications are that the Germans are making energetic preparations to bring the pilotless aircraft sites into operation at an early date."

The next question was, what scale of attack would the modified sites be capable of? In a brief that was prepared on 12th June for the use of the Deputy Chief of Air Staff at a meeting of the Chiefs of Staff on the following day this was assessed at much the same figure as had been arrived at early in February, i.e. an initial heavy attack equivalent to four hundred tons of bombs in ten hours, two repeat attacks of the same scale at intervals of forty-eight hours, and thereafter six hundred tons a month. This, it should be noted, was expected to be the maximum weight of attack: it was not anticipated that the Germans would be able to achieve it, so unreliable were communications between northern France and Germany. Nevertheless, the signs that attack was imminent were not to be ignored, and the Deputy Chiefs of Air Staff intended to ask the Chiefs of Staff on the 13th to agree to attacks on the four supply sites in the area Somme – Pas de Calais.

But by that time the first flying bombs had been launched against the United Kingdom. The threat so long apprehended had at last materialised.

## 18. Survey of Counter-Measures, April 1943 – June 1944.
Between the beginning of the British investigation into German long-range weapons and the commencement of flying bomb attacks fourteen months had elapsed. For the first six months of that period the main problem was that of obtaining information about the development and production work that was going on in Germany. The one exception to this was the identification of the purpose of the heavy constructions that were being built in northern France. In each case the problem was entirely one for the Intelligence staffs to solve.

As far as Germany was concerned attention had from the beginning been directed towards the Baltic coast and by the end of June it had not only been established that Peenemünde was the centre of much new activity but that some form of rocket was being developed there. Not even the powerful arguments of Lord Cherwell could shake the belief of either Mr. Sandys or the majority of the Intelligence Officers who were concerned, that a dangerous weapon was being prepared for use against this country. It was still only a presumption, however, that there was a connection between Peenemünde and constructions in northern France such as that at Watten.

Nor was it known what would be the characteristics of the weapon. Indeed, it is not too much to say that the very principles of its construction were not appreciated in this country until well into 1944. Such estimates of its performance and effect as were made during the summer of 1943 indicated a missile far heavier and more destructive than that which the Germans were actually developing. It was on this account that schemes of civil security remained embryonic; for until it was more certain that the rocket was indeed such as the scientists indicated there was some reluctance to commit the country to massive preparations against it. Certain modifications to the radar organisation were put in hand and something was done to establish a warning system for the general public. Otherwise, concrete measures were few.

But there was at least this to go on: that whatever form the rocket took Peenemünde was a focus of work upon it. Thus, the next important step was the heavy attack on Peenemünde by Bomber Command on the night of 17th August 1943. The precise effects of this raid were difficult to assess but that it delayed development is certain. Shortly afterwards, attacks were made upon Watten by the 8th Air Force with such success that work there was interrupted for the better part of three months. Those measures, and a few attacks upon factories, were the only direct blows at the new weapon until the last few weeks of the year.

The late summer and autumn of 1943, however, saw first, the emergence of the flying bomb as a second long range weapon, and second, the identification of the ski sites in northern France as launching points for it. The processes of intelligence that led up to this revelation have been sufficiently reviewed; and it will have been appreciated that each had a vital part to play in reconstructing what were the German intentions. But it is fair to select the photographic reconnaissance of the Peenemünde area on 28th November 1943 as the final link in the chain.

Thenceforwards it was possible for the first time to plan effective counter-measures without being hampered by the conjectures and controversies that had marked the investigation into the rocket. One, at least, of the projected weapons was now known; and a definite policy of destroying the sites from which it could be launched was embarked upon. This did not mean that the rocket was neglected. The work of investigation went on and was eventually not less successful than in the case of the flying bomb. But it went on quietly as part of the ordinary responsibilities of Air Intelligence: the earlier atmosphere of urgency and alarm, of extraordinary meetings of the Defence Committee and special enquiries, disappeared. Moreover, some of the attacks against northern France were directed against the seven large sites which were thought to be connected with rocket attack.

Broadly speaking, however, from November 1943 to June 1944 the rocket was, as it were, in eclipse. The main concern was the flying bomb and the sites from which it was expected that attack would be launched. The offensive against the latter began on 5th December and lasted until the end of May. The progress that was made in destroying sites was never constant, varying principally according to the weight of attack that was brought to bear. Nor were the arrangements that were made between each of the attacking forces, A.E.A.F. and the 8th Air Force, satisfactory. Nevertheless, by the end of April the ski sites were so badly damaged that their potential rate of fire was no serious menace; and this was the position when the invasion of France began. What was not least notable about this victory was that it had been achieved without interfering to any notable extent with bombardment preliminary to invasion.

This attack on ski sites was indeed an Allied victory in that it forced the Germans first to amend and finally to abandon their original system of sites, none of which, or possibly only one, was actually used. It appears that the Germans appreciated the vulnerability of the ski sites almost as soon as attacks upon them had started – one would have thought they might have appreciated this even earlier – but it was not until the end of March 1944 that they began the construction of the modified type of site which they had designed in the meantime. While this was evidence of the success of Allied bombing it was also proof of the German determination to bring their novel weapon into action; and it was in fact from the modified sites that the main attack upon London was launched. Thus, it cannot be claimed that the victory of the Allied bombers was absolute. On account of the bombing the Germans were forced to alter their plans; but their plans were sufficiently flexible for an alternative system of sites to be constructed and brought into operation. On the whole, however, there was much to be thankful for on 12th June 1944. For the invasion of France had been successfully launched and Allied troops were established there; whereas when the threat from the new German weapons had first appeared there seemed to be the possibility that it would force at least the amendment of the invasion plans if not their abandonment.

# Part IV

# The Attack on London from Northern France: 13th June – 15th July 1944.

**19. The First Attack**.

The first flying bomb to fall in the United Kingdom fell at 0418 hours on 13th June at Swanscombe, four and a half miles west of Gravesend. (A.W.A.S. Summary[30]) Six minutes later a second fell at Cuckfield in Sussex and was followed a minute afterwards by one at Bethnal Green, where the L.N.E.R. bridge over Grove Road was demolished. A fourth bomb fell at 0506 hours at Platt, near Sevenoaks. The only casualties were at Bethnal Green where six people were killed and nine seriously injured.

These were the only flying bombs to fall on British territory until the night of 15th June. First reports from the radar station and the Royal Observer Corps indicated that as many as twenty-seven were launched, including four from the Cherbourg peninsula towards Lyme Bay; but after analysis this figure was altered to eleven. A well-informed prisoner who was captured in April 1945 said that only four or five were dispatched; while according to the War Diary of Flak Regiment 155W, seven were launched, four of them unsuccessfully.

What is beyond doubt, however, is that the attack was not a mere trial. It was intended to be the beginning of a full offensive[31], with piloted bombers of the G.A.F. participating in at least the initial attack. One Me.410 was certainly over the London area on the morning of the 13th, and was shot down by anti-aircraft fire near Barking at 0305 hours; but the enemy found it impossible either to carry out the joint operation or to bring more than one or two sites into action[32].

**20. Action taken in the United Kingdom**.

At the morning meeting of the Chiefs of Staff Committee on 13th the Chief of the Air Staff reported that it was not certain whether the attack had come from such ski sites as were complete or from modified sites. On the whole, the evidence pointed to the latter; the question was, therefore, whether the modified sites should be attacked. Forty-two of these had been identified in the Somme – Pas de Calais; and it was estimated that some three thousand Fortress sorties or five thousand Marauders would be required to neutralise them, which meant a large diversion from the needs of the battle on land. On the other hand, the four supply sites in the same area – Domleger, Beauvoir, Sautrecourt and Renescure – might be neutralised in nine hundred to a thousand Fortress sorties. Consequently, although there was still no established connection between this type of site and either the ski or modified sites, the Chief of the Air Staff recommended that the four sites in question should be heavily attacked immediately and that all launching sites should also be attacked whenever effort could be spared. He made it quite clear that the needs of the Battle of France should not be prejudiced.[33]

A new series of attacks against supply sites was initiated by aircraft of the U.S. VIIIth Air Force when they bombed Beauvoir and Domleger on the 14th. Results were poor, however, in each case. Another attack on Beauvoir on the 15th by Fortresses was unsuccessful, but on the 16th, Bomber Command reported good concentrations of bombs on each of the four sites. No modified sites were attacked; and it is true to say that between the 13th and 16th the Germans were able to complete their preparations for the start of heavy attacks without interference from bombing.

On the defensive side equally little was done. The defences allotted to the invasion ports and bases were in position and nothing was done to weaken them in order to protect London. Air Marshal Hill did not press for it; it would indeed have been surprising if so light an attack had been made the occasion for the large and complicated deployment which was entailed in the existing plan of defence against flying bombs. From the 13th, however, intruder aircraft of A.D.G.B. were sent out to patrol the area of the launching sites. For the same reason – that the attack was so light – the War Cabinet at their evening meeting on the 13th decided to wait for a heavier attack before any announcement of the arrival of the new weapon was made to the general public. It was agreed that the term 'Southern England' should henceforth be used in reporting any incidents that occurred south of a line from the Bristol Channel to the Wash.

## 21. The Attack of 15th/16th June.

On the night of 15th June, a heavy and sustained attack began. Between 2230 hours and 2239 hours on the following night 151 flying bombs were reported by the defences,[34] 144 crossed the coast of England and 73 reached the London area. Of those that fell outside London 14 were shot down by anti-aircraft guns, seven by fighters and one was destroyed by combined gun and fighter action. Anti-aircraft guns of the Inner Artillery Zone were in action and brought down eleven flying bombs inside the built-up area. There were a number of gross errors in accuracy. One flying bomb fell near Chichester, and another as far north as Framlingham in Norfolk. Inside London seventy per cent of the bombs fell south of the river.

## 22. Counter-measures of 16th June.

*a. By the War Cabinet and the Chiefs of Staff.*

Clearly the country was faced with a very different situation to that of 13th June. The Germans had obviously got sufficient sites in action to subject London to a serious scale of attack; though how long the attack could be continued was, of course, not known. The Home Secretary made a statement in the House of Commons on the morning of the 16th, which not least had the merit of correcting the more extravagant speculations of Londoners. The Chiefs of Staff agreed on the morning of the same day that the 'Diver' deployment of guns and balloons should be put into effect. The searchlights demanded by the plan were already deployed as part of the ordinary defences of the south-east. The full deployment of balloons was expected to take about a fortnight to complete; but some of the guns which it had been intended to use were still in their 'Overlord' positions and the Deputy Chief of the Air Staff, as the officer responsible in general for 'Crossbow', did not give a date by which the gun deployment would be completed.

On the evening of the same day a Staff Conference was called by the Prime Minister and the following decisions were made:

"1. To request the Supreme Commander, Allied Expeditionary Force, to take all possible measures to neutralise the supply and launching sites, subject to no interference with the essential requirements of the battle in France.

2. That the air raid warning should not be sounded on the approach of a single pilotless aircraft. At night, the sounding of the siren should be reduced to the minimum and the warning should be only sounded on the approach of the first 'covey'.

3. That for the time being, pending further experience, the anti-

aircraft guns, both inside and outside the London area, should continue to engage pilotless aircraft.

4. That the Air Marshal Commanding, A.D.G.B., in consultation with the G.O.C.-in-C., Anti-Aircraft Command, should re-distribute the gun, searchlight and balloon defences, as necessary, to counter the attacks.[35]

5. That the Air Marshal Commanding, A.D.G.B., should consider the use of armed cables on those balloons deployed against piloted aircraft."

In short, these decisions meant that counter-measures were to be applied immediately; the defensive deployment was to go ahead as planned; counter-bombing was to be begun on as big a scale as possible so long as the battle in Normandy did not suffer; and the general public were to be encouraged to carry on as normally as they could.

*b. By the Operational Commands.*

Fighters of A.D.G.B. and guns of Anti-Aircraft Command were both in action on the night of the 15th and the following day. Eleven fighter squadrons, including two of Mosquitos which operated at night, carried out eighty patrols. The London guns and those deployed between London and the coast were frequently in action and claimed twenty-seven flying bombs destroyed. Thirteen of these, however, came down inside the London area, which profited little.

On the same day the first moves were made to put the planned deployment into effect. The project entailed moving 192 heavy and 192 light guns and 480 balloons. Not much could be done until the evening of the 16th owing to the needs of invasion traffic. On the following day, however, Anti-Aircraft Command reported that one regiment had taken up its new positions in the early hours of the 17th and that three regiments of each type of gun would be deployed by that night. It was expected that the full deployment would have been completed within three or four days. For the time being all guns were drawn from Anti-Aircraft Command.

Balloon Command also reported on the same day that their deployment was going ahead and would be completed in about a week. It was, in fact, completed on 21st June, whereas under the Concurrent Plan a full fortnight had been allowed.

Energetic offensive action was also called for by the opening of the attacks, the more so as the deployment of the defences would take some time. On the 16th itself, however, not much was done. Air Chief Marshal Leigh-Mallory had by then been informed by Air Ministry that the four supply sites in the Pas de Calais were regarded as priority targets, followed by eleven of the original ski sites, then twelve modified sites which were believed to be in operation; and in response to this he arranged with Air Chief Marshal Harris that the four supply sites should be attacked that same night. But beyond a warning to Air Marshal Coningham that the fighter-bombers of 2nd Tactical Air Force might have to be diverted to the attack of modified sites he gave no further instructions.

This is not surprising. In the first place, the same bad weather that was hindering the invasion expedition in Normandy made it impossible to launch effective attacks against targets in the Pas de Calais. But in any case, it was still not clear what were the best targets to attack. The target list issued by the Air Ministry, with its specifying of ski sites, is proof enough that we were not yet aware that only modified sites were in action. It was not until the following day that Air Chief Marshal Leigh-Mallory was informed of the true state of things. Meanwhile on the night of the 16th, and again on the following night, Bomber Command attacked the four supply sites – it was thought with great success. Otherwise there was no bombing of any type of site.

### 23. Amplifying of Counter-Measures, 17th – 23rd June.
There was a decline in the scale of flying bomb attack in the twenty-four hours following dusk on the 16th. Only eighty-three flying bombs crossed the coast, of which forty-eight came down in London. But the next twenty-four hours saw as heavy an attack as that of the 15th/16th; and the efforts to establish effective counter-measures continued.

*a. The Formation of the War Cabinet 'Crossbow' Sub-Committee.*
On the evening of the 18th the Prime Minister held another Staff Conference to review what had already been done and what was planned. Again, it was emphasised that the supply and launching sites (including the large sites) should be hit as hard as the Battle of Normandy would allow; every effort should be made to improve the efficiency of the various arms of defence; and the public should be encouraged to carry on as usual, with the proviso that they should sleep in as safe a place as they could find. The Prime Minister also decided that he would hold a daily meeting at which the departments and operational Commands most concerned in countering the attack would be represented.

It appears to have been the Prime Minister's intention to preside over this body himself, giving it that same powerful authority as earlier special committees that he had established to consider vital operations: as, for example, the Night Air Defence Committee and the "Battle of the Atlantic" Committee, which had not, however, met daily. On 19th June such a meeting was held: Field Marshal Smuts, the Home Secretary, the Secretary of State for Air, the three Chiefs of Staff and the Deputy Supreme Commander, were amongst those present. But on the 20th after consulting the Chiefs of Staff, the Prime Minister came to the conclusion that the day to day consideration of plans and policy would be better carried out by a smaller body of less eminent men. The connection with himself, as Minister of Defence, was retained by instructing the new body to report to him as well as to the Home Secretary and the Chiefs of Staff; its chairman was Mr Duncan Sandys, and A.D.G.B., Anti-Aircraft Command, the Air Staff, the Supreme Allied Commander and the Ministry of Home Security were represented on it. It was not an executive body, but as it reviewed the progress of every sort of counter-measure its deliberations form one of the most important records of the campaign.

b. *Expansion of the 'Diver' Defences.*

During this first week of attack the deployment of guns and balloons and the allocation of fighter squadrons to flying bomb patrols was rapidly carried out. As we have seen, the planned balloon deployment had been completed by 21st June. The deployment of guns was also virtually complete by the same date, and eight single seater fighter squadrons of No. 11 Group, A.D.G.B., and four Mosquito squadrons were being employed on flying bomb patrols. But already Air Marshal Hill, General Pile and Air Vice-Marshal Gell of Balloon Command, had appreciated that more weapons were required than the Concurrent Plan had envisaged. By the 21st, Anti-Aircraft Command were examining a plan to increase the number of guns in the gun belt to 376 heavy (almost double the planned deployment) and 540 light (almost treble). Balloon Command, for their part, were organising an increase of their deployed strength from four hundred and eighty to one thousand balloons. No increase in the number of fighters was contemplated. The problem here was not one of numbers but of increasing the efficiency and effectiveness of the equipment already in use; and not only in fighters but throughout the whole system – radar stations, Royal Observer Corps and operations rooms – by which fighter operations were controlled.

c. *Formation of a Bombing Policy: First Effects of Bombardment.*

An analogous examination of what form the counter-offensive should take was being made during the same period by A.E.A.F., Bomber Command and the 8th Air Force under the surveillance of Air Chief Marshal Tedder. The necessary intelligence came to the operational Commands through the Directorate of Operations (Special Operations) at Air Ministry. On 18th June Air Chief Marshal Tedder, with the full approval of the Supreme Commander, directed that a big effort should be made against 'Crossbow' targets in the near future while the battle on land was still going well. The latter was still to have first claim upon the Allied bomber resources; but once needs had been provided for, 'Crossbow' had priority over all other tasks.[36]

Of the various sorts of 'Crossbow' targets, large sites were considered the most important, then came the supply sites and then the forty-seven modified sites that had by now been identified in the area Somme – Pas de Calais. To these was added, on 21st June, a suspected railhead for flying bomb supply at Nucourt, fifteen miles north-west of Paris, and also the electricity system in the Pas de Calais, which was thought to be important to the functioning of large sites and supply sites. This last target was suggested by Lieut.-General Spaatz.

But during this first week of heavy flying bomb attack the counter-offensive was not satisfactory. One reason is clear enough, and nobody could be blamed for it: it was the weather, which severely curtailed flying during most of the week. It was also the case, however, that neither Air Chief Marshal Harris nor Lieut.-General Doolittle, the commander of the 8th Air Force, was convinced that their forces could as yet play a useful part in countering the enemy's attack. Neither was satisfied about the selection of targets. Air Chief Marshal Harris, after Bomber Command aircraft had attacked supply sites on successive nights – 16th and 17th June – intimated that he was unwilling to attack this type of target again until photographic reconnaissance had established the need. Nor were he and Lieut.-General Doolittle happy about the attack of modified sites, which were so many in number that to be sure of limiting the scale of attack a large number of exceptionally accurate attacks had to be carried out. There was also a strong feeling that attacks should be suspended until clear weather[37] gave an opportunity for a very heavy blow. Meanwhile a much more attractive operation, both to the 8th Air Force and Bomber Command, was projected: a massive attack on Berlin by twelve hundred aircraft of the 8th Air Force and eight hundred of Bomber Command. Air Chief Marshal Tedder was in favour of it, pointing out that one of its advantages would be to damp the spirits of the German people which had been temporarily raised by the exaggerated accounts of flying bomb damage in London. In this sense, so it was argued, such an attack would play its part in the flying bomb campaign.[38] But Air Chief Marshal Tedder did not regard it as a substitute for the attack of the flying bomb organisation proper, and on 23rd June he instructed the Allied Air Commanders that they must seize even a fleeting opportunity for the attack of sites. He suggested that the 8th Air Force kept a force permanently standing by for 'Crossbow' work. Lieut.-General Doolittle agreed to set aside two hundred aircraft.

Altogether, up to 23rd June the counter-offensive, for one reason and another, had not, as it were, settled down. But it had not been barren of results. On the 23rd, three supply sites – Domleger, Sautrecourt and St. Martin l'Hortier – were suspended from further attack. Watten, Wizernes, Siracourt and Mimoyecques, all large sites, had been badly damaged. One attack on Watten by No. 617 Squadron of Bomber Command had been particularly successful. This squadron, which was specially trained in bombing with 12,000 lb. bombs, attacked at dusk on 19th June. Fifteen bombs were dropped, twelve falling within a hundred yards of the aiming point. The first attack on a supply depot – Nucourt – was also successful. Two hundred and fifty tons of bombs were dropped by Fortresses of the 8th Air Force on 22nd June. Buildings and railway facilities were damaged and in three places the ground subsided, indicating that the roofs of underground store chambers had collapsed. In addition, at least six and possibly nine ski and modified sites had been made Category A during the week. Much of this was the work of 2nd Tactical Air Force; but the commander of this force, Air Marshal Coningham, was already seeking permission to be allowed to concentrate on the support of the battle on land.

### 24. Problems of Defence.
It was possible to discern some return for the efforts of the Allied bombers in the scale of flying bomb attack during this period; for only on the 17th/18th and 22nd/23rd was there an attack comparable to that of the 15th/16th, when 151 bombs had been reported. The average for each dusk-dusk period over the whole week was 97 bombs.

But if there was any connection between our bombing and the diminished scale of flying bomb attack, it was not one that could be precisely defined. It was certainly not such that there could be any slackening of the effort to create an effective defence of London. It was in fact to this problem that the attention of those responsible for counter-measures was principally directed.

*a. Intelligence on the Flying Bomb Organisation: Characteristics of the Weapon.*
Nor was there any evidence that the Germans were not prepared to maintain the attack. On the contrary, available intelligence, while it was by no means complete, pointed unmistakably to a well-prepared

organisation. Up to 24th June fifty modified sites had been discovered in the Pas de Calais; thirty-four were complete and twenty-one had been identified as having been in operation. Only two modified sites had been spotted between the Seine and the Somme; but it was evident from radar plots that there were other sites in that area that were actually in use.

What was the next link in the chain of the German organisation was not quite clear. Logically it could well have been the supply sites; but even after two such sites in the Cherbourg peninsula – Valognes and Bricquebec – had been captured and inspected it was still not possible to confirm this. It seemed probable that special fuels were stored to supply sites and also that spare parts and equipment were kept there. Air Intelligence however, could not and would not say that the destruction of this type of site would seriously affect the scale of attack; nor did they say that it would not.

Evidence was in fact accumulating during this third week in June that pointed to the direct delivery of bombs and equipment from storage depots[39] at railheads to the modified sites, thus avoiding the use of supply sites. Two such depots – one at Nucourt and the other at St. Leu d'Esserent – had been identified by 24th June, and others were suspected. Supplies were delivered by rail to these depots, which included much underground storage capacity, and from there by road to the modified sites, usually, and probably entirely, at night.

Summing up the position, A.C.A.S. (I) reported on 26th June, "it must be expected that the enemy's scale of attack will be maintained at its present level and might even increase. Against this, however, must be set the damage being done to the supply sites, depots and other elements of the enemy's rear organisation. On balance it seems unlikely that the scale of attack will increase greatly before it declines."

Scale of attack was one thing, the effect of the attack another; and it was the aim of the defenders to reduce the latter even if the former remained the same. Here the first factor to be considered was the performance of the flying bomb itself. First reports indicated two types: one with a wing span of 17 feet 6 inches, another with one of 16 feet, of which the first was thought to have a heavier explosive charge.[40] Height and speed, the two features which most affected the defending guns and fighters, varied appreciably. Bombs were observed at heights of between 1,000 and 4,000 feet, flying at speeds which appeared to vary between 250 and 400 m.p.h. Their accuracy was such that approximately 65 per cent of the bombs launched reached the London area if not interfered with; which meant that the majority of the bombs, after crossing the coast between Beachy Head and the South Foreland, converged upon the line Dorking – Gravesend and thence passed into the London area.

*b. The Time and Space Problem; First Attempts at Solution.*

The speed of the bombs was found to be between 300 and 350 m.p.h.[41] which, combined with their low altitude, made the work of guns and fighters, separately and in co-operation, more difficult than in the case of attacks by piloted aircraft. At a height of 3,000 feet the bomb presented a target almost equally awkward for both heavy and light anti-aircraft gunners, being at once on the low side for the one and too high for the others. The heavy anti-aircraft regiments were trained and equipped principally to deal with attacks by piloted bombers at high altitudes. The flying bomb, however, crossed the field of vision far more rapidly than any bomber flying at normal operational height. G.L. and predictor operators had therefore to work much more quickly than usual to obtain the necessary fire data for the guns, which in turn had to be traversed and elevated at a speed which proved in fact to be too much for manual laying. The light guns suffered from some of the same disadvantages, with the additional one that this type of anti-aircraft weapon is best used for the close defence of specific and small objectives, whereas in these novel circumstances they had to be widely deployed well away from the target area of London. Up to 18th June both the heavy and light guns that were sited for the close defence of London were allowed to engage flying bombs. Thereafter this was prohibited. For one thing, their patent lack of success was not calculated to improve the morale of Londoners; for another, even when successful, the bombs they hit usually came down and exploded in the built-up area.

As for the fighters, their small margin of speed over the flying bombs, coupled with the short time in which interception had to be made, demanded that they should be quickly and accurately directed on to the course of the bomb. Otherwise, the pursuing fighter reached the gun and balloon belts, and London itself, before the flying bomb could be attacked. There was thus a problem of warning and control to be solved of the same sort, though different in degree, as that which the co-ordinated working of radar stations, the Royal Observer Corps and the system of telecommunications and operations rooms had been solving with fair success for the interception of piloted aircraft since the outbreak of war.

The same was true of the defence system as a whole. It was not just a matter of improving the efficiency of the guns, searchlights, balloons and fighters as separate weapons but of co-ordinating their activities so as to obtain the optimum effect. This was especially so in respect of guns and fighters.

All the 'Diver' defences were controlled from the operations room of the Biggin Hill sector – the operations room at No. 11 Group Headquarters was fully occupied in controlling operations over France. To it was passed all information from the radar stations and the Royal Observer Corps and to it were linked the operations rooms of the guns in the 'Diver' area. But the control that was exercised from Biggin Hill was general and not specific. That is to say, it was not analogous to the procedure that had normally been employed in defence against piloted aircraft, where the direction of intercepting fighters was the work of the sector operations room. Instead, the executive control of patrolling fighters was vested in the same agencies as detected and plotted the flying bombs. Thus, radar stations and the Royal Observer Corps Centres at Horsham and Maidstone were used as fighter direction stations. The reason for such decentralisation was, of course, that the time available for interception was shorter than in the case of attack by piloted aircraft. Similarly, Anti-Aircraft Command found that to control the firing of individual batteries from gun operations rooms was impracticable; batteries were allowed to fire independently except where the gun operations room ordered fire to cease, for example, for the safeguarding of friendly aircraft. In both the Biggin Hill operations room and, through the transmission of information, in the gun operations rooms a complete picture of the state of the battle was progressively recorded, but neither was used for the minute control of fighters and guns.

The system needed supplementing by a number of standing orders designed to avoid mutual interference between the guns, fighters and balloons. Weather was an important factor to be considered when framing them.

As early as 16th June, Air Marshal Hill decided that fighters would patrol over the Channel and the land between the coast and the southern limit of the gun belt. They could pass over the gun belt only when in pursuit of a flying bomb, in which case the guns were not to open fire. On 19th June it was decided that on days of very good visibility, only fighters would operate: on bad days, only the guns: on moderate days, guns and fighters would operate, each in their own areas. These principles were expanded on the 26th under the code names, 'Flabby', 'Spouse' and 'Fickle'. The three forms of procedure can be summarised as follows:

Flabby
Condition – Weather suitable for fighters.

Effect – Total prohibition of gunfire.

Spouse
Condition – Weather unsuitable for fighters.

Effect – Complete freedom to guns.

Fickle
Average weather conditions.

Effect – in 'Diver' belt, guns allowed to fire up to 8,000 feet. Fighters prohibited entry except when making a visual interception. Outside the 'Diver' belt, fighters given freedom of action. Light anti-aircraft guns allowed to fire by day against visual targets if no fighters present.

It cannot be claimed, however, that these rules solved the problem. Fighter pilots were frequently reporting that they had been engaged by the guns; the gunners no less frequently reported that fighters had hindered their shooting; and as will be seen, it was not until the whole scheme of defence was radically altered in the middle of July that these difficulties were overcome. Meanwhile, the gunners and the fighter pilots had not that mutual confidence that is essential to the full success of combined operations.

*c. Improvements in Equipment and Tactics.*
The first weeks of the attack were more difficult for the defenders because the equipment that was available proved unsatisfactory in many respects and was subjected to numerous experiments and changes. Moreover, the novel form of attack demanded novel tactics to counter-act it.

Fighters. Tempest Vs, Spitfire XIVs, XIIs and IXs, Typhoons and, at night, Mosquitos were the first type of fighter aircraft to be used. Of the day fighters, the first two were the fastest and, for this reason, the most suitable. The Mustang III was also satisfactory and from 3rd July onwards this aircraft began to play an important part. Mosquitos were used at night with good results to the end of the campaign, but they were not as fast as the job demanded and almost from the beginning of the attack day fighters were also employed at night. They proved unsatisfactory at first, partly because pilots were also required to fly by day, partly because they were not well trained in night flying; and it was not until volunteers from Mosquito squadrons had been given short conversion courses on Tempests that the faster day fighter achieved good results at night.

As for the actual interception of flying bombs, this was largely a matter of obtaining accurate information on the course of the missile and transmitting it rapidly from the sources on the ground through the fighter controller to the patrolling pilot. But it did not end there. The pilot, having been told where to look for his target, had to find it. By day, this was not easy even in good weather, for the flying bomb was small and it travelled fast. Experience quickly showed that it could most easily be identified in twilight; and 'Flabby', i.e. complete freedom of action for the fighters, was frequently instituted at dawn and dusk for this reason. At night, the task of spotting the bomb was relatively easy, thanks to the glare from the propulsion unit, though this also made it difficult to bring accurate fire to bear.

By the end of June, the methods for controlling fighters were of two main sorts, one of which was used solely for controlling fighters over the Channel, the other chiefly for fighters patrolling overland. The first of these – the 'close control' method – entailed the direction of individual fighters by controllers located at radar stations on the coast. Approaching flying bombs were plotted in the control room of the radar station, from which the controller, who was in R/T communication with the patrolling fighter, would issue detailed instructions on course so as to bring the pilot into a position to intercept. The factor limiting the extent to which the method could be used was the number of control points available. Four radar stations – Fairlight (MEW), Fairlight (CHL), Swingate (CHL), Beachy Head (CHL) – were being used for this work by the middle of July. The principle practical difficulty was that existing types of radar station could not, for technical reasons, provide sufficiently early warning of an approaching bomb. The best of the stations rarely detected the bombs at ranges of more than fifty miles; which meant that the fighter had, even in theory, only six minutes to intercept before the bomb reached the coast. In practice it had less: firstly, because there was a time lag between the initial detection of a bomb and the transmission of interception data from the fighter controller to the pilot; secondly, because patrols could not be carried out at the limit of radar detection because of the danger of being surprised by enemy fighters. This was especially the case in the Straits of Dover, where our fighters had at most three minutes in which to intercept a bomb before the Kent coast was reached.

'Close control' was persevered with, however, for where successful it usually resulted in bombs falling harmlessly into the sea. But it was no use overland, where there were no low-looking radar facilities. Here the 'running commentary' method was used. The controllers using this technique were located, some at three radar stations – Beachy Head, Hythe and Sandwich – and others at two Royal Observer Corps Centres at Horsham and Maidstone. In the 'running commentary' method, the position and course of flying bombs was passed by the controller to all patrolling fighters working on the same R/T frequency, who then worked out their own course to their target. The method was used for seaward patrolling fighters also; but it was at its best overland where landmarks, shell bursts, rockets from R.O.C. posts and searchlight beams all helped the pilots to make speedy interceptions. The chief fault that arose was that more than one fighter frequently went after the same flying bomb, a waste of effort which meant that some flying bombs slipped through unmolested.

Engaging and destroying the bomb had also its problems. Chasing a flying bomb from astern meant a long and probably fruitless pursuit unless the fighter pilot had an advantage in height at the moment of sighting. The best method of closing to attack was, therefore, to fly on the same, or nearly the same course, as an approaching flying bomb so that it came to the fighter, rather than the fighter to the bomb. Usually it was possible to employ only brief deflection shots, so high were the speeds at which combat took place; and the vast majority of destructions were the result of fire from astern. In this position the effect of the slipstream of the flying bomb made it difficult to hold a steady aim, and short bursts of fire and frequent aiming corrections were necessary. For the same reason, the shorter the range the more effective the fire, with the proviso that the fighter did not approach closer than two hundred yards, otherwise the blast from an exploded bomb might be fatal. To cap it all, it was found that the flying bomb was robust enough to take a good deal of punishment before exploding or being brought down.

Guns. The problem that Anti-Aircraft Command faced were no less difficult than those of the fighters. During the first fortnight of the attack they were partly matters of organisation arising out of certain modifications in the Concurrent Plan that were found to be necessary. Under this plan the sites that had been selected for the heavy guns were located in hollows and folds in the ground so that Gun Laying radar might be as free as possible from enemy jamming. Counter-measures to jamming which had been taken prior to the invasion of France had reduced this possibility, and sites on higher ground could thus be utilised. This meant relaying the extensive network of telecommunications that had been established under the earlier plan. Signals detachments of Anti-Aircraft Command and the G.P.O. completed the task by 28th June.

Light guns had also to be resited. Originally, the intention was to deploy these at searchlight sights over whole of the 'Diver' Defence Area so that they could make use of the radar equipment of the searchlights for the engaging of unseen targets. But after the attack had started, Anti-Aircraft Command changed their requirement and the light guns were then concentrated in a belt forward of the heavy guns in order to make the best use of their fire power. This redeployment was still taking place on 26th June.

The deficiencies of equipment that rapidly became apparent were mainly the result of the high speed of the flying bomb and, so to speak, its ability to operate at all times and in all weathers. The first deployment of 15th – 21st June had been made entirely in terms of mobile units of Anti-Aircraft Command, which were fully equipped with transport and could therefore move quickly. But the guns with which these regiments were equipped were 3.7" mobile guns which were manually controlled when firing and proved in practice to be slow to obtain good results. Hence it became essential to reinforce them by static 3.7" guns which could be automatically loaded and remotely controlled (i.e. the gun was traversed and elevated electrically as data was fed into it from the predictor). They were also fitted with the No. 11 Mechanical Fuse Setter which allowed a higher rate of fire and greater accuracy. This type of gun, however, took longer to move and emplace than the mobile 3.7". The difficulty was met by the devising of a steel mattress by the R.E.M.E. detachment at Headquarters, Anti-Aircraft Command, which did away with the necessity for an elaborate concrete emplacement. But it was not until 27th June that the first static guns had been placed in position in the 'Diver' belt.

Nor was it until that date that two new items of equipment which permitted the accurate engagement of unseen targets, began to come into service. These were the SCR 584 and the No. 10 Predictor. The first was an American radar set. It was capable of a number of operational functions but for defence against flying bombs it was used entirely for controlling gun fire against both visual and unseen targets. The No. 10 Predictor permitted more rapid and accurate tracking of targets than earlier models.

The introduction of both equipments at a time when operations were in progress involved a large and difficult retraining programme. No drill books, only a few instructors and little training equipment were available; and only a small number of personnel could be spared from a battery for instruction at any one time owing to the need for keeping the guns in action. These two equipments and the VT proximity fuse, which was only used on an adequate scale after the middle of July, were the prime mechanical reasons for the success that eventually attended the work of the guns.

The main development in respect of light guns was to link troops of four guns to a No. 1 Predictor, which was normally used with heavy guns, and thence to a G.L. Radar set. By these means light guns could be usefully employed against unseen targets, whereas with the usual light anti-aircraft predictor, the Predictor No. 3, only fire against visual targets was possible.

Balloons. No component of the defences was the subject of more experiments and suggestions for improvements than the balloon barrage. The arming of balloon cables commenced on 19th June and was completed for the first deployment of 480 balloons by 21st June. The next additions to the barrage, which more than doubled it, were also armed, as was the final strength of 1,750 balloons, though only after serious difficulties of supply had been overcome.

The arming device itself – D.P.L. (Double Parachute Length) was never entirely satisfactory. It had been designed to be actuated when piloted aircraft, travelling at speeds of 250 to 300 m.p.h., hit the balloon cable. But in the case of the flying bomb, which was usually travelling at nearly 400 m.p.h. by the time it reached the balloon barrage, the cable was not infrequently cut through before the D.P.L. could operate. This had been appreciated before the attack; and it was for this reason that the first balloons to be deployed had been unarmed. However, when the D.P.L. did function satisfactorily it was rarely that the bomb escaped destruction; and it was by these means that the majority of the flying bombs brought down through impact with balloons were destroyed.

Other measures that were considered and tried involved the use of kites and the suspension of nets and lengths of piano wire, but none was generally adopted until the attack had been in progress for over a month. Mathematically, the devices increased the chances of impact, but in practice loss of height, handling difficulties and ground obstructions affected their performance. Moreover, the thinner gauge wires had little capacity for destruction. The Admiralty were much to the fore in these experiments, doubtless seeing an analogy between the balloon barrage and the minefield of naval warfare. There was indeed this obvious similarity, that the balloons were sited for the close protection of the enemy's target and were an obstacle that had to be overcome if the flying bombs were to reach London. They were not, however, like the naval minefield, a permanent hazard; for there were often days of bad weather on which the barrage could only be raised for a few hours at a time. At one period the question of keeping the balloons in operation whatever the weather was discussed; but on examining the records of balloon destruction during the war through bad weather it was agreed that unacceptably high wastage might result and the proposal was not adopted. There was one good logistical reason – the shortage of hydrogen – which would have been aggravated by heavy casualties.

On the whole, the balloons did what was expected of them. They were responsible for a comparatively small proportion of the bombs that were destroyed; but they were, of course, presented with fewer targets than the guns and fighters. That the Germans feared them is obvious enough from the steps that they took to fit some at least of the flying bombs with devices for warding off or cutting cables.

Radar. The radar equipment that was located on the south and south-east coasts at the beginning of the attack was found not to be fully satisfactory. Sufficiently early warning of the approach of bombs was obtained for the purpose of public warning; the tracking of bombs was fairly good and made possible the direct control from radar stations of interceptions by patrolling fighters; an indication of the direction and height of attack could also be given to the Gun Operations Rooms or Anti-Aircraft Command. But in none of these resects were results as good as the situation required. In particular, the continuity of tracking was poor and during a heavy attack not all flying bombs were detected. The average range at which continuous tracking was possible was about 36-40 miles, which was less than had been anticipated. In one important respect results were definitely poor, namely the location of the sites from which bombs were being fired. It was especially poor for the area between the Seine and the Somme. Without accurate plotting of this sort the bombing of the sites that were being used by the enemy was so much more difficult.

The first noteworthy measures to improve the efficiency of radar were not taken until the last week in June, which meant that the new developments were introduced after the period that is under review. Some indication here, however, of what form these took will bring out by implication the deficiencies of the equipment that was in use during the early weeks of the attack.

One of the main problems was to distinguish quickly between ordinary aircraft and flying bombs, a problem which was particularly difficult when aircraft were operating in strength over northern France, which frequently happened despite prohibitions to the contrary. Thus, one of the earliest modifications was to provide centimetre height finding equipment at two of the best placed C.H.L. stations – at Beachy Head and Fairlight. This work was completed by 14th July and at two other stations – Swingate and Foreness – by 9th August. The more accurate information that was obtained also facilitated the direction of defending fighters.

The design of a device for detecting propeller modulation was also hastened so as to distinguish between aircraft with a normal airscrew and jet or rocket propelled aircraft. The first models were fitted at the Beachy Head and Hythe stations by 8th August. The trials were disappointing, however, and the effective contribution of the device to the efficiency of the warning system was very small. If it had worked well it would have been especially useful when flying bombs were being launched from piloted aircraft.

The earliest, and possibly the most important addition to existing radar facilities was the re-siting of an American station – the M.E.W. (Microwave Early Warning). This equipment, with its associated British height finding set – the Type 24 – gave a longer range, better continuity of tracking, and also permitted the simultaneous plotting of more targets than any other radar set. It was useful, therefore, for all three of the main functions of radar, viz: obtaining early warning of attack, controlling fighters, and analysing plots so as to locate the enemy's launching sites. It was for this last purpose that the equipment was initially used.

At the start of the attack the M.E.W. was located at Start Point to cover fighter operations over the invasion beaches in Normandy; and it was intended to move it to France as soon as possible. During the third week in June, however, arrangements were made through the commander of the American 9th Air Force for its use against flying bombs; and it commenced operations at Fairlight on 29th June. From 4th August it was used primarily as an interception station with analysis as a secondary function. It could not be withheld from France indefinitely, however, and it was transferred there late in August. Steps had been taken to produce an equivalent British set – the Type 26 – late in June. It was constructed from a dismantled Type 20 station and certain American components which were obtained direct from the United States. It took the place of the M.E.W. at Fairlight during the second week in August. A second Type 26 station was installed at St. Margaret's Bay.

The only other important modification that came into operation during the main attack, was intended, like the introduction of the M.E.W., to improve the location of launching sites. This information was difficult to obtain by visual means under normal operating conditions owing to the weakness of the response from a flying bomb at long range and also because so many tracks were frequently appearing at one and the same time. Special cameras were therefore installed at three stations – Beachy Head, Fairlight and Hythe – to take photographs every few seconds of the responses that were detected. The pictures from two or more stations could then be examined and collated. The technique was not in use, however, until 25th July.

## 25. Progress of Counter-Measures, 17th June – 15th July.
*a. General.*
It is against the background of these changes in tactics and equipment, few of which had yet made their contribution to a more effective defence, that the first month of flying bomb attack should be set. From the night of 16th June, the attack continued on an average scale, in round figures, of one hundred bombs every twenty-four hours. There were considerable daily and weekly variations in the weight of attack. The worst day was the twenty-four hours following dusk on 2nd July, when 161 flying bombs came close to the coast or passed overland. On the two lightest days, 13th and 15th July, the comparable figure was 42 in each case. The week ending 8th July, when 820 flying bombs were plotted, was the heaviest of the whole attack. The following week, however, the total fell by more than a third to 535.

Various factors account for these variations. That the Germans increased the weight of attack during cloudy weather, which hindered the defenders, is certain. We know, too, that the supply of bombs to sites was hindered by inadequate transport, which was partly due to attacks made specifically against 'Crossbow' targets, storage depots in particular, but partly due also to the general Allied offensive against communications. But it is quite impossible at the moment to say how far the irregular scale of attack was the result of German tactics, how far it was due to Allied counter-measures.

The great majority of bombs was aimed at the London area; many, however, owing to the inherent inaccuracy of the missile fell at widely scattered points in the Home Counties and even beyond. The Solent area also received a small number of bombs. There was a definite attack on the night of 25th June when six bombs fell near Portsmouth, most of them to the west of the town, within an hour; other bombs may have been launched against the same area on 19th June; and later on, between 10th and 22nd July, some sixty bombs fell there at various times. They forced the withdrawal of two fighter squadrons from the main area of attack further east; otherwise their effect was negligible. The attack of the Bristol area, which the orientation of certain sites in the Cherbourg peninsula had led us to expect, failed to materialise.

The attack, in short, was almost exclusively directed at London. At what part, or parts of it, is, however, not certain. The mean point of impact of the bombs was regularly calculated by the Operational Research Section at A.D.G.B. Headquarters and by the Deputy Directorate of Science at Air Ministry. From the analyses were excluded all bombs which were brought down by the defences, all bombs aimed at the Solent area and all bombs which fell more than thirty miles from the centre of London. On this reckoning, the mean point of impact for the period up to the middle of July was at Alleyn's School in North Dulwich, the weekly variations being insignificant. In other words, the bombardment chiefly affected the boroughs south of the river in the area Wandsworth – Croydon – Woolwich, which received nearly forty per cent of the bombs falling on Greater London.

Casualties and damage were by no means negligible. Up to 15th July approximately 3,000 people were killed, 10,000 seriously injured and 12,000 slightly injured, and 13,000 houses were irreparably damaged.[42] But there was at least this to be thankful for, that if the mean point of impact had been a few miles further north, where the density of population was greater, casualties would have been appreciably heavier. Moreover, the maintenance of a fairly constant mean point of impact meant that a number of bombs fell in places already devastated or partially evacuated. As the Germans were doubtless out to do as much damage as possible it was assumed at the time that though their aiming point was probably the centre of London, say Charring Cross, most of the bombs were falling short.[43]

To begin with, all bombs were launched from modified sites in northern France and came inland over the coasts of Sussex and Kent as had been expected. Then on the night of 9th July bombs were plotted approaching London on a westerly course from the direction of the Thames estuary. This suggested that sites had been constructed in the area round Dunkerque and Ostend, where there had certainly been no sites prior to the middle of June. Photographic reconnaissance of the area could not be carried out owing to bad weather until 28th July, when no new constructions could be seen. Thus, it was not until 3rd August that it was firmly established that the bombs approaching London from the east were in fact being launched from piloted aircraft. However, the number launched by this method was small compared to those launched from sites on land; and it remains true to say that the attack of London at this period was almost entirely carried out from the sites in northern France.

*b. The Bombing of Sites in Northern France and Related Targets.*
Policy. This being the case, it followed that the bombardment of sites in that area remained a necessary counter-measure, despite the practical difficulties and the many other calls upon Allied bombing resources.
It will be recalled that up to 23rd June bad weather had interfered with both the weight and accuracy of attacks upon 'Crossbow' targets; but there was every intention, at least on the part of Air Chief Marshal Tedder, of carrying out a heavy and sustained offensive. It will also be recalled that at that time the targets to be attacked were, in order of priority, the large sites, the supply sites and the forty-seven modified sites which had been identified in the area Somme – Pas de Calais. On 22nd June a beginning had been made in the attack of storage depots. The electric power system of the Pas de Calais was also to be interfered with.

General bombing policy from 23rd June remained the same: that is to say that after the needs of the land battle had been met the attack of 'Crossbow' targets had priority over all operations. No written directive embodying this policy appears to have been issued by the Deputy Supreme Commander; but on at least two occasions Air Chief Marshal Tedder personally informed the commanders of the bomber forces what were the relative priorities. Moreover, on 29th June, A.E.A.F. Headquarters requested Bomber Command and U.S. Strategic Air Forces to observe the programme, first – 'Crossbow', second – Railways and Bridges, third – Fuel Dumps. Air Chief Marshal Leigh-Mallory, who was still nominally responsible for 'Crossbow' operations, could properly issue such a request; but there appears to have been nothing mandatory about it. Indeed, the organisation of the chain of command was such that the heavy bomber force commanders regarded themselves as under the direct command only of the Supreme Commander or his Deputy.

Even so, although they knew what the views were of the Deputy Supreme Commander, Air Chief Marshal Harris and Lieut.-General Doolittle sent as many aircraft to attack strategic targets as 'Crossbow' targets. One half of the effort of the two forces was exerted against battlefield targets between the middle of June and the middle of July, one quarter against 'Crossbow' and one quarter against industrial towns in Germany, aircraft factories and oil targets. That the attack of this last type of target was more to the taste of both strategic forces is obvious enough. Moreover, the Chief of the Air Staff also considered that to prohibit it in order to bring to bear a heavier scale of attack on 'Crossbow' targets would be unwise. At a meeting of the War Cabinet 'Crossbow' Sub-Committee on 11th July he urged, "that nothing should be done to detract from what appeared to be the war winning policy of air attack on the enemy's oil resources and essential support to the army." He reminded the meeting that while the concentration on railways and communications prior to D-Day might have given the Germans time to complete their preparations for flying bomb attacks it had also prepared the way for the consolidation of the Allied landings in France. He was implying, in other words, that it was vital to keep a sense of proportion about 'Crossbow' and put it against the wider and far more important background of the land battle. But this does not alter the fact that between the formulation of general bombing policy during this period and its execution there was a gap which might have been filled.[44]

If it is indeed the case, as the records of the campaign appear to show, that the bomber force commanders resented the effort that they had to make against 'Crossbow' targets, there is this to be said for their support, that throughout the first five weeks of the campaign, the policy governing the selection of 'Crossbow' targets, for which not they but the Directorate of Operations (S.O.) at the Air Ministry was responsible, was unsatisfactory.

In the first-place priorities for attack were frequently changed between 15th June and 15th July. Large sites, supply sites, storage depots, and storage depots equally with certain production targets in Germany, were at different times first call upon the bombers. This in itself reflected the imperfect current intelligence of the place which each category of target occupied in the German organisation. Large sites were indeed thought not to be connected with flying bombs but with rockets; and their attack was an insurance against what as yet was only a threat. Supply sites were also a doubtful quantity. That they were originally intended to fulfil some function in the attack seemed to be confirmed by what was learned from the supply sites in the Cherbourg peninsula; but the bombing of them gambled on their actually being in use, of which there was no evidence. Nor did evidence to that effect become available during June and early July; yet attacks were made on them until 10th July. Similarly, ski sites were still on the list of targets as late as 27th June, although there was nothing to show that they were being used.

But where the position was most unsatisfactory from the point of view of Bomber Command and the 8th Air Force was in the relative effort to be assigned to modified sites and storage depots. The fact was that the sites were an extremely unpopular target. They were small, hard to find and well defended, and there were a lot of them – forty-one were identified between 15th June and 15th July, making eighty-eight in all. They were, therefore, a difficult target for all type of bombers and, in addition, a dangerous one for fighter-bombers. For heavy bombers both by day and night they were an uneconomical target; for a heavy weight of bombs had to be dropped to ensure the destruction of even a single site which, where there were so many, was no great loss to the enemy. In any case, sites could be repaired, and new sites constructed, very rapidly. Thus, unless a group of related sites, or, better still, all the sites, could be attacked simultaneously, it was difficult to bring about a reduction in the scale of attack; and throughout these first five weeks there was no apparent return for the effort against them.

On the other hand, the storage depots, of which several had been identified by the end of June, covering as they did a large area, could be very effectively attacked by the techniques in current use by Bomber Command and the 8th Air Force; and the commanders of both these forces were strongly in favour of concentrating against them and abandoning the attack of modified sites. These depots, and also supply sites and production targets in Germany, particularly those factories making gyro compasses, which were essential to flying bombs, were suggested as the best 'Crossbow' targets by Lieut.-General Spaatz on 30th June; and on this occasion Air Chief Marshal Leigh-Mallory (who was still responsible for the execution of 'Crossbow' counter-measures) did direct that for an experiment, modified sites should be left alone for a few days. Both the Chief of the Air Staff and Air Chief Marshal Tedder disagreed with the change, however, and on 5th July the attacks were recommenced. Their point of view was that so long as it remained uncertain what were the best targets to attack it was necessary to maintain at least harassing attacks on modified sites; for that these were being used was one of the few points on which we were clear. Thus, on 6th July it was decided that the 8th Air Force should continue to attack modified sites and supply sites while Bomber Command mainly attacked storage depots, which were, however, given priority for attack. A week later the order was still: 1. Storage Depots, 2. Supply Sites, 3. Modified Sites; and again, Air Chief Marshal Tedder resisted a request from Air Chief Marshal Harris that the modified sites should be ignored.

Organisation. Such differences of opinion were, of course, partly a reflection of the inadequate intelligence of what the Germans were doing, which in turn led to a reluctance on the part of Air Intelligence to recommend as coherent a target policy as the operational commanders would have liked. But it was also felt that the best use was not being made of such information as was available. Intelligence and operational counter-measures were still nominally co-ordinated in the

Directorate of Operations (S.O.) at Air Ministry; but whatever the theoretical advantages of this arrangement it was not working well in June and early July. That this was the case was common knowledge; and the matter came to a head on 8th July when Major-General Anderson of the U.S. Strategic Air Forces formally recommended to Air Chief Marshal Tedder that the organisation of 'Crossbow' intelligence should be overhauled, particularly in the sphere of target selection. In the next few days a scheme was agreed upon between Air Chief Marshal Tedder, the Deputy Chief of the Air Staff and Lieut.-General Spaatz. It meant that the routine work of intelligence was henceforth the entire responsibility of Air Intelligence at Air Ministry; and its collation became the responsibility of an officer selected by A.C.A.S. (I). Thence it passed to an Anglo-American committee consisting of representatives of Air Intelligence and the operational staffs of Air Ministry and U.S. Strategic Air Forces. The function of this body was to examine the collated intelligence daily and recommend what targets should be attacked and in what order. It was known as the Joint 'Crossbow' Target Priorities Committee and it held its first meeting on 21st July. The results of its work are, therefore, outside the period under review. What is important for the present is that it was set up to establish a well-defined and authoritative policy of target selection, the absence of which hampered the counter-offensive during those first five weeks of flying bomb attacks.

At the same time a change was made in the structure of operational responsibility for 'Crossbow' bombing. So far Air Chief Marshal Leigh-Mallory has been responsible for operational counter-measures against 'Crossbow'. But in both its defensive and offensive aspects it was little more than a nominal responsibility. His prime task was the organisation of air support for the land battle; and he had neither the inclination not the time for any other tasks. This was recognised as far as defence against flying bombs was concerned; and when the Chiefs of Staff later took exception to certain changes in defensive measures it was Air Marshal Hill who suffered their displeasure, not Air Chief Marshal Leigh-Mallory, although the former was nominally the latter's subordinate. As for the offensive, Air Chief Marshal Leigh-Mallory had little control over the strategic bombers, with the exception that he had 'general direction' of such as were allotted by the Supreme Commander to support the land battle. And as it was these which were the main arm of the offensive against 'Crossbow' (the components of A.E.A.F. being fully committed to the land battle) he asked Air Chief Marshal Tedder on 22nd July if he could be relieved of his 'Crossbow' responsibilities. The Deputy Supreme Commander agreed and decided that the planning of

76

'Crossbow' bombing should henceforth be done by the Combined Operational Planning Committee, a body on which all the bombing forces were represented; though the broad direction of operations remained his own responsibility the change merely clarified a situation that had existed since April, when Air Chief Marshal Tedder had taken up the position of Deputy Supreme Commander, having as such general responsibility to the Supreme Commander for air operations.

Operations. The Allied bombing during these weeks was by no means fruitless. Of the eighty-eight modified sites that had been identified, sixty-eight had been attacked by 15th July. At least twenty-four of these had been made inoperative and eight others seriously damaged. By 10th July damage at the four most important large sites – Mimoyecques, Siracourt, Watten and Wizernes – was such that they were thought unlikely to become operational before the middle of August; they were accordingly withdrawn from the schedule of targets. On the same date, three of the seven supply sites were also suspended from attack; and in fact, no more attacks were made against this sort of target. A number of power stations and transformers in the Pas de Calais were damaged and one chateau housing a headquarters unit was destroyed.

As for the storage depots, Nucourt and St. Leu d'Esserent were each attacked once in the last week in June by the 8th Air Force. Up to 15th July these were the only depots that were scheduled for attack, though others were suspected; and on 3rd July it had been decided that they should be left to Bomber Command. Very heavy attacks were made on St. Leu d'Esserent on the nights of the 4th and 7th, when nearly three thousand tons of bombs were dropped. At the time Air Intelligence believed that up to 70 per cent of flying bomb supplies were being distributed through this depot; and as after the first attacks there were indications that supplies were being moved from there to Nucourt and, after the second, that the depot was unserviceable, it was reckoned that a notable blow had been struck.[45] Nucourt then became more important than ever to the Germans and it was heavily attacked on the night of 10th July. The target area was completely obscured by cloud, the pathfinder force failed to illuminate it and the attack was a failure. A further attack by day on the 15th was also unsuccessful but Bomber Command persevered and hit the target hard that same night.

Altogether, nearly six thousand tons of bombs were aimed at these two targets. They were at once a suitable target for heavy bombers, particularly for Lancasters carrying 12,000 lb. bombs, and they represented a potential bottle neck in the German supply system, on both counts they were more acceptable as targets to the commanders of the heavy bomber forces than small targets such as the modified sites, where the flying bomb organisation was probably least vulnerable. It is significant, too, of the part that heavy bombers were playing in counter-measures that factories that were thought to be connected with rockets or flying bombs were once more being seriously considered as targets for the first time since February. The Volkswagenwerke at Fallersleben (near Brunswick) was one; and it was attacked by the 8th Air Force with excellent results as early as 20th June and again on 29th June. Then, late in June, three plants producing hydrogen peroxide (which was used in the launching of flying bombs), were put down for attack. They were at Peenemünde, Ober Raderach (near Friedrichshafen) and Düsseldorf; a fourth at Höllriegelskreuth (near Munich) was added on 7th July. None of these was attacked, however, until after 15th July.

That there was some return for the Allied bombing during these first few weeks of flying bomb attacks is, therefore, certain. But what was the extent of it nobody could say at the time; nor, as there had been no concentration of effort against any one type of target, was it possible to say where the Germans were most vulnerable. Certainly, there was nothing to indicate that bombing alone could so affect the scale of attack on London that the close defences of the capital would be less important, much less unnecessary. In fact, the fighters, guns and balloons remained the prime means of defence.

*c. The Attack of London: Work of the Defences.*
According to the most reliable statistics, 2,930 flying bombs were reported by the defences between 15th June and 15th July, of which all except about thirty were aimed at London. The number of bombs that came overland amounted to 2,579, of which 1,280 fell inside the London area. 1,241 bombs were destroyed by the defences, most of them falling in Kent and Sussex and the Channel but 65 of them falling inside London. The rest of the bombs represented gross errors in accuracy.

Very few important industrial and commercial objectives, and no military ones, were directly affected by the attack; and there were less than a dozen major fires. This was only to be expected when the weapon was indiscriminate in its nature and relied on blast rather than incendiarism to cause damage. The long catalogue of incidents consisted almost entirely of damage to civilian property – houses, churches, hospitals, schools and the like. Similarly, the number of service casualties was barely five per cent of those suffered by the civil population, though the two most serious incidents of the period – indeed of the whole attack – judged by loss of life, were ones in which service casualties predominated.[46]

Throughout the period the efficiency of the defences as a whole showed a tendency to improve. The percentage of bombs destroyed rose from thirty-three in the week 15th – 21st June to fifty in that of 9th – 15th July. The improvement was almost entirely the result of the efforts of the fighters, whose percentage success doubled from approximately twenty to approximately forty. Guns and balloons, on the other hand, destroyed only some thirteen per cent and eight per cent respectively of their possible targets; nor were there any signs over these five weeks that these results would materially improve. In sum, almost half the bombs that crossed the coast during the period were succeeding in reaching the London area – a proportion that was considered far from satisfactory.

But these weeks were essentially ones of trial and error, in which the various components of the defence were at once bringing more forces into action, adopting new techniques of operation and, in the nature of things, becoming familiar with the peculiar problem that they were faced with.

Fighters. Most of the fighter squadrons that were employed were drawn entirely from the resources of A.D.G.B., and, in particularly, of No. 11 Group, which although it had extensive duties to perform over the Normandy beaches and the shipping lanes across the Channel, was also responsible for the defence of its own area, including the 'Diver' defence area. But it proved to be impossible to avoid calling on other formations for reinforcements; for only the fastest fighters in service were able to register consistent success; and in A.D.G.B. were only three squadrons of Tempest Vs and three of Spitfire XIVs. Air Marshal Hill's first move was to obtain, with the assent of Air Marshal Leigh-Malory, one flight of Mustang IIIs from No. 316 Squadron of the 2nd Tactical Air Force. These aircraft began to operate on 1st July and straightaway began to score successes; consequently, a much larger reinforcement was negotiated whereby three squadrons – a complete wing – of Mustangs III's were transferred to A.D.G.B. They made their first flying bomb patrols on 12th July. By that date thirteen single-engined fighter squadrons – three Tempest Vs, three Spitfire XIVs, one Spitfire XII, two Spitfire IXs and four Mustang IIIs – were being employed. Three Mosquito squadrons were also in use solely for flying bomb work; six others were being used partly for flying bomb patrols, partly for work over the beaches. Two of them were also used by Bomber Command. These two – Nos. 85 and 157 – were with No. 100 Group under the control of Bomber Command when flying bomb attacks began. They were required to accompany the heavy bombers on attacks where night fighter opposition was anticipated; and for this they were equipped with one of the latest types of Mosquito – the Mark XII – and the most up to date model of A.I. – Mark X. But despite the importance of their task Air Marshal Hill felt justified in asking for their use against flying bombs; and they commenced operations on 27th June. However, Air Chief Marshal Harris only agreed with reluctance; and eventually, under a ruling from the Chief of the Air Staff, the two squadrons divided their efforts about equally between bomber support and flying bomb patrols.

Improvements in the equipment that was used consisted chiefly in concentrating the best and fastest fighters available in the south-east and increasing their speed to the utmost by various modifications. Fighters that were exclusively employed on flying bomb patrols were stripped of armour and all unnecessary external fittings; camouflage paint was removed from the fuselage and wings, and the surfaces were polished; engines were modified to use 150 octane fuel and also accept higher boost pressure than normal. The three types of day fighter principally employed were made faster in this way by some 15-30 m.p.h. A number of Mosquito XIIIs were also speeded up. Not all the twin-engined night fighter types were modified, however, as some were required for normal duties.

The alterations inevitably meant an extraordinary strain upon air frames and engines, but this was accepted as speed was quite the most important factor in interception. For the same reason, increasing use was made of single-seater fighters at night both by ordinary squadrons and by a flight of Tempests, manned by volunteers from Mosquito squadrons, which was placed under the Fighter Interception Unit. These aircraft began to operate regularly from Newchurch on 27th/28th June and scored many successes.

As the attack proceeded and our pilots gained in experience, so the comparatively standardised technique of interception and destruction that had already been outlined was formulated. But there was no one procedure for bringing down the missiles. On 23rd June a Spitfire pilot destroyed a flying bomb by tipping it over with his wing tip; and on 27th June a Tempest pilot destroyed another by manoeuvring his aircraft so that its slipstream forced the bomb into a spin. Most bombs, however, continued to be destroyed by less startling methods.

On the whole, the scale of fighter effort and the number of bombs destroyed by fighters was not unsatisfactory. The weather, as was to be expected, proved an important factor. On some days less than a hundred fighter sorties could be flown; and others as many as five hundred. But the ratio of destructions to targets presented, steadily rose; and there was no reason to expect that it would not continue to improve unless the Germans radically altered their tactics. [47]

Balloons. The original five hundred balloons had hardly been deployed before Air Marshal Hill gave instructions for the barrage to be doubled, the intention being not to extend it geographically but to increase its density and thereby improve the chances of impact. The additions entailed eliminating every barrage in the country except six.[48] The move began on 24th June, but owing to the short notice and the necessity of assembling crews from all parts of the country it was completed less quickly than that of the first five hundred balloons. Even so, by 1st July, the thousand balloons were in position.

Concurrently, Balloon Command Headquarters were working out the maximum number of balloons that could be flown; and on 28th June they reported that 1,750 could be provided by 22nd July. Five hundred of the additions this entailed were intended to increase still further the density of the barrage. The remaining 250 were to extend it to the west. The order to move was given on 8th July, and the deployment was completed a day in front of schedule.

While all these broad additions were being planned and executed, certain deficiencies in the original deployment were rectified. It was found that the northern edge of the barrage was so close to the built-up areas on the southern fringe of the London area that a number of flying bombs, after impact with balloon cables, were still doing damage to life and property. A number of key points in Kent and Surrey were also endangered by the barrage. Immediately after the second deployment had been completed, over two hundred balloons were therefore moved from the north-western side of the barrage to the south.[49] A further fifty balloons were withdrawn to allow a clearance of one mile in front of a number of key points.

During earlier operations for the air defence of the country Fighter Command had normally exercised a close control over the flying of balloons so as not to endanger friendly aircraft; and barrages were frequently lowered or grounded for this reason. But this was hardly practicable with a barrage as large as that now deployed. Moreover, the idea behind it was to present the flying bomb with a permanent and inescapable barrier. Consequently, on 23rd June, A.D.G.B. Headquarters issued a warning to pilots to keep well away from almost certainly lethal obstacle that would be in the air continuously. To assist pilots, Royal Observer Corps posts near the barrage were issued with Schermuly ('Snowflake') rockets, which were fired when aircraft approached. Searchlights were also used for the same purpose.

But it was a deliberate exaggeration, made for the pilots' sakes, to say that the barrage would fly continuously. This was certainly the theory, but weather forbad it being the practice. The balloon and hydrogen resources of the country, by the end of June, had been invested almost entirely in the 'Diver' barrage; and the heavy wastage that would have been incurred if the barrage had been flown during a gale or, which would have been even more dangerous, in an electrical storm, could only have been replaced slowly and in part. Thus, there were many periods when the barrage, wholly or in part, was grounded because of weather.[50] The heavy responsibility of deciding whether to fly or not fell upon the Barrage Commander, who was located at the control centre of all the 'Diver' defences, the Biggin Hill sector operations room.

Guns. That the performance of the guns was unsatisfactory up to the middle of July was freely acknowledged by Anti-Aircraft Command. During these first five weeks, those tactical difficulties of controlling fire against the bombs that have already been outlined, were at their worst, and were likely to remain unsolved until the equipment that had been deployed originally was replaced, especially the heavy gun equipment. All turned, therefore, on the speedy emplacement of static, power-controlled guns, SCR 584 radar sets, and No. 10 Predictors.

The necessary static guns, however, could only be found from the less vulnerable gun defended areas of the United Kingdom; which meant a large movement of equipment that had not been designed for mobility. Thus, it was not until 8th July that the first static, power-controlled guns were in position in the 'Diver' gun belt. By the same date sixty SCR 584 sets and forty-eight No. 10 Predictors were available; thirty-six of the latter, but none of the former, were in action.

By the 15th the general position was as follows. There were 376 heavy and 594 light guns in action in the gun belt. On the coast there were a further six hundred 40mm. and 20mm. guns, most of them manned by units of the R.A.F. Regiment, and also 3½ batteries of rocket guns. All heavy gun sites had been equipped with the SCR 584 and the No. 10 Predictors, but only fifty-five power-controlled guns had been placed in position, and only four of these were operational. Nevertheless, Anti-Aircraft Command could look forward to the early operation of a much more accurate and effective barrage than had been possible hitherto; for not only was the new equipment coming through but the programme of retraining men in its use was beginning to show results.

*d. Difficulties of Co-ordinated Defence.*
But the need for new equipment was not the only factor in the unsatisfactory results achieved by the guns. It was also the case that fighters and guns had not been working together with that smooth co-operation that was necessary if the best possible results were to be obtained. It proved in practice very difficult for pilots to recognise the

boundaries of the gun belt and for gunners to cease fire in time to avoid endangering the fighters. Moreover, fighters were frequently fired on by anti-aircraft units outside the gun belt, although the orders against this sort of uncontrolled fire were clear enough. The difficulties were most apparent when condition 'Fickle' applied, i.e. when the guns in the gun belt were allowed to fire up to 8,000 feet and fighters were prohibited from entering the gun belt except when in close pursuit of a flying bomb, and charges and counter-charges of breaking the rules were unhappily frequent.[51]

The first steps towards a solution were taken on 10th July when at a conference called by Air Marshal Hill it was agreed that when both fighters and guns were operating, the guns in the belt would have complete freedom of action and fighters would enter the belt at their own risk. Under this arrangement there was little point in maintaining guns forward of the belt, except for a few that would provide marker gunfire for fighters patrolling over the coast; and at the suggestion of General Pile it was agreed that proposals should be submitted to Air Marshal Hill for withdrawing into the belt most of the guns deployed on or near the coast.

These projected arrangements contributed towards a more effective defence in that they established the principle of mutually exclusive spheres of action for fighters and guns. But within three days' time they were superseded as a result of a decision that maintained the new principle but radically altered the disposition of the whole of the gun defence.

## 26. The Redeployment of the Guns.

In the original 'Diver' deployment, the area in which fighter interceptions had taken place had extended from off-shore of Kent and Sussex to the southern edge of the gun belt. Usually fighters had been directed by the controlling radar stations on to flying bombs as they crossed the coast; and interception and destruction had consequently taken place overland. So long as this was achieved before the built-up metropolitan area was reached the fighter pilot had successfully defended the main target; but it was obviously even more desirable to destroy bombs before they crossed the coast, for although a bomb might be shot down overland before reaching London, it might still do, and frequently did, no little damage in rural districts and small towns south and south-east of the capital.[52]

Up to the middle of July by far the most successes had fallen to the fighters; but more than fifty per cent of them had resulted in bombs falling on land. Some improvement in successes over the sea could be expected when the radar stations obtained longer warning of the approach of bombs: not a great one, however, owing to the small margin of speed that the fighter enjoyed over the flying bomb. Nor, for obvious reasons, could the proportion improve so long as the guns remained sited well inland. There were, therefore, these three related problems: how to destroy more bombs all told, how to destroy more bombs before they crossed the coast, how to improve the performance of the guns.

By 10th July, as already noted, the answer was partly appreciated, i.e. to reduce the interference of guns and fighters by giving each complete freedom to operate within a defined sphere. The decision to do this was taken by Air Marshal Hill, as commander of the air defences as a whole, and his was the responsibility for its success or failure; but it was one that represented, as it were, the gunners' point of view, and was by no means to the taste of the fighter pilots, who had indeed little cause to think highly of the gunners' achievements up to that time.[53] The complete solution, however, was one that involved even more restrictions on the operations of the fighters and a correspondingly greater reliance on the performance of the guns; for it involved scrapping entirely the inland gun belt, moving it forward to the coast (thus bisecting the area in which fighters had hitherto been free to patrol), and giving the guns virtually complete freedom to engage at all times and in all conditions in their new positions.

Yet despite the unsatisfactory results achieved so far by the guns, a decision to this effect was taken by Air Marshal Hill on 13th July.[54] The new arrangements, which were to be put into effect by the morning of the 17th, were as follows.

The gun belt was to be moved from its original position in front of the balloon barrage to a coastal strip between St. Margaret's Bay and Cuckmere Haven, with a zone of 10,000 yards to seaward and 5,000 yards inland. Complete freedom of action against flying bombs was to be allowed to fighter aircraft forward of the balloon barrage and forward of the new gun belt, but not in the area covered by the latter.

Not all the old problems were solved by the new deployment: some indeed were aggravated. The security of coastal towns had to be considered; and gaps were left in the lay-out of the guns near Eastbourne, Hastings, Bexhill, Hythe, Folkestone and Dover so that the risk of bombs being brought down on those places lessened. Restrictions were also imposed on the guns near the radar stations at Beachy Head and Fairlight so as to lessen the chances of bombs falling on these important links in the chain of defence. These gaps had the secondary function of allowing fighters and aircraft in distress to cross overland without flying directly over the guns. Then, such an immense deployment of guns, representing perhaps the densest concentration of anti-aircraft fire anywhere in the world, had obviously to be so controlled that friendly aircraft were not imperilled; at the same time, restrictions on fire would have nullified the very purpose of the deployment. Careful arrangements were therefore made with the bomber force commanders in the United Kingdom to ensure the safe routeing of aircraft and; in addition, non-operational flying in south-east England was prohibited. Instructions were also sent out to all forces to ensure that any friendly aircraft returning to England flew at a height of at least 10,000 feet, and, in order not to confuse the radar stations, at no more than 200 m.p.h., making at least one marked change of course and at no time flying in a direct line towards Greater London.

But from the point of view of the gunners the change solved more problems than it created. It gave them a better sight of their targets; it improved the efficiency of their radar sets, which were not affected to the same extent as inland by ground "echoes"; and it enabled them to use V.T.-fuzed shells without restriction. Above all, it meant a simplified procedure and the chance to concentrate solely on the business of destroying flying bombs.

The task of the fighters, however, was made more difficult by the change. Whereas hitherto there had been an uninterrupted run for a patrolling fighter from the Channel to the southern edge of the gun belt, and even beyond if the fighter was in close pursuit, the new location of the gun belt meant that two separate fighter patrol areas had to be established, one forward of the guns, the other between the guns and the balloon barrage. And as each of these was restricted in space, the chances of successfully pressing home an interception were inevitably reduced.

### 27. Reactions at Air Ministry.
It was partly on this account that the redeployment was unfavourably received at the Air Ministry. A.C.A.S. (Ops.) in a minute to the Chief of the Air Staff on 17th July, said: "I am not in favour of the plan which must inevitably result in a reduction of the number of kills by fighters … It is doubtful whether this reduction will be made up for by an increased or even similar number of successes on the part of the A.A. gunners."

But there were reasons of a constitutional as well as military character that account for the reception of the new scheme. Air Marshal Hill had taken the decision on 13th July; on the same day, Anti-Aircraft Command had begun to plan the redeployment; and by the 14th a massive movement of guns to the coast had begun. On the 15th, Air

Marshal Hill wrote to the Air Ministry to explain his action. He stated that the new plan was in effect only a tactical redeployment of the resources under his control, but as it involved a substantial change in the plan previously approved by the Air Ministry "and the other authorities concerned",[55] he felt it his duty to report his action.[56]

The Air Ministry, however, held that it was not a matter that was within the competence of Air Marshal Hill to decide. Their point of view was that it had always been customary for any major alterations in air defence plans to be agreed upon in consultation with the Air Staff, as the Air Ministry were constitutionally responsible for the air defence of Great Britain. The Chief of the Air Staff made this point at a meeting of the Chiefs of Staff on 18th July, adding that the Chief of Staff had also been consulted when major changes were projected. He said that while he did not suggest that the deployment should be countermanded, he thought the responsibility for its success or failure should now rest with Air Marshal Hill. It is worth remarking here that Air Marshal Hill's claim that the deployment was simply a tactical move (which comes within the province of any commander who is fighting a battle) implied his willingness to accept full responsibility for it.

But it is clear that the Air Staff were not so much concerned that Air Marshal Hill had proceeded improperly on his own initiative, but that the decision had been taken as a result of pressure put upon him by Mr. Sandys' Sub-Committee, with the result that Anti-Aircraft Command had been given undue preference over A.D.G.B. To put it brutally and colloquially, the fighters had been given a raw deal in favour of the guns because Mr. Sandys – himself an ex-anti-aircraft officer – had wanted to give more chances to the guns; and he and General Pile had persuaded Air Marshal Hill (with the implication that it was against the latter's better judgement) to order a deployment that was originally their idea.[57]

This was not the case, Mr. Sandys' Sub-Committee had neither any formal executive authority, nor did it seek to exercise any on this particular matter. The decision was not only the responsibility of Air Marshal Hill, but one which sprang from the work of one of the A.D.G.B. staff officers. That the result might well mean fewer successes for the fighters was an index that he was anxious to obtain the best total results rather than to maintain the superiority of his own service; which was, indeed, no more than his duty, for although he was an air officer, his task was to co-ordinate the operations of all the components of air defence in the most effective way.

In sum, the deployment was not delayed, or in any was amended, but Air Marshal Hill's professional reputation depended on the success that attended it. As events turned out, it marked the end of the experimental period and the beginning of a period when the technique and organisation of defence was largely stabilised. It will be convenient at this point, therefore, to review what had happened and what had been learned during these first five weeks.

## 28. Survey of the Period.

The attack of London had been made so far by only one of the two weapons that we believed the Germans had developed for long-range bombardment. That the other – the A.4 rocket – was still being developed was certain; and concurrently with the attack of London by flying bombs, more, and more precise, intelligence of the rocket was being received. There was little indication, however, of when rocket attacks would begin.

There was, in contrast, good evidence that the attack by flying bombs would continue, on at least the scale already achieved, unless more effective counter-measures were applied or until the launching sites were physically occupied. Our information on the organisation of the production of flying bombs was still by no means comprehensive or detailed as was wished, but the consensus of reports indicated that the rate of production was not less than 1,000 a month. Moreover, it was suspected that large-scale production might have begun as early as the summer of 1943, and that some 8,500 bombs were in stock when the attacks began. Except for the Volkswagen works at Fallersleben the locations of the assembly and component factories were only suspected; and in the absence of precise information, it was difficult to affect the scale of attack by bombing this type of target.

This left the supply system in northern France as the next stage where the German chain of supply, and thus the scale of attack, could be damaged most effectively. Here, too, for most of these first weeks, intelligence was not satisfactory, though more was known than in the case of the organisation of production. By the middle of July, however, it had been established that the supply sites were unimportant and that the main source of supply to the launching sites was the storage depots, which were, therefore, the most profitable of all the different types of target for attack. Not all the depots had been precisely identified by the same date; but this was only a question of time now that our agents knew what to look for.

There was one more stage at which damage could be done before bombs were launched against England: this was the German firing organisation itself. The actual firing sites, i.e. the modified sites, were always considered a difficult target to attack and destroy, a view that was confirmed when those that had been overrun during the first weeks of the invasion were examined; and it was against the wishes of the bomber force commanders that Air Chief Marshal Tedder insisted on the maintenance at least of harassing attacks against them. In addition, the electric power system supplying the sites and the headquarters of the different sections of the German firing regiment were reckoned to be worth attacking.

But even though there were reasonable grounds for hoping that the effects of bombing would increase, the main form of counter-measure remained the close defence of London by fighters, guns, balloons and searchlights.

Owing to the needs of 'Overlord' the planned deployment had only been put into effect, as far as guns and balloons were concerned, after the attack had begun; so it was not to be expected that the best possible results would be obtained until the defenders had settled down in their new positions and become familiar with a type of attack that was different from anything that had been experienced previously. But it was also clear from the beginning of the attack that the deployment was inadequate both in numbers and in the type of equipment that was being employed. Thus, not only was the size of the ground defences extended, with a consequently heavy strain upon supply services and headquarters staffs, but the crews themselves were called upon to meet the attack concurrently with the rapid introduction of new types of weapon and methods of operation.

This was true of all the components of the defence, but especially for Balloon and Anti-Aircraft Commands. By the middle of July almost the whole of Balloon Command was committed to the defence of London. Plans were in hand by the same date to reduce for the same purpose the scale of gun defences manned by Anti-Aircraft Command in other parts of the United Kingdom. The fighter squadrons were not affected to the same extent; for their normal deployment for the defence of London against ordinary aircraft attack needed little altered to meet the new conditions. They, too, however, had their problems of equipment, which principally took the form of finding the extra speed that was required if interceptions were to be pressed home. It was the same factor of speed, allied to the low altitude at which the bombs flew, that was responsible for the adjustments that were found to be required in radar equipment.

It was also appreciated, a short time after the attacks began, that not only were improvements demanded in the various defensive weapons, but that their combined operation was far from perfect. Various means of clarifying the different spheres of operation were introduced, all with the intention of avoiding mutual interference. On the whole, these tended to favour the operations of the fighters; which was not surprising, for as the defences were organised to begin with the fighter was the most successful of the three main weapons. But the fighters could not erect a permanent barrier at all times and in all weathers to the flying bombs. Balloons could not, partly because they had to be grounded in bad weather, partly because of sufficiently dense curtain and sufficiently lethal cables were not available. Nor could the guns: not, at any rate, in their inland positions, where their opportunities for engagement were curtailed and where even the best available anti-aircraft equipment was not most effective. Guns were, however, capable of firing at all times, provided the necessary supplies were available; and the supreme merit of the move to the coast was that something approaching a permanent and lethal barrier, which no flying bomb, launched from the sites in northern France, could escape, was made possible. Moreover, such bombs as the guns might destroy in their new positions would represent a greater success than a similar number shot down inland, for the simple reason that many would fall into the sea and do no damage whatsoever.

As it was, half of the two thousand six hundred bombs that had come overland between 13th June and 15th July had fallen in the London area. The physical damage that was caused to essential war factories and vital communications was small; but some fourteen thousand casualties in dead and seriously injured, some thirteen thousand houses irreparably damaged and over half-a-million more or less damaged was no small prize for London and the south-east to pay.

That the attack was disturbing was natural. There was no certain relief from attack at any hour of the day, in contrast with the almost exclusively night attacks of 1940-41 and the early months of 1944. In addition, the blast effect of the weapon was, seemingly so much more widely spread than in the case of ordinary bombs,[58] and caused more domestic disturbance. This was one factor which, by increasing the rate of absenteeism, accounted for the definite decline in production in the London area, a decline which, in the case, for example, of the radio industry, amounted to over twenty per cent. The other main factors were loss of time in actual working hours through workers taking shelter, and lowered efficiency through loss of sleep and anxiety. An extension of the industrial alarm system and an increase in the labour force available for repairing damaged property was organised during the second week in July, and was expected to mitigate the worst effects of the attack.

And on the whole, the population was deliberately encouraged to carry on with its normal tasks, the Ministry of Health arranging for the evacuation only of the 'priority' classes – children, expectant mothers, old people and invalids. So far, no unusual or disturbing effects on morale had become evident; but as the attacks were likely to continue, adding always to the results of the strain under which people were living and working, morale was not likely to improve unless the defences could appreciably reduce the number of bombs that were falling daily upon the capital. A great deal depended, therefore, on the wisdom of the reorganisation of the defences that was being carried out from 15th July, and on the skill and endurance of those who manned them.

# Part V

# The Attack on London from Northern France: 16th July – 5th September, 1944.

The first weeks of the attack on London had seen the policy of counter-measures in the process of amendment in two important respects. First, the machinery for the selection of 'Crossbow' targets was being overhauled and, it was believed, improved. Second, the system of defence had been re-planned; and when the re-organisation was completed, much better results were anticipated. On the effectiveness of the first, depended the effectiveness of the counter-measures, and thus the possibility of a reduction in the scale of attack; on the second, the higher rate of destruction of such bombs as the enemy succeeded in launching. We shall consider first, therefore what form the counter-offensive took in the weeks immediately following the middle of July, and what effects it had in fact upon the scale of flying bomb attack.

**29. The Offensive against 'Crossbow' Targets, 16th July – 15th August.** Attacks on storage depots at Nucourt and Rilly la Montagne were made on the 16th and 17th by Bomber Command and the 8th Air Force respectively. Neither attack achieved any significant damage. On the 18th, the 8th Air Force sent 415 Fortresses to Peenemünde and dropped 953 tons of bombs on the hydrogen peroxide plant and the experimental station. Results were fairly good. One of the two hydrogen peroxide installations was well hit; bombs fell in the experimental area; and administrative buildings both at Peenemünde and Zinnowitz were also damaged. Attacks on launching sites in northern France continued to be made, chiefly by Bomber Command.

But Air Chief Marshal Tedder was still far from satisfied; and on the 18th he advanced for the first time a project for the attack of all types of 'Crossbow' target on the same day. It was referred to the Combined Operational Planning Committee for examination. Such an attack would have the merit of damaging every part of the flying bomb organisation, simultaneously, or nearly so. It was not launched, however, until early in August.

Meanwhile, the scale of effort against 'Crossbow' remained low, bearing in mind that it was still reckoned second in importance only to the direct support of the battle on land. Between 19th July and 1st August only 7,500 tons of bombs were dropped on 'Crossbow' targets, out of some fifty thousand tons all told dropped by the strategic bombers. Targets attacked in direct support of the armies themselves received a lesser weight of bombs, 11,200, than oil and industrial targets.

Moreover, the tonnage that was dropped on 'Crossbow' only partly reflected the order of importance that was given to the various types of target. These had been closely examined at the first meeting of the Joint 'Crossbow' Target Priorities Committee on 21st July, as a result of which a short list of targets was agreed upon. This gave three storage depots[59] and seven production targets in Germany,[60] as 'first priority' targets. Next came fifty-seven modified sites, with the proviso that only harassing attacks should be made, in which a high proportion of delayed action bombs was to be used. Large sites were completely suspended from attack, except for experimental attacks by the 8th Air Force. Electric power stations and headquarters targets were also suspended. In short, the prime targets that were approved were those for which the heavy bomber force commanders had always expressed a preference.

Yet of the tonnage that was dropped during the rest of July, less than half was directed against storage depots and only one attack was made on a production target in Germany[61] – the hydrogen peroxide plant at Hollriegelskreuth, which was bombed on 19th July by the 8th Air Force. Otherwise, the 8th Air Force, apart from the direct support of the land battle, went for oil targets, aircraft and aero-engine factories, the German munitions industry and marshalling yards on the Franco-German frontier. Similarly, Bomber Command, outside its effort against 'Crossbow' and in direct support of the armies, went for oil targets, railway centres and town centres. Its biggest effort against any one target was against Stuttgart, on which nearly five thousand tons of bombs were dropped on three nights during the last week in July.

However, on 1st August the Combined Operational Planning Committee presented its plan for a general offensive against 'Crossbow' targets. It was based on an effort of 1,500 sorties by the 8th Air Force, 1,000 by Bomber Command and 400 by the Tactical Air Forces. It envisaged three phases of attack, two by day and one by night, all being completed within twenty-four hours. In the first phase, the 8th Air Force would go for Ober Raderach, Düsseldorf, Fallersleben and Peenemünde, and the flying bomb storage depots at Mery-sur-Oise and Rilly la Montagne; simultaneously Bomber Command would attack the suspected 'Crossbow' storage depot in the Forêt de Niepppe, and also six launching sites. In the second phase, which was planned to begin six hours later than the first, the 8th Air Force would attack twenty launching sites and Bomber Command sixteen. The Tactical Air Forces were to make their effort during these two phases, against forty modified sites. The third phase was to be a night phase, when Bomber Command would attack the storage depots at Bois de Cassan and Troissy St. Maximin. In sum, nearly every major 'Crossbow' target and all launching sites which were known or suspected to be active, were to be attacked.

The plan was not in fact carried out. Air Chief Marshal Leigh-Mallory was not anxious to allow the Tactical Air Forces to be taken away from their prime tasks; a moving battle was at last developing, with an abundance of targets for 2nd Tactical Air Force and the 9th Air Force. However, the plan allotted only a minor part to these forces. The heaviest blows were to be struck by the heavy bombers. Here the main practical difficulty was that for a powerful and successful blow to be struck against a series of widely dispersed targets, and targets which varied in type, good weather over practically the whole of northern France and northern and central Germany was required. Early on 1st August there were slight prospects of this for some days to come, nevertheless, it was agreed that the plan should be attempted.

Weather did, in fact, seriously interfere with operations on the 1st. The 8th Air Force could not go into Germany, while of fifteen launching sites that they attempted to attack, only three were bombed, two with no success. Bomber Command sent 719 aircraft to bomb six modified sites and the suspected depot at Forêt de Niepppe, but only 74 aircraft were able to attack. For the same reason, on the following day, the 8th Air Force succeeded in attacking only five out of fifteen sites that they set out to attack. Bomber Command were more successful. Over three hundred tons of bombs were dropped on each of the storage depots at Troissy St. Maximin and Bois de Cassan; six modified sites and the Forêt de Niepppe were also attacked. The first two targets were accurately bombed; but Air Chief Marshal Harris considered that they would require a succession of attacks before they were neutralised. This applied also to the Forêt de Nieppe, where on this occasion results were poor.

In the next four days, therefore, Bomber Command made twelve attacks against these three targets, and one against the storage depot at St. Leu d'Esserent. During the same period, the 8th Air Force attacked Peenemünde and Fallersleben in Germany, a storage depot at Mery-sur-Oise, two depots for flying bomb fuel, and over twenty launching sites. In short, while the original plan of attack was discarded as regards its time element, it was largely carried out within a week.

What the precise results were, it is impossible to say with any authority. Very heavy tonnages were dropped on the storage depots by Bomber Command; 2,650 tons on Forêt de Nieppe, 3,400 on Bois de Cassan, 3,100 on Troissy St. Maximin and 2,200 on St. Leu d'Esserent. At two of these, St. Leu and Troissy, extensive areas over the underground storage galleries subsided; and Forêt de Nieppe was so badly damaged that on 12th August it was judged safe to suspend it from further attack. The 15th Air Force attack on Ober Raderach – a small one of little less than one hundred tons – achieved little owing to bad weather; but Peenemünde, the power station and an electrolytic installation in the hydrogen peroxide plant were heavily damaged by the 8th Air Force. Even more successful was the attack on the Volkswagenwerke at Fallersleben on 5th August. 85 Liberators made the attack, dropping 244 tons of bombs; nearly all the main buildings were directly hit and heavy damage was caused. The factory was therefore removed from the list of 'Crossbow' targets and no further attacks were made upon it. The offensive against launching sites met with only moderate success: nine sites were put out of action, making 41 that were reckoned Category A out of a total of 94 that had been identified up to date.

All told, nearly 15,000 tons of bombs were dropped on 'Crossbow' targets during the week 2nd – 9th August, three-quarters of them upon storage depots, which were still believed to be the most profitable of the various sorts of targets. This represented quite the most determined effort that had so far been made within such a short space of time to damage vitally the flying bomb organisation. It had not, however, embraced the whole system; which was what Air Chief Marshal Tedder had in mind when he initiated the project of heavy attack. Firstly, it was quite certain that not all of the production targets in Germany had been attacked. Secondly, there were good reasons for suspecting that parts of the supply system in northern France had not been affected: intelligence received during the third week of July indicated that the known storage depots were linked only to launching sites between the Seine and Somme; the sites in the Pas de Calais were probably supplied from other storage depots that had not been identified, or by an alternative system to that operative further south.[62] Thirdly, little had been done to interfere with the rail transport of flying bombs from Germany to northern France. This was not through any failure to appreciate the importance of stopping this traffic. Allied agents had been instructed before ever the flying bomb attack began to discover all they could about the size of the traffic, its timing and routeing. Agents of the Special Operations Executive were also briefed to sabotage it where possible. But it amounted to so little – only two or three trains each day – so many different routes could be used, and movement could, and did, take place exclusively at night, that to arrange bombing attacks upon it was next to impossible. To immobilise rail transport from Germany itself required the destruction of a very large number of targets, principally bridges; and the effort could only be afforded if the Supreme Commander decided that it was necessary for the battle of Normandy, in which case the interruption of flying bomb traffic would be an incidental result. Measures of railway interdiction were actually applied from the middle of August in the area Maastricht, Liege and Namur, which was the principle area for 'Crossbow' traffic from Germany to northern France. They may have had some effect; but there is little or no evidence that the scale of attack was sensibly affected.

The week following the heavy 'Crossbow' attacks was one of increasingly rapid deterioration of the German position in Normandy; and the strategic bomber forces exerted most of their effort against targets connected with the battle on land. Strong attacks were made by Bomber Command and the 8th Air Force on 15th August against seven airfields in Holland and Belgium from which aircraft launching flying bombs were thought to be operating.[63] At all of them, heavy damage was caused to the runways. The operation was significant for 'Crossbow', but it was part of a wider onslaught that was carried out on that day against airfields in North-West Europe. After their battering of the previous week, the storage depots were left alone, except for a further attack on Forêt de Nieppe by 126 aircraft of Bomber Command on the night of 9th August. The two depots – Paris/Dugny and Pacy-sur- Armançon – that were thought to be handling flying bomb fuel were attacked again; the first by Bomber Command on 10th August when over six hundred tons of bombs were dropped, the second by the 8th Air Force on the 10th and again on the 11th, when 163 tons of bombs were dropped. At Paris/Dugny three out of five fuel tanks were badly damaged; at Pacy-sur-Armançon railway facilities were badly damaged but the tanks escaped lightly. On the 12th depots were suspended from further attack.

The heaviest single blow of the week was the work of Bomber Command on the night of 12th August against the Opel motor works at Rüsselsheim which had been placed on the secondary list of production targets in Germany only a short time before. Nearly one thousand tons of bombs were dropped on the town and the works. Damage at the latter was described as "widespread but not severe". Of the main, identified components, only the hall for loading and despatch appeared to have been destroyed.

Altogether, some 31,000 tons of bombs were dropped on 'Crossbow' targets between 15th July and 15th August. Insofar as most of this enormous tonnage was dropped in northern France it was in the scale of flying bomb attack at the time that any positive effects of the offensive could be expected to be displayed.

## 30. Scale of German Attack, 15th July – 15th August: Effects of Allied Bombing.

The total number of flying bombs reported by the defences during this period was 2,667, compared with a total of 2,934 in the first five weeks of the attack. In other words, the Germans had, on the whole, succeeded in maintaining the original scale of attack. But there was this that may have been significant about the second period: that the number of bombs reported in the week following the very heavy attacks of 2nd – 9th August fell by more than half[64] compared to that of the previous week. It was impossible to be certain that this decline was entirely due to Allied bombing. The weather, which was good during this particular week, may have had some effect; for the Germans tended to fire most heavily in dull and cloudy weather. But insofar as the decline was due to bombing, it seemed to be due very largely to the attacks on storage depots rather than on launching sites. Some forty-one of the latter had been destroyed by bombing up to the middle of August; but that still left the Germans fifty-three sites, which were more than enough to maintain the average daily scale of attack. Furthermore, the fact that no attempts had been made to repair sites which had been destroyed and damaged was taken to mean that the Germans were not greatly concerned at the rate of destruction and had ample sites in reserve.

In the absence of reliable statistics,[65] the merit of such attacks was still a matter of opinion. To the majority of the Joint 'Crossbow' Target Priorities Committee, however, it certainly appeared that there was at least no proof that the 26,000 tons of bombs that had been dropped on launching sites between the middle of June and the middle of August had achieved anything worthwhile. On the other hand, they were equally convinced that storage depots, communications and production centres in Germany were valuable targets;[66] and on 15th August Air Chief Marshal Tedder was again asked to give a decision on the matter. Once more he stood by his previous ruling that attacks on launching sites must still be made; though he so far deferred to the strong feeling against them as to agree that they should only be carried out when bad weather prevented attacks on other types of 'Crossbow' target.

## 31. The Work of the Defences, 15th July – 15th August.

The nett result of the bombing may, of course, have been to prevent an increase in the scale of attack; but there is no evidence on the point. That it clearly failed to bring about any important reduction, as compared with the first five weeks, meant that the defences of London had still to deal with a dangerous weight of attack.

### a. The Development of the Coastal Gun Belt.

The working of the defence system was last considered at the stage where the decision to move the guns to the coast had been taken. The redeployment began on 14th July and by dawn on 17th July all heavy guns that had been deployed in the inland belt, were in action in their new positions on the coast. All the light guns were in action two days later, having remained in their inland positions longer than the heavy guns to cover their move. The speed of the redeployment was an achievement that was almost beyond praise,[67] especially as the Command had little experience of large-scale movement.

The position on the morning of 19th July was that 412 heavy and 572 light guns were ready for action in the coastal belt; and there were also 168 Bofors guns and 416 20mm. guns of the R.A.F. Regiment, 28 R.A.C. light guns, and 2½ batteries of rocket guns in position. Amongst the heavy guns was one U.S. Army battalion. Thenceforwards, the numbers rose steadily until by 15th August there were 592 heavy guns, including 5 U.S. Army battalions (80 guns) in the coastal belt, and 701 light guns. The R.A.F. Regiment contribution remained much the same, while there were by then eight rocket batteries.

Within this, so to speak, basic deployment and reinforcement, comparable progress was made in the programme of replacing mobile guns by static guns and bringing in SCR 584 sets and No. 10 Predictors, with which a beginning had been made before the move to the coast had taken place. This unavoidably took longer to complete than the initial redeployment. It was not until 22nd July that the first thirty static guns were in position and ready for action. But thereafter progress was more rapid. By the end of the month 288 static guns were ready for action; by 15th August the figure had risen to 379. It was this gap between the completion of the first moves on 17th July and the bringing to bear in force of the most efficient equipment, coupled also with the need to become familiar with the new positions, that accounts for the relatively poor results that were obtained in the week following the redeployment.

b. Defence against Attack form the East.

The immense task of redeployment was also complicated by the need for setting up a new defence system further north. It will be recalled that on the night of 9th July, and subsequently, flying bombs had been plotted as they approached London from the direction of the Thames estuary, in contrast to the majority of bombs which, being fired from the sites in the belt Dieppe – St. Omer, came in from the south and south-east. It was not known for certain until 3rd August that these were being launched from German bombers; but as early as 12th July A.D.G.B. Headquarters had prepared a provisional plan for the defence of the capital against attacks from Belgium and Holland. The same principles as had governed the form of the original 'Diver' deployment were followed. There was to be a belt of balloons west of a line from Rochester – Thameshaven; a belt of anti-aircraft guns east of the balloons and west of a line from the north-east corner of the existing gun belt to Clacton; forward of the guns there would be a patrol area for fighters, which would be manned by squadrons operating from Manston under the control of the radar stations at Sandwich, Foreness and Foulness.

Further progress was held up for a week by the decision to re-deploy the main gun belt; but the matter was again examined at a meeting at Stanmore on 18th July. By then, an alternative plan had been produced. This, like the plan to move the guns to the coast, emanated from A.D.G.B. Headquarters, and was based on a similar appreciation of what was required; for it envisaged the extension of the new coastal gun belt from St. Margaret's Bay – its present northerly limit – to the North Foreland, and thence further north still, across the Thames, by mounting heavy anti-aircraft guns on a line of ships moored in the estuary. Anti-Aircraft Command preferred a more westerly deployment on the grounds that it would allow the continuous engagement of flying bombs by crossfire as they passed up the river. In any case, as the alternative plan depended upon the provision of the necessary shipping, which it was soon clear could not be provided in anything like the necessary quantity, the original plan was adopted as far as it affected the guns.

But another difficulty arose over the disposition of the balloon defences that were required. The A.D.G.B. plan provided for two belts of balloons; one of 106 balloons which would be an extension of the main barrage at its northern end, and another of 307 balloons which was to be deployed to the north of the Thames between Tilbury and Brentwood. Anti-Aircraft Command held, however, that these would hinder the defence of the capital against ordinary aircraft attack, as the balloon cables would interfere with the gun radar sets in and near London. The upshot was that while Balloon Command reconnoitred the sites that would be required north of the river,[68] no balloons were flown from that area. The extension to the main barrage, bringing it up to the south bank of the estuary in the Gravesend district, was proceeded with; and by the beginning of August 265 balloons had been added.[69]

But with this exception, and also that of an increase in the size of the standing patrols of fighters in the Thames estuary area, which was raised from two fighters to ten from 30th July, the defence against attack from due east was largely left to Anti-Aircraft Command and General Pile was given discretion to re-deploy the permanent defences east of London as he thought fit. These consisted chiefly of the guns in the Thames and Medway A.A. zones; and during the last week in July the movement of 64 of these was begun. The new positions that were taken up were in the quadrilateral Rochester – Whitstable – Clacton – Chelmsford, an area which was henceforth known as the 'Diver' Gun 'Box'. AT the same time, four mobile H.A.A. regiments of 21st Army Group, one Anti-Aircraft Command L.A.A. regiment, and a number of R.A.F. Regiment and naval units also began to move to positions in the box. By the end of July there were 136 heavy guns, 120 40 mm. and 324 20 mm. guns in action there.

As in the case of the coastal belt, to build up a high proportion of remotely controlled static guns within the box took longer than to carry out the initial deployment; but by the middle of August 136 of the heavy guns in the box, which by then contained 208 heavy guns all told, were of that type. The number of light guns had been increased by the same date to 174 40 mm. and 404 20 mm. Gunfire could also be brought to bear from a small number of guns on Maunsell forts moored in the estuary, and from barges and converted pleasure steamers. The normal searchlight dispositions in Essex had also been thickened by the addition of two composite searchlight and L.A.A. batteries.

In sum, by the end of July a strong defence, and by the middle of August a very powerful one, had been erected to meet the attack from due east.

*c. Effect of the 'Diver' Deployments upon the A.A. Defences of the United Kingdom.*

The deployment that had been put in force when the attack had first begun, had entailed the move of five hundred balloons and 192 heavy and 192 light guns. But then, as the inadequacy of these first defences was appreciated, successive reinforcements had been brought in. The strength of the balloon belt had risen to a thousand by the end of June and nearly two thousand by the end of July. The number of heavy guns had risen to four hundred by the first date, and six hundred and fifty by the second; and there had been a comparable increase in that of light guns. The effect on Balloon Command had been to force the elimination of practically all barrages in the rest of the United Kingdom. Anti-Aircraft Command, however, was not so seriously affected.

During the second week in July General Pile asked Air Marshal Hill's approval to very large withdrawals from the rest of the United Kingdom so that the 'Diver' belt could be rendered more efficient.[70] He proposed to withdraw guns first from areas to the north and west of a line from St. David's Head – Humber – Falkirk. This reduction, amounting to 204 heavy guns, meant that the remaining defences were manned only by Home Guards and small cadres of regular troops. The risk to the districts concerned, however, was small in view of the weakness of the German bomber force. But the requirements of the gun belt could not be met without also withdrawing guns form the south and east of the line; and General Pile proposed to obtain 276 guns from twenty-five towns in these areas. The risk involved, for reason of simple geography, was higher than in the case of the more northerly towns. But it seemed to Air Marshal Hill to be an acceptable one; and he approved the proposals.

When the coastal belt was established, and a beginning made with the formation of the 'Diver' Gun 'Box', most of the batteries that were thus obtained from other parts of the country were immediately absorbed and fresh batteries for reliefs and reinforcement were therefore needed, amounting, according to Anti-Aircraft Command's calculations, to 27 batteries – 216 guns. Once again it was necessary to reduce the gun defences of the rest of the United Kingdom. On this occasion the datum line was drawn from the Solent to the Humber. From north and west of it, 17 batteries were withdrawn, principally from the north-east coast, Bristol, Merseyside and Belfast; from south and east of it, eight were withdrawn, from London, Chelmsford, Ashford and Canterbury. The remaining two batteries were available from resources already earmarked for 'Diver'. When these withdrawals had been made, Anti-Aircraft Command had committed 704 heavy guns and 708 light guns[71] to 'Diver', leaving 1,269 heavy guns and 1,613 light guns for the defence of the rest of the country.

*d. The protection of London.*
It has already been noted that during the four weeks succeeding the redeployment to the coast, the general scale of enemy attack was much the same as in the previous weeks. In another respect, too, the position remained much the same: the mean point of impact of all the bombs falling in London was, as before, in the Dulwich district, approximately one mile east of Alleyn's School. The brunt of the attack, therefore, continued to fall on the boroughs south of the river. The toll of houses damaged and destroyed continued to rise, being near one million by the middle of August. Casualties, however, were lower by one half than in the first five weeks; which reflected the evacuation that had been going on, especially south of the river. Nor were there any single incidents so destructive of life as some of those that had occurred earlier in the attack. The three most serious were at Leyton, Kensington and Watford, where some thirty people were killed in each case. The period was notable for quite the heaviest day's attack so far launched, that of dusk on 2nd August to dusk the following day, when in dull, cloudy weather, 210 flying bombs crossed the coast and 103 fell in London. But this was an exceptional day, not only in weight of attack but in the proportion of bombs that penetrated to the capital. For the period as a whole only a little over 33 per cent of bombs reported by the defences succeeded in reaching their target, compared to 44 per cent for the first five weeks of the attack.

That this was so, was largely due to the improved performance of the guns. Between 17th and 24th July, the first week in which guns were operating in their new positions on the coast, the percentage of bombs destroyed by anti-aircraft fire was only slightly better than in the previous most successful week for the guns. The next week, however, saw a notable improvement. Out of nearly six hundred possible targets, the guns destroyed 140, which represented a destruction of 24 per cent compared to 16 in the previous week. There was a further slight improvement in the period 31st July – 7th August, which was a week of consistently bad weather and one in which the Germans launched more bombs than in any previous week. Then, in the week 7th – 14th August, the guns destroyed 120 of the 305 flying bombs that were presented to them as targets; and for the first time their percentage of successes exceeded that of the fighters.

The steady improvement reflected the introduction of the new equipment, but it reflected also the success of the gun detachments in familiarising themselves with the new drills that were entailed. This was the case with the light guns as well as the heavy; for in order that 40 mm. guns could be fired at unseen targets, the No. 3 Predictor, which hitherto had been used exclusively with the heavy guns, was adapted and brought into use by L.A.A. Regiments. It was not least among the achievements of the Command that the soldiers' traditional prejudice against novel equipment was overcome so quickly.

But if the performance of the defences as a whole showed a notable improvement on the first weeks of the attack, the successes of the fighters had diminished; as, indeed, it had been feared they would when the redeployment of the guns had been decided upon. It was recognised that fighters patrolling over the sea would be compensated for the bisection of their patrol area by the gun belt only if an improved technique of control was achieved by the radar stations. For this, the radar stations had regularly to detect flying bombs at least sixty miles away, track them thenceforth continuously and accurately, and provide the fighter pilot with precise information on the course of his target. All this had to be done sufficiently quickly to allow the pilot time to make interception and destroy the bomb before it reached the coastal gun belt. For once that happened, the bomb became within the exclusive sphere of the guns where all pilots were expressly forbidden to trespass.

In the event, the problem was never satisfactorily solved. The American M.E.W. set at Fairlight and its successor the British Type 26, were the most successful stations; but the proportion of possible targets destroyed by seaward patrolling fighters during these four weeks was only one in ten, compared with one in three during the first five weeks, when the fighter patrol area had extended from the Channel to the balloon belt inland. What was particularly significant was that the degree of success remained much the same week by week, despite the fact that pilots and controllers alike became very familiar with the problem. In other words, the failure was a failure of equipment rather than training or individual skill.[72]

Overland the difficulties of interception were not so great. Basically, the problem was the same as over sea, i.e. to give the fighter the necessary information, sufficiently early, for interception to be made and pressed home. Nor was there much difference in the relative size of the two patrol areas. But it was found in practice that the gunfire from the guns on the coast gave the patrolling pilots an excellent indication of the course of the bomb; and very often pilots could, as it were, wait behind the guns to fall on these bombs that passed unscathed through the barrage. In addition, there were facilities for aiding interception over land that were absent at sea. The Royal Observer Corps Centres at

Maidstone and Horsham were used for the control of patrolling fighters – the advantage being that this cut out the transmission of information to the Group operations room from the R.O.C. Centres, which was the usual procedure when piloted aircraft were being plotted. R.O.C. posts, and a number of searchlight units were also used to speed up the passing of information to the patrolling pilot. They were equipped with white Schermuly rockets which they fired to mark the course of a flying bomb. The use of red rockets by the R.O.C. and selected R.A.F. Wireless Observer Units, and searchlight beams to mark the southern boundary of the balloon barrage – by the end of July a more fearsome obstacle than ever – was continued. Searchlight beams were also extensively used to mark patrol lines.

The result was that many more flying bombs were shot down overland than over the sea in these four weeks – the relative figures were 395 and 231 – and there was no great decline from the rate of destruction that had been achieved by fighters in the first phase of the attack.[73]

There was actually an increase in the number that was destroyed by fighters operating at night overland. This was partly explained by the move of the guns to the coast which left the landward approaches to London free for the unimpeded operations of night fighters and searchlights, whereas previously operations overland at night had frequently been restricted to the guns. But it was partly due also to increased skill and efficiency on the part of night fighter crews and searchlight detachments, aided by the ground controls. It was significant that the most consistently successful night squadrons were those that specialised in the work – Nos. 96, 418 and 605 Squadrons, using Mosquitos, and the Tempest of F.I.U. The first of these was second only to two Tempest squadrons – Nos. 3 and 486, which flew chiefly by day – in the number of bombs destroyed. The other successful Mosquito squadrons, which normally operated as 'Intruders', were first employed over the launching site area in northern France in order to spot the sites that were in action. They had little success, and from the middle of July usually patrolled to seaward of the gun belt. All told, eleven Mosquito squadrons and two U.S.A.A.F. night fighter squadrons,[74] as well as detachments from day fighter squadrons, were called upon for night patrols; but with the exception of the four mentioned above, none had any notable success.[75]

One other component of the defences improved on its performance prior to the middle of July: this was the balloon barrage. By the end of July, the planned total of 1,750 L.Z. balloons and 265 Mk.VI balloons was deployed. Weather remained the chief factor affecting the flying of the barrage. In the last week of July, when the weather was very bad, the whole barrage was grounded for nearly one-fifth of the time. The following week, when the weather was better but still far from good, this figure fell to one-twentieth, while in the excellent weather of 9th-15th August the barrage was fully operational for the whole week.

Destruction of bombs through impact with balloon cables reflected the expansion of the barrage. Expressed as a percentage of bombs destroyed to bombs passing into the barrage, it rose from 8 during the second week in July to 15 in the next; it fell to 11 during the bad weather of the last week of the month and then rose again to 18 in the first week of August and 19 in the second. Altogether, 147 flying bombs were brought down by balloons during the period, compared to 55 in the previous five weeks.

This was not due simply to the thickening of the barrage. Certain modifications to the balloons were beginning to show results. By the beginning of July experiments and trials carried out at the Balloon Development Establishment, Cardington had reached the stage where various devices intended to increase the lethality of the barrage could be tried on a large scale. They consisted of attaching either one or two extra wires to the balloon cable. By the end of the month 590 balloons had been fitted with one extra wire, and 69 with two. Two developments sponsored by the Admiralty were also coming into operation by this date. They were known as 'Whiskers' and 'Nets'. The first consisted of suspending light wire in a near-horizontal position from the cable by means of parachutes. The second was an assembly of wires fitted between two adjacent balloons. By the middle of August, 1,540 sites were equipped with one additional wire; the two-wire assembly had been withdrawn pending further trials; 87 sites were equipped with Admiralty 'Whiskers' and six with 'Nets'. The 'Nets' up to that time had enjoyed no success; the 'Whiskers' had brought down two flying bombs; the single wire assemblies had destroyed at least fourteen, possibly as many as twenty; and in twelve other cases flying bombs after an initial impact with light wires had crashed after a second impact later in their flight. Altogether, Balloon Command was at last obtaining a worthwhile return for its strenuous efforts since the attack began.

## 32. Survey of the Period.
This was patently true of the whole field of Allied counter-measures. There was by the middle of August a general feeling amongst those who were responsible for operations, particularly defensive ones, that an ascendancy over the new weapon was being achieved. Not that there

was undue optimism. Air Chief Marshal Tedder pointed out that one factor in the fall in the scale of flying bomb attack during the second week in August might have been the enormous transport difficulties that the battle on land was making for the Germans, and if the position stabilised the attack might intensify. Little or nothing was being said, it is interesting to note, about the position stabilising only when the launching sites had been overrun.

There was also, of course, the possibility that the Germans might adopt new and more effective tactics or modify the flying bomb to give it added speed and range. So far, we had discerned little that was new in either respect. From about 20th July many flying bombs had been fired in salvoes in an attempt to saturate the defences, but with little success. Fighters were slightly less successful against this form of attack than against spasmodic shooting, guns were slightly more. The Germans also took more advantage of weather conditions than during the first weeks of the attack. Early morning, when sea fog and mist over land hindered the defences, was often the busiest time of the day. Here too, however, the advantage to the enemy was unimportant.

The attack from the direction of the Thames estuary, where the Germans had certainly sprung a surprise, had not so far been embarrassing. According to the best British figures, only 107 flying bombs were launched by air from 9th July to the middle of August, all of them by night.

Such modifications to the weapon itself as were reported consisted of alterations to its explosive content. It was during these four weeks that a proportion of warheads was filled with Trialen, a more powerful explosive than that which was normally used. A few bombs were also reported to contain a number of 1 kilogramme incendiary bombs. Range, speed and operational height, however, remained much the same, though there were occasional reports of bombs being seen at heights of 7,000 feet.

The attack had, therefore, remained static, as it were; whereas the counter-measures to it had notably developed. This was not so obviously true of the bombing counter-measures as of the direct defence of London; and at the moment of writing it is still impossible to say how far the Germans were hindered by them. But at the end of July a more clearly formulated bombing policy had been worked out: one bearing a more precise relation to the state of intelligence on the enemy's flying bomb organisation that had been the case previously. Moreover, while the continued attack of the actual launching sites was still insisted upon, the main weight of the offensive had been switched from sites to storage depots, which were not only a probable bottle-neck in the German system of supply but were more suitable targets than the sites of attack by heavy bombers.

The only really obscure feature of the picture which the intelligence officers were constructing remained the machinery of production. Here, little more information that was positive and trustworthy had been obtained. The one known assembly factory was Fallersleben; and accordingly, it had been attacked. But it was certain that there were others; and the absence of dependable intelligence was a serious handicap to an effective counter-offensive.[76] Peenemünde, Ober Raderach and the other hydrogen peroxide plants, were useful targets. Hydrogen peroxide, however, had only a limited use with flying bombs, namely in the launching procedure; and the prospects of destroying so much of the capacity to produce it that not even the small quantities required for launching would be available were remote.

But the contribution of the bombers was not to be assessed only by the damage that was caused to specific 'Crossbow' targets. There were also the effects of the Allied air offensive on the German economy in general to be taken into consideration. Similarly, the land battle, by imposing a strain upon the enemy's capacity to make war, was making an indirect contribution; while the direct threat from the Allied armies to the areas from which bombs were being launched was, of course, potentially the most effective of all Allied counter-measures.

When we turn to the progress of the defences during this first month succeeding the redeployment, more positive statements can be made; for the success of the defences can be assessed by the simple equation of bombs destroyed and bombs reaching London with the number of bombs that the Germans had launched. Clearly, there had been a most marked improvement compared to the early weeks of the attack. The chief reason is not far to seek: it lay in the more effective shooting of the guns, though the balloons had also increased its percentage success. But a further factor was that the defensive system as a whole was working with far more smoothness than in the earlier phase.[77] Dozens of fighters, hundreds of guns and balloons were now operating with little mutual interference in an area little more than fifty miles deep against targets that could cross the area in five to six minutes.

The guiding principle was to restrict the fire of the guns in the belt as little as possible; and by the middle of August even such few restrictions as had been imposed when the redeployment took place had been abolished or modified. The safe areas that had been instituted in front of coastal towns and radar stations were reduced in size. The gap in the barrage over Hastings, which allowed fighters to pass between the two fighter patrol areas, was abolished on 11th August. Instead, Anti-

Aircraft Command accepted a prohibition on fire above 6,000 feet; and aircraft passed over the guns above this height.

But with these small exceptions the guns were free to fire when and where they liked; and the responsibility for avoiding their fire fell upon the fighter pilots. It was a measure of their success in this that few cases were notified between July and the end of August of fighters being damaged by anti-aircraft fire. In sum, provided that the form of the German attack did not change, A.D.G.B. were confident that an effective system had been organised and that the combined efforts of all arms would result in still better results.

## 33. The Offensive against 'Crossbow' Targets, 16th August – 5th September.

General bombing policy during what was to prove the last fortnight of the main flying bomb attack, i.e. that launched from the belt of modified sites between the Seine and the Pas de Calais, showed little change compared to that of previous weeks. Air Chief Marshal Tedder still had difficulty in obtaining from the 8th Air Force as big an effort against 'Crossbow' targets as he wished.[78] Bomber Command's 'Crossbow' effort was also small. During the week 16th – 22nd August, only eleven hundred tons out of a total of nearly twelve thousand dropped by the two heavy bomber forces fell on 'Crossbow' targets; only a little more than two thousand was aimed at battlefield targets. During the week, 23rd – 29th August, the proportionate effort was higher: 4,528 tons were dropped on 'Crossbow' targets out of a total effort of more than seventeen thousand tons.

'Crossbow' bombing policy itself was complicated by the reappearance of targets connected with rocket as distinct from flying bomb attack: which was a result of the more precise intelligence on rocket development and the imminence of rocket attack that had been received during the previous six weeks. Thus, the large sites at Watten and Mimoyecques were returned to the schedule of 'Crossbow' targets and were very heavily attacked by Bomber Command on 25th and 27th August, respectively. The radio and armament factory at Weimar/Buchenwald, which was suspected of making rocket components, was also added to the list and was attacked by the 8th Air Force on 24th August. Five 'Benito' W/T stations in the Somme – Pas de Calais area, operating in a frequency band which, it was expected, would also be used for tracking the rocket, were recommended for attack in order to clear the air and so make listening for enemy rocket signals easier. Two of these stations were lightly attacked during the last week in August, as were five small liquid oxygen plants in northern

France and Belgium. In addition, as the Allied armies advanced to the Seine, the storage depots in the Paris area were suspended from attack and the forward storage depots, rearward of the belt of modified sites, were substituted. These smaller depots were thought to be for rocket rather than flying bomb storage. In attacks on rocket targets between 16th and 29th August two thousand tons of bombs were dropped, leaving only some three thousand that were dropped on targets connected with flying bombs, quite the smallest effort in any fortnight since flying bomb attacks had begun.

These attacks opened with one of the rare contributions of the 15th U.S. Air Force to 'Crossbow' counter-measures. On 16th August 89 Liberators, operating from airfields in the Foggia district, attacked the hydrogen plant at Ober Raderach and dropped 170 tons of bombs. Excellent results were obtained: the hydrogen plant was demolished and the oxygen plant probably damaged by blast; and photographic reconnaissance after the attack indicated that the plant was out of action. A week later it was suspended from further attack.

Apart from the light attacks by the 8th Air Force against the fuel depot at Pacy-sur-Armançon and the airfields at Eindhoven and Roye-Amy, which have already been mentioned, and light attacks by Bomber Command against modified sites, on which less than two hundred tons of bombs were dropped, the only other 'Crossbow' attack during the week 16th – 22nd August was made by Bomber Command on 18th August against a storage depot at Forêt de l'Isle Adam in the Oise valley north-west of Paris. Over seven hundred tons of bombs were dropped and the target area was well covered with craters. The density of trees in the area made any detailed assessment of damage difficult. This was, however, the last attack that it was deemed necessary to make against the group of storage depots in the area, Paris – Beauvais – Compiègne – Rheims, which was daily in greater danger of being cut off from the modified sites by the advance towards the Seine.

During the week 23rd – 29th August a larger effort was made against modified sites: 1100 tons of bombs were dropped on twenty sites, with some success in five cases. All the sites were north of the Somme; which reflected the change in the situation on land. Three airfields in Holland – Venlo, Eindhoven and Deelen – and Le Culot airfield in Belgium, all of which were thought to be in use by flying bomb launching aircraft, were lightly attacked; 150 tons of bombs were dropped, chiefly by the 8th Air Force.

The main attacks of the week were against Peenemünde and the Opel works at Rüsselsheim. The 8th Air Force sent 180 aircraft to Peenemünde on 25th August, 319 tons of bombs were dropped and further damage was caused to the hydrogen peroxide plant. This was the fourth and last occasion on which Peenemünde was attacked. The same night, Bomber Command sent 412 aircraft to Rüsselsheim and 1,554 tons of bombs were dropped. Bombing was well concentrated on the Opel works, very little weight falling on the residential districts nearby. Severe damage was caused throughout the plant; almost all major units, including three assembly sheds, were hit. No further attacks needed to be made on the factory.

These attacks marked the end of the efforts of the heavy bomber forces to diminish the scale of flying bomb attack from northern France. They were not the only 'Crossbow' attacks that were made before the Germans were forced to abandon their launching sites. On 31st August and 1st September Bomber Command sent out very strong forces to attack nine forward storage depots in the Pas de Calais, dropping in all nearly three thousand tons of bombs. These were attacked, however, for the part they might be playing in the enemy's preparations for rocket attack.

## 34. The Contribution of Ground Forces.

In any case, thanks to the advance of the Allied armies, there was not at this time as great a need for the bombing of targets associated with flying bombs as there had been previously. As early as the middle of August the Germans had begun to withdraw from the launching sites south of the Somme, even though the Allied ground forces had not yet reached the Seine. These sites had probably been evacuated by 20th August. At any rate, from dusk on that day only the sites north of the Somme remained operative. What the Germans appear to have done was to withdraw the third and fourth Abteilungen of Flakregiment 155(W) from their original dispositions south of the Somme, and redeploy them in the area north of the river where the first and second Abteilungen had been operating.[79]

The end came rapidly; so rapidly, indeed, that an airborne expedition to land troops in the Pas de Calais on 3rd September was cancelled.[80] By the 30th, the 11th British Armoured Division was in Amiens, and the 3rd U.S. Army was well past Laon. The sites in the Pas de Calais were not occupied by these moves, but their communications with Germany were obviously about to be cut. Thus, on 1st September the sites ceased operating and personnel and equipment were moved east and north-east while there was yet time to escape.

## 35. Scale of German Attack, 16th August – 5th September.

These last weeks showed a substantial reduction in the scale of attack on London – amounting almost to one third – compared to previous weeks.

Between 16th August and 1st September 1,115 flying bombs were reported, representing an average daily rate of 74 bombs. There were, however, considerable variations from day to day. The two heaviest attacks were in the dusk-to-dusk periods of 22nd/23rd and 23rd/24th August, when 103 and 127 bombs respectively were reported. There were two unusually light periods, 17th/18th and 24th/25th August, when 15 and 14 bombs were plotted: on both these days weather was good. On the last day of the attack from modified sites, 31st August/1st September, only eight bombs were reported. From then until the early hours of 5th September there was no activity. Then, between 0500 and 0600 hours on the latter date, nine flying bombs, all of them launched from He.111's, were reported in an attack that marks the end of the main offensive. With the exception of five bombs on the night of 30th/31st August these were the only ones reported as launched from aircraft during these final three weeks, compared with about one hundred and twenty during the previous month.[81] This may have been due to the concerted attack which Bomber Command and the 8th Air Force made on 15th August against airfields in north-west Europe, including seven from which aircraft were operating against London. Otherwise, it is difficult to trace any relation between the scale of attack during this period and the 'Crossbow' counter-offensive; though, as the attack ceased so early in September, it is not to be wondered that there was no visible return for the attacks against production targets in Germany, which received the major part of the 'Crossbow' bomb tonnage during the period and which were, so to speak, long-term targets.

The mean point of impact of flying bombs, which, it will be recalled, had not shown any significant variations during the first two months of the attack, changed considerably during the second half of August. In the week 11th – 18th August, it moved appreciably to the north-east, falling just south of West Ham. The following week showed an even greater variation, the main point of impact falling in Chiswick. For the last week of the main attack it was plotted at a point in the Lambeth – Newington area, north of the Camberwell – Dulwich districts where it had fallen during every week but three. Whether the Germans deliberately changed their aiming points, or whether the evacuation of the sites south of the Somme and the approach of the Allied armies affected the accuracy of their shooting, is not known.

## 36. The Defence of London, 16th August to 5th September.

The decline in the scale of attack would have meant a corresponding alleviation in the weight of bombs falling on London even if the performance of the defences had not improved. As it was, the rate of improvement which was noticed in the month following the redeployment of the guns to the coast was well maintained. By the middle of August, the defences had reached their greatest strength. Fifteen day fighter squadrons and six night fighter squadrons of A.D.G.B. were engaged entirely on 'Diver' patrols, and two more night fighter squadrons were engaged on the work part time. The balloon barrage consisted of 2,015 balloons, of which over sixteen hundred were equipped with light wire armament. In the coastal gun belt, there were 592 heavy and 922 light guns, and over six hundred rocket barrels. In the gun 'box' there were 208 heavy and 178 light guns, four hundred 20 mm. guns and 108 rocket barrels.[82]

Only 17 per cent of the 1,124 bombs that were reported between 16th August and 5th September fell in the target area, compared to 33 per cent during the previous month and 44 per cent during the first five weeks. During the last four days (i.e. excluding the small air-launched attack of 5th September), when 192 bombs were reported, only 28 fell in London. The most successful day for the defences was 27th – 28th August, when, out of 97 bombs reported, no fewer than 87 were destroyed and only four fell in London. During these twenty-four hours the anti-aircraft guns destroyed 62 bombs, fighters 19, balloons two, and guns and balloons shared the destruction of a further four.

The relative successes of the three sorts of defence on this day reflected the trend throughout these last three weeks. The percentage successes of the guns rose from 40 in the second week in August to 55 in the third, 57 in the fourth, and 63 in the final four days before the enemy abandoned their launching sites.[83] Altogether, between 16th August and the end of the attack the guns destroyed 791 flying bombs, compared to 669 during the whole of the previous nine weeks.

Over the same period the successes of the fighters showed little variation. They destroyed 15 per cent of all possible targets until the last week, when their successes fell to 11 per cent probably because of the small number of bombs that was despatched. 263 flying bombs were destroyed by fighters in the three weeks, bringing their successes since 13th June to 1,771.

The balloons maintained the improved rate of destruction that had followed the completion of the full barrage and the equipping of the majority of the balloons with additional wires. 45 flying bombs were brought down by the barrage after 15th August, making a total for the whole of the main attack of 232.

Certain changes in deployment and tactics were made during the period to meet the enemy's involuntary concentration on launching bombs from his more northerly sites. The number of bombs fired from sites south of the Somme was very small from as early as 14th August onwards. By the 21st it was appreciated that further launchings from this area were unlikely; and the movement of a number of guns from the western end of the coastal belt began. By the 25th the full extent of these redispositions had been decided upon: 182 heavy and 48 light guns were to be moved from positions west of Covehurst Bay to thicken the eastern sections of the belt and slightly extend it, and were in fact moved by the end of the month. A similar change was made in the balloon barrage. 246 balloons were withdrawn from its western end; some were used in the area immediately south of the Thames which had until then been defended by the MK.VI balloons, while the remainder were redeployed within the barrage to increase its density. Instructions for the transfer were received by Balloon Command on 22nd August; and the move was completed by the 28th.

The new concentration of fire proved a disadvantage to the fighters. Although the area to be patrolled was no longer extensive, the warning obtained, especially of bombs launched from sites near the Straits of Dover, was necessarily shorter than in the case of those fired from sites south of the Somme; in other words, fighters patrolling to seaward had even less time in which to intercept. Significantly, while the fighters patrolling inland of the gun belt maintained their rate of destruction during these last three weeks, those operating out to sea were somewhat less successful. Their score fell from an average of over 10 per cent for the first two weeks of August to 6 per cent for the third week, and to 9 and 6 per cent respectively for the last two weeks of the attack.

Little could be done to remedy this. On 23rd August A.D.G.B. Headquarters suggested to No.11 Group that it might be possible to make interceptions east of Cap Gris Nez. No.11 Group, however, held the idea impracticable on these grounds: it would be impossible to keep the fighters out of the areas in the Pas de Calais that were strongly defended by anti-aircraft guns, and they would sooner or later be shot down; if the patrolling fighters flew above the ceiling of the enemy's light flak, i.e. at about 6,000 feet, they would have little chance during daylight of seeing a flying bomb launched, and little more at dusk and dawn; even if they did, they could not carry out an attack, owing to the danger from flak, until the French coast had been cleared, which would give them little or no advantage over the fighters already patrolling over the Straits. Moreover, even if had been considered worthwhile to run the hazards of the German ground fire, insufficient aircraft were available at this time. The proposal was, therefore abandoned.

The last of these weighty objections to the scheme arose from the fact that from 26th August the number of day fighter squadrons that was available for full-time employment on flying bomb patrols had been cut down from fifteen to ten. On that day Air Chief Marshal Leigh-Mallory had instructed Air Marshal Hill to release a number of Spitfires for fighter-bomber operations in the Lille – Arras – Douai area, which in turn would release the 9th Air Force for the attack of railways further east and south-east. Five squadrons[84] were accordingly withdrawn from 'Diver' work but were retained on their airfields in Kent on the understanding that they could be re-employed in their old role if the flying bomb situation warranted it.

Air Marshal Hill accepted this reduction of the forces employed against flying bombs for two reasons: first, the shrinkage of the German launching area meant a reduction in the patrol area which the A.D.G.B fighters had to cover; second, by this time the guns were achieving splendid results, and achieving them in all conditions of weather.

This was so much the case, that the operational instructions that had been evolved to meet the conditions created by the coastal gun belt were still further modified in favour of the guns during the last week in August. From 26th August all safety lanes that had been established for the passage of friendly fighters and distressed aircraft were abolished; the coastal gun belt and the gun 'box' were declared prohibited areas for flying below 7,000 feet, leaving the guns complete freedom of action at all times up to 6,000 feet. Fighter airfields within the gun areas continued to be used; but to safeguard the aircraft it was laid down that they should approach from landwards. Aircraft in distress were also provided for by passing warning of their approach to Biggin Hill or North Weald sector operations rooms from the fighter control stations, and thence to the Anti-Aircraft Command gun operations room at Chatham or Southend depending on whether the aircraft was approaching the guns in the coastal belt or those in the 'box'. These rules were in being when the main attack came to an end.

They signified, of course, that for defence against flying bombs, the anti-aircraft gun was the most effective weapon; and fighters were for this purpose, no longer the principle arm of the air defence of Great Britain to whose operations all other arms had to conform. It had taken over a month of heavy attack for this change to be appreciated; but it was greatly to the credit of A.D.G.B. Headquarters that without prompting from Anti-Aircraft Command they had seen its necessity and revised the scheme of defence accordingly. The result was that London, the enemy's target, was much more effectively protected, to the extent during the last three weeks of the attack only one out of every seven flying bombs that the enemy launched actually reached the capital.

# Part VI.

# Rocket and Flying Bomb Attacks on the United Kingdom, 8th September 1944 – 25th November 1944.

**37. Introduction.**

The last flying bombs to be launched from the modified sites in the Pas de Calais fell in Kent in the early afternoon of 1st September. By that date the position on land in northern France was such that within a day or two the whole of the Pas de Calais would have been overrun. Indeed, British forces were beginning their drive on Antwerp; and there was little to stop them reaching the Scheldt. Already, the Germans had begun to evacuate the last of the sites which had been troubling us for so long; and as, to our certain knowledge, no sites had been constructed east of the Pas de Calais there was little likelihood of further bombs being launched against London from sites on land.

The possibility that air-launched attacks would continue could not, of course, be discounted. But here also there were good grounds for optimism; for such was the Allied ascendency over what remained of the German Air Force in the Low Countries, and so swiftly was the whole situation changing in the Allied favour, that few attacks were expected from this source unless the position on land stabilised before Belgium and Holland had been occupied.

As for attacks by rockets, it was known that the weapon had reached a stage of development and production where it could be used operationally. But it was believed that the Allied ground forces would soon have occupied so much of western Europe that no firing points for rockets could be established within range of London.

The first week of September was notable, therefore, for some most sanguine statements on what was to be expected from V-weapons. On 6th September, the Vice-Chiefs of Staff reported that all areas from which flying bombs or rockets might be launched against London had been, or were about to be, occupied by Allied troops; and that "there should thus shortly be no further danger to this country from either of the causes, except for the possibility of the airborne launching of flying bombs." On the following day, Mr. Duncan Sandys, in a lengthy review of the attacks that had taken place, spoke to the Press of the Battle of London being over, "except possibly for a few last shots."

In fact, the battle was far from over. During the next six months over a thousand rockets and nearly five hundred flying bombs fell in the United Kingdom. To understand how this came about, and how far the defences were caught unawares, it is necessary to trace the developments in our intelligence of the German preparations since the early months of 1944.

**38. Intelligence on the Rocket, January – July 1944**.
In the sphere of Allied air operations, the eclipse of the rocket by the flying bomb was complete from December 1943 – June 1944, except for a small number of attacks on the large sites in the Cherbourg peninsula and the Pas de Calais. The intelligence investigation into the rocket, however, continued.

By December 1943, both weapons – the flying bomb and the rocket – had been identified. But as the development work on each was concentrated at Peenemünde, and as the constructional works required for the operations of each were being carried out in the same area – northern France – there was still some confusion between the two in the intelligence that was being received.

*a. Activity at Peenemünde.*
As far as was known at the time, Peenemünde remained the centre both of flying bomb and rocket development during the winter of 1943. To find out exactly what was happening there was, however, even more difficult than it had been in the previous summer. German security noticeably improved after the raid of August. All foreign workers were transferred elsewhere, leaving as the sole intelligence agents in the district the sources which were investigating the activities of the Air Signals Experimental Regiment. Their work on flying bombs was of great value, as we have

seen; but all that was learned from them about rockets during the winter of 1943 was that firing trials were being carried out on a small scale. Photographic reconnaissance during the winter also added little to what was known, beyond establishing that Peenemünde was a production centre for hydrogen peroxide as well as an experimental establishment. All the most important questions – what was the weight of the rocket, how was it launched and controlled, what was its performance, what organisation would control its operations – remained unanswered.

*b. The Polish Trials.*

In March 1944, however, a fresh field for investigation came to light. When the great attack on Peenemünde had been planned in the summer of 1943 it had been appreciated that it might prove almost too successful if it resulted in the evacuation of the station and the dispersal of the work that was going on there. As it was, development work was continued at Peenemünde after the raid, but a measure of dispersal was carried out. In November – December 1943, an organisation was set up at Blizna, near Dębica, about 170 miles west of Warsaw, for testing and firing V-weapons, in which capacity it became as important as Peenemünde. It was controlled by the S.S., which reflected the growing importance of that organisation in the retaliation campaign. The value of the move from the German point of view was not only that Blizna was unlikely to be attacked from the air but that it permitted firing overland and the recovery of the missiles for inspection.

Intelligence in the United Kingdom, however, was unaware of this new station until March 1944, when, thanks to the sources that had been covering the trials on the Baltic coast, it became clear that a flying bomb launching site had been built at Blizna and that bombs were being fired. It was principally from these same sources that it then emerged that trials of a second long range weapon were being carried out at Blizna. To establish beyond doubt that this was in fact the A.4 rocket took many weeks. The Peenemünde sources, the Polish S.I.S. and photographic reconnaissance all contributed; but it was not until July that the matter was settled by the identification of a rocket at Blizna shown on a photograph taken on 15th May. Concurrently with establishing this point much valuable information on the size, nature and effect of the rocket, and on the amount of firing the Germans had been carrying out, was transmitted by the Poles.

*c. Evidence from Prisoners of War and the Swedish Rocket.*

In the meantime, fresh evidence had arrived from two directions, one of them entirely unexpected: from prisoners captured in Normandy and from the examination of a rocket, fired from the Peenemünde area that accidently fell near Malmö in Sweden on 13th June. In other respects, too, the invasion of France marked the beginning of the solution of the problem; for it released for work on the rocket many of the officers of Scientific Air Intelligence whose energies had been devoted up to D-Day in preparation for the invasion.

Evidence from prisoners who had been associated with V-weapon development was useful chiefly in indicating that the rocket firing point was a very simple affair and not the big and cumbersome mortar-like erection which had seemed to follow from the scientists' estimate of a rocket weighing sixty tons or more.

In addition, information was obtained that led to the discovery of three rocket storage depots, two of them underground, in northern France; which in turn, from the layout of their buildings and storage tunnels, provided valuable confirmatory evidence of the length and width of the rocket.

Something was also learned of the unit – LXV Army Corps – which the Germans had formed specially for their retaliation campaign; though beyond the fact that such a formation was in being, this side of the enemy's organisation was to remain obscure to us even for some time after rocket attacks had begun.

With these advances in knowledge of what the Germans were doing in northern France came new information on the technical aspects of the rocket. Arrangements were made for two technical intelligence officers of A.I.2(g) to go to Sweden to examine the remains of the rocket that had fallen there. Some useful information came from this inspection. In particular, the impression that had hitherto been held, that hydrogen peroxide was the main constituent of the fuel of the rocket, was, corrected; instead liquid oxygen was indicated. However, it was decided that the most satisfactory way to exploit this fortunate occurrence was to arrange for the transport of the parts of the rocket to England for detailed examination and reconstruction. All this took time and was not in fact completed until the middle of August.

*d. Further Contributions from the Polish S.I.S. and from Captured Documents.* Until this examination was finished the two main sources of intelligence were the Polish S.I.S. and German documents captured in France. The genius of the Poles for clandestine organisation proved invaluable. They set up an organisation to reach the sites of rocket incidents before the German search parties, and collect any small fragments of interest and photograph anything too large to be carried away. They also planted agents in Blizna camp itself. By the end of

June, they had succeeded in transmitting information which made it almost certain that A.4 rockets were being fired from Blizna. The Poles reported that they were about forty feet long and six feet in diameter (similar dimensions to the rockets photographed at Peenemünde in 1943), and that radio control was employed. Their work was crowned by an exploit in which their leader was picked up in Poland and brought to the United Kingdom, by way of Italy, in a Dakota aircraft with all the documents and parts that he was able to carry.[85] He arrived on 28th July. He was able to clarify several points of detail in the reports that had previously been sent. In particular, he cleared up one point that had proved very puzzling: namely, that many of the rockets fired from Blizna had burst high in the air. Previously, this had been thought to mean that a proximity fuse was fitted; but from what the Polish leader said it was clear that the bursts were premature. In other words, although the A.4 rocket had reached an advanced stage of development it had not yet been perfected.

Before all the Polish evidence, and that from Sweden, had been absorbed, valuable information was revealed by a study of a series of captured documents on the rocket sites in northern France. As a result, more firing sites and rocket storage depots were found and an outline drawing of the rocket itself. Other documents showed what vehicles were required by a rocket firing unit, including the fuel vehicles; from which it appeared that one of the main constituents of the fuel was almost certainly liquid oxygen. By relating this to something that had been transmitted earlier by our Peenemünde sources, certain more positive conclusions were possible regarding the weight of the rocket and its warhead – the most important feature of the rocket from the point of view of those who were likely to be its target.

However, it was not until August that this emerged, by which time the rocket had again become the major concern of the Government that it had been in the summer and autumn of 1943. Counter-measures against it had recommenced; and something of the earlier atmosphere of urgency regarding it had returned to the councils of the War Cabinet and the Chiefs of Staff. It is to what happened in this sphere from June to August that we must now turn.

### 39. Renewed Interest of the War Cabinet.

Although the first five months of 1944 had seen real progress in rocket intelligence there was so much that was incomplete and unsubstantiated that up to the arrival of the flying bomb on 13th June little had been done to acquaint the Chiefs of Staff that rocket

118

development vigorously continued.[86] The advent of one of the two V-weapons altered the position in that attacks upon the large sites recommenced. But these were attacks on suspicious constructions which it was as well to destroy before they were virtually invulnerable, more than upon targets known for certain to be connected with the rocket. And with their exception active counter-measures against rocket attack necessarily waited for the crystallization of the intelligence that was coming from Peenemünde, Sweden and Poland.

Inevitably, however, the arrival of the flying bomb had led to a concern about the rocket and a natural demand from the departments concerned with the defence of the country for some statement, as authoritative and comprehensive as possible, on the possibilities of rocket attack. Dr. R.V. Jones, A.D.I. (Science), was therefore required in the second week of July to prepare a report. He did so with some reluctance: all the results of the examination of the Swedish rocket were not yet to hand, photographic cover of Blizna was not complete, and the S.O.E. operation to pick up the leader of the Poles investigating Blizna, while planned, had still to be carried out. Consequently, his report, which was circulated to the Chiefs of Staff on 16th July, emphasised the gaps in our knowledge, in particular on the launching points for the rocket, the radio control stations, the nature of the radio control, and also on the production and supply system and the field organisation. But he made it clear that the rocket had reached the stage of series production, and that while it had not been perfected it could probably be used operationally on a small scale. He went on to say that there were few indications of when bombing might begin. On the weight of the rocket he said only that judging from craters seen at Peenemünde and Blizna its warhead might weigh between three and seven tons. He repeated the opinion, shortly to be corrected, that hydrogen peroxide was the main constituent of the fuel, and also the mistaken view, which the Polish leader was to put right, that the rocket embodied a proximity fuse.

There was sufficient in the report, however, for the Prime Minister to come to the next meeting of the War Cabinet 'Crossbow' Sub-Committee on 18th July, where he was somewhat critical of the Air Ministry's work on the rocket and their attitude to it, suggesting that they had been caught napping. He directed Dr. Jones to keep his Scientific Advisor, Lord Cherwell, fully informed of all developments in intelligence.

He was no less critical at a further meeting of the Sub-Committee a week later. The previous day, a scientific sub-committee which Mr. Sandys had set up under Professor C.D. Ellis. Scientific Advisor to the

Army Council, to study the rocket, had reported its opinions, through Mr. Sandys. The report embodied intelligence that had recently arrived indicating that the firing point for the rocket was merely a slab of concrete[87] and that its fuel was composed chiefly of liquid oxygen and, possibly, ethyl alcohol. It was more downright than Dr. Jones had been concerning the weight of the rocket and advanced as approximations a total weight of thirty to forty tones and a warhead of five to ten tons at a range of 150 miles. It concluded with the observation: "Although we have as yet no reliable information about the movement of projectiles westward from Germany, it would be unwise to assume from this negative evidence that a rocket attack is not imminent."

At the meeting on the following day the Prime Minister, and also the Home Secretary, expressed surprise that so immediate a threat was not disclosed earlier. They were concerned lest Intelligence had failed in its duty; for the Government was now confronted with the information that the Germans had produced a thousand rockets (this was the number indicated by the Swedish and Polish evidence) which could be fired from a simply constructed platform at ranges of 150 miles.

The suggestion that our Intelligence had been weak was strongly resisted by A.D.I. (Science) who pointed out that the most significant advances in intelligence had only come through in the past week (he had in mind the fuller report on the Swedish rocket and the arrival of the Polish leader). Nor would he accept that adequate warning of attack had not been given; attacks had not yet begun, nor was there any evidence of the movement of supplies towards northern France that would herald them. The Prime Minister, however, made it clear that the scientific committee under Professor Ellis was to be kept fully informed of developments in the sphere of Intelligence.

## 40. The Two Approaches to the Problem.

During the next four weeks additional intelligence was received which, in conjunction with what was already known, made it possible to establish finally the chief characteristics of the rocket; and during that period close liaison was maintained between Professor Ellis's committee and Intelligence. The main contribution of the former was in confirming, by their special knowledge, the technical data that emerged from intelligence reports; but it is worthy of note that it was through the latter that the final and authoritative reconstruction was possible. This was no reflection on the competence of the scientists. It was the duty of Intelligence to discover precisely what the Germans were doing and that this was somewhat different from what British scientists might have done in the same direction is not surprising.

The difference between the two approaches – the scientific and the intelligence – is well illustrated by the varying estimates of the weight of the rocket. The most reliable agents' reports on this aspect during 1944 had never put the total weight at more than twelve tons, nor that of the warhead at more than two. There was, however, a serious objection on the grounds of simple common-sense to accepting weights of this order: i.e. they indicated a rocket too small to offer a sufficient return for the technical difficulties that were involved in designing and producing it. After all, it was abundantly clear by July 1944 that the Germans had invested much time, skill and materials in rocket development; yet, if the intelligence reports were to be believed, they had constructed something which delivered a weight of explosive little if any greater than that contained in the flying bomb, a much less elaborate weapon and one that was thought to be as accurate for all practical purposes as the rocket.

The scientists' estimates during 1943 and early 1944 of sixty-ton rockets can be explained by their ignorance of the technique on which Germans scientists and engineers were working. But even when, as was the case by the end of July 1944, there was good information of the principles of the construction of the rocket, the methods of launching and control, and the fuel that was used, their estimates were still larger than those of Intelligence; and indeed with reason, once granted that such estimates came within their province. Thus, against a tentative suggestion from Intelligence in the last week in July that the rocket might weigh no more than twenty tons, Professor Ellis maintained that this was less than the crucial size below which the rocket would not be worthwhile. Instead, he advanced want seemed to him to be the more reasonable estimate of 28-35 tons, including a warhead of five to seven tons.

In the light of the fuller report on the Swedish rocket, which became available shortly afterwards, he reduced the estimate somewhat and advanced on 2nd August a weight of no more than 24 tons with a warhead of at least four tons. A week later he reduced it still further in the light of the intelligence that was being received, and suggested that the rocket might have a range of 200 miles with a one-ton warhead and 140 miles with one of two tons. In short, he was forced by the intelligence evidence to accept a rocket which was 'unreasonable'.

**41. The Final Reconstruction of the Rocket.**
Nevertheless, it was a rocket with these approximate characteristics that the Germans had developed. The final links in the chain of intelligence were forged, as was typical, through the collation of several separate

pieces of evidence. The general confirmation of the agents' reports of a comparatively low total weight came from the discovery from Swedish and Polish evidence that the fuselage of the rocket was simply a hollow metal shell which left as much space as possible for fuel, radio apparatus and explosive. What was the weight of the fuel was the next problem to be solved. From the Peenemünde sources it had been learned that 4.3 tons of the main fuel was required for normal long-range shooting. The exact nature of the fuel was unspecified, but the most likely possibilities, after the hydrogen peroxide theory had been exploded, were thought to be liquid oxygen or alcohol. If it was the former then it could be calculated, the dimensions of the rocket being fairly exactly known from photographs and other evidence, that the total weight lay between 9 and 14 tons; if the latter, it might be as high as twenty tons. The examination of the Swedish rocket in July indicated the former, which fitted in with numerous agents' reports and information from prisoners. However, it was not until documents captured in Normandy were examined during the second week in August that liquid oxygen could be regarded as almost certainly the main fuel. It was only then that A.D.I. (Science) would advance what he considered a reliable estimate of weight: he did this on 10th August at a meeting of the 'Crossbow' Sub-Committee, giving the total weight of the rocket as approximately twelve tons and that of the warhead as one ton.

This was so much lower than any previous authoritative estimate that the Sub-Committee demurred at accepting it. Within the next fortnight, however, confirmation came from a British source, the Royal Aircraft Establishment at Farnborough. Here, since 31st July, work had been proceeding on the reconstruction of the rocket that had fallen in Sweden. On the basis of the fragments of this missile, and a few dimensions from the documents captured in Normandy, the occupation of the volume of the rocket was accounted for. This gave a total weight of 13½ tons, with a warhead of 1900-2000 lbs. What made this particularly important was that the Swedish rocket was known to be the result of series production; it was also fairly certain that it was rockets of this type that were to have been handled in the storage depots which had been captured in France. Moreover, there was no important evidence from intelligence sources pointing to a warhead heavier than that of the Swedish rocket. Air Intelligence thereupon committed itself to the view that the rocket with which the country was threatened was similar to that which had now been reconstructed. Certain modifications to the latter, giving it a warhead weighing up to three tons, were technically possible; but there was no indication that they had been made.

The position by 24th August was, therefore, that the characteristics of the only rocket that the Germans were likely to fire against the United Kingdom in the near future were known with sufficient accuracy for the threat to be regarded with a good measure of objectivity: it was at least quite clear that unless Intelligence had failed completely the rocket was not the intolerably devastating projectile that it had been made out to be when the threat was first apprehended.

## 42. Report by A.D.I. (Science) 27th August 1944.

The steps by which the problem had been solved, the state of our knowledge of the rocket, and an indication of when and on what scale attack might begin, were displayed in a lengthy report prepared by A.D.I. (Science) during the last week in August. This was the most detailed statement on the rocket and the organisation that lay behind it that was prepared before rocket attacks began. It was circulated on 27th August to every department and formation that had a direct interest in rocket attack; and although it was shortly withdrawn from circulation it thus ensured that every authority concerned knew what to expect. It is, therefore, a valuable document, particularly insofar as it is evidence of the extent to which Air Intelligence had succeeded in discovering what the Germans were planning.

The dimensions of the rocket were here given as 46 feet long and 5 feet 7 inches diameter. It structure was divided into four parts: the warhead, which it was reckoned, was normally 5 feet 7 inches long and weighed one ton; the apparatus compartment, which was 4 feet 7½ inches long and contained all the radio gear and gyrostabilisers; then came the two main fuel tanks in the middle part of the rocket, which was 20 feet 2 inches long; lastly, the tail containing the propulsion installation, the four fins of the rocket being attached to the tail. It was thought that the Germans would use their best explosive filling in the warhead, possibly trialen. With the normal warhead of one ton the range was reckoned to be 200-210 miles, which would be less if a heavier warhead was used.

The method of launching was known to need no elaborate firing point: simply a slab of concrete and a platform about six feet square into which fitted the bases of the four fins. But nothing definite was known about the trajectory of the rocket after firing. There were three possibilities, and the object of all of them was for the rocket to finish burning while travelling upwards at an angle of 45°, with as high a speed as possible, having already covered some useful distance towards the target. It was known that the rocket started vertically with low acceleration, and that its time of flight at a range of 200 miles was about six minutes.

The examination of the Swedish rocket had revealed a well-equipped radio compartment, which would certainly be used to help in tracking the rocket and probably also in controlling its flight. In addition, there was sufficient equipment in the form of gyroscopes, jet rudders and aerodynamic rudders, for rough aiming to be possible even if radio control was jammed. What accuracy the German control system allowed was not known. During 1943, several agents had given the intended accuracy as 1 kilometre at a range of 200; but the Polish evidence strongly indicated that control was one of the main practical difficulties. For example, on 22nd July, 1944, seven rockets were fired form Blizna, but by early evening only one had been found. It appeared, therefore, in the words of A.D.I. (Science), that 'the accuracy is not impressive'.

In sum, a good deal was known about the weapon itself. To that extent, Intelligence had given some fore-warning to the Civil Defence authorities. There was also something of value – if only negative value – to air operations in the knowledge that the rocket firing points were small and simply constructed; for this obviously meant that they would be hard to identify by photographic reconnaissance and even harder to destroy by bombing. In addition, what was known of the radio control of the rocket was useful in indicating in what ways radio counter-measures might be applied.

But the most effective counter-measures would be the destruction of experimental stations, factories engaged on rocket production, and the field organisation that was responsible for rocket operations. Here, the only detailed and reliable information related to Peenemünde and Blizna. Blizna was no longer a target by August 1944 as the Russian advance in Poland had forced its evacuation; nor was Peenemünde as profitably attacked as it had been in 1943 as the experimental work on the rocket was no longer so important. It was information on production and the supply and firing organisation that was most needed; and it was precisely here that least was known.

There were indications that production was at the rate of 500 a month and that about 2,000 had been built by the end of August 1944; but where production was going on was doubtful. That it was widely dispersed, with numerous factories sending components to a few main assembly plants, was fairly clear. The Rax works at Wiener Neustadt and the Maybach works at Friedrichshafen had been associated with assembly; but there were also reports of evacuation from both places to new factories. Half a dozen other factories had been mentioned by agents, including one at Klausthal, where the explosive may have been in production, a Siemens works at Arnstadt Thuringen making the radio control, a factory near Weimar and an underground factory in Central Germany.

In the field, two main types of rocket storage depot had been discovered in northern France during July, one above ground and one below. Judging from the single instance of the former – at Bois de Baugy, eight miles south-west of Bayeux – the Germans had relied on heavily wooded surroundings for concealment: the others, of which there were two examples known to us – at Hautmesnil, between Caen and Falaise, and La Meauffe, near St. Lô – took advantage of existing quarry workings; they were served by a main railway. The Hautmesnil depot was estimated to have a capacity of about one hundred rockets. Local underground shelters for storing up to ten rockets were also discovered in Normandy. All this proved very useful, but as far as the German field organisation was concerned, it simply indicated what had been planned for the area that had been liberated. Outside that area – i.e., by the fourth week in August, everything north of the Seine – there were no certainties, only suspicions. These concerned six underground depots near the lower Seine and twelve between Compiègne and St. Omer; some of the latter group were to be bombed in August and early September. Nothing was known of any storage and supply system the Germans had built, or were building, outside France.

As for the formations of the German Army that were responsible for rocket operations it was certain that these came under LXV Army Corps which had been formed specially to control the retaliation campaign. But the components of this Corps – the firing batteries, maintenance units and their equipment and location – were matters of conjecture based on very scanty information. Similarly, little was known of the number of sites that had been constructed or could be brought into operation. Such as there were would, of course, be within two hundred miles of London; but none had been identified north of the Seine up to the end of August.

In the absence of information of this kind it was only possible to advance opinions, rather than estimates of any precision, on the likely scale of attack that London might suffer in the near future. In any case, the enemy's effort would obviously depend on the date of attack. This, it was believed, had been repeatedly postponed: chiefly for technical and production reasons. But by August 1944 series production of rockets had been under way for some months. Moreover, production type rockets had been fired in Poland during the early summer and presumably could have been fired from France if the Germans had wished, or if they could have transported them there. That they had not done so was thought to be due to their desire to attack on an impressive scale. Not even the invasion of France had forced the German's hands, possibly because one V-weapon, the flying bomb, could be more easily brought into operation. With the breakout from Normandy, however, the Allied ground forces threatened the whole of the area north of the Seine in which rocket firing points had been constructed. Therefore, the report of A.D.I. (Science) concluded, "the Germans will launch the rocket against us as soon as they can amass sufficient effort; this may be soon, but the still existing technical defects, the relatively small warhead, the increasing difficulties of supply, and our threat to the operational area, all lead us to believe that the magnitude of the menace is small."

In respect of when and on what scale the Germans might launch rocket attacks the report was not the last word before attacks actually began. But it marks the end of a phase: that in which Intelligence had been seeking to identify the characteristics of the weapon with which the country was threatened. The search had been successful – so Intelligence officers believed. However, the planning of operational counter-measures and the execution of certain of them had gone on during the summer of 1944 concurrently with the Intelligence investigation.

### 43. Counter-Measures against Rocket Attack, June – August 1944.

These are best considered under three headings: Civil Defence, Radar and Radio, and Air Operations.

*a. Civil Defence.*

It will be recalled that from June to November 1943, Civil Defence preparations against rocket attack had been an important aspect of counter-measures. A warning system had been devised; reserves of Morrison shelters were concentrated near London and the Solent area; and plans covering evacuation of certain classes of the population from the threatened areas had been prepared. The plans were made on the understanding that London was to remain the seat of Government and that essential war production in the London area was to be maintained. But as the investigation into the rocket continued during the summer and autumn of 1943 without confirming any of the earlier alarming reports about the danger and imminence of rocket attack the War Cabinet decided in November that all plans for Civil Defence should simply be completed on paper. Then, with the emergence of the flying bomb as by far the more likely weapon for retaliation, all rocket plans were set aside early in 1944; and only when, at the meetings of the War Cabinet 'Crossbow' Sub-Committee on 18th July and 25th July, Air Intelligence reported that the rocket was in series production were Civil Defence arrangements again reviewed.

Mr. Morrison, as Home Secretary and Minister of Home Security, acted quickly. On 26th July he placed a memorandum before the War Cabinet in which he drew attention to the report that, "1,000 rockets with a range of possibly 200 miles were believed to be in an advanced state of preparation and that the warhead weighs probably 7 tons.[88] The latest theory is that no elaborate launching sites are necessary and it is therefore reasonable to assume that the enemy will mount an attack on a fairly considerable scale, as he did in the case of flying bombs, even though the frequency and density may be less." So far, the Civil Defence services were coping satisfactorily with flying bomb attacks; though repairs to houses were hardly keeping abreast of the task. On the basis of the original plans for dealing with rocket attack it was, however, quite clear that Civil Defence resources mobilised to their fullest extent would be exhausted after three or four days of attack at hourly intervals by rockets. Whether rocket attacks would be as frequent as this was uncertain; but on the basis of calculations made by the Research and Experiments Department of the Ministry of Home Security it appeared that if the 1,000 rockets that the Germans were believed to have manufactured were fired against London about 18,000 people would be killed, and at least as many, if not thrice as many, seriously injured. Material damage from a single rocket, assuming a 7-ton warhead, was expected to demolish or render uninhabitable all houses within a radius of 400 yards.

The implications were very serious. It seemed to the Home Secretary that the economy of London would be grievously strained if serious rocket attacks began, especially if flying bomb attacks continued. Hospital services might be swamped; the Civil Defence services would need considerable military assistance; a much bigger force than was already engaged on house repairs would be needed; and the police, railways and such emergency arrangements for accommodating and feeding evacuees as were in being might be overwhelmed by the exodus of people from the capital.

Nor were the effects likely to be confined to the civil population: they might well affect the conduct of Allied military operations. Here, the Home Secretary argued thus: "As the areas of sheer devastation grow under continued bombardment, I fear that the public will become angry, though whether the anger will be directed solely against the enemy may be doubted. We have boasted rightly of our air superiority and military strength. We shall be expected to use our resources to eliminate attacks on the Metropolis by the new weapons as we have virtually eliminated raids by ordinary aircraft. It will be difficult to give convincing reasons why this cannot be done. In my view, the rocket attack must from now onwards be regarded as a major effort by the Germans to avoid sheer defeat. It must be met by us by a corresponding effort both in active attack and passive defence, and not regarded as fatalistically inevitable or even as a by-product of enemy activity to be dealt with by the resources of the Fighting Forces which are not otherwise required to prosecute the war."

Clearly, the Home Secretary was not disposed to minimise the gravity of the threat. Offensive counter-measures he did not attempt to deal with, but as for defensive preparations he concluded his paper by asking the War Cabinet to give a decision on the vital question of evacuation, the policy for which would largely dictate what was done in other spheres of civil defence. He himself, also Mr. Willink, the Minister of Health, felt that plans should be made to deal with an exodus considerably greater than that of the half million people for whom plans had been prepared in the summer and autumn of 1943; in which case some public announcement about the rocket would be desirable as a stimulant to voluntary evacuation before attacks actually began.

The Home Secretary's memorandum was considered by the War Cabinet on 27th July.[89] Its recommendations were accepted, it being agreed that, "plans should be made to meet the contingency of rocket attacks on the scale which now seemed possible; and certain action should be taken at once". Immediate action covered such matters as the evacuation of priority classes from London; shifting production, especially vital war production, from London to factories outside; evacuation of patients from London hospitals; and moving 10,000 Government employees from their present shelterless accommodation to safer premises either in London or elsewhere. The question of advising newspaper editors in confidence of what might happen was considered; as was the advisability of extending double summer time beyond the agreed date of 13th August. Mr. Churchill also did something to prepare the public in a speech in the House of Commons on 2nd August.[90]

Other action that was contemplated covered the evacuation of up to two million people from the London area and the control of a large-scale exodus on foot; the reinforcement of the force already engaged in repairs; the co-ordination of civilian evacuation with the shifting of production; the evacuation of non-essential Government staffs and the allocation of the best protected accommodation to the staffs who would have to remain in London. A ministerial committee – the Rocket Consequences Committee – consisting of the Home Secretary, and the Ministers of Labour, Production, Health and War Transport, was set up to co-ordinate all departmental action; while a committee of permanent officials was established to work out problems of staff accommodation.

Throughout the whole of August, the work of planning and preparation went ahead vigorously. The position at the end of the month was as follows.

The areas earmarked for evacuation had been extended to include 27 boroughs and urban districts around the Metropolitan area, and facilities for evacuation had been made available to all mothers with children of school age or under, as well as to the usual priority classes. Organised and private evacuation had continued, and on 31st August it was estimated that nearly 1½ million people had left London: most of them doubtless because of flying bomb attacks. A "Voucher Scheme" designed to regulate the flow of refugees through the London stations was prepared; while to handle those who would move out of London by road in the event of heavy attack temporary accommodation had been prepared in Rest and Reception Centres within forty miles of the centre of London for a maximum of 700,000 people. It was a measure of the Government's appreciation of the problem that the possibility of providing accommodation for an even larger number of refugees was being examined.

Within the general plan of civilian evacuation, and co-ordinated with it, were other schemes for the evacuation of industrial workers and Government staffs and their dependants. The principles underlying industrial dispersal were that only unique, or nearly unique production should be interfered with, or production of special importance for current operations or production largely concentrated in the London area. All moves were to be of personnel rather than plant, with the workers going to reception factories in safe areas.

The plans for Government departments visualised the evacuation of about 85,000 of the 130,000 employed at headquarters in London. 13,000 were to stay in London in well protected accommodation; the rest were to be dismissed or "stood off". It was intended to carry out this very difficult transfer gradually.

Also, by the end of August, good progress had been made in evacuating patients from London hospitals and thus leaving large numbers of beds vacant for receiving rocket casualties. 15,734 patients and staff had been evacuated and 28,249 beds in London hospitals were ready for casualties. A further 8,179 beds could have been made available at a few hours notice by discharging patients to their homes.

Other features of the preparations that were being made were as follows. For repair work to houses and essential services, demolition and clearance work, a force of up to 120,000 men could be brought into action: double summer time had been extended to 17th September: a scheme had been prepared for clamping down on all sources of information for at least 48 hours after the first rocket attack.

In short, a good deal of time and energy had been expended on preparations of one sort or another. How far these would have helped London to withstand attack on the scale for which they were designed it is, of course, impossible to say. For during the second half of August two new factories emerged which altered the whole situation. The first was the success of the Intelligence investigation into the rocket, which pointed to a much less destructive weapon than had been appreciated in July. The second was the advance of the Allied armies in France, which increasingly threatened to drive the Germans from those areas of northern France from which it was presumed that rocket attacks would be launched.

As soon as Air Intelligence committed itself to a reliably low estimate of the weight of the rocket Mr. Morrison asked the Chiefs of Staff what effect this might have on the possible scale of attack, taking into account also, so far as possible, the effect of the advance in France. He himself felt that some of the preparations which the Rocket Consequences Committee had sanctioned were scarcely justified in view of the latest intelligence. In response to this request an appreciation was obtained on 28th August from Mr. Sandys who advanced as a basis for planning the possibility of up to sixty rockets falling daily on London during the first month of bombardment, reinforced by about twenty flying bombs.[91] The reaction of the Civil Defence authorities was to amend their plans on the principle that the more drastic measures that had been envisaged should be discontinued or remain plans on paper.

Then, as the first few days of September saw the situation further improve – the cessation of flying bomb attacks being only one of many good features – Mr. Morrison on 7th September recommended to the War Cabinet that such evacuation schemes as were actually being carried out should be stopped and all preparations suspended, except where, as in the case of the dispersal of some of the London production, it would be more trouble to reverse what was being done than to complete it. The War Cabinet agreed. Thus, the period of preparation in the sphere of Civil Defence ended on a note of optimism that was in sharp contrast to the sober urgency with which the Rocket Consequences Committee had begun its work in late July.

*b. Radar and Radio.*

Amongst the first counter-measures against the rocket that were contemplated was the use of radar. Five stations between the Isle of Wight and the North Foreland – Ventnor, Poling, Pevensey, Rye and Swingate – were specially fitted with Cathode Ray Direction Finding and photographic equipment to observe the flight of rockets; and a continuous watch had been maintained at them until March 1944. The watch was renewed on 13th June, immediately after the first flying bomb attack.

Their equipment was the best that was readily available at the time but it only permitted observation up to a height of about 50,000 feet. During the early months of 1944 equipment was therefore prepared for covering altitudes between 50,000 and 100,000 feet. Two stations utilising it were established at Martin's Mill, near Dover, and Snap Hill, near Pevensey, by the third week in August. By the same date, five more stations – at Ramsgate and Dymchurch on the south coast, and Bromley, Bawdsey and High Street on the east – had been equipped to the standard of the original stations. In addition, eleven army radar sets – G.L. Mark II – were modified for the same purpose and deployed at intervals between Pevensey and Harwich. Special aerials, giving cover up to 400,000 feet, were also under construction at this time; four stations were to be fitted but were not expected to be ready for operations before October.

It was intended to use radar for two purposes: early warning and firing point location. As to the first, under the best conditions, i.e. if the attack was from northern France, if there was no jamming by the enemy and no interference through the presence of aircraft in the area under observation, a warning of about 3½ minutes was expected from the Cathode Ray Direction Finding stations, one of 4 minutes from the stations at Martin's Mill and Snap Hill, and one of 1½ minutes from the G.L. sets. But as to the second – firing point location – not much was expected from the equipment that was available: location with a mean radial error of two miles was the very best that was anticipated. From the middle of June units of the 11th Survey Regiment, Royal Artillery, were deployed near London and in the Margate – Hastings area to help in this work with their flash-spotting and sound-ranging equipment.

To make the best use of such warning as radar might give, the necessary telecommunications were installed to give direct speech between the radar stations and the Filter Room of No. 11 Group. From there, the warning system for the general public was to be put into effect.

It was appreciated that such a system, if effective, would be of some help to the defence of the country. Accurate firing point location would also be useful in that it would be a first step towards the identification of the sites from which rockets were being launched and hence to their attack. However, it was so far doubtful, in July and August, that much would be accomplished in either sphere that much of the attention of the scientists, technicians and officers concerned was directed towards another aspect of radio science which, if its application proved practicable, would notably hamper the enemy. This was to jam the radio control of the rocket. Radio counter-measures of this sort were the responsibility of the Director General of Signals at the Air Ministry who worked in co-operation with Sir Robert Watson-Watt's Interdepartmental Radiolocation Committee.

An essential preliminary step before any jamming measures could be carried out was to discover what signals were being transmitted by the Germans, and for what purpose, when rockets were being fired. As early as May 1944 a listening station had been set up to identify any signals that could be associated with the firing of rockets from Peenemünde. No information had been obtained from it up to the beginning of July, by which time an extensive programme of investigations, to be carried out chiefly from the United Kingdom, had been instituted.

This entailed listening to and jamming enemy signals from ground stations, mostly in the United Kingdom, and from Allied aircraft. Listening from the air was naturally directed to the Blizna and Peenemünde districts. Suitable aircraft – Lightnings (P.38s) – for covering Blizna were provided by the U.S.A.A.F. during July but owing to the Russian advance in Poland they were never used. During August, the Baltic area was visited by Halifaxes of No. 192 Squadron, R.A.F. Their operations were arranged to coincide with periods when Air Intelligence believed that rocket firing would be taking place at Peenemünde. However, no signals were intercepted.

During these same two months ground stations were also listening for enemy signals. Four stations of the R.A.F. "Y" Interception Service were engaged on this work in the United Kingdom. Negotiations for the establishing of a listening station in southern Sweden were begun in late July, but nothing was settled before rocket attacks began. Nor was anything useful learned from the British stations. At one time it was thought that significant signals had been received, but on analysis they turned out to have no connection with rocket firing.

Neither ground not air listening, therefore, had contributed to our knowledge by the end of August; and jamming measures were thereby made more difficult. It had been appreciated, however, at the beginning of the investigation into jamming, that high-powered transmitters would be necessary if interference was to be effective. Accordingly, action was taken in July to provide twenty 50-kilowatt transmitters. Two were already available; others could be obtained by modifying equipment in the hands of the B.B.C.; three more were ordered from the United States; the rest were to be manufactured in the United Kingdom. Eight such transmitters were in position by the end of August: a battery of six at Crowborough and two more at Brighton. A large number of smaller transmitters were also ready for operation; but they were regarded as stop-gaps until the more powerful equipments were in service. All radio counter-measures were controlled by No. 80 (Signals) Wing of the Royal Air Force from a special control room which was established first at Beachy Head and later at Canterbury.

Airborne jamming had the advantage over jamming from ground stations that less power was required. On the other hand, the difficulties of installation, maintenance and operation of the equipment required was greater. But the chances of jamming effectively from ground stations were reckoned so small that great emphasis was placed upon fitting aircraft for this work, especially when the examination of the Swedish rocket indicated that jamming from the ground would be even more difficult than we had thought. By the middle of August, the action that was being taken was to prepare four squadrons of heavy bombers which would powerfully reinforce the one R.A.F. squadron – No. 192 – that was available for such work. A small number of aircraft had been fitted with transmitters by the end of the month.

Thus, a good deal of preparatory work had been carried out by the end of August for combating the anticipated attack by means of radio science. But the location of much of the ground equipment had been dictated by the expectation of attack from northern France. The swift advances in that area during the last days of August and early September accordingly rendered abortive some of the dispositions that had been made. However, no immediate and startling results had been expected from the equipment that was available. This was true for all the tasks of which radar and radio were theoretically capable: it was particularly true of the location of rocket firing points and of interference with the radio control of the rocket.

It could not be said, therefore – and was not – that all was satisfactory in this sector of the defences. But with the increasing likelihood that the Germans would be unable to fire any rockets before the whole of northern France was occupied it was possible to hope that the worst dangers had been avoided and extensive radio counter-measures would not be required.

*c. Operational Counter-Measures.*
The preparations in Civil Defence and radio warfare during July and August had their parallel in the sphere of operations. These were of two sorts: plans for operations which would only be undertaken when attacks began, and actual operations against German targets that were known or suspected to be connected with preparations for rocket attack. In each case the emphasis was almost wholly on what could be done by bombing; the sole exception was the arrangements that were made for giving warning of rocket attack to the general public. The reason is obvious enough: the rocket was not a weapon that could be repelled by fire power from aircraft once it had been launched. In other words, there was some chance of destroying the wasp's nest; there was none of swatting the wasps.

Public Warning System.

A scheme for giving warnings to the public had been one of the earliest counter-measures that had been pursued, and a system had been devised by the autumn of 1943. The problem was basically a radar problem; for only radar could hope to detect a rocket sufficiently early in its time of flight of five to six minutes for a warning of sufficient length to be useful to be sounded. The need for speed also demanded that the number of channels through which radar information passed before reaching the public in the shape of an audible warning should be as few as possible. For the same reason, the warning itself had to be such that it could be operated centrally for the whole of a threatened area; it had also to be sharper and more arresting than the siren to galvanise people into taking what shelter they could in the short time before the rocket arrived. The system that was established, therefore, was as follows.

The specially equipped radar stations that, from 13th June, were keeping a watch for rocket firings were allotted landlines for their exclusive use that linked them to the Filter Room of No. 11 Group.

To the same room 140 maroon-firing equipments in the London area and 21 in the Portsmouth/Southampton area were directly linked and could be fired by operating a single switch in the Filter Room. The procedure that was laid down was that on receipt of warning by code-word "Big Ben" from the radar stations the Controller on duty in the Filter Room operated the switch and fired the maroons. Both areas would be put under warning, it being impossible for the radar stations to distinguish which was being attacked. If the system worked as it was intended to work a warning of at least 1½ minutes and at most 3½ minutes would have been given to the public.

However, although the system could have been put into operation at any time during July and August 1944 the preliminary announcement which was necessary if the public were to know what to do was never made. There were a number of good reasons. In the first place, at best the warning was only short, and there was some doubt whether it would be worthwhile except if attacks were heavy. Then, the system itself could not be regarded as perfect: it depended entirely on the extent to which the radar stations detected rockets shortly after they had been fired, and what their proportionate success might be was doubtful. If only there had been fair certainty of the scale of attack, or even whether attacks would be launched at all, these limitations might have been accepted. But in the circumstances, nothing was done to warn the public and no decision was taken as to when the warning system might be brought into effect. It was, however, decided on 5th September, by which time northern France was largely cleared, that no warning need be given in the Portsmouth/Southampton area until there was evidence that the enemy intended to attack it.

*d. Offensive Action and Plans.*
Up to the middle of July the bombing of targets connected with rocket attack was confined to four of the large sites – those at Mimoyecques, Watten, Siracourt and Wizernes[92] – which were amongst the first targets associated with V-weapon attack in general to be bombed after the first flying bombs had landed in the United Kingdom. Such success attended the bombing that on 10th July the sites were suspended from further attacks except for certain special projects which did not in fact add to the damage.[93] Then, after an interval of nearly six weeks, photographic reconnaissance revealed that construction was still going on at Watten and Mimoyecques; and a further heavy attack on each, on 25th and 27th August respectively, was carried out by Bomber Command. The results appeared inconclusive at the time; but it was to be found when the sites were later examined that bombing over the whole period had very seriously retarded the progress of construction. Altogether, 7,469 tons of bombs were dropped on the large sites between the middle of June and their capture by Allied ground forces.

But it was only with the important advances in intelligence from early July onwards that other types of target were attacked. At that time, hydrogen peroxide was thought to be one of the main constituents of the fuel of the rocket as well as necessary for the launching of flying bombs; and attacks on the hydrogen peroxide plants at

Höllriegelskreuth and Ober Raderach were carried out with this in mind. The three attacks on Peenemünde in July and August were also directed against the hydrogen peroxide plant there as well as the experimental station. The attack of the other main experimental station at Blizna would have been a very difficult operation and was hardly considered as the Russians during July advanced steadily closer to the place. Instead, arrangements were made to send a mission to inspect it as soon as it was in Russian hands.[94]

Altogether, with one further exception, bombing operations during July and August were concentrated against targets within the areas, or near to them, from which it was expected that rocket attacks would be launched. The exception was an attack against a factory adjacent to the notorious Buchenwald concentration camp near Weimar. There was good evidence that the factory was making rockets, flying bombs and radio components; and it was attacked on 24th August by 121 Fortresses of the 8th Air Force who dropped 266 tons of bombs. Interpretation of photographs taken after the attack showed that a great part of both the armaments and the radio sections had been destroyed; the concentration camp had escaped lightly (as, of course, was intended); but great damage was done to the S.S. camp and offices. Some damage had also been done in the underground storage area; but it was impossible to assess its effect.

As for targets in France and Belgium, the most remunerative appeared to be liquid oxygen plants and the forward storage depots between Rouen and St. Omer. A study of the former had been begun at the end of July when evidence was accumulating that the main fuel of the rocket was liquid oxygen rather than hydrogen peroxide. Attention was concentrated on possible sources of supply in France and Belgium rather than in Germany. There were two reasons: first, it was felt that the Germans would be more likely to make use of plants near the areas from which rockets would be fired in order to avoid relying on the overstrained supply routes between Germany and western Europe: second, it was impracticable to attack the large number of small plants that were in Germany itself.

But it was not until the last week in August, when there was reason to fear that the Germans would mount the best attack they could before the Pas de Calais was lost to them, that attacks were carried out. In these circumstances, 'short term' targets in the rocket firing areas were preferable to industrial targets in Germany. On 25th August, 430 tons of bombs were dropped on five liquid oxygen plants in France and Belgium by the 8th Air Force. On 31st August and 1st September no less than 2897 tons were dropped by Bomber Command on nine of the forward storage depots. In addition, there were light attacks on 'Benito' W/T stations at Boulogne and Cassel. The railway interdiction that was being imposed at this time for the battle on land was also affecting the lines of supply that the Germans would use to bring up rockets to northern France.

Otherwise, the main interest of the period lies in the planning of counter-measures that would be applied when rocket attacks were about to begin or had actually begun. The preparation of a plan was started by the Joint Crossbow Target Priorities Committee early in August, and was completed by 20th August. The aim of the plan was to reduce the scale of rocket attack in the shortest possible time.

The launching sites themselves were reckoned unprofitable targets; but the plan gave priority to armed reconnaissances in the area of the launching sites and near the rocket storage depots so that any fleeting chance might be taken of attacking any installations, vehicles or troops concerned with the transport, servicing firing and control of the rocket.

Next, sustained attacks against nine forward storage depots and three rearward storage depots in the Rouen – Compiègne region were recommended, and also against a total of eighteen liquid oxygen plants in France and Belgium. Seven of the latter were selected as primary targets.

The attack of the transport communications which the Germans would probably use for rockets was next in importance. Transport by rail was to be interfered with by attacks against what was known as "The Third Ring of Rail Bridges". This consisted of thirty bridges on or near the frontiers of Belgium, France and Germany; roughly, they lay along the line Antwerp – Liège – Namur – Verdun – Conflans – Besançon. If these were cut, all railway traffic from Germany westward would be practically immobilised. The more northerly sections of it were brought under attack during the last week in August as part of the air support of the battle on land.

Interference with road and water transport was also advocated. M.T. vehicles, particularly those carrying fuel, were to be attacked. Twelve lock gates were selected which, if destroyed, would stop water traffic into the launching and forward storage areas.

Fifteen production centres in Germany were also selected; though they were only to be attacked if forces were available after the other and more important counter-measures had been catered for.

Such, in outline, was the bombing plan that was recommended. The armed reconnaissance of the rocket firing points that was so pronounced a feature of it depended on the speed with which sorties could be organised; for it was appreciated that unless vehicles and attendant personnel were sighted whilst they were grouped round the firing points it would only be rarely that targets of this sort would be presented to our pilots. The bombing plan, therefore, was co-ordinated with extensive arrangements made in July and August for giving immediate warning of the areas from which attacks were being made. The arrangements were as follows.

All radar warnings that were passed to the No. 11 Group Filter Room were to be transmitted immediately to the headquarters[95] of all the authorities that were concerned in rocket counter-measures. Action would be taken immediately to despatch jamming aircraft of No. 100 Group, if aircraft were not already patrolling; No. 106 Group would despatch photographic reconnaissance aircraft to the firing areas; A.E.A.F. Headquarters was responsible for organising armed reconnaissance. The Air Commander-in-Chief of A.E.A.F. was responsible for co-ordinating all counter-measures.

The position of the firing points that were in use was expected to follow the first warning at an interval of either 30 minutes or 90 minutes, depending on whether the photographing of the cathode ray tubes at the radar stations was necessary. The positions were to be calculated by a Scientific Officer at the No. 11 Group Filter Room and thence passed to the same series of headquarters as the initial warning. In the light of this new data further reconnaissance would be carried out. It was also intended that the firing point positions would be passed through Air Ministry to the Air Warfare Analysis Section where the "Oboe" and "G.H." co-ordinates necessary for blind bombing attacks would be calculated. This presumed a degree of accuracy in the detection of firing points which was not in fact obtained.

The first of a series of trials to test these arrangements was held on 21st August. It proved satisfactory; though inevitably the initial radar data on which the effectiveness of the system would depend in practice, was synthetic.

### 44. Events Immediately Prior to the First Rocket Attack.

Thus, up to the end of August extensive preparations were under way in each of the main fields in which counter-measures to the rocket might be applied. During the second half of August there had been no slackening, although the speed of the Allied advance steadily increased and threatened the areas from which rocket attacks were expected. Indeed, precisely because the developments in the land battle might force the Germans to attack, more active counter-measures were taken during the last week in August: Bomber Command carried out heavy attacks against the forward storage depots on northern France and

"Benito" stations and liquid oxygen plants were attacked. Also, from 30th August, fighters of A.D.G.B. and 2nd Tactical Air Force carried out sweeps over southern Belgium and the Pas de Calais to detect any signs of imminent attack and to attack suspicious vehicles and installations. The crucial period, it was felt, would be the first fortnight in September.[96]

But as the first three days of September saw no check to the Allied advance in northern France or much likelihood of one for some time to come the future came to be regarded far more optimistically. The change was registered in a number of ways. On 1st September the Rocket Consequences Committee called a halt in the bigger Civil Defence preparations. On 4th September the reconnaissances that A.D.G.B. had been carrying out were discontinued, and the Chief of the Air Staff recommended the cessation of the bombing of the German rocket organisation.

On the following day the future policy for 'Crossbow' counter-measures was outlined in a memorandum by the Vice Chiefs of Staff which was agreed to by the Chiefs of Staff Committee. As a result, all bombing attacks against 'Crossbow' targets were discontinued, except for attacks, as part of the general offensive against the German Air Force, against airfields from which aircraft launching flying bombs were known, or suspected, to be operating. No drastic changes in defensive organisation were contemplated since there was a possibility of a few more flying bombs being launched from the Pas de Calais before it was completely overrun; but a review of the defences was to be undertaken to arrange for their reduction and re-disposition. Radio counter-measures were not to be closed down immediately, not because they might be useful for the defence of the United Kingdom but because, as the Vice Chiefs of Staff put it, "there is rather a remote possibility of attacks against targets on the continent". Experimental work in this sphere was therefore to continue. Experimental work was also to be the gauge by which continued production of special equipment required for defence against 'Crossbow' was to be measured. If not important for this purpose production was to be closed down.

Now, so rapid was the Allied advance, and so few the signs of effective German resistance, that the shelving of preparations against rocket attack is easily understandable. Nevertheless, we are entitled to say it was premature, even granted that future operations such as the capture of the Rhine crossings at Arnhem, which had been decided upon by 6th September, were successful: it appears as if the first opportunity was taken for discounting a threat which had always been an irritating diversion from the last great offensive.

For it was known that the range of the rocket was 200-230 miles, which left within range of the centre of London the whole of Holland west of a line from Amsterdam due south to the Belgian frontier. This area, and part of Belgium also within 230 miles of London, was not in Allied hands on 6th September. Thus, the view, which seems to have been held by the Air Staff, that the rocket had ceased to be a threat, was not entirely acceptable; and in fact, it was not accepted by the Intelligence Staff at A.D.G.B. Headquarters without a reservation. On 6th September they drew attention to the fact that the range of the missile was known to be such that, so long as the Germans held western Holland, attacks on London were possible. On that date the area still in German hands from which rockets could reach the capital included the whole of Holland west of a line from Amsterdam to the Belgian frontier, as well as a part of Belgium. The success of the Arnhem operation would see the occupation of that area; but in the meantime, its use for the launching of a rocket attack was at least theoretically possible.

As for how likely the Germans were to use the area for this purpose, on 4th September the Chief of the Air Staff said, "they would have to make certain preparations of which we have no evidence and which in present circumstances are extremely unlikely." This is a surprising statement for two reasons: first, it was well known that rocket firing points and storage depots could only be detected with great difficulty – such evidence of preparations for firing as had been discovered in northern France amounted to little more than half a dozen concrete slabs and two or three storage depots of which there was little or no information until they were actually occupied; second, Holland had not been covered for signs of German preparations to anything like the same extent as northern France.[97] In short, the argument from silence was a dangerous one; and events were soon to prove it so.

## 45. Reactions to the First Rockets.

It was, therefore, without any prior warning from Air Intelligence, such as had preceded the flying bomb offensive, that the first rockets fell in the London area. The first fell at Chiswick at 1840 hours on 8th September, the second sixteen seconds later at Parnwood Wood, Epping.[98] Three people were killed and twenty injured, ten seriously, at Chiswick, but there were no casualties at Epping. From examination of the damage and fragments at Chiswick it appeared that the rocket used was essentially the same type as the Swedish rocket; such differences as there were, were thought to be due to the modifications necessary before a prototype could be produced in large numbers. The warhead was much the same as Air Intelligence had forecast, i.e. a total weight of just under 2,000 lbs. of which 1600 lbs. was high explosive. The radar stations, although on watch, failed to give warning of the two rockets; but later examination of the photographic records of the C.H. station at Bawdsey showed that plots had been obtained of one of them. Sound ranging equipment in Kent gave good information of the Chiswick rocket, poorer information of the other. From both sets of data, it was thought that one launching had been from the Rotterdam area, and the other from somewhat further north.

On the morning of 9th September, the Chiefs of Staff considered what counter-measures should be adopted. It is clear from the minutes of the meeting, though these only sketch the discussion, that they were not disposed to adopt any elaborate counter-measures while the situation on land was so promising. Moreover, only two rockets, little more destructive than flying bombs, had fallen in the country, and a strong counter attack was not yet called for. They advised the War Cabinet not to make any public announcement for the time being (none had been made by the Germans) and not to apply the drastic censorship measures which the original plan for security in the event of attack had envisaged. It followed that the public warning system would not be put into operation: in any case, the radar stations specially equipped for observing rockets had been selected with attack from northern France in mind and were unsatisfactory for giving warning of rockets fired from Holland. Mr. Sandys, who was present at the meeting, suggested that mobile radar or sound ranging equipment should be sent immediately to Belgium to give better information of further firings than could be obtained from England. It was typical of the tenour of the meeting that Lieutenant General Nye, the V.C.I.G.S., thought that by the time such equipment had been transported across the Channel and up the lines of communication to Belgium the firing area would have been neutralised by the ground forces. However, the Chiefs of Staff invited the Air Ministry to convene a meeting of the departments concerned to suggest measures for locating the firing points and providing an early warning system.

### 46. First Counter-Measures.
No recommendations for counter-measures by air forces were made by the Chiefs of Staff. Operations had begun, however, soon after the first rockets had fallen. On the night of the 8th intruder aircraft, and on the following morning, day fighter squadrons of A.D.G.B. were despatched on reconnaissance over south-west Holland, the beginning of an activity that was to continue until the last rocket had been fired against the United Kingdom; P.R.U. aircraft began daily photographic

reconnaissances over the suspected firing area; and aircraft of No. 100 Group, R.A.F., were sent up to listen for and jam any radio signals which might have some connection with rocket firings. The listening and jamming stations of the radio counter-measures organisation that had been established in the United Kingdom carried out similar duties. On the Continent, the Dutch resistance movement, through the Special Operations Executive, was briefed to provide intelligence of the location of firing points and the transport of rockets and fuel. As early as 11th September a report was received in London which gave the location of three launching sites in the Wassenaar district north-east of The Hague.

After the rockets which had fallen on the evening of the 8th, the next were reported from Frambridge, seven miles north of Southend, at 2130 hours on the 10th, from Lullingstone, near Dartford, at 0907 hours on the 11th, and from Magdalen Laver, six miles north-east of Epping, at 0930 hours, also on the 11th. Only one person was injured in the three incidents, in two of which the rocket was reported to have exploded in mid-air. Between the 11th and midnight on the 16th, a further fifteen rockets fell on land and three were reported to have fallen in the sea off the Essex coast. All told, therefore, twenty rockets fell in the United Kingdom between the 8th, when the attack began, and the 16th. Only ten of them fell within the London Civil Defence region.

During these nine days the foundations of a policy of counter-measures were laid. General responsibility for it lay, as for the flying bomb, with the Deputy Chief of the Air Staff: the Air Staff Directorate which was the channel between him and the operational formations concerned was the Directorate of Operations (Air Defence).[99] Air C.-in-C., A.E.A.F., was ultimately responsible for the control of offensive air operations against the rocket organisation; but the rapid advance on the Continent, with its consequent strain on airfields and communications, and the continued importance of the land battle during September, meant that the active participation of the Tactical Air Forces was necessarily limited. It was, therefore, upon home-based air forces that the bulk of the effort against rockets fell. Air Marshal Hill at A.D.G.B. was responsible for directing and co-ordinating their activities; and as in the case of the flying bomb, it was the squadrons directly under his command that were the most active of the Allied air forces.

## 47. Counter-Measures Prior to Arnhem.

What was done and planned during these early days of the attack represents a policy of counter-measures not so elaborate as that which had been planned during August, when a heavy scale of attack from a more destructive weapon than actually arrived on 8th September was feared. The decision that had been taken towards the end of the flying bomb attack from the sites in northern France to stop the bombing of 'Crossbow' production targets by heavy bombers was not rescinded, and altogether, heavy bombers had little place in the counter-measures that were applied at this time. The arrangements for the control of operations gave Air Marshal Hill the right to approach Bomber Command direct if he wanted a target attacked that was unsuitable for his own forces; but there was nothing mandatory about such requests. One attack was made by Bomber Command on 14th September against a suspected rocket storage point near The Hague. Thirty-seven aircraft dropped 190 tons of bombs in an accurate and concentrated attack; how far, if at all, it affected the rocket organisation could not be ascertained.

Otherwise, armed offensive action from the air was confined to patrols by day and night by A.D.G.B. aircraft over and near the launching area, which by the 10th was known to be the stretch of wooded country between The Hague and Leiden. Between the 8th and 16th nearly nine hundred sorties were flown by A.D.G.B. A variety of targets – road, rail and water transport, suspected storage and launching points – was attacked by cannon and rocket fire.

Liquid oxygen plants, as providing the main fuel of the rocket, were also considered as targets; but there was so little evidence on which of the many plants in north-west Europe were connected with the rocket organisation that a systematic offensive against them was held to be unwarranted so long as the scale of rocket attack remained small. Intelligence reports during September had specified three small plants near Schiedam as producing liquid oxygen for rockets. Their bombing, however, raised a question which was to limit offensive action for the duration of the attack, namely, the safety of the Dutch people. The three plants were small and were in built-up areas and could not be attacked without inflicting casualties on civilians. Bombing was, therefore, ruled out. In its place, the Special Operations Executive was asked to arrange for their sabotage.

Defensive counter-measures in the air had been confined, up to the middle of September, to a 4-hour patrol every 12 hours by a Fortress of No. 100 Group from which all suspicious radio signals had been jammed. A continuous patrol for this task was organised during the third week in September, subject to the overriding claims of Bomber Command for the support of these aircraft and their specially trained crews on bombing operations. In addition, Halifaxes of No. 100 Group maintained a listening watch over the North Sea; but nothing significant was heard. From this, and from evidence from fragments of rockets examined in the United Kingdom, it was beginning to appear that radio control was not essential.

Where most progress was made was in the provision of equipment both in England and on the Continent for providing early warning of attack and for locating firing points. Certain measures had been put into operation by the middle of September; others were in process of being carried out.

In England, three radar stations had been added to those covering Holland, making six between Dover and Lowestoft. One of them, Bawdsey, had been converted to a higher power, and two others were about to be converted. A number of Army G.L. Mk. II sets were also deployed in this area. No. 11 Survey Regiment, R.A.F., continued to employ its sound ranging and flash spotting equipment in Kent, and brought a small number of balloons into use to assist its observations. Thirty-nine low power and four high power ground transmitters for jamming were also in action by the middle of September. They were controlled from the control centre set up under No. 80 (Signals) Wing, R.A.F., at Eastbourne, which also controlled listening stations at Coulsden and at Capel, near Tonbridge.

This considerable organisation had little to show for its activities. The radar stations and the survey unit had provided useful data for the location of firing points; but as these were thought to be changed frequently, the information was little use for briefing purposes. Nor was the existing organisation reliable as a means of providing early warning of attack: in only six out of the first twenty incidents could a warning have been given to the public. As for the listening and jamming stations, they, like the aircraft engaged on radio counter-measures, had obtained only negative information.

The fact was that the original programme of radar and radio counter-measures had been based on the assumption that rocket attacks would be launched from northern France; whereas attacks from Holland required both the radar stations that had been specially equipped for observing rockets and the survey unit to operate beyond the range at which reliable and efficient working would have been possible. The performance of radar in the United Kingdom was eventually improved; but what the situation demanded in September 1944 was that an organisation similar to what had been prepared in England should be set up on the Continent as close as possible to the area which the Germans were using.

Something was being done in this direction before the attack on Arnhem had been launched, even though success there might mean the

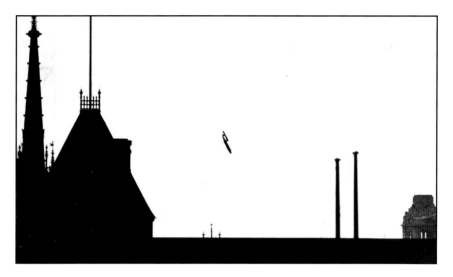

Above: A V1 flying bomb diving on to the streets of London, 28 June 1944. The buildings in the foreground are the Royal Courts of Justice on the north side of the Strand, though the missile truck the Peabody Buildings in Wild Street. (Historic Military Press)

Below: The ruins of the Guards' Chapel at Wellington Barracks in London. The chapel was destroyed on Sunday, 18 June 1944, when a direct hit by a V1 caused the roof to collapse onto the congregation. A total of 121 people were killed and 141 injured (military and civilians) in what was the worst V1 incident of the war. (Historic Military Press)

Above: Another one that got through – a V1 flying bomb in the last few seconds of its flight before it fell on to the streets and buildings of London somewhere in the vicinity of Piccadilly Station. (Historic Military Press)

Below: The aftermath of a V1 flying bomb incident in the Aldwych on 30 June 1944. The V1 is reported to have cut out over Waterloo Station and then went into a steep dive. It exploded at 14.07 hours in the street just outside the Air Ministry at Ad Astral House. Forty-six people were killed and at least 200 others suffered serious injuries. Many of these were inflicted by flying glass fragments from hundreds of shattered windows. (Historic Military Press)

Above: The V1 flying bomb that caused the damage seen here exploded in York Road near Waterloo Station at 09.36 hours on 23 June 1944. According to one account, it 'destroyed general railway offices, 2 air shafts [and] an 8-car train; 100 feet of track were damaged and 5 streets suffered severe blast damage across 400 yards square'. (Historic Military Press)

Below: The aftermath of the explosion of a V1 flying bomb in Medlar Street, Camberwell, at 03.21 hours on 17 June 1944. The blast caused severe damage to Nos. 1-21 Medlar Street, and the railway bridge was badly damaged and collapsed, wrecking a section of a laden goods train. (Historic Military Press)

Above: A Handley Page Halifax pictured over the V1 flying bomb site at Siracourt, codenamed Wasserwerk St. Pol, during the Bomber Command daylight attack on 6 July 1944. The original caption states: 'The whole surrounding area including serving roads and railways has been completely obliterated by hundreds of bombs. Very heavy bombs were dropped by RAF aircraft at 08.00 hours on the morning of 6 July 1944.' (Historic Military Press)

Below: An air-launched V1 on a Heinkel He 111 H-22.

Above: Evidence of the V-weapon campaign can still be seen. Seen here are the ruins of the Church of St Mary at Little Chart, Kent, which was hit by a V1 flying bomb just after 20.00 hours on the evening of 16 August 1944. (Historic Military Press)

Right: A V2 rocket is prepared for firing on the launch pad at Peenemünde. (Historic Military Press)

Left: The moment that a V2 rocket is test-fired. The first launch of a V2 occurred on 13 June 1942, on which occasion the rocket pitched out of control and crashed as a result of a propellant feed system failure. (Historic Military Press)

Below: The scene in Staveley Road, Chiswick, after the detonation of the first V2 rocket to come down on British soil at 18.43 hours on Friday, 8 September 1944. (Historic Military Press)

Right: A young girl stands amid the ruins of her home in Battersea following a V2 incident on 27 January 1945. It left 17 people dead, 20 houses destroyed, and dozens more damaged. Listed as Big Ben incident No.625, the rocket exploded at 16.01 hours at the north-west end of Usk Road at the junction with York Road. (NARA)

Below: A V2 rocket struck Smithfield Market, hitting a building at the junction of Charterhouse Street and Farringdon Road, at 11.30 hours on 8 March 1945. A total of 110 people were killed. (Historic Military Press)

Above: A view of 88 Kynaston Road, Orpington, Kent (the left-hand half of the building), which was hit by a V2 rocket at 16.54 hours on 27 March 1945. This was the last V2 to hit the UK in the Second World War. One of the occupants, Ivy Millichamp, was killed, aged 34. (Historic Military Press)

Right: The headstone marking the last resting place of Ivy Millichamp. As the inscription on the headstone states, she was the last civilian killed in the UK through enemy action in the Second World War. (Historic Military Press)

end of the bombardment of London. On the 17th, the Deputy Chief of Air Staff reported to the Chiefs of Staff that 21st Army Group had provided a survey regiment – No. 10 Survey Regiment, R.A. – for employment in Belgium as an extension of the existing lay-out in the United Kingdom. It was intended to be in operation in the Antwerp area by 23rd September, though landlines connecting it to the Canterbury headquarters of the system could not be provided until later. 21st Army Group also agreed to provide three G.L. Mk. II sets which, with two high-looking Type 9 Mk. III stations, would form an early warning system on the Continent. Sites for the former had been selected, and the crews and necessary additional equipment were in transit to the Continent by 17th September. The Type 9 stations were expected to be ready to move by 23rd September. By the same date, a 'Y' Service unit and a number of jamming transmitters were being prepared for Continental service.

For the best use to be made of all these measures it was essential that some form of control centre should also be set up in Belgium. For this purpose, a special unit, No. 105 Mobile Air Reporting Unit, was formed in A.D.G.B. during the second week in September: its headquarters were to be at Malines. It was to be an advanced element of A.D.G.B., responsible for the transmission of rocket warnings to No. 11 Group Filter Room at Stanmore and for the correlation of all data received from the survey, radar and radio counter-measures units that would eventually come into operation on the Continent. The whole system was expected to give more reliable information than that from the units in the United Kingdom.

## 48. Effect of the Attack on Arnhem.

On the morning of 17th September, the airborne operations against the Lower Rhine were launched. Rockets continued to be fired from The Hague area throughout the day; five fell in England, all but one in the London region. This was the heaviest attack on one day since the bombardment had begun. Between the night of 17th and the morning of the 19th, when the Chiefs of Staff held their usual weekly meeting to consider 'Crossbow' policy, only one rocket fell – at Lambeth on the evening of the 18th. At that meeting a decision taken by the War Cabinet the previous evening was noted. This was that no public announcement about rocket attacks should be made for a week, during which time an appreciation should be made of the prospects of the continuance of the bombardment. Obviously, this entailed a forecast by the War Office of the situation on land by the 25th. The Chiefs of Staff, therefore, asked that this should be made and that the Deputy Chief of Air Staff, in consultation with Mr. Sandys, should prepare an appreciation of what threat would remain in the light of the War Office estimate.

This appreciation, which also took account of flying bomb attacks, was circulated to the Chiefs of Staff on 23rd September and was considered at their meeting on the 25th. By then two things had happened: first, the British forces had been checked at Arnhem and there was no immediate prospect of an advance across the Rhine; second, there had been no rocket incidents in the United Kingdom since the evening of the 18th. The two, as it were, balanced each other. From the first, it might follow that the attacks would continue as the launching area would remain in German hands. From the second, it appeared that the area had already been evacuated; there were, in fact, reliable intelligence reports that rocket supplies had been moving eastwards from The Hague and that the order to evacuate the area had been given on the 17th, the day the airborne attack was launched. It is now known that this information was correct.

There was a further factor to be considered: even though the launching area remained in German hands, could they maintain a firing organisation there? The Deputy Chief of Air Staff and Mr. Sandys thought it would be difficult and they reported, "owing to the general state of dis-organisation especially as affecting communications in this area it seems likely that few more rockets will be fired at London".

In sum, before any important alterations to 'Crossbow' policy could reasonably be made a further period was required for observing how the situation developed. The Chiefs of Staff agreed, therefore, that it would be best to wait a week before any public announcement about rocket attack was made; though they also placed on record their view that in general it was sound policy to keep the public informed. They also considered the question of giving a public warning of attack. Up to date, the performance of the radar and sound ranging units had been such that, if warnings had been based upon it, only once out of 16 times would the warning have been followed by an incident in London, and only once out of 6 times by an incident anywhere in the country. Moreover, on three occasions between 14th and 18th September incidents had occurred where no warning could have been given. The warning system that was being set up in Belgium was expected to improve the rate of probability; but in the meantime, it was decided that no warnings were to be given in the United Kingdom.

Similarly, nothing was done at this stage to increase the scale of Allied counter-measures. Armed reconnaissances continued to be made by A.D.G.B. aircraft, though on a reduced scale owing to the effort that A.D.G.B. made in support of the airborne operations. Some four hundred sorties were made in the week 16th-23rd September, less than half of the effort of the previous week. A number of barges, locomotives and lorries were destroyed; and on the 19th storage installations and a suspected firing point were attacked by three squadrons of Spitfires. Another suspected storage depot, at Eikenhorst, was attacked by thirty aircraft of Bomber Command on 17th September: 172 tons of bombs were dropped in an accurate attack which caused a heavy explosion in the target area.

**49.Switch to the Attack of Norwich: Rocket Attacks on the Continent.**
The lull in attacks on the United Kingdom continued throughout most of 25th September. Then, at 1910 hours a rocket fell at Hoxne, in Suffolk. The next to fall came down nearly twenty-four hours later at Ranworth, eight miles north-east of Norwich. The next day, three more fell within nine miles of Norwich. This city, therefore, appeared to be the target; and from 25th September to the night of 3rd October, sixteen rockets were reported from this district. No rockets were reported during the period from the London area.

Radar information and intelligence reports first established that the new direction of attack was from an area some ten miles west of Appeldoorn. Later, it appeared that an area in the south-west corner of Friesland was in use and possibly Vlieland and Terschelling in the Friesian Islands. As the most southerly of these areas was just over 250 miles from London, and as London would obviously be attacked if possible, the bombardment of Norwich signified that the maximum operational range of the rocket was certainly under 250 miles. If London was again to be attacked the Germans would therefore have to return to south-west Holland.

There was no indication of such a move for over a week after the attacks on Norwich had begun; and counter-measures continued after the pattern of the previous fortnight. 667 sorties were flown by A.D.G.B. aircraft over the suspected launching areas between 23rd and 30th September: barges, railway engines and lorries were damaged and destroyed and particularly good results were obtained in strafing railway rolling stock. No attacks against rocket targets were made by heavy bombers. Photographic reconnaissances over western Holland continued.

During the week No. 105 Mobile Air Reporting Unit was established at Malines; two of the G.L. Mk. II sets that 21st Army Group had provided were set up in the Ostend area; and No. 10 Survey Regiment, R.A., was deployed around Antwerp. Radio counter-measures were maintained from ground stations in England and in Belgium, and aircraft of No. 100 Group continued to listen, and occasionally, to jam suspicious signals.[100] There was still no evidence, however, that the Germans were using radio control.

The scale of attack against the United Kingdom was such that counter-measures involving any diversion of force from the offensive against Germany were unwarranted. But on 14th September a number of French and Belgian towns began to suffer rocket attacks. More than twenty incidents were reported between the 14th and the 25th, the majority in or near Lille and Liège. Up to the end of the month, no reliable reports of the areas from which the attacks were being made had been received in London. A week later, however, by which time there had been more than eighty Continental incidents, an area near Enschede on the Dutch – German frontier was indicated. This was only 120 miles from Liège and less than two hundred miles from Lille, and the accuracy of attack against both places was better than in the attacks that had so far been made against London and Norwich.

Not surprisingly, therefore, the view was expressed by the Chief of the Imperial General Staff at a meeting of the Chiefs of Staff on 2nd October that henceforth the main targets for rocket attack might well be areas important for 21st Army Group, such as Brussels and Antwerp. The observation was made when a request from 21st Army Group for the return of No. 10 Survey Regiment from its rocket duties was being discussed.

About this time, however, the Supreme Commander, A.E.F., was also becoming concerned at the potential threat to his forces not only from rockets but also flying bombs; for intelligence was received late in September that the Germans were preparing flying bomb launching sites south-west and east of Cologne and Bonn. During October, therefore, a special section was set up in S.H.A.E.F. for the control of a Continental 'Crossbow' organisation. All the radar and signals units that had been sent to Belgium to improve the defence of the United Kingdom were transferred to General Eisenhower's control, although the signals link between No. 105 Mobile Air Reporting Unit at Malines and No. 11 Group Filter Room was maintained. A number of Fighter Command officers experienced in defence against V-weapons was transferred to the new section of S.H.A.E.F. As part of the general arrangement, No. 10 Survey Regiment returned to its normal duties with 21st Army Group, but its place was taken by No. 11 Survey Regiment from England. This unit could be spared from England as the performance of the British radar stations had noticeably improved since the end of September; very few rockets were not being observed and in nearly all cases the area from which firing had taken place was being indicated.

## 50. Renewed Attacks on London.

The decision to release the survey unit was taken on 7th October by which time the direction of attacks against the United Kingdom had once more been changed. The lull in the bombardment of London that had set in on 19th September had coincided with intelligence reports that the German firing batteries had moved from The Hague north-east towards Utrecht; and it had been from the northern half of Holland, as we have seen, that rockets had been fired against Norwich. On 3rd October, however, a report was received from an agent that certain launching crews had returned with equipment and rockets to south-west Holland and that rockets might be expected soon from an area south of The Hague. The intelligence was promptly confirmed that same night when a rocket, which was subsequently plotted as coming from near The Hague, fell in Leytonstone at 2305 hours.

Between then and 14th October both Norwich and London were under fire, with more attention being paid to London as the period advanced. 39 incidents were reported, 21 the result of rockets aimed from The Hague area at London. The accuracy of the German fire was poor. More than half the rockets fell nearer to Southend than to London. But the attack had recommenced and there was no prospect of it ceasing until such time as south-west Holland was liberated or some counter-measures more effective than any that had been employed so far, were brought to bear.

## 51. Further Attacks by Flying Bombs.

Any increase in counter-measures had to be considered in relation to the air offensive against Germany and to weight and effectiveness of attack on England. So much depended on the first that to reduce it in order to strike at the German V-weapon organisation would be justified only if the second was such as to impair seriously the Allied offensive effort. What was needed, therefore, about the middle of October, when it was clear that the Germans would be holding most of Holland until the early spring, was as reliable a statement as possible of the scale of future attacks. This question, however, could not be answered in terms of rocket attacks alone; for flying bombs were still reaching England. It is these attacks that must now be considered.

*a. The German Effort, 15th September – 14th October.*

It will be recalled that what has here been termed the main phase of the flying bomb attack on London came to an end in the early morning of 5th September 1944 when eight flying bombs fell at scattered points north and east of London, the target at which they were aimed. They were the last of a considerable number[101] of bombs which had been launched since 8th July, concurrently with launchings from sites in northern France, by He. 111s of I/K.G.53[102] operating mainly from airfields in Holland.

The optimism of the first week in September in the United Kingdom was tempered by the realisation that similar attacks might continue; though it was thought that their scale would be so small that no modifications need yet be made to the existing scheme of defence. And as during the next ten days Air Intelligence regularly reported an intensifying of trial launchings in the Baltic area, it was no surprise when air-launched flying bombs again came over England. This was in the early morning of 16th September, the ten-day lull since the last attacks being accounted for by the move of I/K.G.53 from its Dutch bases to airfields in north-western Germany, of which Varelbusch, Aalhorn and Rheine were thought to have been taken over. About fifteen He.111s participated in the attack which took place between 0530 and 0630 hours. Seven flying bombs were reported by the defences. Two came down in London; the rest fell at various widely separated points in Essex.

Attacks continued to be made on most nights during the rest of September; and by the end of the month eighty bombs had been plotted by the defences on twelve nights. Of these, seventy-two came overland but only fourteen reached the London area. Twenty-three bombs were destroyed: ten by fighters – two over the sea; ten by guns of Anti-Aircraft Command – three over the sea; two by naval gunfire from H.M. ships at sea; and one was shared by the guns of Anti-Aircraft Command and the Navy.

The attack continued on a similar scale in the next fortnight. Sixty-nine flying bombs were plotted, of which fifty-three came overland and twelve fell in the London area, a slightly higher proportion of those that were plotted than in the previous fortnight. However, against this, the defences had been almost exactly twice as successful. From 15th – 30th September, 29 per cent of the flying bombs plotted had been destroyed; whereas in the period 1st – 14th October this figure had risen to 55 per cent. Thirteen bombs were shot down by fighters – three over the sea; twenty-three by Anti-Aircraft Command – eleven over the sea; and two by naval gunners.

*b. Counter-Measures, 15th September – 14th October.*
These figures reflect a departure from the 'stand fast' defensive policy which, in default of anything better, had followed the end of the main attack from northern France. When air-launched attacks recommenced

the great majority of the guns of Anti-Aircraft Command that had been in action against flying bombs were still deployed in the Gun Belt on the south-east coast and the Gun Box in Essex. The latter, it will be remembered, had been established expressly to deal with air-launched attacks against London from the outer Thames estuary. Some of the renewed attacks were also launched from this direction. Others, however, were made from further north, the bombs crossing the coast between Clacton and Harwich.

The first defensive measures to be taken – apart from interception sorties by A.D.G.B. night fighters – therefore involved the reinforcement of the Gun Box and the deployment of additional batteries along the coast between Clacton and Harwich. Altogether, between 16th and 19th September, sixteen heavy and nine light anti-aircraft batteries were ordered to move. This was a considerable force, but it was not the intention at this stage to establish a coastal gun belt in East Anglia similar to that which had been so effective in the south-east. The scale of attack was not sufficient to warrant the great concentrations of fire that had been employed in the south-east. Moreover, to permit unrestricted fire during darkness – and it was expected that the German attacks would continue to be made exclusively at night – would endanger the aircraft of Bomber Command which normally flew out and home over the East Anglian coast. Accordingly, the rules for engagement for guns in the Clacton – Harwich strip permitted 'seen' fire at flying bombs below 6,000 feet but 'unseen' fire only when the No. 11 Group Controller was certain that there were no friendly aircraft in the area. Night fighters, however, were instructed to regard the new deployment as they did the Gun Box and Gun Belt: that is to say, they were not to pursue flying bombs closer than six miles to the coast from seaward and five miles from landward. Additional searchlights were set up near the coast to mark the boundaries of the area.

A conference was held at A.D.G.B. Headquarters on 21st September to consolidate these first measures and work out a comprehensive plan for defence against the new attacks. By that time, it was clear that the use of what can well be described as a highly mobile launching site – the bomber aircraft – conferred a great advantage on the enemy: he could launch flying bombs from any point over the North Sea so long as it was within 130 miles – the range of the flying bomb – from London. Indeed, by the 21st there was good evidence that flying bombs aimed at London had crossed the coast even further north than Harwich. But to protect the whole coast of East Anglia round to the Wash was reckoned unjustifiable. Instead, it was decided to establish a coastal gun zone, 5,000 yards deep, from Clacton, where the existing Gun Box had its northerly limit, to Great Yarmouth. It was to embrace the permanent anti-aircraft defences of places like Harwich, Lowestoft and Great Yarmouth. The total number of guns to be deployed, including those already in the Gun Box and in permanent defences, was 516 heavy guns and 611 light. Forward of the gun zone, patrol areas for Mosquito night fighters were established. Inland of the zone, Tempests of No. 501 Squadron were to operate in co-operation with searchlights.

The order to redeploy to the north of Harwich was issued to all batteries concerned in the early morning of 22nd September. Some preliminary work in selecting sites and in preparing stocks of steel mattresses for static guns had already been done; and it was intended to complete the move by 26th September. On the 23rd, General Pile, allowing himself a little grace, informed the War Cabinet 'Crossbow' Sub-Committee that the deployment should be complete by the 30th, with the majority of guns statically emplaced.

But the deployment was unsatisfactorily handled. The needs of the forces in Europe limited the amount of railway and road transport available, and the staff work of Anti-Aircraft Command and Nos. 1 and 2 A.A. Groups was not as well done as in the great deployment to the south-east coats in the middle of July. It was not until 13th October that the deployment was substantially complete. On that day 498 heavy guns and 609 light guns were ready for action in the Gun Box and the new Gun Strip.

There were important differences between the new situation and that which had applied when flying bombs had been coming from sites in northern France. First, in the earlier attack all bombs aimed at London had had to fly over a comparatively restricted stretch of coastline; whereas in an air launched attack a much wider area had to be covered. Second, in the earlier case a permanent 'attack in progress' had been assumed; in the new one there were restrictions on fire. Third, in the new form of attack flying bombs were crossing the coast often as low as 1,000 feet, compared to 2,000-3,000 feet in the attacks of the summer, and this created a difficult problem of low-angle engagement for the 3.7 guns and for searchlights. Fourth, the enemy aircraft were approaching at very low altitudes, usually below 300 feet, which meant that there was frequently little warning of attack. Moreover, the radar equipment of the night fighters operating out to sea was not at its best when searching for aircraft at very low altitudes. Frequently, contact was first obtained only when the launching aircraft climbed to 2,000 feet or so, prior to releasing its bomb. After release the aircraft usually dived to sea level and flew hard for home, which again made its interception difficult. Various measures were adopted during October to meet some of these difficulties. Radar and R/T facilities were improved at the stations at Trimley, Hopton and Greyfriars; other stations in East Anglia were modified later. The possibility of using naval fighter-direction ships was examined; but nothing came of it until the following month. Also, to improve fighter interception, the development of a Wellington aircraft, fitted with A.S.V. Mk.VI to act as an airborne fighter control station was put in hand. It was not until January 1945 that it was ready for operations.

To assist guns to engage at very low altitudes a new control equipment – R.O.3 – was brought into service. Its supply, however, was slow, and by the middle of October only some forty guns could be controlled by it. The normal fire-control instruments with which the rest of Anti-Aircraft Command was equipped were specially sited for controlling low-angle fire, though to do this meant some sacrifice of early warning. The problem as it affected searchlights was met by substituting a spacing of 3,000 yards for the normal one of 6,000 yards within a belt 16 miles wide from Saffron Walden and Sudbury in the north to Southend and Brigtlingsea in the south. Over and near this swathe of country patrol lines were established for Tempest night fighters.

Rules for the engagement of flying bombs by the guns in the Gun Box and Gun Strip were agreed upon by the third week in October. They marked a compromise between the views of Bomber Command on the one side and Fighter and Anti-Aircraft Commands on the other. Flying below 6,000 feet over the box and strip areas was normally prohibited during the hours of darkness, and the guns were free to engage flying bombs up to a height of 4,000 feet. But provided Bomber Command gave prior warning to Fighter Command, aircraft could fly at any height over the Gun Strip, though not the Gun Box. At such times the guns were permitted to engage only those bombs below 4,000 feet which could be visually recognised. Finally, the Fighter Command Controller had the right to restrict or withhold fire to safeguard any friendly aircraft which was forced to fly over the Gun Strip.

Yet despite the difficulties which hampered the defence a high proportion of the flying bombs which came overland or approached the coast during the first month of the attack was destroyed. Altogether, between 15th September and 14th October, 149 flying bombs were plotted by the radar stations and Royal Observer Corps; 125 of these came overland but only twenty-six fell in the London area. Sixty-one bombs were destroyed, and the rest fell short, chiefly in Essex. Casualties were small: only 91 people were killed and 217 seriously injured.

Moreover, there was evidence from Air Intelligence that I/K.G.53 was finding the operations no little strain. Up to 14th October, No. 25 Squadron – the Mosquito night fighter unit that was employed up to this date to intercept launching aircraft – claimed four He.111s destroyed, two probably destroyed and two damaged. These were not heavy casualties for a unit thirty aircraft strong to have suffered in the course of a month. But in addition, it was believed that it was incurring a high accident rate; and not surprisingly, for the He.111 pilots were required to operate at very low altitudes with an overloaded aircraft.

However, no immediate diminution in the scale of German attack was expected. Throughout late September and the first half of October Air Intelligence was regularly reporting intensive training in the Baltic area in the launching of flying bombs; and there was reason to believe that one, possibly two Grüppen were being prepared to supplement the operations of I/K.G.53.

The airfields from which the latter was operating were an obvious target for counter-measures by bombing. They were, in fact, the only possible targets without striking deep into Germany at factories concerned in flying bomb production. Varrelbusch, Zwischenahn, Aalhorn and Münster/Handorf were the airfields principally in use. Regular photographic reconnaissances were flown over them from the middle of September, and Bomber Command and the 8th Air Force were asked to collaborate in their attack. Few attacks were made, however, during this first month. Münster/Handorf was attacked by twenty-three aircraft of Bomber Command on the night of 23rd September, but results were poor. Five light attacks, in which 217 tons of bombs were dropped, were made by Bomber Command and the 8th Air Force during the first week of October against the same airfield with better results: photographs showed many craters on the runways and two He.111s severely damaged. On 12th October a big strike by Liberators against airfields in north-west Germany, including Varrelbusch and Zwischenahnn, was planned but bad weather prevented bombing.

In sum, by the middle of October, a defensive system had been brought into operation which was succeeding in restricting to insignificance the number of flying bombs that were reaching London. In those circumstances more powerful counter-measures by bombing were not called for; and on 10th October, in reply to a suggestion by Mr. Sandys that there might have been "an imperceptible slackening-off" in counter-measures, the Chiefs of Staff made it clear that they had no intention of interfering with what was being done unless the attack increased in strength.

**52. Rocket and Flying Bomb Attacks, 15th October – 25th November.**
This was the point of view of the Chiefs of Staff and Air Ministry at this
time on the whole question of the air defence of the United Kingdom.
They preferred to wait for developments in the German attacks rather
than approve further counter-measures of a precautionary nature that
might prove unnecessary. For there was no certainty that the scale of
bombardment of the United Kingdom would notably increase. There
was, as we have noticed, evidence that more German units might soon
be employed in launching flying bombs from the air; but their likely
dispositions were such that they could be used against Continental
towns as much as London. Moreover, the building of launching sites
for flying bombs in western Germany and the already heavier scale of
rocket attack against French and Belgian towns than against England,
indicated that any increase in the total V-weapon effort of the enemy
might affect the Continent rather than Great Britain. It was, of course,
appreciated that the Germans would continue to attack London, for
political and psychological reasons, for as long as they could. But they
could do themselves more good, militarily, by concentrating upon
towns along the lines of communication of the Allied armies, especially
Antwerp whose proper functioning as a base port was essential to
future Allied operations.

*a. Relative Effort against England and the Continent.*
During the third week of October there was little to show how the
Germans would allot their effort. The scale of attack against British and
Continental targets was small. Only eight rockets fell in Great Britain: all
were launched from The Hague area and were widely scattered
between London and Southend. Rather more were launched against
Continental towns; and for the first time Antwerp was a target, the first
rocket being reported from there on 13th October. Flying bomb attacks,
however, up to 21st October, continued to be made exclusively against
London. The week 14th – 21st October was, in fact, the heaviest since the
attacks had recommenced: 84 flying bombs were reported of which only
five got through to London.

Then, on 21st October, flying bomb attacks began against Continental
targets from the sites which the Germans were known to have been
preparing in western Germany. For the first three days Brussels was the
target, where some twenty incidents were reported. On the night of the
23rd, the attack switched to Antwerp which was to be the sole target
for the next fortnight. Over one hundred incidents were reported from
that district before the end of October. About the same time, the enemy's
rocket attacks against Continental targets were concentrated on

Antwerp; nearly one hundred rockets were reported between 21st October and the end of the month. In short, Antwerp had become the main target for attack by V-weapons.

The next few weeks confirmed this. By 25th November, 245 rockets had been recorded as falling in the United Kingdom, or sufficiently near its shores to be reported. Of these, about two hundred had been aimed at London, the rest at Norwich. Rocket incidents reported on the Continent up to the same date, attacks having started in strength a week later than against London, amounted to 559, of which 430 fell in or near Antwerp. In short, the Germans were making twice the effort against Antwerp that they were against London.

The records of flying bomb incidents showed that even more attention was being paid to Antwerp than to London. The scale of attack against the latter remained fairly constant. Between 16th September and 21st October, when London was the sole target, 233 flying bombs were reported by the defences. Between 21st October and 25th November, when London and also continental targets were being attacked, 237 flying bombs were reported in the United Kingdom, but no less than 698 on the Continent, about eighty per cent being aimed at Antwerp.[103] That is to say that nearly three times as many flying bombs were being launched against Antwerp as against London.

*b. Counter-Measures to Flying Bombs.*
German activity over the whole period was to some extent conditioned by the state of the moon, the heaviest attacks being launched on clear nights of little or no moon. The fluctuations over the six weeks, in terms of those bombs that were plotted weekly by the defences, were as follows: 84, 40, 12, 108, 42, 35. According to Air Intelligence the long-expected second G.A.F. unit commenced preparations during the period – 31st October was thought to have been the date of its first attack – and during the week following more bombs were reported than in any other week since 16th September. However, the increased effort was not maintained. An attack on the night of 5th November, when a number of bombs crossed the Kent coast, was thought to have been the work of the new unit. The novel direction of attack was put down to the unit's inexperience rather to any intention of outflanking the gun defences.

Such alterations as were made to the defences were matters of detail. From 5th November a regulation came into force, by agreement between Bomber and Fighter Commands, by which all friendly aircraft, other than night fighters, were prohibited from flying during darkness below 500 feet over an area bounded by Southend and Cromer and extending some seventy miles out to sea. Within the area night fighters were permitted to engage any aircraft flying below 300 feet without first establishing its identity. The purpose of the regulation was to help night fighter pilots and observers, and operators at coastal radar stations, to take action against launching aircraft without delay.

For the same purpose various modifications were made during November to seven radar stations – Bawdsey, Hopton, Happisburgh, Trimley, Neatishead, Patrington and Greyfriars – on the East Anglian coast: the object was to improve the range of the stations at the low heights at which the He.111s were operating. A very flexible system of fighter control was introduced by which any radar station detecting a suspicious "echo" could immediately take over the direction of the nearest Mosquito.

Trials were also carried out during November in controlling fighters from a frigate – H.M.S. *Caicos*. Early results were disappointing – the effective range of the ship's radar being only some twenty to thirty miles; but the trials were persevered with.

There was one important alteration to the system of fighter interception inland where Tempests were operating in conjunction with searchlights. It was found in practice that it was more of a hindrance than a help to have a thick carpet of searchlights; for the danger of a pilot, flying a single-engined fighter at high speeds and low altitudes, being dazzled by the beams was considerable. Moreover, the altimeter of the Tempest was not as accurate as it ought to have been. So, by the end of November all searchlights that had been moved into Essex to improve the spacing between lights were kept doused. It was found that searchlights operating at the normal interval of 6,000 yards gave a sufficiently good indication of the course of flying bombs for a high proportion of interceptions to be made.

In the Gun Box and Gun Strip only minor alterations were made. There was a reduction in the number of light guns deployed, which were comparatively ineffective, and an increase in that of heavy guns, which by the middle of November totalled 540. But it was with some difficulty that these were kept in action. Manpower cuts, replacement of all men under 35 who were medically A.1 by older or less fit men, and the need for building winter quarters for the great majority of sites, created grave administrative problems. Manning the guns, however, was simplified to some extent as operations, in contrast to those of the summer, took place entirely at night.

The results achieved by the defences were very good. out of the 321 flying bombs that were reported between 14th October and 25th November, 248, or seventy-seven per cent, were destroyed. Of the rest, only twenty-five landed in the London Civil Defence Region, though some of those which fell short, and some which were shot down overland, caused damage and casualties in East Anglia. Most of the destructions went to the credit of Anti-Aircraft Command; and as the majority of fighter interceptions fell to the aircraft patrolling inland of the guns, the greater the successes of the guns the fewer those of the fighters. Altogether, 203½ were destroyed by Anti-Aircraft Command, 40½ by Fighter Command and four by naval gunners. In addition to these last destructions 127½ of the successes of the guns and fifteen of those of the fighters were obtained over the sea. Mosquitos of Nos. 25, 96, 68 and 488 Squadrons, in addition to these fifteen flying bombs, claimed nine He.111s destroyed, two probably destroyed and one damaged. No bombing attacks were made during this period on the airfields from which the launching aircraft were operating; though a number of Intruder sorties were flown over them.

The only other counter-measures took the form of interference by R.C.M. transmitters with the medium-wave beacons that I/K.G.53 was thought to be using.

### c. Counter-Measures to Rockets.

Just as counter-measures against flying bombs fell largely upon the air defences of Great Britain, so those against rockets were principally carried out by Fighter Command. 2nd Tactical Air Force assisted in the work of armed reconnaissance by attacking transport targets over much of Holland, leaving the rocket launching areas used for the attack of London to Fighter Command. But these activities were part of the constant offensive by continentally based aircraft against communications between the battle area and western Germany; and while they were useful in straining communications and supply between the rocket launching areas and Germany a detailed consideration of them is more appropriate to the subject of the air support of the Allied armies.

The heavy bomber forces were not used in this period directly against rocket targets. Even if it had not been the case that there were many better targets – notably oil plants, railway centres and the enemy aircraft industry – claiming their attention, there were two factors that would have reduced their 'Crossbow' effort to very small proportions. They were, first, the paucity of targets connected with the production of rockets; second, the difficulty of finding suitable targets in the launching areas.

Something was learned during October about rocket production from a factory in Luxembourg which had been making one of the components. It appeared that the Germans had planned to produce over 12,000 rockets by October 1944 with an eventual rate of production of 1,000 a month. Production had certainly fallen short of this; nevertheless, it was likely that at least 2,000 rockets had been produced by the end of September and that something approaching the planned output each month was being achieved. Therefore, allowing for an expenditure of some seven hundred rockets on trials and operations up to the end of October, a substantial reserve existed for the scale of effort at that time.

Documents discovered at the factory, supported by evidence from prisoners, suggested that a very important, if not the only component assembly plant was located at Niedersachswerfen, near Nordhausen in the Harz Mountains. It was at any rate the only assembly factory of which there was positive and irrefutable evidence and inevitably the question of its attack arose.

It had been under consideration for some time as a producer of Jumo jet engines, and the difficulties of attacking it were known to be very great. To reach the plant was not the main problem so much as to damage it effectively. It consisted of two parallel tunnels about one mile long which had been constructed in former gypsum[104] quarries and lay for the most part under some two hundred to three hundred feet of this material. The only bombs available to the Allied air forces which might penetrate to the tunnels were the 12,000 lb. "Tallboy" bombs used by Bomber Command. Production of the bombs during the autumn of 1944 was small and such as there were were needed for the attack of the 'Tirpitz', whenever the opportunity arose, and for certain vital communication targets in Germany. The attack of Niedersachswerfen was therefore shelved.

The great majority of targets in the areas from which rockets were being fired at the United Kingdom were no less difficult for heavy bombers, but for different reasons. The areas themselves were known, lying between The Hague and Leiden and The Hague and Hook of Holland. Much of this country was heavily wooded and the precise location of firing points and storage depots was not always known. And where the hand of nature was not an obstacle that of man was; for certain possible targets lay in or near built-up areas and could only have been attacked by heavy bombers at the cost of civilian life. The less devastating attacks of fighter-bombers against targets of this type were also prohibited, out of concern for the Dutch population, for most of this period.

In these circumstances the offensive took the form of sweeps and reconnaissances in which fighters and fighter-bombers attacked targets of opportunity rather than specific, pre-selected objectives. This was work better suited to 2nd Tactical Air Force than Fighter Command: first, because to be effective a large number of sorties was needed – and 2nd Tactical Air Force was a much stronger force than Fighter Command; second, because 2nd Tactical Air Force was continentally based within easy reach of the areas to be attacked, whereas Fighter Command Squadrons had to fly over a hundred miles across the sea before they reached western Holland. The sorties flown over Holland and north-west Germany by the two forces reflect the differences: for the period 15th October – 25th November they were only six hundred by Fighter Command and nearly ten thousand by 2nd Tactical Air Force.

Much German transport was destroyed in this offensive: forty barges, forty locomotives, over two hundred railway vehicles and nearly two hundred motor vehicles were claimed as destroyed, by the two forces. It is unlikely that the German rocket batteries were unaffected by these attacks – though there is no evidence either way at the time of writing – but those by 2nd Tactical Air Force were not carried out specifically for that purpose. Insofar as they were affected it was as a by-product of the larger purpose of preparing for the final offensive against Germany. Their real strength in and near The Hague was not directly attacked.

This was far from being a satisfactory situation to Fighter Command. It was appreciated that the scale of rocket attack was low and did not warrant any important diversion of bomber forces; it was appreciated also that the heavy bombers and tactical air forces had more important tasks than the bombing of 'Crossbow' targets. But there was intelligence evidence during October that the Germans were accumulating supplies of rockets near The Hague which might be the prelude to a heavier attack. Air Marshal Hill argued, therefore, in a letter to the Deputy Chief of Air Staff on 24th October that a small offensive effort immediately might avoid a heavier effort later at a time when it might be embarrassing to the conduct of the offensive against Germany.

There were, in particular, two areas near The Hague which were believed to be actively employed both for firing and storing rockets. They were at Bloemendaal and Ockenburg Klinier which adjoined and together covered about 600 x 500 yards well away from any important built-up area. They were recommended as targets to Bomber Command on 17th October. By 10th November their importance was judged to have diminished and they were withdrawn from the list of targets. They were not attacked during these three weeks.

Fighter Command had no better response from 2nd Tactical Air Force to requests made on 16th and 18th October for the attack of two stations at Leiden, through which rocket supplies were thought to be passing, and the Hotel Promenade at The Hague which was used as a vehicle park.

However, a better argument than the wisdom of insuring against heavier attack for direct action against targets near The Hague came to hand at this time in the form of an increase from 26th October in the German fire against London; though the fact that this occurred is proof of the validity of the representations of 24th October. In the twelve days from 15th – 26th October only nineteen rocket incidents had been reported in the United Kingdom. All were from rockets aimed at London but only two fell in the London Civil Defence Region. But on the 26th alone, eight incidents were reported and nine on the following day; and by 4th November a further twenty-seven incidents had occurred. The attack was not only heavier than any hitherto made in a similar period, it was also more accurate. Thirty-three of the incidents were in the London Civil Defence Region and a further seven within twenty-five miles of Charing Cross. The mean point of impact of these forty rockets fell in Poplar.

The attack did not slacken. In the fortnight following 4th November it increased a little, sixty-two incidents being reported in the United Kingdom. Accuracy, however, fell away, only twenty-six of the incidents occurring in the London Civil Defence Region. During the week ending 25th November the accuracy of fire again improved as did its weight: forty-five incidents were reported in the United Kingdom, thirty-three of them in the London area.

Casualties in the weeks following 25th October rose sharply. In the seven weeks up to that date rockets had killed only 82 people and injured 164 in the United Kingdom; whereas in the month following 406 people were killed and 1002 injured. The first single incidents causing heavy loss of life were recorded during these weeks. Seven incidents each caused the deaths of more than twenty people; while on 25th November there was a terrible incident in New Cross Road, Deptford, when at twenty-five minutes past twelve a rocket hit a crowded Woolworth's store. One hundred and sixty people were killed and one hundred and eight injured.[105]

By that time the rocket had been publicly recognised by the Government. On 8th November the German Home Service for the first time announced that 'V.2' attacks were being made on London. Two days later, Mr. Churchill made the long-delayed announcement, without specifying that London was the German target. No decision had yet been taken to give warning of attack to the general public. For one thing, nine G.L. Mark II sets which were a part of the system by which rocket warnings might have been given were transferred to

S.H.A.E.F. in the middle of November to complete the radar cover of Brussels and Antwerp. But even if they had remained in England the prospects of establishing within a short time an efficient warning system were not good. The difficulty was not, as it had been earlier in the attack, that particular rockets might escape observation, though this still occasionally happened, as that a large number of unnecessary warnings would have been sounded in London.

The general position, however, by the middle of November was such that when A.O.C.-in-C., Fighter Command, again raised the question of direct attacks on the launching areas near The Hague the response was more favourable than before. Air Marshal Hill wrote to the Air Ministry on 17th November, making his letter the occasion for a thorough review of the difficulties under which Fighter Command had been operating. He pointed out that armed reconnaissances had to be carried out by Spitfires in daylight whenever weather permitted, and as winter approached their scale of effort was being seriously affected. Moreover, the majority of sorties had to be flown at low altitudes if the pilots were to identify suitable targets and attack them with cannon and machine-gun fire; and this in an area where the Germans had deployed a large number of light anti-aircraft guns was a dangerous proceeding. Altogether, armed reconnaissance seemed to him to be ineffective unless combined with other forms of offensive action.

Here, Bomber Command and 2nd Tactical Air Force could help, though so far, they had done very little. A number of sorties were also being flown by bomb-carrying Spitfires of Fighter Command whose pilots were, however, under strict instructions not to bomb if there was any risk of causing civilian casualties.

It was particularly in this last connection that Air Marshal Hill wanted a revision of policy. He maintained that the positions of certain targets were known accurately and that the civilian population had been moved away from rocket launching points. In his view, therefore, it was "a question of balancing the certain injury to British civilian life and property against the possible injury to Dutch civilian life and property"; and he asked that bombing attacks should be permitted in spite of the risk. He also asked for suitable rocket targets and the airfields used by aircraft launching flying bombs against England to be placed on a higher priority for attacks by Bomber Command.

The whole question was considered at a conference on 21st November under the chairmanship of the Deputy Supreme Commander. Air Marshal Hill and members of the Dutch Government were present. The latter agreed that if bombing attacks on launching points and storage sites were indeed considered necessary and likely to prove effective, they would raise no objection at this stage. Air Marshal Hill was therefore given authority to undertake such attacks even against targets near built-up areas, provided he considered them "reasonably discriminating".

This applied only to Fighter Command and its fighter and fighter-bomber aircraft. No alteration was made in 'Crossbow' policy as it affected 2nd Tactical Air Force and Bomber Command. Air Chief Marshal Tedder put the claims of the battle on land on 2nd Tactical Air Force higher than the needs of rocket counter-measures. However, the current operations of this force included attacks on the railway bridges at Deventer, Zwolle and Zutphen, which carried communications to The Hague. 2nd Tactical Air Force was therefore considered to be making a contribution to defence against rockets.

As for Bomber Command, their operations were to continue to be governed by the instruction from the Combined Chiefs of Staff whereby the greatest possible effort, particularly by visual bombing – and it was this sort of attack which was needed for 'Crossbow' targets – was to be made against oil targets and communications, especially those affecting the Ruhr. This did not absolutely rule out attacks against other targets, and the airfields of I/K.G.53 were still on the Bomber Command list of targets. But these would obviously not be attacked if conditions were favourable for attacks on targets within the scope of the directive from the Combined Chiefs of Staff. In any case, according to Air Intelligence at this time, the scale of flying bomb attack on England was likely to remain low.

Although the medium and heavy bombers thus remained inoperative against both rocket and flying bomb targets, the decisions of 21st November mark the beginning of more active counter-measures. They mark also a new interest on the part of Fighter Command in the rocket attacks. Hitherto, apart from its comparatively small effort in armed reconnaissance, its task had been largely passive: i.e. to utilise its system of intelligence and communications for the warning system which, in one important respect, the warning of the general public, had not been put into operation. Henceforth, it was to attempt a specific task, one which was unique in the history of the Command and one more usually undertaken by a bomber force, namely the attack at its source of an organisation itself attacking the United Kingdom.

# Part VII.

# Rocket and Flying Bomb attacks on the United Kingdom. 25th November, 1944 – 29th March, 1945.

### 53. Fighter-Bomber Attacks against The Hague, 25th November – 16th December.

During the first fortnight after Fighter Command had been allowed greater liberty of action the weather was poor and only spasmodic attacks could be made. Conditions improved during the first week in December and a more sustained offensive was undertaken.

No. 12 Group of Fighter Command, being more suitably located than No. 11, had by now been made responsible for operations against The Hague area, and a list of targets suitable for attack by fighter-bombers was issued to it on 29th November. It included a suspected storage area and a depot for motor vehicles in the Haagsche Bosch, suspected storage areas near Wassenaar, at Voorde and Huis le Werve, and a vehicle park and storage area and billets believed to be occupied by rocket-firing troops in the Hotel Promenade at The Hague. Light attacks had been made on some of these targets on 21st November; and between then and 4th December, 13½ tons of bombs were dropped in small bombs of 250 lbs.[106] The accuracy of the bombing was considered very high; but many of the targets were well concealed, particularly in the Haagsche Bosch, and observation of results was often difficult or impossible. Nevertheless, the enemy was at least being harassed, and many targets which had hitherto enjoyed complete immunity were now being attacked for the first time.

164

Attacks on these targets continued during the next fortnight. An attack was also made on 10th December against the main railway station at Leiden, through which rocket supplies were known to pass; four Spitfires dropped eight 250 lb. bombs of which at least four hit the target. Altogether, between 25th November and 16th December nearly three hundred sorties were flown by Fighter Command over Holland and 25 tons of bombs were dropped.

2nd Tactical Air Force was also indirectly assisting in the offensive against The Hague area by attacks against German communications south of the Zuider Zee. Railway lines were cut south-west of Zwolle by fighter bombers, a bridge north-east of Rotterdam was destroyed, and Leiden station was bombed by Typhoons. The important communication points at Deventer, Zwolle and Zutphen were attacked by medium bombers.

## 54. Rocket Attacks, 25th November – 16th December, 1944.

Offensive action by Fighter Command during these three weeks was small in weight of bombs dropped; and by that token alone not much could be expected from it in reducing the scale of German attack. But it was in this way that the new policy of counter-measures could be most strikingly justified; and there was, therefore, no little interest in the size of the German effort at this time.

In the first week of the period, 25th November – 2nd December, forty-five rocket incidents were reported in the United Kingdom; in the next week, thirty-five; and in the next, twenty-nine. Activity, therefore, decreased as Fighter Command's efforts increased. But whether the two were directly connected was not demonstrable. It was perhaps evidence against it that the scale of rocket attack against Antwerp increased as the Ardennes offensive gathered strength. In other words, it was possible that in order to increase the rate of fire against the main Allied base in Belgium while the German offensive was in progress the scale of attack on the other targets had to be reduced. However, it was noticeable that the accuracy of attack against London fell away after Fighter Command began regular bombing. In the first week of the period over half the incidents occurred in the London Civil Defence Region: in the next two, only a third. Perhaps most significant was the fact that whereas up to the beginning of December the enemy effort was fairly equally divided between day and night, in the following fortnight only about one-fifth of the incidents were by day. It seemed fair to assume, therefore, that the more determined efforts of Fighter Command in daylight had forced the Germans to fire mostly at night.

All rockets launched against the United Kingdom continued to come from the general area of The Hague; but a wider dispersal of launching points was discerned at this time. Three districts were in use: one south of Leiden, one in The Hague – Wassenaar district, and one three or four miles east of the Hook of Holland. It was thought that supplies of rockets were brought to Leiden by rail, and were then taken by road to field storage depots near the launching areas for final assembly. Liquid oxygen was believed to be conveyed by rail as far as The Hague itself. Intelligence of the German field organisation made it fairly clear that operational control was being exercised by the S.S. which was known to provide at least one of the eight firing troops in action. Certainly two, and possibly three of these were thought to be firing against England, the others at Antwerp.

## 55. Continued Offensive Against The Hague: Request by Home Secretary for Stronger Counter-Measures.

Fog affected operations in the week 17th – 24th December and only eighty-three sorties were flown over The Hague by Fighter Command. They included, however, the heaviest single attack that had yet to be mounted. This was the work of thirty-three Spitfire XIV aircraft of Nos. 229, 453 and 602 Squadrons against Marlot, a block of flats near the Haagsche Bosch, which was believed to be the headquarters of the rocket firing troops in that district. The Spitfires each carried one 500 lb. bomb in addition to two 250 lbs. Photographs were taken during the attack, which was made on Christmas Eve, from an accompanying Mustang, but they showed only one direct hit. Later photographs, however, showed that considerable damage had been done and shortly after the attack the building was evacuated. One Spitfire was destroyed by anti-aircraft fire.

The German effort against London during this week was also low: there were only twenty-eight incidents, seven in the London area. As in the previous fortnight most of the firing was at night. There were no incidents where there were heavy casualties.

However, on 22nd December, the Home Secretary suggested to the Chiefs of Staff that more powerful counter-measures should be applied against The Hague area. His was the main responsibility for the security of the civilian population, and certain developments in that sphere threatened an effect out of all proportion to the moderate scale of rocket bombardment. These originated from doubts which had been expressed about the safety of the London underground railways under rocket attack. It was feared that rockets might penetrate the tunnels running under the Thames and cause flooding with heavy loss of life, especially at night when thousands of people were sheltering in 'tube' stations. Accordingly, during December the transmission of special warnings to the London Passenger Transport Board was considered so that the under-river floodgates of the 'tubes' could be closed during attacks.

Mr Morrison was anxious, therefore, that rocket attacks should be reduced below even the present low effort. He recognised that the scale of attack had fallen during the first three weeks in December, and this he credited to the attacks of Fighter Command and 2nd Tactical Air Force; but he suggested that heavy bomber attacks upon The Hague launching areas would reduce it still further. He also argued that as, according to the Air Ministry, the morale of all the German firing troops, not only those attacking England, was being affected by the attacks of Fighter Command and 2nd Tactical Air Force, heavy bomber operations against rocket targets would contribute to the security of the lines of communication of the Allied forces in Belgium as well as to the defence of the United Kingdom.

The Home Secretary's views were considered at a meeting of the Chiefs of Staff on 23rd December, who strongly recommended that heavy bombers should not be employed against targets near The Hague. Their reasons were two-fold: firstly, they were sure that the attacks would mean heavy loss of life amongst Dutch civilians and the destruction of much Dutch property without achieving anything more than a temporary interruption of rocket firings; second, for the eight to ten known or suspected targets to be attacked effectively some twelve hundred to fifteen hundred sorties by Lancasters would be needed, and this effort, it was felt, could not be justified.

## 56. Consideration of Stronger Counter-Measures.
Nevertheless, the possibility of widening the scope of counter-measures by bombing was much to the fore at this period. During December the Deputy Chief of Air Staff asked the Economic Advisory Branch of the Foreign Office and the Ministry of Economic Warfare to review again the liquid oxygen factories that might be providing fuel for rockets. A detailed paper was prepared and circulated on 18th December 1944. It emphasised that Germany required liquid oxygen for industrial purposes and for high-altitude flying as well as for rockets and that it was impossible to say what were the requirements for each purpose or what factories provided them. There were indications that the Germans would probably rely for liquid oxygen for rockets on plants producing at least fifteen to twenty tons a day, supplemented by deliveries from such of the smaller plants as lay within fifty miles of rocket launching points. There were in Holland eight plants that the Germans might be

using, five in western Germany and five elsewhere in Germany. None of the German plants, however, could be positively identified as producing for rockets and, consequently, none were attacked. Those in Holland continued to be studied and one, at Loosduinen, was eventually bombed by Fighter Command, but the evidence was never conclusive that the Germans used these plants for rocket fuel.

Another type of target which if successfully attacked might affect the scale of attack from The Hague was studied in January 1945: this was the road and rail communications system between Germany and western Holland. A report on the subject by the Deputy Chief of Air Staff was presented to the Chiefs of Staff on 13th January. Leading from northern Germany to enemy-occupied Holland there were four main railway and four main road bridges, all of which crossed the river Ijssel between Doesberg, near Arnhem and Kampen, near Zwolle. All were strongly constructed, some four hundred yards in length, and heavily defended by anti-aircraft guns. For their destruction, the employment of the tactical air forces appeared most suitable; and it was estimated that about six hundred sorties by fighter-bombers or four hundred medium bombers would be needed to destroy the railway bridges and a similar effort for the road bridges. Even then, the interdiction would not be complete. It would be necessary to prevent attempts to repair the bridges or to convey supplies across the Ijssel by pontoon bridges or barges; the possible diversion of road traffic to the northern route across the Zuider Zee causeway would also have to be reckoned with. For such extensive operations the approval of the Supreme Commander was necessary; and neither the Air Staff at Air Ministry nor S.H.A.E.F. considered that they were justified. Consequently, plans for the full interdiction of supplies to The Hague were left at the paper stage against the possibility that their execution would be necessary if rocket attacks substantially increased.

Neidersachswerfen was also re-examined during January 1945, as a possible target. By this time German jet-propelled aircraft were considered to present a real threat to Allied air superiority; and it was as a producer of jet engines rather than rockets that the factory was placed on the current target lists for Bomber Command and the 8th Air Force on high priority. It was felt that although to destroy it would probably be impossible, damage to the approaches, and to the storage sheds and workers' dwellings on the surface might affect production. For two months the best method of attacking it was examined. A detailed model of the target area was constructed and studied by officers of Bomber Command and the 8th Air Force who concluded that the output of the factory could not be stopped with existing types of bomb. It might be reduced by continued attack of the railway system in and near the target area; but this would have meant a very considerable diversion of bombing effort from targets more profitable to the general offensive. On 8th March the Chiefs of Staff finally agreed that attack upon the factory would not be worthwhile.

Thus, no radical change was made in the policy of counter-measures, which remained those carried out by Fighter Command, supplemented by 2nd Tactical Air Force. This applied until all attacks upon the United Kingdom, both by rockets and flying bombs, had ceased.

## 57. Fighter-Bomber Attacks Against The Hague, 17th December 1944 – 16th February 1945.

Up to the middle of January the striking force that Fighter Command maintained for attacks against The Hague amounted to four squadrons of Spitfires, Nos. 453, 229, 303 and 602. All operated under No. 12 Group, chiefly from the Coltishall sector. No operations were flown against the area at night. The intruder resources of the Command were at this time fully committed to the support of Bomber Command; and although the question of using intruder pilots under training was considered nothing came of it.

During the first month of this period operations were affected by the weather: only some three hundred sorties were flown, of which nearly one-third had to be abandoned. As this was also the period in which there was heavy fighting in the Ardennes the effort of 2nd Tactical Air Force was largely confined to the support of the Allied ground forces and few operations were carried out which might have affected The Hague area.

Attacks were carried out, as weather permitted, in accordance with a list of targets agreed upon between Air Intelligence, and the Director of Operations (Air Defence) at Air Ministry and Fighter Command. The list initially comprised eleven targets: seven wooded areas near The Hague, Wassenaar and Hook of Holland which were in use for storing rockets preparatory to firing, one headquarters building at The Hague, one supply depot – the Leiden goods station – one liquid oxygen depot – the Staats Spoor station at The Hague – and the billets and vehicle park at the Hotel Promenade at The Hague. The list was supplemented during the next two months as intelligence indicated fresh targets; and by the middle of February there were seventeen targets between the Hook of Holland – The Hague – Leiden which were judged to be connected with rockets and whose attack had been approved. The main consideration in clearing a target for attack, when its connection with the German organisation had been established, was the danger to Dutch civilians. Very great care had to be taken in briefing pilots, selecting aiming points and planning the method and direction of attacks in order to minimise possible civilian casualties.

During November 1944, there had seemed to be a possibility of carrying out attacks on particular launching sites at times when rockets were about to be fired. It was hoped to make use of the wireless traffic between the headquarters and sub-formations of the German rocket batteries, which was being intercepted by 'Y' units in Belgium, to obtain warning of attacks by individual launching sites. A study of the intercepts up to the end of November indicated that a warning of about an hour would usually be obtained, which was sufficient for aircraft either of Fighter Command or 2nd Tactical Air Force to be over the site at the time of firing. Further study showed, however, that there would be little or no indication of which of the sites within a battery would be firing; and while the wireless traffic proved a valuable source of information on changes in the dispositions of the German firing troops it was never used as a basis for operations against particular sites.

During the weeks 17th December – 16th January, Fighter Command only operated on fifteen days and a high proportion of the sorties that were flown had to be abandoned, in which case bombs were either jettisoned in the sea or brought back to England. Altogether, 258 fighter-bombers were despatched of which 92 were unable to find their targets. In addition, 68 armed reconnaissances were flown in which machine-gun and cannon attacks were made on rocket storage areas and rail and road transport near The Hague. A small number of bombing attacks, four in all, were made at squadron strength (twelve aircraft); but the normal strength both for bombing attacks and armed reconnaissances was four aircraft. There was also the attack by three squadrons on the Marlot flats which were in use as headquarters.

With the exception of the latter attack and four attacks upon the Hotel Promenade at The Hague, all bombing was against storage areas. The Haagsche Bosch, where enemy activity was believed to be heaviest and where rockets were actually photographed from the air during December as they lay in side roads cut through the trees, was attacked on five occasions. Four attacks were made on two more storage areas at The Hague – Voorde and Huis le Verve; three areas at Wassenaar, north-east of The Hague, received nine attacks. Altogether, just under fifty tons of bombs were dropped during the period, mostly consisting of 250 lb. bombs.

It was very difficult for the fighter bomber pilots to assess results at the time of attack. The Hague area was heavily defended,[107] and while losses due to enemy fire during the month amounted to only one

Spitfire it was highly dangerous for pilots to come below 3,000 feet either to bomb or to observe results. Nor, since most of the bombs were dropped in wooded country, was photographic reconnaissance after an attack really fruitful. What appeared undeniable, however, was that the effort against launching areas ought to be as sustained at least throughout the hours of daylight, and, if possible, by night also. Night sorties, as we have seen, were not possible at this time owing to the commitments of Fighter Command in support of Bomber Command's attacks against Germany. Moreover, a sustained effort by day during the winter months meant that a large number of sorties against specific objectives would be failures owing to bad weather.

The scale of attack during the second half of January remained low. Only nine bombing attacks were carried out, all of them against rocket storage areas. A tenth attack was attempted but had to be abandoned owing to cloud. Armed reconnaissances fared no better; seven were attempted but only two were carried out. The weather was particularly bad towards the end of the month and no operations were carried out during the last week. The most notable attack on a suspected rocket target during this period was in fact not the work of Fighter Command but of 2nd Tactical Air Force which, on 22nd January, sent four squadrons of Spitfire fighter-bombers to attack a liquid oxygen factory at Alblasserdam. The target was destroyed. 2nd Tactical Air Force was more active at this time against communications east of The Hague than it had been at any time since the middle of December 1944.

However, the first half of February 1945 saw these attacks, and those of Fighter Command, increase in response to a decision of the War Cabinet on 27th January that Fighter Command should intensify its attacks on The Hague area and that 2nd Tactical Air Force should supplement the attacks on communications which Fighter Command was already planning. Two more Fighter Command squadrons – Nos. 603 and 124 – began to participate in the offensive and a list of secondary targets, more suitable for attack in bad weather than the targets near The Hague, was prepared. These were stretches of railroad and railway junctions in the rear of The Hague, in the area Gouda – Utrecht – Amersfoot: the junction at the latter place was particularly important.

The results were apparent from 3rd February which was the first clear day for nearly a fortnight. In the succeeding fortnight, 3rd – 16th February, thirty-eight attacks, involving 286 sorties, were attempted against targets near The Hague, compared to sixteen attacks and 74 sorties in the previous fortnight. With the exception of three armed reconnaissances all were bombing sorties; forty could not be carried out, some through mechanical troubles but most because of bad weather.

Altogether, thirty-one bombing attacks were carried out, mostly against rocket storage areas. The Haagsche Bosch was attacked on seven occasions, the Staalduinsche Bosch, near the Hook of Holland, on five, and Ruist en Vreugd at Wassenaar on three; four more attacks were carried out on storage areas at The Hague and Wassenaar, and the Hotel Promenade at The Hague was attacked three times. In accordance with the new policy four attacks were made on secondary railway targets.

But the target against which the greatest effort was made was of a type which had not previously been attacked by Fighter Command – a suspected liquid oxygen plant in a former tramway depot at Loosduinen, south-west of The Hague. As a result of the close study of the possible sources of liquid oxygen supply that had been made in 1944 it had appeared that no major offensive against likely plants was possible, but in December Fighter Command had been asked to consider the attack of three factories in Holland which held promise as targets. One of these – Alblasserdam – was attacked by 2nd Tactical Air Force on 22nd January, with great success. Another, at Ijmuiden, consisted of two buildings in the middle of a large factory area and precision attacks upon it would have been exceptionally difficult. The third possibility – Loosduinen – was a difficult target so long as care was taken to avoid Dutch casualties, as there was civilian property on three sides of the factory. It was, therefore, with some reluctance that Fighter Command undertook its attack especially as there was no reliable evidence that even complete success would affect rocket supplies, the Intelligence officers at Fighter Command believed that all the oxygen that was required for the existing scale of rocket attack could be transported from Germany.

Two attacks were made upon Loosduinen on 3rd February, one on the 8th and two on the 9th. In all but one attack the bombing runs were made over the one side of the factory that was free of housing; and the technique of the pilots has been well described as 'trickling their bombs towards the target'. For this reason, five attacks had to be made. Altogether, seventy-eight fighter-bombers, carrying nearly thirty tons of bombs, attempted to attack the factory but only about one-third of their bombs fell in the target area. However, with the last attack the factory was sufficiently badly damaged to be ignored in the future.

In attacks on other targets fifty tons of bombs were dropped, chiefly on the two storage areas most used by the Germans, the Haagsche Bosch and the Staalduinsche Bosch, at which over thirty tons were aimed. The accuracy of bombing was high: only seven tons of bombs were estimated to have fallen outside the two areas. Moreover, 500 lb.

bombs were frequently dropped, whereas previously loads had consisted almost exclusively of 250 lb. bombs. The change had been made possible by an arrangement with 2nd Tactical Air Force that Fighter Command aircraft could land to refuel and rearm at an airfield at Ursel, near Ghent.

But what damage had been done was hard to estimate. Occasionally, heavy explosions in the woods indicated that rockets had been detonated; and it was known that even slightly damaged rockets had to be returned to Germany for repair before they could be fired. What was the number of these, however, was not known. It was, in fact, rather from the indirect evidence of changes in the scale and character of attacks on London than from direct evidence of damage in and near The Hague that the effect of the offensive could best be assessed.

With the exception of the fighter-bomber attack on Alblasserdam and two unsuccessful attempts by medium bombers to deny communications across the Ijssel at Zwolle and Deventer the efforts of 2nd Tactical Air Force over the period 17th January – 16th February took their usual form of attacks on communications south of the Zuider Zee. Over three thousand sorties were flown and impressive numbers of barges, railway locomotives and rolling stock, and motor vehicles were destroyed, and railway lines were cut at no less than 139 points. But as in the case of the operations of Fighter Command the precise effects of this upon the enemy's position in Holland could not be estimated, nor upon his rocket organisation in particular. Again, it was in the attacks upon England that any evidences of success would be apparent.

## 58. Rocket Attacks, 17th December 1944 – 16th February 1945.
### a. Enemy Activity.
During the last fortnight of December 1944, the scale of rocket attack on London remained low. Only 57 rockets were reported compared to 80 during the first half of the month and 86 in the second half of November. The majority of rockets continued to be fired at night, only fourteen incidents occurring during daylight. This alone meant some relief for London as casualties from rockets falling at night tended to be less than in daytime incidents. The accuracy of the German fire also remained poor: only fifteen rockets fell within the London Civil Defence Region. Casualties were, in fact, slightly higher than during the first half of the month – 176 killed and 352 seriously injured compared to 128 and 310 – chiefly because of two serious incidents in Islington and one in Chelmsford in which 124 people were killed and 168 injured. They were, however, less than half of those of the last fortnight in November when the firing troops at The Hague had been operating undisturbed.

On the Continent, in contrast, the scale of rocket attack increased, especially during the last week of December when the Ardennes battle was at its height. Altogether, 217 rockets were reported, all fired at Antwerp, compared to 143 in the first half of the month, a small number of which had been fired at Brussels and Liège.

The comparative lull in the attack of London was soon broken. Beginning with the first week in January 1945, the number of rockets reported weekly in the United Kingdom jumped from an average of 34 for December to 59. There was no decline during the rest of the month when 167 incidents were reported, making a total for the month of 226, compared to 137 for December. On 26th January there were seventeen incidents, thirteen of them in the London area, the highest so far recorded in one day. The first half of February saw still heavier attacks. Up to and including the 16th, 145 rockets were reported; and again, on one day, the 13th, there were seventeen incidents, eleven in the London area. With this increase in fire there was, for most of the period, an improvement in accuracy. During December 1944, only one-third of reported incidents were in the London area. During January 1945, the proportion rose to exactly a half; and this was maintained during the first few days of February. Then, however, during the week 10th – 16th February, which saw the heaviest weeks' activity since the rocket attacks had begun, only a little over one-third of the incidents were in the London area.

Where the total number of incidents was comparatively small no great significance was attached to these variations in accuracy. What was undoubtedly significant, however, was the change in the distribution of the German fire between day and night. Whereas in December only one-third of the incidents in the United Kingdom had occurred during daytime, in January nearly sixty per cent were in daytime, and a similar percentage in the first half of February. It appeared, therefore, that despite the greater activity of Fighter Command over The Hague area the Germans were not restricted to the hours of night for firing so much as they had been when the fighter-bomber offensive opened.

With the improvement in accuracy, the higher rate of fire and the increase in daylight attacks, casualties during this period sharply increased compared to December. Between 1st January and 16th February[108] 755 people were killed and 2,264 seriously injured by rockets, a weekly casualty role twice as high as that of December. There were thirteen incidents, mostly in east and north-east districts of London, in each of which more than twenty people were killed.

The greater weight and effect of the attack during these first weeks of 1945 must be placed against the background of the counter-offensive.

During January the Operational Research Section at Fighter Command Headquarters carefully collated the scale of rocket attack and of the fighter-bomber offensive against The Hague. A simple balancing of the two sets of data was hardly sufficient evidence to support any positive conclusions about the effect of the offensive. It did appear, however, that it was only in the period 4th – 15th December, when Fighter Command had been able to make sustained attacks on The Hague, that the weight of German fire had been affected. Moreover, during that period the accuracy of fire by day had been considerably, and by night slightly, affected; though on the whole it seemed that neither sporadic nor sustained attacks by day had much effect on the enemy's scale of effort or accuracy by night. What was needed was a sustained effort both by day and night, and a recommendation to this effect had been made by the Chief Intelligence Officer of Fighter Command on 22nd January, 1945.

The shortage of suitable night fighters made it impossible to conduct a continuous counter-offensive, but, as we have seen, from the beginning of February the weight of attack by day against The Hague area was notably increased. Even so, the scale of rocket attack remained higher than at any time previously. This was not to say that the counter-offensive was failing. At the least it might be saving London from still heavier bombardment; for even though assessment of the results achieved was not easy it was beyond doubt that damage was being caused to targets in The Hague area that were known for certain to be connected with rocket attacks. However, it was not certain which targets or what type of targets were most precious to the enemy; and on 15th February 1945 the Chief Intelligence Officer at Fighter Command recommended a new target policy which entailed concentrating for a week on one of three main targets – Haagsche Bosch, the woods near Ockenburg, and Staalduinsche Bosch – rather than spreading the effort of the Command over a dozen targets. The recommendation was accepted and the new policy was applied from 20th February. Its results will be considered at a later stage.

*b. Defensive Reactions.*
In the more clearly defensive aspects of counter-measures there were some notable developments between the middle of December and the middle of February. By this time the radar stations in the United Kingdom, through No. 105 Mobile Air Reporting Unit at Malines, were detecting a large number of rockets sufficiently early for warnings to have been sounded in the London region. If a warning of fifty to sixty seconds had been acceptable to the Civil Defence authorities the existing

system would have sufficed. But something better would be required if ever the scale of attack became such that public warnings were essential, and at a meeting on 15th January, Sir Robert Watson-Watt's Interdepartmental Radio Committee was asked to investigate what would be required to permit warnings of up to four minutes. In the meantime, no public warnings were sounded in London.

However, on 2nd January, the War Cabinet decided to put into operation the scheme for issuing special warnings to the London Passenger Transport Board so that the floodgates of the 'tube' railways could be closed. Warnings began to be given on the afternoon of 8th January. During the ensuing months 201 warnings were passed, of which only nine were false; and only four rockets fell in the London region without warning.

The reliability of the warning system also came under review in connection with a project of Anti-Aircraft Command to attempt the destruction of rockets by gun fire. The question was first raised outside Anti-Aircraft Command at a meeting at Fighter Command Headquarters on 19th December, where General Pile indicated the possibilities of predicting the passage of rockets through a pre-defined area which would be covered by anti-aircraft fire and the rockets thus exploded in mid-air. Its success depended on the accuracy of the prediction of the trajectory of the rocket and on the efficiency of the G.L. radar sets which would be employed for the purpose. G.L. sets had improved in performance during the latter half of 1944, but for the purpose in mind it was essential that they should receive a preliminary warning from the C.H. stations of the R.A.F. Close co-ordination of the two types of radar was therefore necessary to give this longer warning and also ensure that virtually all rockets were observed.

A report on the subject was given to the War Cabinet 'Crossbow' Sub-Committee on 15th January 1945, by Sir Robert Watson-Watt. He held that the requirement of comprehensive warning, this being taken as 80 per cent of all rockets, could be met but that at present warnings of only 60 to 75 seconds could be given on those rockets that would fall in London, which left only fifteen seconds for computing where the rocket would fall. Re-siting certain stations might lengthen the time for computation, but this would give rise to certain practical difficulties and increase the danger of jamming by the enemy.

On the chances of a successful engagement there were varied opinions. Professor C.D. Ellis put them at 1 in 100 in theory: Sir Robert Watson-Watt thought them 1 in 1,000. Consequently, until more effective results could reasonably be claimed the Sub-Committee agreed that it would be premature to ask the permission of the War Cabinet for the necessary firing trials. Anti-Aircraft Command were asked to continue their investigation of the scheme and Sir Robert Watson-Watt's committee were invited to examine means for improving existing methods of predicting the course of rockets. The proposition was to be examined again in March.

Radio warfare was the sphere of another important development in defensive measures. It will be recalled that a good deal of care had been taken to build up an organisation for interfering with the radio control which it was expected would be applied to the rocket; and listening for radio signals and jamming them both from ground and air had been amongst the first counter-measures to be applied. By the middle of December 1944, however, there had been no evidence that any rockets fired against either the United Kingdom or the Continent contained radio control equipment. In consequence, existing and proposed radio counter-measures were largely abolished. All listening and jamming stations in the United Kingdom were taken off the rocket watch and the transmitters on the Continent were transferred to operations in support of the bomber offensive, though they were earmarked for a speedy return to rocket work if required. Similarly, aircraft of No. 100 Group, R.A.F., which had been employed in rocket counter-measures, were released for bomber support, but they were so maintained that their reconversion would take only a short time. As a further precaution, a small listening watch was maintained in Belgium.

## 59. The Last Air-Launched Flying Bomb Attacks, 25th November 1944 – 14th January 1945.

*a. Enemy Activity: Attack of Manchester.*
Air-launched flying bomb attacks on London were last considered at a stage when a second German unit had begun to take part in the offensive. The week following its appearance the scale of attack was heavier than in any previous week; but then, in the last two weeks of the period, 11th – 25th November, there had been a sharp decline in the German effort. After the last attack of this period activity ceased for more than a week, probably because of the full moon, and it was not until the night of 4th December that launchings again took place. These were the work of the third G.A.F. unit which Air Intelligence had previously identified as under training. The strengths of these three Grüppen, which together formed K.G.53, was about one hundred aircraft, which should have meant a maximum strength for sustained operations of between sixty and seventy aircraft, each of which could launch one flying bomb. In fact, nothing like that number of bombs was regularly launched. In the week 4th – 11th December, attacks were made

on four nights and only 37 flying bombs were reported.[109] The following week saw one night of heavier activity than usual: this was 17th/18th December when 29 bombs were reported. Otherwise there was activity on only two nights, and the total number of bombs reported during the week was 45. Thereafter, with an exception to be noted shortly, the Germans operated on only four nights – 3rd/4th, 5th/6th, 12th/13th and 13th/14th January. On the night of the 12th, 28 bombs were reported; on the rest only 23 all told. And with the attack of the 13th/14th the last air-launched flying bomb landed in the United Kingdom.[110] That this form of attack had come to an end was not, of course, appreciated at the time. A close watch was kept on Schleswig and north-west Germany from which the German units had been operating; and after a month had elapsed without further attacks being made Air Intelligence reported that while bad weather, unserviceable airfields and a full moon could account for the inactivity of the first week of the month some general limitation, probably of aircraft fuel, had brought about the continued inactivity. Certainly, it seemed hardly likely that a shortage of flying bombs had brought air-launchings to an end, for firings against Continental targets continued on a large scale – during the period 25th November 1944 – 15th January 1945, 1,654 flying bombs were reported. Moreover, there was good intelligence evidence that the enemy held large stocks of bombs. Nor was there any evidence that the aircraft and aircrew losses of K.G.53 had not been replaced.

But before K.G.53 ceased operations it had mounted an attack which, while it caused little material damage, sharply displayed the potential threat from air-launched bombs if the Germans had possessed all the resources for a sustained offensive. The attack took place in the early morning of 24th December and was directed at Manchester. Thirty bombs were reported by the defences and from this, and from intercepted wireless traffic, it appeared that probably about fifty He.111s, nearly the maximum operational strength of K.G.53, took part in the attack. All the bombs reported came overland, and while a number came down over thirty miles from Manchester and only one fell within the city boundary the attack was quite as accurate as any that had been launched against London: six bombs came down within ten miles of the centre of Manchester and eleven within fifteen miles. The casualties were 37 killed and 67 seriously injured. The attack was launched from off the Yorkshire and Lincolnshire coasts between Skegness and Bridlington; the first bomb fell at 0521 hours, the last at 0625 hours. The position of launching and the direction of attack outflanked the guns deployed on the East Anglian coast; and although seven bombs passed over the Humber Gun Defended Area and were engaged, none were shot down. No launching aircraft or bombs were intercepted by fighters.

*b. Defensive Reactions.*

The Germans undoubtedly sprung a surprise. There had been no prior intelligence that the attack would be launched and there were no defences in the North of England suitably placed to intercept it. Nevertheless, the attack was not unexpected. As early as the previous October, when Air Intelligence had reported that additional units of the G.A.F. were training to launch flying bombs, Anti-Aircraft Command had begun to prepare detailed plans for a rapid deployment along the coast north of the Wash, and No. 5 Group of Anti-Aircraft Command had carried out preliminary reconnaissances for the selection of suitable gun sites. On 2nd November, No. 5 Group was ordered to reconnoitre the coast between Skegness and Whitby and by the 19th a plan of deployment had been completed. It provided for what was termed a Gun Fringe between Skegness and Whitby which would be manned by 59½ batteries of guns. No moves had been ordered, however, before the attack on Christmas Eve.[111]

But all this preliminary work proved useful when on the same day as the Manchester attack, and following it, Air Marshal Hill ordered the immediate deployment of sixty heavy anti-aircraft guns between Skegness and Filey. Two days later four troops of light guns were ordered to move to sites in the Gun Fringe and four troops of searchlights were deployed to provide navigational aids to night fighters and bombers flying over the Fringe. Similar rules for the engagement of targets applied in the Gun Strip and Box further south, were introduced. On 11th January a full scheme for the Fringe, involving 212 heavy guns, was approved by the Chiefs of Staff. Schemes were also prepared, but never carried out, for coastal gun zones for the defence of the areas Tyne – Tees and Forth – Clyde. By the end of January 1945, there were 88 heavy and 16 light guns deployed in the Fringe which extended from Skegness as far north as Flamborough Head. Heavy guns were steadily added until the Fringe reached its greatest strength during the first week in March when 152 heavy and 16 light guns were ready for action.

The majority of these guns was found by redeploying guns available in No.5 Group and few calls were made upon the batteries on the East Anglian coast. There, throughout the attacks on London of December and January, the strength of the defences remained much the same. At the beginning of the period, 25th November, there were 346 heavy guns and eight light in the Gun Strip and 138 heavy and 36 light in the Gun

Box. At the end, 14th January, the position was unaltered except that the Gun Strip was stronger by twenty heavy guns.

And it was these guns that were the principal defence against the German attacks on London. Of the 138 flying bombs that were reported as being launched against London during this period 83 were shot down by anti-aircraft fire. Naval gunners shot down three and fighters eight. Over five hundred patrols were flown on patrols inland, over the sea and on intruder work by Fighter Command. Three He.111s were claimed as destroyed and one damaged by Mosquitos over the North Sea and one He.111 was believed to have been destroyed and one unidentified aircraft damaged on 5th/6th January by intruding Mosquitos over airfields in north-west Germany used by K.G.53.

Altogether, 79 flying bombs, excluding the Manchester attack, came overland during this period, but only fifteen of them managed to reach London and explode there. Outside London only one person was killed and six seriously injured. In London the casualties were 61 killed and 151 injured; four incidents accounted for 48 killed and 105 injured. Thus, approximately three bombs were being launched against London for the death of one Londoner: not, by any token, an adequate return for the effort employed.

**60. Heavier Attacks Against The Hague, 17th February – 16th March.** Bad weather during the third week in February coincided with the change in the target policy of Fighter Command whereby bombing was to be concentrated on a small number of targets; and it was not until 21st February that the Haagsche Bosch came under heavy attack. Ten attacks had been attempted on the previous two days, nine against the Haagsche Bosch and one against the Hotel Promenade; but only two were carried out. In one case the primary target could not be bombed and instead attacks were made on road and rail transport in North Holland along the line of communication between the causeway over the Zuider Zee and The Hague area. In the other, six Spitfires of No. 124 Squadron successfully dropped their bombs in the Haagsche Bosch in a typical attack in which the pilots dived down from 11,000 to 5,000 feet before bombing.

Late on the 20th the weather began to clear and the next two days were fine. Fighter Command made the most of them. Twenty-two bombing attacks were carried out on the 21st, and seventeen on the 22nd; only five attacks were against areas other than the Haagsche Bosch. The total number of sorties flown on the two days was 214 and forty tons of bombs were dropped. Only one aircraft was lost.

Bombs were dropped in all parts of the forest, which was nearly two miles long and half a mile wide at its widest point, but particular attention was paid to the north-west corner, where a group of buildings known as the Filmstad was in use as a storage depot. It was first attacked on the morning of the 22nd by twelve Spitfires of No. 453 Squadron. Most of the bombs hit the target and very heavy explosions were caused; and when No. 602 Squadron attacked shortly afterwards the pilots were assisted by a column of smoke rising from the buildings. Their bombing was also accurate. The buildings continued to burn throughout the day and photographs taken later from a Mustang of No. 26 Squadron showed that about eighty per cent of them had been destroyed.

The following day, the 23rd, the weather was bad and only one sortie, on which no bombing was possible owing to cloud, was flown. It was very gratifying, however, after the effort that the Command had made on the previous two days, to observe a marked decline in the scale of German attack. From 17th – 23rd February the attack of London had continued on just as heavy a scale as in the first two weeks of the month: 71 rockets were reported in the United Kingdom of which 31 fell in the London region. But then, between dusk on the 23rd and the morning of the 26th, only one rocket fell in the United Kingdom – on the morning of the 24th. Photographic reconnaissance on that day showed that, for the first time since December, when photographs first revealed rockets in the Haagsche Bosch, there were no rockets to be seen in it. The same photographs showed four rockets in the Duindigt area contingent to the Haagsche Bosch to the north, where there was a racecourse from which rockets were known to have been fired. When firing was resumed on 26th February, after a 62-hour lull, radar evidence indicated that the rockets had come from this area; while on the same day a photograph taken from a Mustang of No. 26 Squadron showed a rocket in position for launching in the woods east of the racecourse. It seemed a fair enough inference, therefore, that storage facilities in the Haagsche Bosch had been so badly damaged that they had been vacated at least temporarily and that while new arrangements were being made launchings had had to cease.

It was some days before this evidence had been sufficiently studied for a new target policy to be formulated. Meanwhile, the main target remained the Haagsche Bosch, particularly the northern part near the racecourse. From 24th – 28th February, 88 attacks were attempted, involving four hundred sorties, all with the Haagsche Bosch as the primary target. The weather was cloudy and twelve operations had to be abandoned. Twenty-eight others were made against secondary railway targets, widely dispersed over the communications system between Gouda, east of The Hague and Alkmeer in North Holland. Three attacks were made on the Ockenburg storage area at The Hague and one on Ruist en Vreugd at Wassenaar, north-east of The Hague. Four attacks on the Haagsche Bosch and Ockenburg were made with cannon and machine-gun fire. The rest, forty in all, were against the Haagsche Bosch. In many of these attacks, after bombing the primary target, our squadrons carried out low-level reconnaissances over western Holland, attacking road and rail transport. The most successful was by No. 602 Squadron, who, on the 25th, destroyed a large number of vehicles in an M.T. park north-west of Rotterdam. The total weight of bombs dropped in all these operations was seventy tons, of which forty were dropped on the Haagsche Bosch and twenty-five on railways. Bombs of 250 lbs. were exclusively employed.

On 28th February, the Chief Intelligence Officer at Fighter Command recommended certain alterations to targets. He did not suggest that the Haagsche Bosch should be removed from the list of targets, although there was still no sign that rockets were being stored there. The aiming points for attack, however, were so selected that the northern portion of the area, including part of Duindigt, would be covered. There was photographic evidence available by this time that a limited number of rockets – up to six, compared with twenty to thirty that had sometimes been seen in the Haagsche Bosch – was being stored under camouflage netting in Duindigt. This area was to be one target. A second was to be the rest of Duindigt, and a third was to be the storage and maintenance area of Ruist en Vreugd. Fifty per cent of the effort of Fighter Command was to be devoted to the first, thirty per cent to the second, and twenty to the third. In the event of bad weather railway targets were to be attacked rather than other storage areas. This policy was approved and all concerned were informed on 1st March 1945.

It was recognised by the Intelligence Section at Fighter Command that there was an element of doubt about the Haagsche Bosch target; and strenuous efforts were made to identify another storage depot which might have taken the very important place which the Haagsche Bosch had hitherto occupied in the German organisation. For even if the Germans had completely evacuated the Haagsche Bosch, which was not absolutely certain, they had found other means for maintaining the scale of attack on London – in the week following the resumption of firing, 26th February – 5th March, 70 rockets were reported in the United Kingdom, 33 of them in London, compared to 71 and 32 in the week before the lull. But until new storage areas were found it was considered worthwhile to maintain the attack on the Haagsche Bosch.

It had certainly proved very useful to the Germans in the past and it might be possible to damage its facilities to such an extent that it could not be brought into use again. The northern portion of the area, where there was a network of roads and also a bridge across a wide and deep anti-tank bridge between the forest and Duindigt, in particular offered good opportunities for denying it to the Germans.[112]

Consequently, on the first two days of March attacks continued to be made almost exclusively against the Haagsche Bosch. Thirty-four attacks were attempted, of which eight could not be made because of the weather; twenty-three were carried out against the Haagsche Bosch and three against other storage areas, including Ruist en Vreugd. On the 3rd, half the twenty-eight attacks that were made were aimed at the Haagsche Bosch, the rest at Ruist en Vreugd and Staalduinsche Bosch, the latter being the storage area for rockets fired from the neighbourhood of the Hook of Holland.

But the 3rd was most remarkable for one of the rare interventions of 2nd Tactical Air Force directly against a rocket target. Arrangements had been made during February that this force should attack the Haagsche Bosch with medium bombers when it had the aircraft to spare; and between 0900 and 0920 hours two wings, Nos. 137 and 139, of Mitchells and Bostons bombed the area.

There was much to be said for such an attack. A much heavier weight of bombs could be dropped simultaneously than by fighter-bombers: heavier bombs could be used and the area deeply and extensively cratered. Altogether, fifty-six aircraft were employed and sixty-nine tons of bombs were dropped. Unfortunately, the bombing was very inaccurate. As far as could be judged the nearest bombs to either of the two aiming points were some five hundred yards away, and the biggest concentration of bombs was over a mile away in a densely populated area. Severe damage to Dutch property and heavy civilian casualties were reported and a strong protest was lodged by the Netherlands Embassy in London. The cause of the accident appeared to be the application of an incorrect allowance for wind which resulted in abnormal bombing errors. Instructions were given by A.O.C.-in-C., 2nd Tactical Air Force that no further attacks by medium bombers were to be made against The Hague.

Nor was the Haagsche Bosch again attacked by Fighter Command. All the intelligence at this stage pointed to Duindigt as the only profitable target, although it was also clear that extensive storage facilities did not exist there. There was some evidence that Staalduinsche Bosch, Ruist en Vreugd and Ockenburg were being used, but not extensively. A target of a different character that was also selected early in March was the headquarters of the Bataafsche Petroleum Company which was believed to be in use as billets and offices by the firing troops in The Hague area. One attack was made upon it on 4th March, by four Spitfires of No. 602 Squadron. It was a difficult target – there was much property on two sides of it – and no bombs hit the building. More successful attacks were to be made later. Otherwise, from the 4th to the 8th of the month the efforts of the Command was devoted to the three storage and firing areas mentioned above, with secondary railway targets being attacked when the weather was poor. Altogether, forty-seven operations were flown, twenty against Ruist en Vreugd, twelve against Duindigt, and the rest against Ockenburg and the Staalduinsche Bosch. Weather, as had been only to often the case during the last four months, seriously interfered. None of the operations on the 6th, 7th and 8th could be pressed home and sixteen of those attempted on the 4th and 5th had to be abandoned. On eight occasions the primary target was obscured by cloud and the railway system in the triangle Hague – Rotterdam – Utrecht was attacked instead.

On 8th March, in the light of the latest intelligence, a new list of priorities was issued by Fighter Command. The first target was to be Duindigt, which remained the only area on which satisfactory information was available; the second was a wood at Ravelijn, a mile to the north of the racecourse at Duindigt, where recent photographic reconnaissance had revealed a small number of rockets; the third was the Bataafsche Petroleum Company's building in The Hague. These were the only targets selected; the railway system east of The Hague was to provide secondary targets. Seventy per cent of the effort of Fighter Command was to be devoted to Duindigt and the rest to Ravelijn. The third target, the Bataafsche Petroleum Company, was to be the object of a single attack, if possible, by a full squadron, which would see its destruction. In fact, it was not attacked until the latter half of March, by which time the target policy of Fighter Command had again been altered; and from 9th – 16th March inclusive, with the exception of three attacks on Ruist en Vreugd on the first day of the period, all attacks were against Duindigt, Ravelijn and railway communications.

A considerable effort was brought to bear during the week, many aircraft landing at Ursel, near Ghent, after a first attack, re-arming and refuelling there, and carrying out a second attack before returning direct to England.

Altogether, 108 bombing attacks and 26 armed reconnaissances were attempted, involving 586 sorties, and 110 were carried out, though not always against the primary target. Secondary railway targets, particularly between Gouda and Utrecht, were attacked as much as the storage area at Ravelijn, nearly twenty tons of bombs being dropped on each. Some seventy tons of bombs were dropped on the Duindigt area, and it was there that there was the most obvious return for the efforts of the Command. Much of the target area was heavily pitted with craters (it was remarked at the time that it looked as if Bomber Command not Fighter Command had been attacking it) and on several occasions heavy explosions followed bombing. To crown it all, from 13th March there was evidence, which was confirmed by photographs on 18th March, that the enemy had abandoned the area.

Throughout all this period, 16th February – 16th March, 2nd Tactical Air Force had been supporting operations on land, and apart from the ill-fated attack on the Haagsche Bosch on 3rd March their efforts had only indirectly affected the German Rocket Organisation. Nearly fifteen hundred sorties had been made against communications in Holland leading to The Hague; a railway bridge between Zwolle and Enschede had been destroyed and over fifty cuts in railway lines had been made. The usual extensive toll of railway and road transport vehicles was claimed.

## 61. Scale of Rocket Attacks, 17th February – 16th March.

During these four weeks in which so much thought and effort had been devoted to the counter-offensive against The Hague a dividend seemed to be discernible not only in the photographic evidence of the evacuation of, first, the Haagsche Bosch and, second the Duindigt area, but also in a reduction in the scale of attack on London. This was not apparent in the first week, 17th – 23rd February, when the comparatively heavy attacks of the first half of the month were maintained: 71 rockets fell in the United Kingdom that week, 31 of them in the London Civil Defence Region. But in the next week, during which a lull was forced on the Germans by the bombing of the Haagsche Bosch, the number of rockets reported in the United Kingdom fell to 57. There was something of a recovery in the week 3rd – 9th March, when 65 rockets were reported; but in the week 10th – 16th March, during which Duindigt was abandoned, there were only 50 rocket incidents, the lowest weekly total for over a month.

For the whole period just under half of the rockets reported fell in London. In the week 3rd – 9th March, the percentage rose to as high as sixty, only to be followed in the next with a fall, coincident with the fall in the scale of attack, to one of forty.

It was perhaps not insignificant that whereas in the first week of the period two-thirds of rocket incidents occurred during daylight the

185

proportion fell as the counter-offensive against The Hague continued. In the second week only forty per cent of rockets were launched in daylight, in the third thirty-seven, and in the fourth twenty-six. Moreover, the hours of heaviest activity were in the early morning before dawn, and the lightest the last hours of daylight and the earliest of night. The implication was not that the presence of Fighter Command aircraft over The Hague almost throughout the day was forcing the Germans to fire at night – this had seemed a fair enough inference in December but had been invalidated in January and February when the majority of rockets had been fired in daylight despite the fighter-bomber offensive – but the enemy's storage facilities had been so affected by the counter-offensive that rockets were having to be brought up to launching points during the night and fired as quickly as possible. In other words, no reserves of rockets were being held in the field.

The perceptible slackening in the German offensive was not accompanied by a relief in the number of casualties. The fall of rockets in London was, as before, chiefly in eastern and north-eastern districts – the point of greatest concentration during the period was in East Ham – and a number of serious incidents swelled casualty lists to figures comparable with those of previous weeks. In the four weeks preceding 14th February, 473 people had been killed and 1,415 seriously injured by rockets in the United Kingdom, of whom only 17 were killed and 107 injured outside London. In the four weeks following that date 580 were killed and 1,220 seriously injured, of whom 50 were killed and 121 injured outside London. How much depended on freedom from really serious incidents was underlined by the fact that whereas 114 rockets fell in London during the four weeks, six rockets alone killed 308 people and seriously injured 318. The heaviest casualties were caused by a rocket which fell on Smithfield Market in Farringdon Road, E.C.1, at ten past eleven on the morning of 8th March: 110 people were killed and 123 seriously injured.

No alterations were made to the warning system during the period beyond the deployment near Lowestoft of an extra G.L. MK. II radar set. Sir Robert Watson-Watt's committee continued its examination of what an effective public warning would entail but the only warnings that were given, were to London Passenger Transport Board.[113]

## 62. The Last Flying Bomb Attacks from sites in German-occupied territory, 3rd – 29th March.
*a. Intelligence Prior to the Resumption of Attacks.*
The lot of Londoners during March was made no easier by a resumption

of flying bomb attacks after an interval since 14th January. Attacks against Antwerp had continued throughout the period, all from sites on land in western Germany and, late in January, from the Rotterdam – Dordrecht area. But there has been no sign of a resumption of air-launched attacks, which were the only means of attacking the United Kingdom unless the Germans increased the range of the flying bomb beyond the 130 miles which had so far been the limit of its operations. Evidence began to accumulate in February 1945, that it was precisely this that the Germans were attempting to do. It appeared that by reducing the weight of the wing of the bomb, by using a large proportion of wood instead of steel in its construction, and perhaps also the weight of the warhead by replacing the usual steel casing with wood, the amount of fuel that could be carried, and therefore the endurance and range of the bomb, had been increased. Wreckage that was recovered in February from flying bombs that had crashed in Belgium indicated that both sorts of alteration had been embodied in production. On 25th February the Chiefs of Staff were informed by Air Intelligence that in view of these changes attacks on the United Kingdom might take place, and that, if London was to be the target, the Germans would have to construct launching sites in south-west Holland. There was so far no evidence that they had done so, but comprehensive photographic reconnaissance of the area was being flown. The Chiefs of Staff were told that assuming the trials of the modified weapon were successful, operations could be expected to start about one month later. What the scale of attack might be was doubtful. As far as was known only one regiment had been trained to fire flying bombs and at least half of it was committed to the attacks on Antwerp. However, Air Intelligence estimated that sufficient crews might be deployed to launch attacks on London on a scale of some thirty flying bombs every twenty-four hours.

On the day following this meeting of the Chiefs of Staff, photographs taken over south-west Holland showed that two launching sites, oriented on London, were being constructed, one near The Hague at Ypenburg airfield, which was no longer in use, the other in a factory district at Vlaardingen, six miles west of Rotterdam. In each case the Germans had taken great care to conceal the components of the site among adjacent buildings. Both sites, therefore, were difficult targets and no attacks were made on them for some time to come.

*b. Defensive Preparations.*
On 26th February a conference was held at Fighter Command Headquarters to consider what could be done about the new threat. It

was significant of the change that had occurred since the question of defence against flying bombs had arisen over a year before, that now without question the guns were allotted the main role. Flying bombs aimed at London from sites on land in south-west Holland could be expected to converge on the capital over the coast between the Isle of Sheppey and Orfordness. Accordingly, the basis of the plan that was made was the reinforcement of the gun defences of this area, which was already covered by the Gun Box and the southern sectors of the Gun Strip, by ninety-six heavy guns, i.e. twelve batteries. These were to be found by redeploying twelve batteries from the northerly sectors of the Gun Strip, half of which would be replaced by mixed R.A. and A.T.S. batteries then under training. Instructions for the move were given on 27th February and on the following day four of the batteries were ready for action in the Gun Box. By 4th March a further two batteries had been added to the Gun Box and three to the southern Gun Strip; and this was the extent of the reinforcement that was carried out. On that date there were 196 heavy guns and 16 light in the Gun Box and 304 heavy and 8 light in the Gun Strip.

The rules governing the fire of the guns were designed to give them almost as much freedom as they had enjoyed in the later stages of the deployment on the south-east coast in the previous August. A permanent "attack in progress" was declared by day and arrangements were made with Bomber Command whereby the Controller at No. 11 Group Filter Room could remove all height restrictions on gunfire if flying bombs were reported and if there was no large-scale friendly activity near the gun zones. The procedure came into effect on the night of 28th February. To reduce the chances of friendly aircraft being fired on flying was restricted over the quadrilateral North Foreland – Gravesend – Orfordness – Ostend.

Considerable fighter defences were planned; for the expectation of thirty flying bombs every twenty-four hours implied a scale of attack approaching half that which had caused so much destruction in the summer of 1944. Six Mustang squadrons were selected to operate by day, three between the guns and London, three to seaward of the guns, and their engines were boosted to give extra speed; No. 616 Squadron, which was equipped with Meteors, was transferred from 2nd Tactical Air Force to Fighter Command for patrol duties overland. By night, two Mosquito Squadrons were to patrol to seaward and the Tempests of No. 501 Squadron overland. To improve radar reporting, the Admiralty was asked to return the fighter-direction ship, H.M.S. *Caicos*; but this proved impossible as there were few ships of this kind to meet extensive naval requirements. For the same purpose, a direct link was laid between radar stations of 2nd Tactical Air Force in Belgium which covered the Dutch coats and No. 11 Group.

*c. The Attacks: Success of the Defences.*

The German attack began in the early morning of 3rd March. The first flying bomb to be reported[114] penetrated the defences and fell in Bermondsey at 0301 hours. Six more were reported in the next three hours, followed by a lull until the middle of the afternoon. Then, from 1430 until 2230 hours, seven bombs were plotted. Another lull ensued until shortly before 11 o'clock on the following morning, when three bombs were plotted in the next hour. There was an even longer pause before the next bombs came over, which was not until 1100 hours on 5th March. So far, therefore, the weight of attack had been nothing like that anticipated.

Of these first twenty-one flying bombs, seven penetrated to London and exploded there, and ten were shot down by anti-aircraft fire – not as high a proportion of destruction as the anti-aircraft gunners had achieved either during the later stages of the attack from sites in France or against air-launched flying bombs. But thereafter the performance of the guns exceeded even their previous best. From the evening of 5th March until the early afternoon of the 29th, when the attacks ceased, 104 flying bombs were plotted. Activity did not continue daily – there were five days, 9th – 13th March, when it ceased altogether – and on days of activity the average number of bombs was less than ten. No less than 81 bombs were shot down, 76 by Anti-Aircraft Command, four by fighters of Fighter Command, and one shared by gunners of the Royal Navy and Anti-Aircraft Command. For the whole of the attack, therefore, out of the 125 flying bombs that came close enough to the coast to be reported 91 were shot down, 86 by Anti-Aircraft Command. Only 13 bombs came down with the London Civil Defence Region. Twenty others escaped destruction but fell outside London. The total number of bombs the Germans launched is unlikely to have been less than one hundred and fifty; therefore, only some nine per cent of their effort reached the target area. Casualties in the United Kingdom were very small: 26 killed and 106 seriously injured, of whom 22 were killed and 83 injured in London. The last flying bombs to fall in London exploded at 0754 and 0755 hours on 28th March at Chislehurst and Waltham Holy Cross respectively. The last to fall anywhere in the United Kingdom was shot down by anti-aircraft fire and fell at Iwade, near Sittingbourne, Kent, at 0959 hours on 29th March. The last to approach the coast was also shot down by anti-aircraft fire off Orfordness at 1243 hours on 29th.

The scale of attack proved to be so much less than had been expected that with the exception of one Mustang squadron and the Tempests of No. 501 Squadron, defence against it was left entirely to Anti-Aircraft Command and the reporting system of radar stations and the Royal Observer Corps. The other Mustang squadrons which had been originally allocated to flying bomb defence reverted to escort duties with Bomber Command early in March and No. 616 (Meteor) Squadron returned to 2nd Tactical Air Force. Radio counter-measures against signals from the transmitters with which a proportion of flying bombs was fitted were applied throughout the attack.

Bombing counter-measures directly against the German flying bomb organisation in south-west Holland were very few; indeed, the success of the close defences of London was such that they were not urgently required. Little was known about the means of supply to the launching sites; there were certainly no storage depots comparable to those that had been established in 1944 in northern France. Vlaardingen and Ypenburg appeared to be the only launching sites that were being employed against London; though shortly after activity had ceased there was evidence that a third site near the Delftsche Canal had also been used. Both Vlaardingen and Ypenburg were attacked, the first by Typhoons of 2nd Tactical Air Force, the second by Spitfires of Fighter Command. Vlaardingen was attacked on 23rd March; one of the essential buildings was destroyed and shortly afterwards the Germans dismantled the launching ramp. Ypenburg was first attacked on 20th March by four Spitfires of No. 124 Squadron, and, later on the same day, in separate attacks, by Nos. 451, 453, 603 Squadrons and again by No. 124, twenty-four Spitfires taking part in all. As a result, in this case also, an essential component of the site was destroyed. On the 23rd two attacks were carried out by twelve Spitfires of No. 451 Squadron. The bombing was accurate; and photographs taken after the attack showed that the launching ramp had been dismantled.

This last flurry of flying bomb activity against London during March was clearly a failure. It is hard to see in it any serious military purpose, other than the testing of a modified type of flying bomb. It did not divert any Allied forces, other than a single Mustang squadron, from the offensive against Germany: such forces as were used against it were part of the air defences of Great Britain and would have continued in that role whether or not flying bomb attacks had been launched.

### 63. The Last Rocket Attacks on London, 17th – 27th March.
*a. Attack against German Railway Communications.*
The month of March 1945 saw also the end of the rocket bombardment

of London. The situation was last considered at the stage which had been reached by the middle of the month when Fighter Command had for some time been attacking the storage areas at Duindigt and Ravelijn which were the only ones for which there was any reliable evidence of employment. However, photographs taken during the second week in March strongly indicated that the Germans had been driven out of both areas. Consequently, in default of any other targets in The Hague area which could be attacked without probable hurt to civilians, an entirely new policy was decided upon, one which was to be applied until the enemy's attacks had ceased.

It took the form of concentrating upon the attack of the railways leading to The Hague, particularly upon the stretches of track between Haarlem and Leiden, Utrecht and Leiden, and The Hague – Gouda – Alphen, along which rocket supplies were known to pass. The policy was not rigidly applied. The large building of the Bataafsche Petroleum Company at The Hague remained on the list of targets; and a garage – the Kurhaus garage – at Scheveningen, where meilerwagen, the long vehicles specially constructed for carrying rockets by road, were believed to be housed, was also selected for attack. Also, Duindigt and Ravelijn received a small number of attacks between 17th and 19th March, as an insurance against resumption of activity there, and from the 24th, by which time there was evidence that firing, though not storage, had been resumed in the Duindigt district armed reconnaissances were flown daily over the area. However, during the rest of March, no other targets associated with either the storage or the firing of rockets were bombed. There was a report late in the month that a large hall at Rynsburg, near The Hague, in happier times a flower market, was being used for storage; but the evidence was not held to be sufficient to justify its attack.

The Bataafsche Petroleum Company's building was attacked on 18th March by six Spitfires of No. 602 Squadron. The attack appeared to the pilots to be very accurate. Six 500 lb. and twelve 250 lb. bombs were dropped and only one cluster missed the target. Later, photographs indicated that the damage was not as great as had been thought; though an intelligence report of 25th March stated that the German organisation occupying the building had been evacuated. A further, and heavier attack was made on 30th March by No. 603 Squadron. Twelve Spitfires took part, each refuelling and re-arming at Ursel after the first attack and bombing again on the homeward journey. Over ten tons of bombs were dropped; at least six direct hits were scored on the building and eight near misses.

The Kurhaus garage at Scheveningen was also accurately bombed in the heaviest single attack made by Fighter Command during the whole of its offensive against The Hague. This took place on 22nd March when 24 Spitfires of Nos. 603 and 453 Squadrons, each carrying one 500 lb. bomb and two 250 lb., attacked the garage section by section. The squadrons refuelled and re-armed at Ursel and attacked again just over three hours later. In all, over twenty tons of bombs were dropped. The full extent of the damage was not apparent; but a ramp leading from the roadway to the first floor of the garage collapsed under the bombing and the approaches were heavily cratered. A nearby transformer station was also hit. Intelligence officers at Fighter Command were doubtful whether the Germans had been driven out of the garage but no more attacks were made upon it.

With these exceptions the efforts of the Command were entirely directed against railways. Between 17th March and 3rd April, which was the last day on which any bombing attacks were made, a total of 1,572 sorties were flown by Fighter Command against western Holland. Nearly fourteen hundred were against railway targets; the rest, including the attacks on Ypenburg, were against specific objectives directly connected with the German firing troops. Against the latter targets some seventy tons of bombs were dropped compared to over four hundred tons on railways. The weight of bombs dropped in this period of less than three weeks was in fact higher than at any other stage of the offensive, partly because the weather was better and partly because more use was made of Ursel airfield for refuelling and re-arming, which allowed double attacks to be made and 500 lb. bombs to be carried.

The effect of the offensive was next to impossible to estimate. Many cuts were made in stretches of track – according to the interpretation of photographs no less than 220; three railway bridges and two road bridges were destroyed and fourteen more damaged. But little movement was taking place on Dutch railways at this time (it was significant that while 84 M/T vehicles were claimed as destroyed by Fighter Command during this period the score of railway vehicles was only 14) and it was hard to say whether this was because the Germans did not need or want to use them or because they could not. Certain stretches of railway remained unrepaired after being broken; others were repaired shortly after bombing.

There was, however, some evidence that the Germans were at least inconvenienced by the attacks. Since the autumn of 1944 the Intelligence officers concerned had accepted that Leiden was the only railhead for rocket supplies; and the stations there had not been attacked only because of the congestion of civilian property in the neighbourhood.[115] But on 18th March 1945 photographs taken by No. 26 Squadron of

Fighter Command revealed both at Leiden and The Hague the easily recognisable long railway wagons on which rockets were transported. Five days later a similar train was photographed in Rotterdam station, and others were seen at Amsterdam in the latter part of March. The evidence was slight enough but it bore the interpretation that the direct lines from western Germany through Amersfoort and Utrecht to Leiden were being interrupted and that other routes, and possibly railheads additional to Leiden, were being improvised.

On the basis of this intelligence the effort of Fighter Command during the last few days of March and the first three days of April was concentrated on the railways Leiden – Woerden, Hague – Gouda, Amsterdam – Hilversum and Amsterdam – Utrecht. Special attention was paid to a bridge at Elinwijk which carried the Utrecht – Woerden railway over the Merwede Canal and to a junction of tracks on the line Woerden – Brendijk. Repair work was vigorous at both places and although many hits were scored photographs taken on 2nd April, when the offensive was almost over, indicated that the lines were still serviceable.

Throughout the period 2nd Tactical Air Force was operating further to the west in support of the advance across the Rhine and also scored many hits on railway communications. Again, the damage that was caused would not make the Germans' task in bringing up rockets for firing any easier; but to what extent the rate of fire was affected by these attacks, as by those of Fighter Command, is still not known.

*b. Enemy Activity: Reactions of the Defences.*
After the abnormally low scale of attack during the week 10th-16th March when only 50 rockets had fallen in the United Kingdom there was a slight recovery, and between 17th and 23rd March 62 rockets were reported. 24th March was a day free of incident. On the 25th, 26th and 27th, 7, 9 and 2 rockets fell, the last at 1645 hours on the 27th in Kynaston Road, Orpington, making the 1115th rocket to be reported in the United Kingdom. And that was the end.

Of these 80 rockets, 34 fell in London, representing a gross accuracy similar to that of earlier weeks, and making a total of 518 rockets in the London Civil Defence Region since 8th September 1944. The tendency to fire principally at night which had been noticed towards the end of February and which was an index of the effectiveness of the counter-offensive remained very marked: only thirty-six per cent of these last rockets fell in daylight.

Casualties would have been light during the period compared to earlier weeks but for the ill-fortune which saw the last rocket but one fall on a block of workers' flats, Hughes Mansions, in Stepney. The flats were hit at 0721 hours on the 27th; 134 people were killed and 49 seriously injured. Casualties for the last fortnight totalled 308 killed and 604 seriously injured compared to 394 killed and 763 seriously injured in the previous fortnight. These brought the total casualties from rockets for the whole period of attack to 2,511 killed and 5,869 seriously injured in London and 213 killed and 598 seriously injured elsewhere.

The system for warning the London Passenger Transport Board remained in operation to the end of the attacks. Only five rockets escaped detection during these last days and warnings were transmitted in all other cases. If these had been given to the general public in London it would have meant seventy-five warnings for a total of thirty-four rockets falling in London. In other words, approximately twice as many warnings than were strictly necessary would have been sounded. This was one of the factors affecting the findings of the Inter-departmental Radio Committee on the feasibility of an effective public warning system. A warning time of some four minutes could have been obtained by reliance on existing C.H. stations but the number of warnings given to the London area for rockets that fell outside would have been over sixty per cent of all warnings sounded. A more reliable system would have needed considerable scientific and technical effort for the development of special equipment; and in the general circumstances this was held to be unwarranted.

A similar verdict was passed on the scheme of Anti-Aircraft Command for shooting at rockets which was again considered during the last week in March. On 21st March, General Pile wrote to Mr. Duncan Sandys, the chairman of the War Cabinet 'Crossbow' Sub-Committee, and asked for permission to carry out experimental firing as the time available was clearly becoming very short. He did not advance any scientific estimate of the chances of detonating rockets as there were so many imponderables;[116] but an improved G.L. radar set had recently been developed and he considered that the chances of predicting where rockets would fall were sufficiently high to justify opening fire. A meeting of the 'Crossbow' Sub-Committee was held on 26th March as a result of which a panel of scientists was set up to prepare an agreed statement on the probable chances of success. They reported the same day that on the assumption of Anti-Aircraft Command that 400 rounds would be fired against any one rocket the chances of securing a hit were at best 1 in 30. Immediately General Pile again asked for permission to fire, pointing out the possible value in the future of the experiment and stating that he would attempt to treble the number of rounds fired and thus treble the chances of a hit. The proposal came before the Chiefs of Staff on 30th March when it was decided that the chances of success were too small to justify the possible adverse effect on public morale, and permission was therefore refused.

*c. Withdrawal of the German Batteries: Cessation of Counter-Measures.*
By 3rd April it was obvious that further rocket attacks on the United Kingdom from Holland were unlikely (though it was to be late in April before there was positive evidence that the launching troops had been withdrawn); and on that day Air Marshal Hill stopped all fighter-bomber attacks against western Holland and substituted armed reconnaissance. These were maintained by sections or pairs of fighters until 25th April. Flying bomb attacks were even less likely in view of the photographic evidence that the sites at Vlaardingen and Ypenburg had been dismantled and that no new sites were being constructed.

Both flying bomb and rocket attacks against Antwerp had also come to an end at much the same time as those against London: in each case the last were fired on 28th March. The flying bomb sites in the Deventer – Hengelo area of Holland, which were the last in action against Antwerp, were destroyed in the last days of March. To complete the picture of retreat and abandonment there was good evidence that K.G.53, which had last launched flying bombs in the middle of January, had been disbanded. As for rocket-firing troops, as early as 21st March units previously attacking Antwerp had begun to withdraw to avoid being trapped by the Allied advance across the Rhine.[117] It was believed at the time that they had instructions to retire to Nordhausen in the Harz mountains where the higher headquarters of the rocket organisation had been concentrated.

April, in consequence, was a month of reduction and, finally, of standing down of all formations engaged in rocket counter-measures. On the 13th the watch for rockets was discontinued at all C.H. radar stations. On the 20th the Chiefs of Staff agreed that all flying restrictions over the flying bomb defence zones could be cancelled. They also instructed the Joint Intelligence Sub-Committee to report the possibilities of further attacks on England. On receipt of the report, which stated that there was no rick of flying bomb attack and only a very slight chance of rocket attack, they approved the discontinuance of all counter-measures.

# Appendix I

## Note by the Vice-Chief of the Imperial General Staff on German Long-Range Rocket Development.

11th April, 1943.

War Cabinet
Chiefs of Staff Committee

German Long-Range Rocket Development
Note by the Vice-Chief of the Imperial General Staff

It is felt that the Chiefs of Staff should be made aware of reports received in the War Office, since the end of 1942, of German experiments with long-range rockets. Five reports have come from several independent sources of varying reliability, and their number indicates a foundation in fact, however inaccurate their details may be.

   2. Particulars of these rockets, and an appreciation of the potentialities of such a weapon, are at Annex of which essential points are:

     (a) Each rocket might carry an amount of explosive at least equal to that carried by the German 1,000 kg. (2200 lb.) bomb.

     (b) The extreme range would seem to be about 130 miles.

     (c) Owing to the inaccuracy of the rockets at long ranges an efficient attack would necessarily be limited to an area target, such as London.

     (d) While we might hope that the preparation of the projector installations would not be successfully concealed from aerial observation, should we fail to detect and destroy them an attack could fall without any warning.

     (e) Bad weather conditions are no deterrent.

   3. Even though we have no proof or even indication of action to employ these rockets against us, so far, it is considered that the

indications are sufficient to justify taking certain actions in view of the powerful moral and surprise effect of such weapons.

In general, the main thing is to forestall any employment of this weapon, and we must therefore try to ensure, by aerial reconnaissance, that the preparation of projector installations is detected at an early stage, and that detection is followed by action to prevent these weapons being brought to a state of readiness.

4. I therefore recommend that:

(a) air photographic cover obtained of likely areas should continue to be closely examined for signs of projector installations: a plan for future cover and interpretation should be worked out carefully;

(b) all South Eastern Observer Corps and R.A. flash spotting stations be instructed to report any unusual phenomena which might be connected with rocket projectiles, since initial ranging experiments would probably have to be carried out before fire for effect;

(c) a detailed plan should be prepared by which a concentrated attack on projector installations could be delivered at short notice from the air.

(d) the Ministry of Home Security should be given warning of the possibility of this form of attack and the precautions being taken. I do not consider it desirable to inform the public at this stage, when the evidence is so tangible;

(e) the Minister of Defence should be informed.

(Intld.) A.N.
V.C.I.G.S.

War Office,
9th April, 1943.

## Annex

German Long-Range Rocket Development

1. Historical.

As far back as September 1938 unconfirmed reports were received of the development of weapons to project by electro-magnetic means projectiles of a weight from 100 to 3000 tons to a very long range,

London being specified as the eventual target. These were considered unlikely and nothing has been heard of them since the end of 1939.

By July 1940 there had been sufficient reports on the development of rockets by the Germans for the possibilities of such weapons, even though relatively short ranges were then involved, to be considered as an aid to invasion.

By the end of 1940 the German Army had in service a heavy rocket weapon, with a bomb weighing 180 lbs. and a range of just over a mile. A few months later a slightly lighter weapon with a bomb weighing 70 lbs. and a range of about 3¾ miles was in service. Variations on these two have been introduced since.

Since the beginning of this year there have been unconfirmed reports of heavy rockets with a range of 130 miles, again with England specified as the target.

2. Latest Reports.

The general trend of the reports received from various sources in the first three months of this year, although all as yet unconfirmed, suggest very strongly that the Germans have been doing considerable development work on the subject of long-range rockets. The reports mention rockets containing 5 tons of explosive, and with ranges of 130 miles. Gyroscopic and radio control have both been mentioned.

Technical opinion considers that it is possible to attain this range, but that while the weight of the complete rocket would be of the order of 9½ tons, the weight of the explosive head is unlikely to exceed 1¼ tons, containing about 1600 lbs. of explosive. Such a rocket would have a diameter of about 30 inches and a length of about 95 feet. The projector would have to be some 100 yards long, unless an extremely accurate method of directional control in flight has in fact been developed.

3. Appreciation of potentialities.

(i) While the exact form of this projectile is not known it should be recognized that the basic problem is that of projecting a large weight of H.E. a long distance. The following estimations are based on one particular possibility which has been studied in some detail by C.P.D., but the order of magnitude of the resulting figures would apply to any form the projectile may take.

(ii) The effectiveness of the explosive head of a rocket must be taken as comparable with that of a bomb, and the H.E. content of a head weighing 1¼ tons might be about 1600 lb., i.e. slightly more than that of the normal 1000 kg. bomb. The total damaging effect would, however, be greater owing to the heavier weight of the projectile and its higher terminal velocity. The effectiveness of these long-range rockets as a weapon must, therefore, depend principally on the degree of accuracy which can be achieved.

(iii) The principal advantages of long-range rockets compared, as an offensive weapon, with action by bomber aircraft are:

(a) The rocket attack cannot be the subject of an early warning as can aircraft.

(b) The rocket cannot be intercepted in flight by fighters or attacked with A.A. weapons.

(c) Bad weather conditions are no deterrent. A rocket can be used when aircraft would be grounded.

(d) There are no losses in trained personnel in the form of air crews.

(e) Heavy attack in daylight is possible.

The principal disadvantages from which the long-range rocket suffers are:

(i) The total expenditure of much labour and material in metal and propellant with each shot fired. In the case considered it would amount to a total of nearly 10 tons, including at least 4 tons of propellant, for every 2800 lb. effective weight of bomb fired.

(ii) The relative inaccuracy as compared with bomber aircraft. At 130 miles range, the mean lateral deviation is estimated to be at least 2½ miles either side of the target, very probably more, depending on the degree of accuracy in manufacture. The lateral 50% zone would probably be at least 8 miles, and the smallest profitable target for a concentrated attack would be an area of about 64 square miles.

(iii) The substantial labour involved in installing each projector, which, unless very carefully concealed, cannot be expected to remain free from attack.

Disadvantage (i) can perhaps best be illustrated by comparison of a 1000 rocket attack with a raid by 500 heavy bombers carrying an average of 2½ tons each, both attacks thus having equal H.E. effect. The total expenditure of material for such a bomb raid, in round figures will be:

| | |
|---|---|
| Bombs | 2½ x 500 = 1250 tons |
| Fuel | 1.9 x 500 = 950 |
| Aircraft | 8 x 50 = 400 tons (assume 10% loss) |
| | |
| Total | 2600 tons |

On this scale of raid some 250 – 300 aircrew personnel would also be lost (based on scale of 10% of aircraft lost).

The comparable expenditure in long-range rockets will be:
9½ x 1000 = 9500 tons

Disadvantage (iii) is brought out by considering the forms the projector could take, assuming control in flight is not provided. There seem to be three alternatives:

(i) Employment of a favourably sloping hillside, on which a path to carry the projector rails, at least 100 yards long, must be prepared.

(ii) Boring of a shaft down into the ground at a suitable angle, again laid on the target and again permitting no traverse. Preparations in this case might be effectively concealed.

(iii) Employment of a structure in the open, with a track length of 100 yards, strong enough to carry the moving load of 9½ tons and to support itself. Assuming an angle of about 45° from the ground is necessary, the height of the "muzzle" end of the structure would be about 200 feet in the air. Such an arrangement with the provision of suitable gear could be adapted to permit of traverse.

Each of the three types of installation will require a crane for the handling of the projectile, and since transport of the rocket complete, will be difficult owing to its length (95 ft.), some sort of assembly point will be required in the neighbourhood.

Conclusions.

(i) A rocket roughly equivalent in effectiveness to a 1000 kg. bomb with a range of 130 miles is technically possible, but considerations of accuracy limit employment to the attack of area targets.

(ii) The Germans have been pursuing development towards the production of weapons of this type.

(iii) In terms of material expended it is a wasteful project, but given certain conditions a heavy attack on a big target might be considered profitable.

(iv) If the preparations were not subjected to serious interference, an attack could be launched without any early warning, and there are no means of intercepting it.

(v) The only satisfactory counter-measure appears to be destruction or damage to the projectors before they can be used.

# Appendix II

Memorandum by Mr. Duncan Sandys, Joint
Parliamentary Secretary, Ministry of Supply, on the
division of responsibilities in investigations into
German long-range rockets.

Annex to C.O.S. (43) 323(O), 19th June, 1943.

Division of Responsibilities.

1. Intelligence.
   (a) Reports from Agents.
   (b) Information from prisoners of war.
   (c) Reports from the Continent on economic aspects.
Responsibility for Action:
The M.I. Branches concerned and the Ministry of Economic Warfare will
continue to supply Mr. Sandys with all available information on this
subject. Mr. Sandys will pass on such items of this information as may
be necessary to the Committees concerned with the different aspects of
the problem.

2. Photographic Interpretation.
Responsibility for Action:
The Intelligence Staff, Air Ministry D. of I. (O) will continue to inform
Mr. Sandys of any conclusions they may reach as a result of the
examination of aerial photographs relating to this problem and will
furnish him with such other advice or assistance within their sphere as
he may require.

3. Operational.
   (a) Reconnaissance Flights.

(b) Bombing attacks upon development establishments, factories or projector emplacements.
(c) Operation of R.D.F. and Signals equipment and special training of personnel.
(d) Fighter interception of enemy spotting and reconnaissance planes.

Responsibility for Action:
The Air Ministry will be responsible for the co-ordination of all these operational aspects of the problem. For this purpose, a Committee has been set up under the Chairmanship of A.C.A.S. (Ops.). The Air Ministry will receive from Mr. Sandys recommendations for action under (a), (b) and (c), which will be addressed as follows:
(a) D. of I. (O)
(b) A.C.A.S. (Ops.)
(c) D.G. of Sigs.

4. Radiolocation.
(a) Technical study of radio methods of locating the site from which the rocket has been projected.
(b) Technical study of the possibilities of diverting or jamming the rocket, if radio-controlled.
(c) Technical study of methods for communicating warning and operational data to all authorities concerned.
(d) Preparation of plans for putting into effect methods evolved under (a), (b) and (c) above.
(e) Supply and erection of any additional equipment required.
Responsibility for Action:
The Ministry of Aircraft Production in consultation with the other Departments concerned, will be responsible for the necessary technical planning and for the provision of any additional equipment required. An Inter-Departmental Committee has been set up for this purpose under the Chairmanship of Sir Robert Watson-Watt.

5. Deception, Security and Civil Defence.
(a) Preparation of plans to deceive or, failing that, to confuse the enemy as to the effect of his fire.
(b) Recommendations on policy to be adopted in regard to public warnings, security and censorship.
(c) Special Civil Defence measures.
Responsibility for Action:
These aspects of the problem will be dealt with by an Inter-

Departmental Committee of the Home Defence Executive under the Chairmanship of Sir Findlater Stewart.

6. Co-ordination.
Responsibility for Action:
Mr. Sandys will be responsible for co-ordinating action under the various heads above and for rendering periodically to the Chiefs of Staff a consolidated report setting out the progress made over the whole field and recommending any further action necessary.

# Appendix III

## Formation of a Directorate in the Air Ministry to be concerned with Intelligence and Operational Aspects of 'Crossbow'.

As the result of recommendations by the Chiefs of Staff the Minister of Defence has decided that the Air Ministry in the person of the D.C.A.S. shall centralise the work of the Joint Intelligence Committee and the operational staffs concerned with counter-measures against rockets, pilotless aircraft and glider bombs directed against the United Kingdom.

2. To assist the D.C.A.S. in this task a special directorate has been formed. The responsibilities of the Directorate are as follows:

(i)   to co-ordinate within the Air Ministry all intelligence work with all work connected with evolving and putting into effect counter-measures to meet the enemy's employment of rockets, pilotless aircraft and glider bombs directed against this country.

(ii)  as affecting the defence of this country, and in conjunction with the Intelligence staff and appropriate technical and scientific experts to study the development of rockets, pilotless aircraft and glider bombs.

(iii) as affecting the defence of this country, and in conjunction with the Intelligence staff and appropriate technical and scientific experts to study and appreciate the construction and development of projector sites suitably placed for the bombardment of targets in this country.

(iv)  to keep in closest touch with the Intelligence staff and particularly to advise on the operational requirements of air reconnaissance and other forms of intelligence.

(v)   as a result of these studies and in conjunction with the

Intelligence staff to appreciate the scale and nature of these special forms of possible bombardment of this country and the probable timings of attacks.

(vi)  to consider with the appropriate Directors and as necessary with other Departments and appropriate advisers all possible means of countering or delaying these special forms of attack.

(vii)  in conjunction with the appropriate Directors and Departments to prepare outline plans and through A.C.A.S. (Ops.) institute executive action for:

(a) offensive counter-measures by air forces.

(b) defensive measures so far as Air Ministry responsibility is concerned. This includes normal forms of air defence as well as radio counter measures.

(viii)  to review at frequent intervals the progress and results of offensive counter-measures and, in the light of these reviews, to make recommendations as to further action.

Expert scientific advice.

3. The Director is authorised to call on outside authorities for whatever expert technical and scientific advice he considers necessary. A great deal of advice on these subjects has been afforded in the past by the Ministry of Supply as well as by M.A.P. It is most desirable that the experience of these authorities should not be wasted or the useful functions which they have performed in the past be checked or abandoned. The Director should, therefore, see that the maximum value is obtained by continuing to consult them on matters appropriate either to the Intelligence aspect of the problem or on the technical and scientific aspects of counter-measures as appropriate. Where advice and assistance is required from authorities in the Ministry of Supply, application will be made to the Joint Parliamentary Secretary of the Ministry of Supply through his Military Staff Officer.

Special Duties.

4. In order to facilitate co-ordination between the Intelligence staff and the Operational staff, the Director has been appointed Chairman of the special Sub-committee of the J.I.C. established to consider all intelligence matters connected with this subject. So far as the work of this committee is concerned, the Director will report jointly to the J.I.C. and to the D.C.A.S.

5. So far as his purely Air Ministry duties are concerned, he will report to the D.C.A.S. but for the initiation of approved counter measures he

will deal with the appropriate operational directors through A.C.A.S. (Ops.). On matters of intelligence he will deal with the Directors of Intelligence (O) or (R) and A.D.I. (Science) as appropriate or if he considers necessary, directly with A.C.A.S.(I).

Composition of the Directorate.
6. The Directorate will initially consist of:
   1 Air Commodore (Director)
   1 Wing Commander (Assistant Director)
   1 Squadron Leader
   2 Flight Officers or Section Officers
   Civilian assistants.
Air Commodore Pelly, M.C. has been appointed Director, and Wing Commander Lamb is filling the appointment of Assistant Director. Action is being taken to establish the Directorate.
Location.

7. Until accommodation can be found in the Air Ministry, Whitehall, the Director is provisionally accommodated at Horseferry Road.

*D.C.A.S.*
*23rd November, 1943.*

# Appendix IV

## Possible Effects of Flying Bomb Attack on the Invasion of France.

Headquarters COSSAC,
The Secretary,
Chiefs of Staff Committee,
Offices of the War Cabinet.

20th December 1943.

Interim Report by COSSAC on the Effects of 'Crossbow' on 'Overlord'.

Object.
1. In accordance with the instructions of the Chiefs of Staff:
   (a) To consider what effect an attack by 'Crossbow' on the ports on the South Coast would be likely to have upon the launching of 'Overlord'.
   (b) If it is considered that the effects would be serious, to examine whether any steps could be taken to mount 'Overlord' from bases out of range of 'Crossbow': and, if so, by what date a decision to do so would have to be made.

Assumptions.
2. It is difficult to estimate the full effect of this form of attack in default of further intelligence, particularly on the following points:
   (a) Whether, in fact, the weapons can be directed on targets other than those which are indicated by the present information as to the alignment of their construction, i.e. on London (90%) and Bristol (10%).
   (b Whether the extreme range is limited to 140 miles.

208

(c) The limits within which lower ranges are possible.

(d) The capacity for sustained attack.

3. For the purposes of this examination, the following assumptions, based on COS (43) 760 (O), have been made:
  (a) That 100 'Crossbow' sites would be used against 'Overlord'
  (b) That 100% effort is equivalent to 2,000 tons of bombs per 24 hours sustained throughout the 24 hours.
  (c) That a warhead of 1,200 lbs. is used.
  (d) That the accuracy of the attacks would not exceed that of previous GAF bombing attacks on this country.
  (e) That the extreme range is limited to 140 miles.
  (f) That the weapons can be directed onto any area within range.
  Areas Liable to Attack.

4. It will be noted that London and Portsmouth are within the 100% strike zone, the Thames Estuary in the 90% zone, Ipswich and Felixstowe in the 70% zone, Southampton and the Solent in the 30% zone and Bristol and Plymouth in the 10% zone. This last zone includes the coast from Lymington Westwards to Plymouth inclusive.

### Part I

Effects of 'Crossbow' on Assault and Follow-up.

Effect of Attack on Launching Assault and Follow-up.
6. During the assembly period prior to embarkation, the ports between Newhaven and Plymouth will be filled to capacity with ships and craft taking part in the Assault; the heaviest concentration being in Portsmouth and Southampton where the threat would be considerable. The berthing and assembly plans for these ports will therefore require revision in order to introduce an acceptable degree of dispersion. The full implications of this will require time to investigate. The follow-up forces assemble for loading in the Thames and Bristol Channel areas and consist of Landing Ships and Craft, M.T. Ships and coasters. A fair degree of dispersion is ensured, but here again further dispersion will be necessary.

7. During the loading period the LST and LCT hards afford a considerable measure of dispersion. The marshalling areas for the embarking troops are within 5 or 10 miles of the embarkation points but are generally outside the port towns themselves. The main assembly areas for the Naval forces and craft after loading are in the vicinity of the

large ports, e.g., the Solent and Spithead in the case of Southampton; their extent ensures a fair degree of dispersion for craft.

8. It is concluded that owing to the small size of the ships and craft composing the assault forces and the degree of dispersion of the embarkation points and in the naval assembly areas, 'Crossbow' attack would not preclude the launching of the assault from the South coast. There must be, however, a risk of casualties both to embarking personnel and to craft, numbers depending on the scale, density and continuity of the attack. It is desirable therefore to investigate the possibility of launching the Assault from outside the 30% zone, i.e., West of Southampton.

Courses of Action Open.
9. Two courses of action must be considered:
   (a) To remove the threat by mounting the assault from bases out of range of 'Crossbow'.
   (b) To reduce the threat by reducing the concentration of forces in the vulnerable central sector and effecting the maximum dispersion to the less vulnerable sectors of the South Coast.
   Course (a).

10. Bases out of range of 'Crossbow' comprise those on the South Coast to the West of Plymouth, on the West Coast those North of and including the Bristol Channel ports and on the East Coast those North of Southwold.

11. It has not been possible in the time available to carry out a detailed examination of the potential bases on the East and West Coasts North of the 'Crossbow' area. Generally speaking, however, either by reason of their size or their present functions they possess small berthing and accommodation capacity. This would entail splitting the assault forces into small units with a consequent adverse affect on training, and may also encroach upon existing activities.

12. In general also the almost complete absence of hards and the difficulty of finding suitable assault training areas and beaches would have an additional serious affect on the training of the forces.

13. To launch the assault from such bases it would be necessary for the forces on the East and West Coast to sail a considerable time before D

day, certainly well before a reliable weather forecast for D day could be made, in order to allow for bad weather on the passage round Lands End and for delay due to the probability of enemy interference on the East Coast by minelaying, light surface craft and air attack. In these circumstances it would be difficult, if not impossible, to ensure the necessary accurate timing of the assault.

14. The above conditions would necessitate turning 'Overlord' into a long sea voyage operation for which a large proportion of the assault forces (in particular the LCT and support craft) is unsuited. The initial assault could therefore be only on a very reduced scale and could be undertaken only against weak opposition.

15. From the above it is concluded that 'Overlord' cannot be launched in its present form unless the assault forces finally assemble on and sail from the South Coast.
Course (b).

16. It would be possible to reduce the threat to the assault forces by reducing the concentration in the central South coast sector. Considerable dispersion could be achieved by spreading the short-range craft over the whole South coast.

17. From a preliminary examination it would appear possible to spread the forces based on Portsmouth and some of those at Southampton to the Plymouth area and ports further West where some reserve capacity exists: and those based in the Thames to the Ipswich area. This course, however, has the following implications:
    (a) The landward arrangements for assembly and loading would have to be completely re-planned. It is doubtful if the execution of the actual work could be completed in the time available.
    (b) Considerable fresh work on fuelling and maintenance arrangements in the South-West would be necessary.
    (c) More hards may be required if sites for them can be found.

18. From the above it appears doubtful if it would be practicable in the time available to revise the plan to any appreciable extent. It is therefore concluded that, in the main, the existing plan for launching the assault and follow-up must stand, but that the maximum degree of dispersion of ships and short-range crafts must take place during the period prior to loading, and the risk of casualties during embarkation and assembly be accepted.

## Part II

Effect of 'Crossbow' on the build-up and stores movement.

19. The build-up is sailed partly in naval ships and craft from the same areas as the assault and partly in MT ships and coasters from London, Southampton and the Bristol Channel ports, the centre of gravity being the Southampton – Portsmouth area. Stores shipment by coaster and stores ship is practically entirely from the same ports.

20. The considerations in paras. 7 and 8 apply to the sailing of naval ships and craft from the South Coast as in the case of the assault forces. Any movement to the Westward would result in a longer turn-round and consequent slowing of the build-up.

21. The loading of the MT and Stores shipping depends on adequate civil dock labour. It is considered that it might be just possible to maintain the build-up and stores shipment through London and Southampton for 'Overlord' in conditions similar to the raids of 1940/41. If, however, 'Crossbow' results in a 24-hour bombardment sustained over a number of days, the difficulty of housing, feeding and transporting dock labour to their work and the interruption of essential services and communications, would probably make it impossible to maintain the full scale of build-up and stores shipment through these ports.

22. It is therefore necessary to examine whether it would be practicable to handle the MT and Stores shipping without the use of the ports of London and Southampton.

23. To do this will involve the increased use of the Bristol Channel and possibly the use of the Mersey. A detailed examination will be necessary to determine whether it is practicable. It can however be said at once that the diversion of this proportion of the MT shipping to Western ports would have to following repercussions:
   (a) It would either necessitate the provision of considerable extra shipping or would result in a decrease in the rate of build-up.
   (b) It would involve considerable changes in the plans for the concentration of Army formations and their movement to ports of embarkation.
   (c) It would involve new arrangements for the staging and assembly of troops and probably additional constructional work.
   (d) It would raise complications in the assembly and control of

convoys and probably also in the arrangements for the sea and air escorts.

24. It is recommended that a detailed examination be made immediately.

## Part III

Summary of Conclusions.

25. (a) That it is not possible to launch 'Overlord' in its present form unless the forces assemble on, and sail from, the South Coast.

   (b) That 'Crossbow' attack would not preclude – though it might prejudice – the launching of the assault from the South Coast; the probability of casualties to embarking personnel and craft makes it desirable to move the assault forces, if practicable, West of Southampton.

   (c) That the movement of assault forces to bases out of range of 'Crossbow' would have serious repercussions on training, with consequent loss of efficiency.

   (d) That the movement of the assault force to the Westward would have such implications as to make it doubtful whether the landward arrangements could be revised in the time available, and consequently that, in the main, the existing plan for the assault and follow-up must stand, and the risk of casualties be accepted. Within the limits of practicability, however, the maximum degree of dispersion must take place in the period prior to, and during, embarkation.

   (e) Since the handling of MT and Store ships depends largely on civilian personnel, it is undesirable to rely on the full capacity of the ports of Southampton and London for this purpose. In view of the implications of this on the provision of shipping and rate of build-up, a detailed examination of the proposal should be made forthwith.

   (f) That if the plan is to be altered a decision must be made at once in order that the provision of landward facilities for embarkation and fuelling and maintenance arrangements in the South-West area can be initiated. However, no movement of naval forces need take place until the assembly period, unless the nature of the threat has previously declared itself.

*F.E. Morgan*
*Lieutenant General,*
*Chief of Staff to the Supreme Commander (Designate)*

# Appendix V

Memorandum by Sir Findlater Stewart, Chairman,
Home Defence Executive, on Civil Preparations
against Flying Bomb and Rocket Attack.

Norfolk House,
S.W.1.

18th February, 1944

'Crossbow'
Civil Preparations.

## I. Introduction.

The fundamental difficulty in making plans and preparations to meet
'Crossbow' attack is the lack of any firm information as to the precise
nature of the threat with which we are faced. The enemy is known to be
developing a number of weapons of the rocket or jet-propelled type, and,
while we have now a fair amount of information as to the potentialities
of some of these, we cannot be certain which of them will be turned
against the United Kingdom. It is, however, becoming clear that there
are really only two weapons in the field so far as the immediate future
is concerned – the long-range rocket and the pilotless aircraft.

To take the latter first, the Air Staff are satisfied that the enemy
intends to use this weapon against us as soon as he is in a position to
launch an attack on a sufficient scale to make it worthwhile. The
weapon is simply a pilotless plane with some form of automatic control,
and the weight of the warhead of high explosive will probably be of the
order of 1 ton and is certainly not likely to exceed 2½ tons. At the time
of writing the Air Staff give the following estimated scale of attack,
assuming no serious interference by bombing with the constructional
work on the projectors (an unlikely assumption):

By mid-March not exceeding:

(i)  an initial "blitz" equivalent to 400 tons of bombs spread over a period of 10 hours. This is approximately the same scale of attack as that experienced in the blitzes of April and May, 1941.

(ii) two repeats of (i) above at 48-hour intervals.

(iii)  thereafter, 600 tons a month of which 400 at most can be in one "blitz" of 10 hours.

   If sustained attack is adopted, 20 tons per day.

To the above must be added the weight of bombs which might be dropped by the G.A.F., which is now thought unlikely to exceed 250 tons in a heavy attack, or 100 tons on two or three nights per week.

The maximum combined scale of attack by pilotless aircraft and bombers is, therefore, considered unlikely to exceed the equivalent of some 650 tons spread over a period of ten hours, and the maximum sustained rate, some 120 tons on two or three nights per week.

It will be clear that there is no fundamental difference between attack by pilotless aircraft and by ordinary bombing planes, except that the attack might be continuous throughout the 24 hours; the weight of the warhead is not likely to be greater than that of the heaviest bombs, and the speed of approach (estimated at 300-400 miles per hour) is not such as to vitiate altogether the existing public warning system.

This is not the case when we come to consider the long-range rocket. Our information on this subject is much less definite than that on the pilotless aircraft, and this notwithstanding that it was the first threat to emerge. There is, however, little doubt that the enemy is preparing to use a weapon of this kind against us. Bombardment with such a weapon presents a very different problem from that of the air-raid or even the attack with pilotless aircraft. Like the latter, it could be continuous day and night; but the size of each individual "incident" might be enormously increased, and moreover the high speed of approach would render the existing public warning system useless.

Partly because the long-range rocket was first in the field, and partly because for the reasons given it faces us with a much more difficult problem, we have tended to concentrate on it rather than on the pilotless aircraft when considering 'Crossbow' plans. The greatest difficulty has always been the lack of any firm appreciation of the probability of attack, to set against the cost in effort and material of making ourselves ready to meet it; but the problem is primarily one of insurance, and whatever the probability of attack the possible consequences of non-insurance are so serious as to justify the payment of a reasonable premium.

Broadly speaking, preparations to meet the new danger are of two types – firstly, there are those measures which will have to be implemented immediately the attack starts, whatever its strength or duration, and secondly there are the measures which we will be forced to take in case of serious and persistent bombardment. Preparations of the first type must be complete; for example, the warning signal will have to operate from the time the first projectile is fired, and must therefore be held ready to go into operation at any moment. The Cabinet have approved a number of such preparations; but, as regards plans to meet prolonged bombardment, they have decided that these can for the moment be kept at the paper stage, and that material and effort must not be diverted to them to the detriment of other war needs.

In considering which is the most likely objective against which the enemy will direct the new weapons, it should be realised that the fire will almost certainly be inaccurate; it has been estimated that roughly no more than 50% of the missiles only would fall within a circular area 4 miles in radius. The margin of error of these dimensions clearly points to a large target as the most likely objective, and it is generally agreed that, while there are other important targets within range, the weapon is most likely to be used first against London. The basic assumption throughout this paper is that London will be attacked. The Air Staff are, however, of the opinion that Bristol is the second probable target. Portsmouth, Southampton, Poole and Weymouth are all possible objectives.

## II. Security.

(a) Information of Government Officials.

The Cabinet have ruled that those Ministers responsible for preparing plans to meet the 'Crossbow' danger should be given discretion to inform such of their officials as they think necessary of the possible employment by the enemy of new forms of weapons to attack London and the South-East of England. In conveying this information, it was to be made clear that it was not certain that such an attack would take place, and that consequently preparations involving diversion of effort must be kept to the absolute minimum.

Much has appeared in the Press on the subject of the enemy's new weapon, but this has all been unofficial, and, if it were to get about that the Government themselves were disturbed by the new threat, the effect on public opinion might be serious, and the enemy would be forewarned as to our preparations. In implementing the Cabinet decision Departments generally have therefore made every effort to keep the number of people with full knowledge of the danger as small as possible consistent with adequate planning.

In the particular case of Regional staffs, it is clearly necessary that Departments should be governed by a common doctrine; difficulties are bound to occur, if, of officials of the same standing attached to different Departments, some knew of the new danger and some did not. It has therefore been agreed that all Departments should tell their "Regional representatives" in the areas likely to be subjected to attack (Regions 4, 5, 6, 7 and 12). In some cases, it has been necessary to go further than this – for example, the Ministry of Home Security have had to tell all Regional Commissioners, since, while some Regions will not themselves be likely to suffer bombardment, they may well be called upon to provide Civil Defence reinforcements for a less fortunate Region. Similar considerations apply in the case of the Regional Controllers of the Supply Departments, the Ministry of Production and the Factory and Storage Premises Control, any of whom may be called upon to make emergency arrangements to carry on production which may have to be moved from the target area either beforehand or as a result of the attack. It is also very likely that, in planning, inter-department contact may be necessary at levels lower than the Region. To meet this point it has been agreed that Regional representatives should themselves be responsible for initiating such contacts, and that, subject to general directions from their Departments, they should have discretion to inform their own subordinates of the danger when inter-department contact at a level lower than Region is clearly desirable; the Regional representatives will be warned to tell any subordinate to whom they impart this knowledge that it should not be passed on to anyone without their authority. In the same way, Service authorities desiring to make contact with their opposite numbers on the Civil side will go through the Regional representatives of the Civil Departments.

(b) Control of the Press.
(1) Under Long-Range Rocket Attack.
In view of the fact that there may, if the worst happens, be some delay between the explosion of the first rocket projectile and its notification (see iii) below, it will only be possible to safeguard ourselves adequately against the publication of material of use to the enemy by issuing prior notice to the Press when the use of the new weapon appears likely. Editors have already been informed by the Home Secretary of the new danger at two Press Conferences and in a confidential letter, and it will simply be necessary to remind them of this when the time comes and to ask them not to print anything on the subject other than official

announcements for a period of 48 hours after the first attack; this will give a breathing space in which the Government can decide the form which the necessary public announcement on the subject should take, and consider what further guidance for editors is required.

There are three possibilities:

(i) we may get clear evidence that rocket bombardment is about to start.

(ii) we may get no such evidence, the first warning being the detection by radio location of the firing of the first projectile; or

(iii) we may know nothing at all until the first projectile arrives.

Draft private and confidential letters to editors have now been prepared. The first of these will be used if there is no prior warning of the attack, and will simply ask editors to publish nothing about it for at least 48 hours. The second draft, for issue if and when it is decided that rocket attack is imminent, asks editors to maintain press silence in the same way for 48 hours after the first attack; and it adds that, since it may in practice be difficult to distinguish between the bursting of the projectile and that of a bomb (or an explosion at an ammunition dump or cordite factory) all possible precautions should be taken to ensure that nothing is published about any unusual incident which might be due to the rocket. A third draft of lines very similar to the second will be used if the warning to editors is made at the same time as a public announcement about the new danger.

(2) Pilotless aircraft attack.

In the event of pilotless aircraft attack there are two possibilities:

(i) we may get clear evidence that pilotless aircraft attack is about to start.

(ii) we may know nothing at all until the first projectile arrives.

(i) As it is possible that this form of attack might not be at once distinguished from an air raid, or might occur at the same time as an air raid, it will be necessary to take steps to modify the existing instructions to the Press on the subject of the reporting of air raids. A draft letter to Editors covering all the points involved is being prepared by the Ministry of Home Security and the Ministry of Information in consultation, and this would be issued on information being received that pilotless aircraft attack was imminent. As in the case of the long-range rocket the letter will impose a stop on publication for 48 hours.

(ii) For the arrangements in the event of attack without warning, see under III.

(c) Postal and telegraph censorship.

It will not be possible to guarantee the prevention of any leakage of information to the enemy about the effect of his fire through postal and telegraph channels, and the most we can hope to do is to delay such leakage as long as possible.

   (i)  In the case of mail, the main danger of leakage is in letters to Northern Ireland – there is 100% censorship on letters to Eire and neutral countries, and, in the case of letters to the U.S.A. and the Dominions, the time of transit is such that a considerable delay would automatically be imposed. Postal and Telegraph Censorship will not be able with their existing staff to impose 100% censorship on all letters from Great Britain to Northern Ireland, because of other commitments of operational importance; it will however be possible to impose a selective approximate 100% censorship on mails from any part of southern England, which covers all the likely targets.

  (ii)  Telephone communication between Great Britain and Ireland presents considerable difficulties, since Allied and neutral diplomats are permitted to speak in their own language. The Foreign Office have however agreed that during the period of the emergency, Allied (except U.S.) and neutral diplomatic callers will be told by telephone operators that their calls to Ireland can only be accepted if they are made in English; and instructions will be given by the Postal and Telegraph Censorship Department to interrupt any such calls in a foreign language. The Press have private telegraph lines to Ireland not subject to normal censorship control and special measures to prevent leakage of information through this channel have been taken.

(iii) In the case of telegrams, at least 96 hours delay already exists in personal (but not foreign government or commercial) telegrams to the Iberian Peninsula, Sweden, Switzerland and Turkey. Other overseas personal telegrams to insecure destinations can be made subject to a similar delay, for a period which might in all cases be extended unofficially to a limited extent without undue comment. In addition, The Foreign Office have agreed to issue to Allied (except U.S.) and neutral diplomatic staffs in London a circular asking them to refrain from any references to the 'Crossbow' attack in their cypher telegrams, and warning them that these telegrams may be delayed. Postal and Telegraph Censorship Department will give instructions for outward Allied (except U.S.) and neutral diplomatic telegrams (overseas and to Eire and

Northern Ireland), in cypher or foreign language, to be delayed for 48 hours.

(iv) Travellers to Eire and neutral countries also constitute a possible danger, particularly when they make the journey by air. Leakage through this channel could only be stopped by delaying the travellers, and the objections to this are substantial.

In short, while there is little hope of eliminating altogether the risk of leakage, it is fairly safe to assume that information of value to the enemy will take some time to get there. The problem of Ireland is difficult; but on the other hand, it is understood that the enemy has not in Eire an organisation comparable to that which exists in neutral countries capable of collecting the minor indiscretions of individuals and piecing them together to obtain an important piece of information.

It is relevant here to consider the arrangements which Postal and Telegraph Censorship can make to maintain their work if and when London is heavily bombarded. In the case of postal communications, outgoing surface and air mails will be diverted to provincial centres such as Manchester, Liverpool and Birmingham for examination; until such diversion becomes necessary, the intention is that, so long as the staff now working in London are able to reach their places of work, they should continue to do so. In the case of telecommunications, the telegraph censorship examiners will work in the protected accommodation available at the Central Telegraph Office and at the cable stations – there is of course no possibility of routing to convenient examination centres in the provinces, since the examination must take place at the point of transmission. If the cable stations in London are rendered untenable, the censorship will be carried out at the emergency cable stations which exist in the outer London area, and if necessary also at the W/T Stations belonging to Cable and Wireless Ltd., in East Anglia and the West of England; and if these too are put out of action, the telegraph censorship will despatch its staff to operate at the actual cable heads on the South West coast unless it should be decided that the Cable Companies should operate at some new intermediate points. Postal and Telegraph Censorship have requested the General Post Office to discuss these changes of location for telegraphic operations with Cable Companies, both British and foreign, so that the censorship plans can conform; in these discussions there will be no specific references to 'Crossbow', and the approach will be made with reference to the Prime Minister's recent statement in Parliament that an intensified bombardment of London is to be expected. Telephone censorship will continue to be conducted in London as long as possible; and if the London centre became untenable the external telephone circuits will at that stage have to be routed outside London for censorship at provincial centres.

**III. Prior Warning of Attack, and Notification of First Projectile.**
The Air Staff, in consultation with the Joint Intelligence Committee, are responsible for co-ordinating reports from photographic reconnaissance and intelligence sources, and will keep the Chiefs of Staff informed of the situation. It seems therefore reasonable to hope that at some stage the Chiefs of Staff will be in a position to say that the attack with the new weapon is imminent. If this should be possible the Cabinet at that stage will be asked to consider the question of a public announcement (see section V below) and the issue of the appropriate letter to editors (see Section II (b) above). If the public announcement is in the event made, the Ministry of Home Security will at once take steps to bring the special public warning system for long-range rockets (see Section IV below) into operation.

On the other hand, it is possible that, if the enemy decided on a short experimental attack in the near future, this would come without it being possible to give any prior warning.

(1) Long-range rocket.
There are two possibilities:
  (a)  the firing of the first projectile might be detected by radio location at one or more of the special Radar stations on the South Coast;
  (b)  the Radar watch might fail to record the first projectile, in which case the first we should know of it would be its arrival at its target.
If the first of these alternatives happens, H.Q., A.D.G.B will at once inform Home Secretary War Room, who will thereupon watch for any reports of abnormal explosions. Such an explosion will be reported at once to Fighter Command, and as soon as it can be confirmed that it was in fact due to a rocket the main operating Departments will be told; at this stage the Ministry of Information will issue the appropriate letter to editors, and the Ministry of Home Security will prepare the public announcement for immediate issue.

If on the other hand the Radar watch fails to record the first projectile, the initial warning will be the abnormal explosion caused by its arrival at its target; the Ministry of Information have arranged to hold up any reports of such explosions until they have been checked with the Ministry of Home Security, and the latter Department have arranged to report any abnormal explosions to the Air Ministry and the Ministry of Information. Confirmation will be obtained as soon as possible that the abnormal explosion is due to a rocket, and thereafter the same procedure as before applies. These arrangements will operate for notifying the firing of the first projectile whether or not there has been any prior warning.

(2) Pilotless aircraft.

In the case of pilotless aircraft attack without prior warning, the first we should know of it would be the arrival of the projectile. The attack might not be at once distinguished from an air raid, or might occur at the same time as an air raid. In the event of an isolated incident occurring which was suspected to be due to pilotless aircraft arrangements have been made whereby the Ministry of Home Security would inform the Ministry of Information of the fact that an incident was suspected to have been caused by pilotless aircraft and the Ministry of Information would take steps immediately on receipt of this information to ask the press not to publish anything about the incident for 48 hours, as the incident was being investigated. The same procedure would be adopted in the event of an attack involving a number of pilotless aircraft incidents, whether first reported as an air raid or actually in conjunction with an air raid.

## IV. Warning Signal.

As explained above, the existing air raid warning system will, it is hoped, prove effective in the case of pilotless aircraft (see Section I above). In the case of the long-range rocket, however, it is desirable that some special warning should be provided since the speed with which the rocket will travel will be so great that a warning could not be given in time by means of the ordinary air raid warning machinery. It has been argued that, on the sounding of such a warning, the public might give way to panic in a rush for cover, with consequent loss of life; but on the other hand there will undoubtedly be strong public demand for a warning of some kind, which will enable people to take cover and on balance save many lives. The time between the sounding of the warning and the arrival of the rocket must of necessity be very short, since the rocket is estimated to reach its target some three minutes after projection. The arrangements which has been made is that maroons with whistles attached will be fired automatically on selected A.A. gun and Balloon Barrage sites and certain Police Stations by means of a network of communications controlled from Fighter Command; rocket flares will follow in a few seconds, so that the warning will be both audible and visible. In addition, one wail of the siren may be used as a reinforcement of the maroons. A warning system on these lines is provided for the London area and the Portsmouth – Southampton area.

Most of the arrangements for this special warning signal have been completed, and it could be put into operation at any moment. It will clearly be essential to inform the public of the warning before it is introduced, and this will be done if and when the public announcement is made (see Section V below)

In addition to explaining the nature of the warning, the announcement will emphasise that the warning period is not likely to last more than one minute, and therefore that the best thing to do is to take cover immediately on hearing it; it will also have to be pointed out that there can be no "All Clear", and the suggestion made that one need only remain under cover for a period of 5 minutes after the sounding of the warning, unless in the meantime a second warning has been sounded.

### V. Public Announcement.

Up to the present the Cabinet have ruled that no public announcement on the subject of the new weapon should be made. The Press have been informed in confidence that the Government is considering measures to deal with them should they be used; and a good deal of information on the subject has appeared in the Press in correspondents' reports, particularly from those neutral countries. While any official announcement on the subject is still clearly premature, there are advantages to be gained by making it in advance of the actual attack; the shock of a new and terrifying attack would be likely to be greater the more unexpected it was, and while the unofficial material in the Press has no doubt done something to prepare the public against this, there is no doubt that an official statement will be taken much more seriously. Since any considerable refugee movement from a place the size of London would present an unmanageable problem, the announcement could also be used to exhort the general public to stand firm. An announcement of some kind will of course be essential before the public warning system can be operated. (See Section IV above).

A draft announcement has been prepared, and will be submitted to the Cabinet for approval at the stage when the Chiefs of Staff decide that the attack is imminent. It has been kept in skeleton form so that it can be altered suitably according as it goes out as a Press notice or is embodied in a speech in the House or a broadcast statement by a Minister.

### VI. Evacuation.

The Cabinet have agreed that there should be no organized evacuation other than of the 'priority classes' for whom evacuation plans have been operated in the past, in relation to the risks of air raids. These classes are

(a) unaccompanied school-children, (b) mothers with children of school age or under, (c) expectant mothers, (d) limited numbers of unaccompanied children under 5.

The scheme for evacuation by private arrangement, under which free travel and billeting allowances are provided for those who can find their own accommodation, is in continuous operation and will be allowed to continue. It covers a wider range of 'priority classes' than the organised scheme, including aged, infirm and blind persons, and it would reduce to some small extent the population of the threatened areas.

Organised evacuation can be put into operation at short notice in any evacuable area. But under Cabinet approval, detailed plans for the organised evacuation of priority classes from London (i.e. Greater London evacuable area), Southampton, Portsmouth and Gosport have been completed. These plans cover the registration, assembly and transit of evacuees to the London terminal stations, (so far as it is practicable to settle details at this stage), and their removal to pre-arranged reception areas in accordance with prepared railway timetables. The plans so far made provide for the removal of 100,000 persons from London and 20,000 from Southampton, Portsmouth and Gosport combined in a period of ten days. If the demand for evacuation should exceed these numbers, further plans will be prepared, to operate after the initial movement has been completed.

Simultaneously with evacuation, all schools situated within 8 miles of central London will be closed, and possibly also those within the danger areas at Portsmouth and Southampton; schooling will continue in the remainder of the London area, subject to further consideration later in the light of developments.

## VII. Maintenance of Machinery of Government.

Some time ago the Cabinet considered what steps would be necessary to maintain essential work at the headquarters of offices of Government Departments if London were subjected to heavy 'Crossbow' bombardment; they then agreed that the "black" plan for the evacuation of Government Departments should not be reviewed, but that the accommodation of the citadel type available should be investigated, and arrangements made for the essential work of Government Departments to be continued in London in the event of 'Crossbow' attacks.

Starting from the principle of no "black" move, it then becomes necessary to consider what are the likely problems we will have to meet. Assuming a steady and continuous 'Crossbow' bombardment, we may have to face the gradual devastation of London, building up, within a period of time which would depend upon the weight of attack, to a point at which the available Civil Defence and restoration services are no longer able to cope with the situation. Since the weapons are not accurate ones, the enemy could not select particular areas of London as his target, and the projectiles would probably be spread at random over the whole Greater London area; therefore, while individual Government Offices might receive a direct hit, the weapons would not be concentrated on Whitehall. The main problem is not therefore the damage to individual buildings so much as the gradual disintegration of London which, through the growing disorganisation of essential services such as road and rail transport, would make it increasingly difficult for Government staffs to attend their offices. The solution is therefore to revive the plan for keeping essential staffs at their offices day and night and standing off all non-essential staff.

A survey has been made of the amount of protected accommodation, including citadel accommodation, available in Government offices; as a rough standard, the degree of protection in such accommodation is that provided by the strengthened basement of a building fully or partly framed in steel or reinforced concrete with strong floors. The total amount of citadel and other protected accommodation available for Government staffs is not sufficient to house all the essential staff, even though the latter has been calculated as the minimum of personnel necessary to keep the machinery running for a short emergency (two to three weeks). Though a few Departments have a surplus of protected accommodation, the majority have a deficit; in many cases this could probably be squeezed into the available accommodation, but in others the amount of the deficit is too great for this. Since there is no question of constructing further protected accommodation, such essential staff as cannot be squeezed into the available accommodation will be housed in the next safest part of their building; thus, when the time comes to stand-off non-essential staff, and reduce work to the essential minimum each Department will transfer as much of its essential staff as possible into the protected accommodation and put the rest of the essential staff in the next safest place.

When the time comes for non-essential staff to be stood off an arrangement on the lines of that made in the early days of the war will be introduced whereby staffs are told to report at suburban railway stations or Post Offices, or, in the case of Ministry of Labour staff, at the Employment Exchanges nearest their homes, for instruction.

Each Government Department with any essential staff has been asked to review its arrangements for feeding that staff; it may either maintain an emergency stock in its canteen or, if it has no canteen may obtain Army 'Compo' packs sufficient to feed the essential staff for 4 days. Departments have also been asked to review their arrangements for heating drinks etc. in the protected accommodation.

When any Government office is hit during rocket bombardment, it will be re-housed by the Ministry of Works in the normal way. The Ministry did at one time maintain in London a 10% reserve of accommodation with a complement of furniture and provided with adequate tele-communications. This was whittled down by increase of staff to something nearer 4%, and in view of the new danger it is clearly advisable to increase it once more to the old level. The Minister of Works has requisitioned further reserve space and the minimum work necessary to make the accommodation suitable for occupation on an emergency basis is in hand and as each group of newly requisitioned buildings is made habitable, the Post Office is providing telephones with a switchboard and exchange lines, on a small scale to meet immediate needs on first occupation. The additional accommodation obtained is not of first-class standard, and consists mainly of blocks of large houses since there is no further steel-framed accommodation which could be taken.

As indicated above, the rough standard of protected accommodation is the strengthened basement of a building fully or partly framed in steel or reinforced concrete. Accommodation of the citadel type is of course very much safer than this; the Cabinet have always held that citadels should be provided for the essential nuclei of the main operational Departments, since the essential war communications of the departments must be protected as far as possible against sustained heavy bombardment – with their associated deep tunnels, the citadels provide security for telecommunications. Citadel accommodation was included in the general survey described above, but only the Service Departments, the War Cabinet Offices and the Ministry of Home Security have citadels – except that accommodation of the citadel type has been provided for the main military headquarters in London, namely S.H.A.E.F. and E.T.O.U.S.A. and a limited amount of deep shelter accommodation is being prepared as reserve accommodation for the London Regional War Room, Combined Operations etc.

It was indicated above that essential staffs have been calculated on the assumption that the emergency would be of two to three weeks' duration; for a more prolonged emergency the figures are of course much greater – if indefinitely prolonged it could in fact scarcely be much less than the total staff of the Departments; and might indeed have to be greater. From the point of view of present planning the short period is the most important and the one for which the completion of plans is essential; until 'Crossbow' bombardment starts, we cannot say what is likely to happen after a long period of it – it may well be that it will not be possible to carry out anything like normal administration from London with reduced staffs, especially since the situation in London would throw heavy additional burdens on a number of departments. A partial solution of the long-term problem would be for those departments with strong Regional organisations to de-centralise, and preparations to this end are in hand; but a bombardment of the severity contemplated over a long period would raise many other serious problems besides this particular one of maintaining the Government machine.

## VIII. Shelters.

There are no special shelter problems to be faced under attack by pilotless aircraft. In the case of the long-range rocket, however, in view of the shortness of the period between any public warning of the firing of a rocket and its actual explosion, it would not be possible, even if sufficient deep shelters were available, for the general mass of the public to reach them in time. It is thought that the enemy will most probably aim at the maximum blast effect with this weapon – in view of its inaccuracy concentration on maximum earth shock is not likely, since bombs so devised are generally used against small targets such as big buildings not vulnerable to blast. Against blast Morrison and reinforced surface shelters offer adequate protection, and fortunately shelters of this type are well dispersed.

The Minister of Home Security has concentrated in London a greater proportion of the existing stock of Morrison shelters. The London reserve has been made up to 68,000 and an additional 44,000 are stored sufficiently close to London to enable a large proportion of them to be moved rapidly into the London area. The Cabinet have additional 100,000 shelters, and 50,000 of these will, it is hoped, be delivered in time for the anticipated emergency. They have also authorised the Minister to complete with all possible speed the strengthening of all surface shelters in London and this work is proceeding.

For the present it has been decided that the deep tube shelters shall not be made available to the public and the Ministry of Home Security have in hand a scheme for blocking up the public entrances to these shelters, a scheme which could be put into effect at short notice.

## IX. Civil Defence Services.

The adequacy of the available Civil Defence Services obviously depends on the weight and concentration of the attack which the enemy is able to bring to bear; broadly speaking, if an attack approaches in intensity anything like the estimates which have been made, it is clear that the Civil Defence Services available in the vulnerable areas, and in particular in London, would very soon be exposed to a severe strain which might well prove beyond their capacity. It is not considered that any fundamental change in the operational control of the existing Civil Defence Services is required, but special attention is being paid by the Ministry of Home Security:

(i) In consultation with the Ministry of Health and the Home Office, to the possibility of reinforcing from other areas the Civil Defence Services, the Police and the National Fire Service, and

(ii) in concert with G.H.Q. Home Forces, to the possibility of provision of military assistance (including Home Guard assistance) for rescue work, traffic control, etc. (See Section X for military assistance in demolition, clearance and repair).

## X. Demolition, Clearance and Repair.

The Ministry of Works estimate that there are approximately 70,000 building and civil engineering operatives in London, of which 14,000 could be added immediately to the labour force at present engaged on demolition and clearance and repairs to public utility undertakings, houses and factories. In addition, approximately 10,000 men should become available owing to unemployment caused by the incident. This total of 24,000 within the London Region could be transferred to essential works as the need arises. It is considered that these arrangements will cover urgent demolition, clearance and restoration of services, as, with the conditions envisaged under rocket bombardment, it is unlikely that much repair to buildings would be possible. Machinery also exists for a further 40,000 men to be drafted into the Region in four weeks and the Ministry of Home Security, in conjunction with the Ministry of Works, are providing emergency quarters for 10,000 of these men.

Arrangements have been made by the Ministry of Works for the urgent construction (if and when required) of hutted camps at various points on the East and South coasts and at Bristol and Cardiff to house building-trade workers whom it may be necessary to import as reinforcements. This shelter would become available in a matter of days. Permanent camps of this type already exist at Fareham and Farlington.

If civilian resources become stretched to the limit, it will obviously be necessary to turn to the military for assistance. G.H.Q., Home Forces have made arrangements to reinforce the troops available in two phases. Phase 1 is the recreation of Special Force London, which was made available to the Regional Commissioner in the 1940 – 1941 air raids on London for demolition, clearance and repair. Phase 2 is the reinforcement of any of the London Sub-Districts with extra military assistance from outside London District, and will be initiated by G.H.Q. on the recommendation of Headquarters, London District. Arrangements for the movement, location, equipment and control of reinforcing troops have been made.

A third phase will consist of organised assistance by Home Guard. Arrangements have been made with the War office for the issue of special instructions in the event of the services of the Home Guard being required to supplement the military assistance to be given in Phase 1 and Phase 2.

## XI. Accommodation of the Homeless.

Rest centres in the London Region provide accommodation, with feeding facilities for 150,000 people. To supplement this provision, all available buildings suitable for the accommodation of homeless persons on the lowest practicable standard (e.g. Schools, Churches, Cinemas etc) have been listed. A proportion of these providing accommodation for over 500,000 people (187,500 in the County of London and 315,000 in the remainder of the Region) have been prepared as reception centres and plans made for their use in case of need.

Billeting accommodation in the Region is estimated to be sufficient for the reception of 1,250,000 persons of which number 750,000 could be accommodated in the part of the Region outside the County of London.

Both Rest Centre and housing accommodation are, of course, liable to be considerably reduced by the effects of bombardment. On the other hand, any substantial exodus of population, under the Government Evacuation Scheme or otherwise, will tend to ease the pressure on housing.

The problem has also been considered for Portsmouth, Gosport and Southampton. There is available in Southampton rest centre accommodation for 13,000 persons, and for Portsmouth and Gosport the figure is 10,000. The homeless will be accommodated in these rest centres in the first instance, and subsequently billeted. It the attacks are heavy and persistent, and billeting accommodation in the target areas were saturated, the existing arrangements provide for homeless persons to be transferred from rest centres in the target areas to rest centres and billets in the hinterland. Temporary hostels in the form of hutted camps have been provided in the neighbourhood of Southampton and Portsmouth to supplement accommodation for the homeless. These are primarily intended for essential workers, who must be kept within reach of their places of work; the temporary hostels provide accommodation for 8,000 persons equally divided between Southampton and Portsmouth.

## XII. Relief of Distress.

In the event of 'Crossbow' bombardment the Ministry of Labour and National Service and the Assistance Board will be concerned with making money payments:

(a) Of war damage compensation to persons who are in urgent need of replacement of clothing, furniture, workman's tools etc.;

(b) of war injury allowances to civilians and certain classes of Civil Defence volunteers;

(c) to persons who lose their employment as a result of destruction of their place of work;

(d) to "evacuees" (other than unaccompanied schoolchildren who will be billeted with board and lodging) who are evacuated under the Government scheme and who, after being billeted by the local authority are in need of cash payments for maintenance;

(e) to "refugees", viz., persons who flee en masse to the country and who, being unable or unwilling to return to their homes, are billeted by the local authority and are in need of cash payments for maintenance.

Considerable number of people may have to be dealt with, and the Assistance Board in particular will have to carry a greatly increased load. The Board have therefore made plans which provide for:

(i) The loan of about 1,000 staff from other Government Departments, most of whom have recently had preliminary training in their work;

(ii) the transfer of staff from other Regions to bombarded areas;

(iii) the suspension of all less essential work;

(iv) the introduction of a special emergency procedure for payments;

(v) special arrangements with the Ministry of Works for alternative accommodation when offices are put out of action;

(vi) the obtaining of emergency supplies of cash at any hour.

As regards the payments referred to in Section XII (a) and (b) above, these are made by the Assistance Board at the administrative centres set up by local authorities as well as at offices of the Board. As regards payments to evacuee and refugees – Section XII (d) and (e) above, these are made in the first instance by the Ministry of Labour at their Local Offices or at special premises taken for the purpose; the procedure provides for dealing with large numbers with the greatest possible speed and the main problem will be that of finding premises for additional pay stations where they are needed in the reception areas and of allocating staff to the pay stations. Unless and until the attack takes a very intensive form the Ministry of Pensions will continue payment of a Special Temporary Allowance to Widows, but if circumstances make it impossible to continue such payments the Ministry of Pensions Regional Staff will reinforce the staff of the Assistance Board and the widows of those killed will be dealt with through the general Assistance Board machinery.

## XIII. Refugees.

A Committee of the Departments principally concerned has examined the problem which will be presented by large scale refugee movements from London in the event of 'Crossbow' bombardment; the Committee proceeded on the following assumptions:

  (1)  that every effort will be made by encouragement and exhortation to induce the population to stand firm, but that nevertheless it is necessary to make such arrangements as are practicable to deal with the possibility of a large-scale exodus of refugees from London;

  (2)  that it would be undesirable, and in any case, most difficult to attempt to arrange for any substantial organised evacuation of any classes of the population other than the priority cases; i.e. women and children, for which detailed plans have been completed; and

  (3)  that the nature of the provision which should be made to deal with the possibility of such an exodus of refugees should be governed by two considerations; on the one hand, that it must be such as is necessary to enable public order to be maintained, to prevent panic movements from developing, and to avoid public scandal or criticism of the Government on the ground of inadequate preparations or forethought; and on the other hand, that it must not be so attractive as to encourage the movement of refugees out of the Metropolis.

It is thought probable that by far the greatest number of refugees will have recourse to rail transport, and the main problem therefore is that of coping with a rush on the main line termini, particularly those in the northern and western parts of the capital. It is not considered that it would be practicable to shut down these termini entirely, or to close them to passenger traffic; the problem therefore reduces itself to the control of crowds at railway stations, and this will be handled by the police in consultation with the Ministry of War Transport and the railway authorities. A special problem arises in the case of the tube railways, in view of the fact that many of these are used as shelters from raiding at night; it will not be practicable to stop all the trains and use the tubes merely for shelters, and on the other hand there would be serious political difficulties, in view of the use of the tubes for shelter at present, in the way of the prohibition of their use by the public during 'Crossbow' bombardment. If it is practicable to get the number of shelters within limits, the best course from an operating point of view would be to continue to run something like the normal service; and the police and other authorities concerned are considering the question of the arrangements necessary for this purpose.

It is not considered that it will be necessary to take any special measures to control refugees leaving by road transport. There only remains therefore the problem of an exodus from London on foot. It will be quite impracticable for the police to prevent any such large scale exodus; all that the police could do would be to shepherd pedestrians along the road in such a way as to prevent traffic congestion, to disperse them along as many roads as possible so as to avoid the effect of a continuous stream of refugee traffic, and, as they proceed towards the outer perimeter of London and beyond, to get them so far as possible turned aside into Rest Centres.

For the accommodation of refugees, use will have to be made of the Rest Centres and Reception Centres in and near London; in the out-County portion of the London Region there is accommodation of this kind for 384,000 persons, and in the Home Counties there is further accommodation within 40 miles of London for 216,000 persons in Rest Centres; there is also a reserve of accommodation such as cinemas, village halls, churches, etc., which can be used if the need arises. It is considered that this accommodation should be sufficient to cope with the problem of a refugee exodus, provided every endeavour is made to persuade those who have been temporarily accommodated there to return to their homes. Where this cannot be effected, and the Rest Centres become overcrowded, it will be necessary to resort to billeting as far as practicable in the neighbourhood. It will be necessary in places where there are genuine homeless people, as distinct from refugees, to distinguish so far as possible between the two classes; while the former are entitled to be billeted, and require as sympathetic treatment as can be given, the latter should, in pursuance of the general principle stated above, receive no more than the bare minimum.

Some of the second- and third-line Rest Centres and Reception Centres which may be used for the accommodation of refugees are not equipped for the preparation of hot meals on the scale required. Therefore, arrangements have been made by the Ministry of Food for

Semi-Mobile Kitchen units to be set up where required to distribute meals in hot containers to the Rest and Reception Centres accommodating refugees. The principle has been adopted that the Ministry of Food will distribute the meals to the buildings in which the refugees are accommodated. Otherwise there would be the danger that large numbers of refugees might be attracted towards the kitchens and Emergency Food Centres and that it would be impossible to provide accommodation for these people in such areas.

As regards other cities in the South of England, the places most likely to be evacuated are Portsmouth, Gosport and Southampton. The available provision of accommodation and food for refugees from these places is the same in general character as in the case of London, and could be operated without serious difficulty.

## XIV. Food.

The major problems which 'Crossbow' may bring for the Ministry of Food are first the maintenance of food processing and of wholesale and retail distribution in event of widespread damage to factories, warehouses and retail shops in the London or other large target areas, and secondly, the organisation of emergency feeding services (including shelter feeding) for people within the target areas and for refugees who may move elsewhere.

The following plans to meet the above emergencies have already been completed:

(1) Arrangements have been made to maintain the output of processed foods by stepping up production elsewhere or by bringing into operation shadow factories, where available, if factories in the target areas should be damaged or destroyed.

(2) A full review has been made of the bulk stocks held by the Ministry in the target areas. So far as the heavy pressure on cold storage and warehousing space will permit the stocks of certain key foodstuffs in London are being limited or dispersed within the area.

(3) Special arrangements have been made to ensure the supply in the London area of the three main perishable foodstuffs: milk, meat and bread. Adequate reserves of condensed milk and canned meat are available should the supplies of fresh milk and fresh meat fail. In event of widespread destruction of plant bakeries in this area, a nationwide scheme for the mobilisation of bread for London and the adjacent Home Counties has been prepared.

(4) Arrangements for the maintenance of wholesale distribution in the event of widespread destruction of traders premises in

London have been reviewed. So long as transport (either road or rail) and labour are available wholesale distribution both within London and to the areas normally served by London will be maintained from emergency depots already established outside London. It has always been the Ministry's policy to secure the widest dispersal of food stocks; as a special precaution against failure in distribution within the target areas, stocks of essential foodstuffs (i.e. flour, sugar, tea, canned meat, condensed milk and margarine) have been increased in the Southern part of England.

(5) Plans have been prepared in conjunction with other Departments concerned for large-scale emergency feeding in London and the adjacent Regions. Reserve equipment has been concentrated in safe areas near the capital. A scheme has been prepared for the rapid expansion of the shelter feeding services in London.

(6) Arrangements already made for the provision of reserve stocks for the essential personnel of Government Departments and also for key factories working for Supply Departments in the London area have been reviewed.

(7) Arrangements have been made with the Home Guard Directorate for the feeding of Home Guard units called upon to assist the Civil Authorities. Arrangements are also being made for any additional measures necessary for the feeding of personnel moved into London by the Ministry of Works or by the Civil Defence Services.

## XV. Postal and Telephone Communications.

In preparing to meet the danger of 'Crossbow' bombardment the Post Office have:

(1) Accelerated the transfer of certain key cables in the London Telecommunications network to deep level tunnels.

(2) Arranged for the photographic apparatus used by the Post Office in connexion with outgoing Airgraphs to be dispersed between two buildings and for the photographic apparatus at Messrs. Kodak's works at Harrow used in connexion with incoming Airgraphs to be similarly dispersed.

(3) Reviewed the machinery necessary for decentralising the work of the Post Office Savings Bank and Accounting Departments should it become impossible for them to function in London.

(4) Reviewed the special transport arrangements for getting telephone and telegraph operating personnel and key officers to their posts in the event of normal transport failing.

(5) Confirmed the state of readiness of emergency scheme for

essential trunk telephone services in the event of the London Trunk Exchange being destroyed or seriously damaged.

(6) Ensured that arrangements for the staffing of reporting centres for civil servants (see Section VII above) are understood so far as the Post Office is responsible for them.

(7) Under review, in collaboration with the Censorship Authorities, the position which would arise should it become necessary to transfer the Foreign Mails Division and the Ships Division of the Post Office from London to the provinces.

## XVI. Production.

The Prime Minister has given authority for:

(a) the removal from London of any particular manufacture (or part thereof) which represents the only capacity of its kind;

(b) the general reduction of stocks of very important articles in the London area.

The Supply Departments are as far as possible taking the action considered necessary under (b) and as regards (a) the action directly related to 'Crossbow' is the acceleration of the construction of three valve factories by M.A.P. as well as the dispersal by them of certain production units outside the London area, and the earmarking of reserve accommodation outside the area. Under their normal placing arrangements Employment Exchanges will divert as necessary workpeople who become unemployed so far as to meet demands for labour elsewhere. The individual Supply Departments will take up direct with the Ministry of Labour as occasion demands any questions of transferring labour between particular factories.

## XVII. Transport.

The Ministry of War Transport have considered the probable effect of 'Crossbow' bombardment on transport in the London area, and the steps which they can take to mitigate this.

As regards railways, experience during heavy raids has shown that while damage was extensive, it could, with few exceptions, be repaired fairly rapidly; the types of damage creating the longest interruption were damage to bridges or viaducts, tunnels and power stations. It has been possible to safeguard the electrified railways against damage to power supplies to some extent by linking up to alternative sources of supply, though the varying cycles in use on the different systems prevent the achievement of complete interchangeability of power supplies by linking with the grid. The only serious new problem with which the railways will be faced arises in connection with the flooding of the deep-running tubes through breaches of the under-river tunnels; the water-tight bulkheads which isolate the under-river sections of tubes during air raids takes four minutes to close, if time is allowed for the clearance of trains, and in the case of the rocket the warning period will be much shorter than this. It might, therefore be necessary to close the under-river tunnels permanently if and when rocket bombardment begins.

In the case of road transport, the road system is so widely dispersed that, while it would undoubtedly suffer heavily in a highly concentrated bombardment, occasional and scattered projectiles would be unlikely to produce a sufficiently general effect to stop road movement otherwise than purely locally. The worst effect would probably be the curtailment of the power supply for trams and trolley buses, and even this difficulty might be met very quickly from alternative sources of power.

# Appendix VI

## The last Intelligence Report to the Chiefs of Staff before the beginning of Flying Bomb Attacks.

C.O.S. (44) 317 (0)
12th June, 1944

War Cabinet,
Chiefs of Staff Committee,
'Crossbow'.

Supplementary Report by Assistant Chief of Air Staff (Intelligence).
Modified Pilotless Aircraft Sites.

1. After a gap of 7 days, photographic cover of a number of modified pilotless aircraft sites in the Pas de Calais area, North of the River Somme, was obtained on 11th June. Immediate interpretation of photographs of 9 of these sites shows:
   (i)   Much activity at 6 sites.
   (ii)  Rails have been laid on the ramps at 4 of these sites and are now heavily camouflaged.
   (iii) The square building is complete in 6 cases.

2. The discovery that launching ramps, complete with rails, have been erected on prepared foundations in a period which in one case certainly, is not more than 7 days, and our knowledge that the square building can progress from the foundation stage to completion in something under a fortnight, tends to confirm the belief, already stated, that the Germans are using pre-fabricated structures for these two essential elements of the sites. It also confirms the theory that, once these foundations are laid, sites can be brought to a state of structural completion very quickly.

3. The foundations for the launching ramp and square building are complete at 20 of the 42 modified sites so far found in the Pas de Calais

237

area. This number includes the 4 on which rails have been observed. It is therefore possible that at least 20 sites aligned on London could now be structurally complete. Arrangements have been made for photographic cover to be obtained of all modified pilotless aircraft sites and all supply sites in the Pas de Calais area North of the Somme, today if weather permits. It is hoped that the results of immediate interpretation will be available on the morning of 13th June.

4. A report has also been received from a usually reliable source that, on 9th/10th June, a train consisting of 33 wagons, each 18 metres (58½ feet) long, and each loaded with 3 "Rockets" passed through Ghent. The destination was given as Tourcoing. According to the same report, further trains were expected. Taken in conjunction with photographic evidence, some credence can be given to this report. From the description given, it is possible that the objects seen were the fuselages of pilotless aircraft, and not rockets for delivery to the large sites.

5. Without further evidence no definite conclusions can be arrived at in regard to the intended scale and timing of an attack on this country, but the indications are that the Germans are making energetic preparations to bring the pilotless aircraft sites into operation at an early date.

*Offices of the War Cabinet, S.W.1.*
*12th June, 1944.*

# Appendix VII

## Report to the War Cabinet by the Chief of Air Staff on the First Flying Bomb Attack against England.

W.P. (44) 320
13th June, 1944

War Cabinet,
'Crossbow',
Report by the Chief of Air Staff.

Last night the enemy launched an attack by pilotless aircraft against this country. Full and accurate reports of the details of the attacks are not yet available. From information obtained from Radar plots and the Royal Observer Corps, it appears that up to 27 pilotless aircraft may have been employed. The weather was bad at the time, making accurate visual observation difficult; the enemy operated normal aircraft intermittently over the S.E. and S.W. coast and the movement of our own aircraft made accurate plotting difficult.

2. According to reports, the first wave of pilotless aircraft appeared off Folkestone between 0407 and 0440 hours and penetrated Kent, Surrey and Sussex, four penetrating as far as Greater London. The second wave, reported to consist of thirteen aircraft, appeared over the Channel between Dungeness and South Foreland between 0458 and 0520 hours. Nine of these operated over Kent, Surrey and Sussex. The third wave, about which there is still considerable uncertainty, is reported to consist of two to four aircraft, which made landfall between Lyme Regis and Bridport from 0501 to 0535 hours. There was some movement of our own aircraft in this area at the time, and since no incidents have been reported, it may turn out that the aircraft reported were not all pilotless aircraft.

3. The aircraft were first reported to be coming in at a height of about 1,000 feet and rising gradually to a height of 4,000 feet. Their speed was

estimated at between 230 and 250 m.p.h. and the path of flight of some of them was reported as being erratic.

4. Reports from the Royal Observer Corps describe the aircraft as having a long nose, small wings and showing a brilliant white light behind. This corresponds generally with the description of the pilotless aircraft based on a report on wreckage of a German pilotless aircraft recently examined in Sweden.

5. Incidents reported by the Ministry of Home Security as being due to pilotless aircraft occurred at:

   (i)   Bethnal Green where the L.N.E.R. Railway Bridge over Grove Road was demolished and 200 persons rendered homeless. Casualties were 2 killed and 28 injured.

   (ii)  Stone (near Dartford)   }

   (iii) Platt (near Sevenoaks)  } Where slight damage, but no
                                         casualties, was caused.

   (iv) Cuckfield (Sussex)    }

6. It is not possible to state whether these pilotless aircraft attacks were delivered from the few "ski" sites which remain not completely damaged, or from the newly discovered modified sites which recent photographic reconnaissance has shown in some cases to be approaching a state of completion, permitting discharge of pilotless aircraft. Radar plots indicate, however, that most of the pilotless aircraft operating over the South East area were probably launched from sites in the Pas de Calais immediately north of the Somme. It is in this area that activity at the modified sites was recently reported and where some sites appear to be reaching an advanced stage of completion.

7. In view of the difficulties attending the attack of the small and well camouflaged sites, the Chiefs of Staff recently considered the desirability of attacking the supply sites which were suspected of constituting the servicing depots and rail heads for the modified launching sites.

8. I now feel that it would be advisable to recommend to the Supreme Allied Commander that these supply sites should be heavily attacked immediately, and that all launching sites capable of operation should also be attacked whenever effort can be spared. I am of the opinion that, in view of the present inaccuracy and light scale of attack of these pilotless aircraft, the air effort diverted should, at present, be limited to what can be spared without prejudicing in any way the urgent needs of the Battle of France.

*(Intld.) C.P.*
*Air Ministry, S.W.1.*
*13th June, 1944.*

# Appendix VIII

## The Redeployment of Flying Bomb Defences.

Headquarters, Air Defence of Great Britain,
15th July, 1944.

Defence of London Against Flying Bombs.

As a result of a new comprehensive examination of the defensive problem raised by the enemy's use of Flying Bombs against London, it was decided, at a meeting held at this Headquarters on the 13th July, 1944, to carry out a rearrangement of the defensive plan with a consequent alteration in the rules for the co-ordination of action by fighters, A.A. guns and balloons.

2. The new rules, which come into force w.e.f. 0600 hours, 17th July, 1944, have now been set out in this Headquarters' Operational Instruction No. 15/1944 copies of which are attached hereto.

3. It is a matter of urgency and great importance that these rules should be fully understood by all concerned, and it is therefore desired, in this letter, to point out the main alterations involved. These alterations are set out below, but the detailed rules must be obtained from the Operational Instruction, and not from the broad statements set out in this letter. The alterations are:

(i)  The cancellation of previous instructions detailed in this Headquarters' letter ADGB/S. 38621/Ops. 5B dated 22nd June, 1944, involving the use of code words "Flabby", "Fickle" and "Spouse".

(ii)  The removal of the 'Diver' Gun Belt from its original position immediately in front of the anti-'Diver' balloon barrage to a coastal strip between St. Margaret's Bay and Cuckmere Haven.

(iii) Complete freedom of action against Flying Bombs will be allowed to A.A. guns at all times and in all conditions, within the

241

boundaries of the new 'Diver' Gun Belt.
(iv) Complete freedom of action against Flying Bombs will be allowed to fighter aircraft forward of the balloon barrage, but excluding the area of the 'Diver' Gun Belt.
(v) The freedom of action allowed in sub-paragraphs (iii) and (iv) involve:
(a) the prohibition, subject to certain exceptions, of all flying within the 'Diver' Gun Belt, up to a height of 10,000 feet.
(b) the prohibition of engagement of Flying Bombs directed at London by shore based A.A. gunfire outside the 'Diver' Gun Belt.

4. The strict co-operation of all Commands in the application of these rules is of the greatest importance, and would be appreciated by this Headquarters.

*W.B. Callaway.*
*Air Vice Marshal,*
*Senior Air Staff Officer,*
*Air Defence of Great Britain.*

Air Defence of Great Britain Operational Instruction No. 15/1944.

Action by co-ordination of Fighters, A.A. Guns and Balloons in Defence of London against Flying Bombs.

Information.

Introduction.

The defensive resources available to Headquarters, A.D.G.B. to counter the enemy attack on London by Flying Bombs commenced deployment on 16th June, 1944, and thereafter have been in action in areas allotted to the respective arms under rules crystallised in this Headquarters' latter A.D.G.B./S.38621/Ops.5B, dated 22nd June, 1944.

2. In the light of experience gained, a review of the defensive problem raised by the enemy's use of Flying Bombs has been carried out, and as a result, it has been decided to rearrange the defensive measures against Flying Bombs directed at London, and to adjust the rules for the co-ordination of action by the various arms concerned.

3. It is considered of the highest importance that the action of fighters and A.A. guns against Flying Bombs should be co-ordinated and controlled with the greatest care, and all relevant authorities are

therefore requested to co-operate to the fullest extent by prohibiting the engagement of Flying Bombs by fighters, A.A. gunfire, and small arms fire unless covered by the rules set out in this Instruction.

Intention.

4. To define the rules for the co-ordination of action by fighter aircraft, A.A. guns and barrage balloons in the defence against Flying Bombs directed against London.

Execution.

5. In this Instruction, the terms set out below will bear the following meanings:

(i)   Flying Bombs – Enemy Flying Bombs, previously referred to or known as 'Diver' aircraft or pilotless planes.

(ii)  London 'Diver' Defence Area – An area in which the anti-'Diver' defences of London will mainly be expected to operate. This area lies within the following points:
Clacton-on-Sea
Knocke
North Coast of Belgium and France to St. Valery en Caux
Brighton
Slough
St. Albans

(iii) 'Diver' Balloon Area – An area in which a special deployment of balloons for defence against Flying Bombs has been effected. This area lies within lines joining the following co-ordinates:
WR.0694 – WR.1583 – R.1580 – WR. 1079 – WR.0067 – WQ.7859 – WQ.7460 – WQ.7371 – WQ.7872 – WQ.7975.

(iv)  'Diver' Gun Belt – An area in which a special deployment of A.A. guns for defence against Flying Bombs is effected, and in which A.A. guns have special freedom of action. This area lies along the South Coast between St. Margaret's Bay and Cuckmere Haven, and extends in depth between lines running parallel to the coast, 10,000 yards out to sea, and 5,000 yards inland.

(v)   'Diver' Sea Area – The sea area between the coast of England and the coast of Belgium and France and between lines joining Clacton to Knocke and Brighton to St. Valery en Caux.

(vi)  "Day" – Half an hour before sunrise to half an hour after sunset.

(vii) Eastern 'Diver' Balloon Area – An area in which it is under consideration to deploy balloons for the Eastern defence of London against Flying Bombs. This area will lie to the West of a line Chelmsford (WM.1525) – Thameshaven (WM.1800) – Rochester (WR.1887) – Wouldham (WR.1583).

(viii)Eastern 'Diver' Gun Box – An area in which a special deployment of AA. Guns for the Eastern defence of London against Flying Bombs is to be effected. This area lies within lines joining:

Clacton-on-Sea (WM.6132)
Whitstable (WR.5585)
Wouldham (WR.1583)
Rochester (WR.1887)
Thameshaven (WM.1800)
Chelmsford (WM.1525)

Application of this Instruction.

6. The rules as set out herein apply only to the defence against Flying Bombs directed at London. The area, therefore, in which they apply is limited, and is referred to in this Instruction as the "London 'Diver' Defence Area".

7. The engagement of Flying Bombs outside the London 'Diver' Defence Area is under consideration, and, pending instructions being issued, will be subject to the normal rules for the engagement by A.A. guns of hostile aircraft, as set out in A.D.G.B. Operational Instruction No.5/1944, except:

(i) no A.A. guns or fighters will engage a Flying Bomb so as to be likely to cause it to fall within a built-up area or on installations of national importance;

(ii) by night, a flying bomb will always be treated as an "Unseen" target under the terms of A.D.G.B. Operational Instruction No.5/1944.

Effective Date.

8. The rules set out in this Instruction will be brought into effect as from 0600 hours, 17th July, 1944.

General Rules.

9. Nothing set out in this Instruction will be taken to override the general instructions set out in S.D.158, except in regard to the control of fighters where it is specifically so stated.

10. Except where specifically stated, nothing in this Instruction affects the engagement of hostile aircraft by fighters or A.A. guns.

11. The areas between Brighton and Clacton-on-Sea which are specified as being safety lanes for the approach of low flying friendly aircraft in accordance with paragraph 10 (iii) of A.D.G.B. Operational

Instruction No.5/1944 and S.D.533, Appendix 'E' should no longer be regarded as such safety lanes. Stops are being taken to amend these instructions as necessary.

12. Troops not trained in A.A. defence are subject to the rules set out in S.D.158 (Part I), paragraph 38 (ii) and are therefore prohibited from engaging Flying Bombs in any circumstances.

Restrictions on Flying.

13. The 'Diver' Gun Belt and Eastern 'Diver' Gun Box up to a height of 10,000 feet are being declared a prohibited area for flying, in accordance with the rules set out in S.D.158 (Part 2), paragraph 10 (i) and (iv), except that:

(i) The prohibition will also apply to fighters in pursuit of the enemy.

(ii) Fighters engaged in anti-'Diver' operations may cross the 'Diver' Gun Belt at any height through a corridor over the town of Hastings, and lying between lines drawn at right angles to the coast at co-ordinates WR.2326 and WR.2728.

Restrictions on Gun Fire.

14. Within the London 'Diver' Defence Area no shore based A.A. guns will engage Flying Bombs, except:

(i) Those A.A. guns in the 'Diver' Gun Belt or Eastern 'Diver' Gun Box which are connected to an A.A. Command G.O.R. and subject to control therefrom.

(ii) Any guns outside the 'Diver' Gun Belt that have been specially deployed or nominated in an anti-'Diver' role, such deployment or nomination to be made only with the consent of Headquarters, A.D.G.B.

15. A.A. guns, no matter where deployed, will not engage Flying Bombs so as to be likely to cause them to fall in built up areas or on installations of national importance.

16. Within the 'Diver' Gun Belt, A.A. guns specially deployed in an anti-'Diver' role will not engage any aircraft above a height of 8,000 feet.

17. A.A. guns will not engage Flying Bombs in the Hastings corridor detailed in paragraph 13 (iii) above, except by day in good visibility when no friendly aircraft is within 2 miles of the target.

18. A.A. guns will be restricted when this is necessary for the safety of aircraft in distress. These restrictions will be imposed as necessary by the Controller at an appropriate forward control point, who is to be responsible for ensuring that aircraft returning towards the English coast which he knows or suspects are in distress are not engaged by A.A. fire. For this purpose, the following special circuits are being provided:

From
Beachy Head C.H.L. Controller
To
New Haven G.O.R.

From
Fairlight M.E.W. Controller
To
Bexhill G.O.R., Hastings G.O.R., Rye G.O.R.

From
Hythe Type 16 Controller
To Littlestone G.O.R., Dover G.O.R.

From
Dover A.S.R. Controller
To
Littlestone G.O.R., Dover G.O.R.

Special Rules for Co-Ordination of Action by Fighters and A.A. Guns against Flying Bombs.

Freedom of action for fighters.
19. Fighters will have complete freedom of action in all conditions against Flying Bombs in the London 'Diver' Defence Area:
   (i) Forward of the seaward boundary of the 'Diver' Gun Belt.
   (ii) Between the 'Diver' Gun Belt and the 'Diver' Balloon Area.
   (iii) Forward of the Eastern boundary of the Eastern 'Diver' Gun Box.
Subject to such restrictions as may from time to time become necessary to counter Flying Bomb attacks from bases in Belgium. Such restrictions, when considered necessary, will be specially notified.

Marking of Gun Belt and Balloon Area.
20. (i) 'Diver' Gun Belt.
Marker floats are being moored in the positions set out below and those, besides acting as orbit positions for fighters, should give pilots out to sea an indication when they are approaching within a few miles of the 'Diver' Gun Belt. The positions are as follows:
   WR.5927, WR.5723, WR.4819, WR.4417, WR.3713, WR.2605, WR.2102, WW.1598, WW.0898, WW.0297.
   (ii) 'Diver' Balloon Area.
Red 'Snowflake' rockets will be fired from selected R.O.C. posts near

the 'Diver' Balloon Area, as a warning to pilots that they are approaching the balloon barrage. Owing to the wide dispersal of R.O.C. posts, complete reliance should not be placed on this warning by pilots, and by night this warning is being supplemented by exposure of searchlights.

Freedom of Action for Guns.

21. Subject to the provisions of paragraphs 9-12 and 15-19 above, A.A. guns will have complete freedom of action to engage Flying Bombs in the 'Diver' Gun Belt and Eastern 'Diver' Gun Box in any weather conditions both by day and night, and will not be expected to withhold fire owing to the presence of friendly fighters in the vicinity of the flying Bombs.

In this respect, however, attention is drawn to the provisions of paragraphs 18 and 19 above.

Rules for Ships at Sea.

22. Ships at sea will not engage Flying Bombs within the 'Diver' Sea Area, except:
   (i)   By day; and
   (ii)  in conditions of visibility of not less than 3 miles; and
   (iii) provided the Flying Bombs are clearly recognised; and
   (iv)  no friendly fighter is within 2 miles of the Flying Bomb.

Illustration of areas referred to above.

23. Attached at Appendix 'A' hereto is a map setting out for ease of reference the various areas referred to in this Instruction, and defined in paragraph 5 hereof.

Cancellation of previous instructions.

24. The instructions set out in Headquarters' A.D.G.B. letter, reference ADGB/S.38621/Ops.5B, dated 22nd June, 1944, and the signals referred to in paragraph 1 thereof, will be cancelled and destroyed w.e.f. the introduction of these rules.

*W.B. Callaway*
*Air Vice Marshal*
*Senior Air Staff Officer,*
*Air Defence of Great Britain*

*15th July, 1944.*

247

# Appendix IX

## Minute from A.C.A.S. (Ops.) to the Chief of Air Staff on the Redeployment of the Anti-Aircraft Defences.

Deployment of Defences against Flying Bombs.

The new plan for the deployment of anti-aircraft and fighter defences to counter the flying bomb was not submitted to the Air Ministry for approval. The matter appears to have been raised at the Fourth Meeting of the Cabinet Crossbow Committee on the 7th July when Sir Frederick Pile said that in general the guns were only unrestricted in the worst weather and record showed that on the average each gun was only firing 10 rounds per day due to the many restrictions which had had to be placed upon them. In particular, coastal guns were frequently restricted from firing at a bomb which was not followed by fighters. He felt that it was essential to work out some system by which guns would be less restricted as otherwise the enormous effort which had gone into this gun deployment would be largely wasted.

After further discussion the Chairman announced his intention of paying an early visit to the gun belt and thereafter discussing the problem further with Sir Roderic Hill and Sir Frederick Pile.

2. At the next meeting, on 14th July, "Sir Frederick Pile said that an entirely new deployment of guns had now been decided upon….."

3. In paragraph 10 of his Fifth Report the Chairman of the Cabinet Crossbow Committee says "In the light of the operational experience gained up to date, the lay-out of the defences has been reviewed. As a result, it has been decided to make a number of important changes in our deployment plan for guns and fighters. I shall circulate a separate report on this subject."

4. It seems therefore that as you say, the re-deployment has been made largely as a result of representations by General Pile and that co-ordination between A.D.G.B. and A.A. Command was effected at a

meeting of the two Commanders-in-Chief with the Chairman of the Sandys Committee. Since by its terms of reference, the Committee is charged merely with reporting on the effects of Crossbow, and on the counter-measures to meet it, the re-deployment appears to have been decided upon without proper authority.

5. The advantages and disadvantages of the new plan have been set out by Air Marshal Commanding, A.D.G.B. and G.O.C.-in-C., A.A. Command in C.B.C. Papers Nos. (44) 23 and (44) 21. Neither of these reports remarks on the effect of the gun belt area on aircraft making contact with flying bombs over the Channel and having to give up the chase before they have had time to close the range. Results show that by far the greater proportion of flying bombs destroyed by day fighters come down on land and it is fair to assume that the actual engagements take place in or shortly behind what is now to be a prohibited zone.

6. Reference is made in the A.D.G.B. report to the difficulty of identifying aircraft in distress, and fighters returning from patrol over the sea, but the solution of this problem does not seem to be provided for in the immediate future. In the meantime, the new plan was due to be introduced as from 0600 hours today.

7. I am not in favour of a plan which must inevitably result in a reduction in the number of kills by fighters since it is doubtful whether this reduction will be made up for by an increase or even similar number of successes on the part of the A.A. gunners.

8. A.D.G.B. have now for the first time informed us of the plan and have asked for covering approval. I am informing A.D.G.B. that, for the reasons set out above, approval cannot be given.

*A.C.A.S. (Ops.)*
*17th July, 1944.*


Secret

# Appendix X

## Report of Attack on the United Kingdom by Flying Bombs 12th June 1944 to 29th March 1945.

This form of attack was in three distinct phases. Except for one attack in the Manchester area on the night of 23rd/24th December 1944, London was the main target.

Phase:
(1). 12th June 1944 to 1st September 1944 – Land-launched from the coast of France between Dunkirk and Etretat.
(2). 4th September 1944 to 14th January 1945 – Air-launched mostly off the coast of East Anglia.
(3). 2nd March 1945 to 29th March 1945 – Land-launched from Holland.

This report deals with these three phases as a whole. During the whole period 9,251 Flying Bombs were in operation, 5,890 crossed the coast, 2,563 reached the London area and 4,262 were destroyed. There were 2,420 incidents reported in the London Region and 3,403 incidents on land elsewhere.

Casualties (Operational Figures):

Killed:
London – 5,375
Elsewhere – 462

Seriously injured and detained in hospital:
London – 15,258
Elsewhere – 1,504

In addition to these figures, Service casualties reported were:

Killed:
London – 207
Elsewhere – 95

Seriously injured and detained in hospital:
London – 280
Elsewhere – 197

# Appendix XI

## Fall of Flying Bombs on Greater London, 1944-45.

| | | 1944 | | | | | | | 1945 | | |
|---|---|---|---|---|---|---|---|---|---|---|---|
| | Jun | Jul | Aug | Sep | Oct | Nov | Dec | Jan | Feb | Mar | Total |
| **Group 1:** | | | | | | | | | | | |
| Chelsea | 2 | 1 | | | | | | | | | 3 |
| Fulham | 3 | 9 | 2 | | | | | | | | 14 |
| Hammersmith | 4 | 6 | 4 | | | | | | | | 14 |
| Hampstead | 5 | 2 | 2 | | 1 | 1 | | | | | 11 |
| Kensington | 4 | 11 | 6 | | | | | | | | 21 |
| Paddington | 3 | 1 | 1 | | | | | | 1 | | 6 |
| St. Marylebone | 3 | 7 | 2 | 1 | | | | | | | 13 |
| St. Pancras | 5 | 10 | 4 | | 1 | | | | | | 20 |
| Westminster | 12 | 13 | 6 | | | | | | | | 31 |
| | | | | | | | | Group Total | | | 133 |
| **Group 3:** | | | | | | | | | | | |
| Bethnal Green | 3 | 3 | 3 | 1 | | 1 | | | | | 11 |
| City of London | 4 | 11 | 2 | | 1 | | | | | | 18 |
| Finsbury | 2 | 3 | | | | | | | | | 5 |
| Hackney | 7 | 22 | 8 | | 1 | | | | | | 38 |
| Holborn | 2 | | 2 | | | | | | | | 4 |
| Islington | 4 | 8 | 3 | | | | | | | | 15 |
| Poplar | 9 | 18 | 9 | 1 | | | | | | | 37 |
| Shoreditch | | 3 | 7 | | | | | | | | 10 |
| Stepney | 5 | 15 | 10 | | | | | | | | 30 |
| Stoke Newington | 2 | 3 | 2 | | | | | | | | 7 |
| | | | | | | | | Group Total | | | 175 |
| **Group 4:** | | | | | | | | | | | |
| Bermondsey | 9 | 12 | 8 | | | | | | 1 | | 30 |
| Deptford | 8 | 16 | 5 | | | | | | 1 | | 30 |

| | Jun | Jul | Aug | Sep | Oct | Nov | Dec | Jan | Feb | Mar | Total |
|---|---|---|---|---|---|---|---|---|---|---|---|
| Greenwich | 21 | 41 | 11 | | | | | | | | 73 |
| Lewisham | 39 | 52 | 25 | | | | | | 1 | | 117 |
| Woolwich | 29 | 26 | 25 | 1 | 1 | | | | | | 82 |
| | | | | | | | | Group Total | | | 332 |
| | | | | | | | | | | | |
| Group 5: | | | | | | | | | | | |
| Battersea | 10 | 20 | 4 | | | | | | | | 34 |
| Camberwell | 21 | 39 | 20 | | 1 | | | | | 1 | 82 |
| Lambeth | 18 | 38 | 12 | | | | 1 | | | | 69 |
| Southwark | 9 | 4 | 1 | | | | 1 | | | | 15 |
| Wandsworth | 42 | 63 | 19 | 1 | 1 | | | | | | 126 |
| | | | | | | | | Group Total | | | 326 |
| | | | | | | | | | | | |
| Sub-Group 6-A: | | | | | | | | | | | |
| Cheshunt | 1 | 3 | 2 | | 3 | | | | | | 9 |
| East Barnet | 1 | 3 | 3 | | | | | | | 1 | 8 |
| Edmonton | 1 | 5 | 1 | 1 | 1 | | | | | | 9 |
| Enfield | 4 | 8 | 7 | 2 | | | | 1 | | 1 | 23 |
| Friern Barnet | 1 | | | | 1 | 1 | | | | | 3 |
| Hornsey | 4 | 9 | 2 | | | 1 | | 1 | | | 17 |
| Potters Bar | 1 | | 1 | 2 | | | | | | | 4 |
| Southgate | | 4 | 2 | | | | | | | | 6 |
| Tottenham | 2 | | 2 | | | | 1 | | | | 5 |
| Wood Green | 3 | 2 | | | | | | | | 1 | 6 |
| | | | | | | | | Sub-Group Total | | | 90 |
| | | | | | | | | | | | |
| Sub-Group 6-C: | | | | | | | | | | | |
| Barnet Urban | | 2 | 1 | | | | | | | | 3 |
| Bushey | | 1 | | | | | | | | | 1 |
| Elstree | 1 | | | | | | | | | | 1 |
| Finchley | 3 | 2 | 1 | | | | | | | | 6 |
| Harrow | 6 | 4 | 2 | | 1 | | 1 | | | | 14 |
| Hendon | 1 | 4 | 8 | | | | | | | | 13 |
| Ruislip & Northwood | 3 | 1 | | | | | | | | | 4 |
| Uxbridge | 2 | 1 | 2 | | | | | | | | 5 |
| Wembley | 1 | 8 | 5 | | | | | | | | 14 |
| Willesden | 4 | 6 | 5 | | | | | | | | 15 |
| | | | | | | | | Sub-Group Total | | | 76 |
| | | | | | | | | | | | |
| Sub-Group 6-D: | | | | | | | | | | | |
| Acton | 4 | 1 | 1 | | | | | | | | 6 |

| | Jun | Jul | Aug | Sep | Oct | Nov | Dec | Jan | Feb | Mar | Total |
|---|---|---|---|---|---|---|---|---|---|---|---|
| Brentford & Chiswick | 2 | 5 | 6 | | | | | | | | 13 |
| Ealing | 5 | 4 | 5 | | | | | | 1 | | 15 |
| Feltham | 2 | 1 | 2 | | | | | | | | 5 |
| Hayes & Harlington | 1 | 3 | 2 | | | | | | | | 6 |
| Heston & Isleworth | 3 | 9 | 3 | 1 | | | | | | | 16 |
| Southall-Norwood | 1 | 3 | 1 | | | | | | | | 5 |
| Staines | 5 | 1 | | | | | | | | | 6 |
| Sunbury | 4 | 2 | 2 | | | | | | | | 8 |
| Twickenham | 8 | 10 | 8 | | | | | | | | 26 |
| Yiewsley & West Drayton | 1 | 1 | 1 | | | | | | | | 3 |
| Sub-Group Total | | | | | | | | | | | 109 |
| | | | | | | | | | | | |
| **Group 7:** | | | | | | | | | | | |
| Barking | 8 | 17 | 12 | 1 | | | | | | 1 | 39 |
| Chigwell | 6 | 8 | 6 | 1 | 1 | | | | | | 22 |
| Chingford | 3 | 5 | 1 | 1 | | | | | | | 10 |
| Dagenham | 5 | 10 | 11 | | 1 | 1 | | | | 1 | 29 |
| Ilford | 14 | 14 | 8 | | | | | | | | 36 |
| Leyton | 3 | 13 | 8 | | | | | | | | 24 |
| Waltham Holy Cross | 4 | 4 | 4 | 1 | | | | | | 1 | 14 |
| Walthamstow | 5 | 6 | 7 | 1 | | 1 | 1 | | | | 21 |
| Wanstead & Woodford | 5 | 12 | 5 | | | | | 1 | | | 23 |
| West Ham | 11 | 32 | 13 | 1 | | | | | | | 57 |
| East Ham | 8 | 18 | 10 | | | | | | | | 36 |
| Group Total | | | | | | | | | | | 311 |
| | | | | | | | | | | | |
| **Group 8:** | | | | | | | | | | | |
| Beckenham | 20 | 37 | 12 | | | 1 | | 1 | | | 71 |
| Bexley | 5 | 12 | 5 | | | | | | | | 22 |
| Bromley | 14 | 14 | 6 | | | | | | | | 34 |
| Chislehurst & Sidcup | 12 | 24 | 11 | 1 | | | | 1 | | 1 | 50 |
| Crayford | 4 | 7 | 1 | | | | | | | | 12 |
| Erith | 4 | 6 | 2 | | | | | | | | 12 |
| Orpington | 16 | 25 | 21 | 2 | | | | 2 | | 1 | 67 |
| Penge | 6 | 8 | 4 | | | | | | | | 18 |
| Group Total | | | | | | | | | | | 286 |
| | | | | | | | | | | | |
| **Group 9:** | | | | | | | | | | | |
| Croydon | 46 | 67 | 26 | | | 1 | | | | | 140 |
| Banstead | 12 | 19 | 5 | 1 | | | | | | | 37 |
| Barnes | 1 | 3 | 5 | | | | | | | | 9 |

| | Jun | Jul | Aug | Sep | Oct | Nov | Dec | Jan | Feb | Mar | Total |
|---|---|---|---|---|---|---|---|---|---|---|---|
| Beddington & Wallington | 9 | 17 | 9 | | | | 1 | | | | 36 |
| Carshalton | 6 | 14 | 5 | | | | | | | | 25 |
| Coulsdon & Purley | 18 | 26 | 13 | | 1 | | | | | | 58 |
| Epsom & Ewell | 6 | 16 | 5 | | | | | | | | 27 |
| Esher | 12 | 11 | 13 | | | | | | | | 36 |
| Kingston | 2 | 5 | 1 | | | | | | | | 8 |
| Maldon & Coombe | 8 | 8 | 4 | | | | | | | | 20 |
| Merton & Morden | 7 | 20 | 8 | | | | | | | | 35 |
| Mitcham | 14 | 25 | 5 | 1 | | | | | 1 | | 46 |
| Richmond | 6 | 1 | 3 | 1 | | | | | | | 11 |
| Surbiton | 9 | 13 | 1 | | 1 | 1 | | | | | 25 |
| Sutton & Cheam | 11 | 17 | 4 | | | 1 | | | | | 33 |
| Wimbledon | 16 | 12 | 7 | | 1 | | | | | | 36 |
| | | | | | | | | Group Total | | | 582 |
| | | | | | | | | | | | |
| Total for Region | 696 | 1106 | 539 | 14 | 27 | 10 | 4 | 11 | - | 13 | 2420 |

# Appendix XII

## Fall of Flying Bombs – Counties.

| Region | County | No. of Flying Bomb Incidents | Total for Region |
|---|---|---|---|
| 1 | Durham | 1 | 1 |
| 2 | Yorkshire | 7 | 7 |
| 3 | Northamptonshire | 4 | |
| | Derbyshire | 3 | |
| | Rutlandshire | 1 | |
| | Leicestershire | 1 | |
| | Nottinghamshire | 1 | |
| | Lincolnshire | 2 | 12 |
| 4 | Essex | 412 | |
| | Suffolk | 93 | |
| | Hertfordshire | 82 | |
| | Bedfordshire | 10 | |
| | Norfolk | 13 | |
| | Cambridgeshire | 5 | |
| | Isle of Ely | 3 | |
| | Huntingdonshire | 2 | 620 |
| 6 | Hampshire | 80 | |
| | Oxfordshire | 4 | |
| | Buckinghamshire | 27 | |
| | Berkshire | 12 | 123 |
| 10 | Cheshire | 6 | |
| | Lancashire | 8 | |

|    |            |       |    |       |
|----|------------|-------|----|-------|
|    | Shropshire | 1     | 15 |       |
| 12 | Kent       | 1,444 |    |       |
|    | Sussex     | 886   |    |       |
|    | Surrey     | 295   |    | 2,625 |

Total Incidents – 3,403

# Appendix XIII

## Serious Flying Bomb Incidents in the United Kingdom.

| Date | Time | London Area | | Casualties: Seriously | |
|------|------|-------------|---|------------------|------------|
| | | | | Killed | Injured |
| **1944** | | | | | |
| 18 June. | 1120 | Westminster, Wellington Barracks | | 58 | 20} |
| | | Royal Military Chapel | H | 63 | 48} |
| 19 June. | 0232 | Kensington, Clydesdale Road | | 21 | 25 |
| 19 June. | 1200 | St. Pancras, Whitfield Street | | 21 | 79 |
| 19 June. | 2204 | Southwark, Union Street | | 38 | 54 |
| 22 June. | 0020 | West Ham, Barking Road/Beckton Road | | 17 | 31 |
| 24 June. | 0631 | Finsbury, Killick Street | | 16 | 27 |
| 28 June. | 1740 | Camberwell, Glebe Estate | | 14 | 35 |
| 30 June. | 1410 | Westminster, Melbourne House/ | | | |
| | | Bush House | | 48 | 150 |
| 30 June. | 1215 | Tottenham Court Road, Howland Street | | 20 | 29 |
| 1 July. | 1535 | Fulham, Harwood Terrace/ | | | |
| | | Bagley's Lane | | 15 | 12 |
| 1 July. | 2358 | Fulham, Lewis Trust Buildings, | | | |
| | | Lisgar Terrace | | 14 | 5 |
| 1 July. | 1850 | Bermondsey, Gainsford Street | | 13 | 37 |
| 3 July. | 0747 | Chelsea, Turks Row | | 10 | -} |
| | | | H | 64 | 50} |
| 5 July. | 1313 | Willesden, Ivy Road | | 10 | 25 |
| 7 July. | 1459 | Hayes, H.M.V. Works | | 34 | 18 |
| 9 July. | 1230 | Leyton, Norlington Road/Claude Road | | 18 | 47 |
| 10 July. | 1445 | Bethnal Green, Grove Road | | 14 | 8 |
| 13 July. | 0945 | Lewisham, Southend Lane | | 15 | 35 |
| 18 July. | 2033 | Beckenham, Elmers End Road | | 10 | 33 |
| 23 July. | 0917 | Hackney, Marcon Place | | 12 | 38 |
| July. | 0443 | Willesden, Kilburn Street | | 15 | 30 |
| 27 July. | 1805 | Leyton, Vansittart Road | | 34 | 24 |

| | | | Killed | Seriously Injured |
|---|---|---|---|---|
| 28 July. | 1332 | Kensington, Earls Court Road | 30 | 44 |
| 5 Aug. | 1640 | Camberwell, Lordship Lane | 16 | 36 |
| 16 Aug. | 0952 | Walthamstow, Junc. of High Street and Hoe Street | 17 | 62 |
| 17 Aug. | 0924 | Bermondsey, Rotherhithe Street | 10 | 43 |
| 17 Aug. | 1330 | Battersea, Beauchamp Road | 12 | 25 |
| 20 Aug. | 1204 | Feltham, Twickenham Road | 11 | 13 |
| 21 Aug. | 1247 | Willesden, College Road | 20 | 25 |
| 21 Aug. | 2017 | St. Marylebone, Wharncliffe Gardens | 29 | 58 |
| 23 Aug. | 0445 | Hammersmith, White City Estate | 14 | 24 |
| 23 Aug. | 0801 | East Barnet, Oakleigh Road | 21 | 190 |
| 16 Sept. | 0555 | Barking, St. Audrys Road | 13 | 17 |
| 9 Oct. | 0056 | Hornsey, Barrington Road | 17 | 20 |
| 18 Oct. | 2329 | Edmonton, Fore Street | 12 | 29 |
| 31 Oct. | 0650 | Coulsdon, Olden Road/Dale Road | 17 | 10 |
| 15 Nov. | 0030 | St. Pancras, Grafton Road | 18 | 20 |
| 15 Nov. | 0058 | Sutton, Frogmore Gardens | 11 | 18 |
| 25 Nov. | 0504 | Hampstead, Kingsbury Road | 12 | 29 |
| 10 Dec. | 1903 | Tottenham, Fairfax Road | 13 | 30 |

**1945**

| | | | | |
|---|---|---|---|---|
| 5 Jan. | 2226 | Beckenham, Fairfield Road | 11 | 22 |
| 5 Jan. | 2245 | Lambeth, Richbourne Terrace | 14 | 36 |
| 14 Jan. | 0155 | Southwark, Horsman Street | 10 | 17 |
| 14 Mar. | 0923 | Ealing, Belvue Road | 12 | 22 |

| Date | Time | Elsewhere | | Casualties: Killed | Seriously Injured |
|---|---|---|---|---|---|
| **1944** | | | | | |
| 19 June. | 0205 | Reigate, Surrey | | 10 | 17 |
| 24 June. | 0630 | Charing, (Newlands Camp) Kent | H | 47 | 28 |
| 30 June. | 0337 | Westerham, Kent | | 30 | 9 |
| 3 July. | 0251 | Marden, Kent | H | 11 | 8 |
| 15 July. | 0012 | Portsea Island, Hants | | 15 | 35 |
| 30 July. | 0305 | Watford, Herts | | 33 | 18} |
| | | | H | 2 | -} |
| 30 July. | 2347 | Swanscombe, Kent | | 13 | 22 |
| 5 Aug. | 1858 | Snodland, Kent | | 11 | 21 |
| 6 Aug. | 1710 | Dartford, Kent | | 10 | 12 |
| 19 Sept. | 0433 | Hornchurch, Essex | | 10 | 8 |
| 10 Oct. | 0500 | Hatfield, Herts | | 8 | 30 |
| 24 Dec. | 0615 | Oldham, Lancs | | 26 | 37} |
| | | | H | 1 | -} |

H = Service Casualties

259

# Appendix XIV

## Fall of Long-Range Rockets on Greater London, 1944–45.

| | 1944 | | | | 1945 | | | Total for War |
|---|---|---|---|---|---|---|---|---|
| | Sept. | Oct. | Nov. | Dec. | Jan. | Feb. | Mar. | |
| *Group 1:* | | | | | | | | |
| Chelsea | | | | | 1 | | | 1 |
| Fulham | | | | | | | | - |
| Hammersmith | | | | | | 1 | | 1 |
| Hampstead | | | | | | 1 | 2 | 3 |
| Kensington | | | | 1 | | | | 1 |
| Paddington | | | | | | | | - |
| St. Marylebone | | | | 1 | | | | 1 |
| St. Pancras | | | | | | 1 | 1 | 2 |
| Westminster | | | | 1 | | | 1 | 2 |
| | | | | | | | Group Total | 11 |
| | | | | | | | | |
| *Group 3:* | | | | | | | | |
| Bethnal Green | | | | 1 | | 1 | | 2 |
| City of London | | | | | | | | - |
| Finsbury | | 1 | | | | 1 | 1 | 3 |
| Hackney | | 1 | 2 | 2 | | 5 | | 10 |
| Holborn | | 1 | | | | | | 1 |
| Islington | | 2 | 1 | | 5 | | | 8 |
| Poplar | | 2 | | | 1 | 4 | 2 | 9 |
| Shoreditch | | | | | 1 | | 1 | 2 |
| Stepney | 1 | 2 | 1 | | 4 | | | 8 |
| Stoke Newington | | | | | | 2 | | 2 |
| | | | | | | | Group Total | 45 |

*Group 4:*

| | | | | | | | | |
|---|---|---|---|---|---|---|---|---|
| Bermondsey | | 2 | 2 | | | | 3 | 7 |
| Deptford | | 1 | 2 | | 2 | 1 | 3 | 9 |
| Greenwich | | | 3 | 2 | 6 | 4 | 7 | 22 |
| Lewisham | 1 | 1 | 3 | 2 | 3 | 1 | 1 | 12 |
| Woolwich | 1 | 2 | 6 | 2 | 3 | 6 | 13 | 33 |
| | | | | | | | Group Total | 83 |

*Group 5:*

| | | | | | | | | |
|---|---|---|---|---|---|---|---|---|
| Battersea | | | 1 | | 1 | | | 2 |
| Camberwell | | 1 | 2 | 2 | 3 | 1 | | 9 |
| Lambeth | 1 | | | 1 | 1 | | | 3 |
| Southwark | | | | 2 | 1 | | | 3 |
| Wandsworth | | | 2 | | 2 | 2 | | 6 |
| | | | | | | | Group Total | 23 |

*Sub-Group 6-A:*

| | | | | | | | | |
|---|---|---|---|---|---|---|---|---|
| Cheshunt | | | | | 3 | 2 | 2 | 7 |
| East Barnet | | | | | 1 | | | 1 |
| Edmonton | | | 1 | | 4 | 1 | 3 | 9 |
| Enfield | | | | 3 | 4 | | 2 | 9 |
| Friern Barnet | | | | | 1 | | | 1 |
| Hornsey | | | 1 | 1 | 2 | | | 4 |
| Potter's Bar | | | | | 1 | | | 1 |
| Southgate | 1 | 1 | 1 | 1 | | | | 4 |
| Tottenham | | | | | 1 | 1 | 1 | 3 |
| Wood Green | | | | | 1 | 1 | | 2 |
| | | | | | | | Sub-Group Total | 41 |

*Sub-Group 6-C:*

| | | | | | | | | |
|---|---|---|---|---|---|---|---|---|
| Barnet Urban | | | | | | | 1 | 1 |
| Bushey | | | | | | | | - |
| Elstree | | 1 | | | 1 | | | 2 |
| Finchley | | | 1 | | | | | 1 |
| Harrow | | | 1 | | 1 | | 2 | 4 |
| Hendon | | | 1 | | 1 | | | 2 |
| Ruislip & Northwood | | | | | | 1 | 1 | 2 |
| Uxbridge | | | | | | | | - |
| Wembley | 1 | | | | | | | 1 |
| Willesden | | | | | 2 | | 2 | 4 |
| | | | | | | | Sub-Group Total | 17 |

| | 1944 | | | | 1945 | | | Total for War |
|---|---|---|---|---|---|---|---|---|
| | Sept. | Oct. | Nov. | Dec. | Jan. | Feb. | Mar. | |
| *Sub-Group 6-D:* | | | | | | | | |
| Acton | | | | | | | | - |
| Brentford & Chiswick | 1 | | | | | | | 1 |
| Ealing | | 1 | | | | | | 1 |
| Feltham | | | | | | | | - |
| Hayes & Harlington | | 1 | | 1 | | | | 2 |
| Heston & Isleworth | | | | | | 1 | 1 | 2 |
| Southall-Norwood | | | | | | | | - |
| Staines | | 1 | | | | | | 1 |
| Sunbury | 1 | | | | | | | 1 |
| Twickenham | | | | | 1 | | | 1 |
| Yiewsley & West Drayton | 1 | | | | | | | 1 |
| | | | | | | Sub-Group Total | | 10 |
| | | | | | | | | |
| *Group 7:* | | | | | | | | |
| ·Barking | | 2 | 2 | 4 | 6 | 3 | 4 | 21 |
| Chigwell | | 4 | 4 | | 2 | 1 | 6 | 13 |
| Chingford | | 1 | 1 | | 2 | 6 | 1 | 11 |
| Dagenham | 1 | | 2 | 2 | 3 | 7 | 4 | 19 |
| Ilford | | 1 | 6 | 2 | 5 | 14 | 7 | 35 |
| Leyton | | 1 | 1 | 2 | 3 | 3 | 2 | 12 |
| Waltham Holy Cross | | | 1 | 1 | 4 | 6 | 3 | 15 |
| Walthamstow | 1 | 2 | 4 | 1 | 2 | 6 | 2 | 18 |
| Wanstead & Woodford | | 3 | 2 | 2 | 4 | 2 | 1 | 14 |
| West Ham | | 3 | 7 | 1 | 4 | 6 | 6 | 27 |
| East Ham | 1 | | 2 | | 4 | 6 | 1 | 14 |
| | | | | | | Group Total | | 199 |
| | | | | | | | | |
| *Group 8:* | | | | | | | | |
| Beckenham | | | | | 2 | 1 | 2 | 5 |
| Bexley | | | 5 | 2 | | 3 | 2 | 12 |
| Bromley | | | 1 | | 2 | 2 | 1 | 6 |
| Chislehurst & Sidcup | | | 1 | 2 | 3 | 5 | 6 | 17 |
| Crayford | | | | 2 | | 3 | | 5 |
| Erith | | | 5 | 2 | 1 | 6 | 3 | 17 |
| Orpington | 3 | | 3 | | 1 | 1 | 6 | 14 |
| Penge | | | | | | | | - |
| | | | | | | Group Total | | 76 |

| | 1944 | | | | 1945 | | Total for War |
|---|---|---|---|---|---|---|---|
| | Sept. | Oct. | Nov. | Dec. | Jan. | Feb. | Mar. | |

*Group 9:*

| | Sept. | Oct. | Nov. | Dec. | Jan. | Feb. | Mar. | Total for War |
|---|---|---|---|---|---|---|---|---|
| Croydon | | 1 | | 1 | 2 | | | 4 |
| Banstead | | | 1 | | 1 | | | 2 |
| Barnes | | | | | 1 | | | 1 |
| Beddington & Wallington | | | | | | | | - |
| Carshalton | | | | | | | | - |
| Coulsdon & Purley | 1 | | | | | | | 1 |
| Epsom & Ewell | | | | | | | | - |
| Esher | | | 1 | | | | | 1 |
| Kingston | | | | | 1 | | | 1 |
| Malden & Coombe | | | | | | | | - |
| Merton & Morden | | | | | | | | - |
| Mitcham | | | | | | | | - |
| Richmond | 1 | | | | | | 1 | 2 |
| Surbiton | | | | | | | | - |
| Sutton & Cheam | | | | | | | | - |
| Wimbledon | | | | | | | | - |
| | | | | | | Group Total | | 12 |
| Total for Region | 16 | 27 | 87 | 46 | 113 | 114 | 114 | 517 |

# Appendix XV

## Serious Rocket Incidents in the United Kingdom.

| Date | Time | London | Casualties: Killed | Seriously Injured |
|------|------|--------|--------|--------|
| **1944** | | | | |
| 1 Nov. | 0510 | Camberwell, Friern Road | 24 | 16 |
| 1 Nov. | 1830 | Deptford, Shardeloe Road | 31 | 47 |
| 5 Nov. | 1713 | Islington, Grovedale Road | 32 | 85 |
| 10 Nov. | 1420 | Stepney, Goulston Street | 19 | 97 |
| 11 Nov. | 1838 | Greenwich, Shooters Hill | 24 | 21 |
| 19 Nov. | 0831 | Wandsworth, Hazelhurst Road | 33 | 23 |
| 19 Nov. | 2116 | Bromley, Southborough Lane | 23 | 63 |
| 22 Nov. | 1941 | Bethnal Green, Totly Street | 25 | 44 |
| 24 Nov. | 2032 | Poplar, McCullam Road | 18 | 53 |
| 25 Nov. | 1225 | Deptford, New Cross Road | 160 | 108 |
| 30 Nov. | 0110 | Greenwich, Sunfield Place | 23 | 16 |
| 6 Dec. | 0235 | Camberwell, Varcoe Road | 20 | 9 |
| 7 Dec. | 0124 | Hackney, Canley Road | 22 | 8 |
| 14 Dec. | 1718 | Southwark, Great Dover Street | 14 | 50 |
| 26 Dec. | 2126 | Islington, Mackenzie Road | 68 | 99 |
| 31 Dec. | 2340 | Islington, Stroud Green Road | 15 | 34 |
| **1945** | | | | |
| 4 Jan. | 1230 | West Ham, Plaistow Road | 20 | 33 |
| 4 Jan. | 1612 | Hackney, Woodland Street | 15 | 102 |
| 4 Jan. | 2029 | Lambeth, Westminster Bridge Road | 41 | 26 |
| 9 Jan. | 1930 | Deptford, Adolphus Street | 14 | 51 |
| 13 Jan. | 0600 | Islington, Salterton Road | 29 | 36 |
| 13 Jan. | 1258 | West Ham, Freemason Road | 15 | 35 |
| 20 Jan. | 1052 | Potters Bar, Southgate Road | 21 | 26 |
| 20 Jan. | 1315 | East Barnet, Calton Road | 12 | 59 |

| | | | Killed | Injured |
|---|---|---|---|---|
| 20 Jan. | 1954 | Tottenham, Osman Road | 23 | 48 |
| 22 Jan. | 1714 | Southwark, Borough High Street | 30 | 76 |
| 27 Jan. | 1602 | Battersea, Usk Road | 15 | 43 |
| 28 Jan. | 0044 | West Ham, Grosvenor Road | 28 | 2 |
| 1 Feb. | 0306 | West Ham, Barney Street | 30 | 15 |
| 2 Feb. | 0826 | Deptford, Finland Road | 24 | 22 |
| 9 Feb. | 1608 | St. Pancras, Tavistock Place | 31 | 54 |
| 13 Feb. | 1644 | Wood Green, Pelham Road | 15 | 40 |
| 13 Feb. | 1852 | West Ham, Queen Street | 28 | 23 |
| 14 Feb. | 1000 | Camberwell, Trafalgar Avenue | 18 | 29 |
| 14 Feb. | 2159 | Hammersmith, Wormholt Road | 29 | 41 |
| 16 Feb. | 2344 | Leyton, Crownfield Road | 25 | 10 |
| 19 Feb. | 1420 | Walthamstow, Black Horse Road | 18 | 35 |
| 6 Mar. | 0310 | West Ham, Upperton Road | 31 | 8 |
| 7 Mar. | 0323 | Deptford, Folkestone Gardens | 52 | 32 |
| 7 Mar. | 1247 | Poplar, Ide Street | 25 | 40 |
| 8 Mar. | 1110 | Finsbury, Farringdon Road | 110 | 123 |
| 16 Mar. | 0638 | Leyton, Albert Road | 23 | 18 |
| 21 Mar. | 0936 | Heston, Great West Road | 33 | 98 |
| 25 Mar. | 2301 | Enfield, Broadfield Square | 7 | 100 |
| 27 Mar. | 0721 | Stepney, Hughes Mansions | 134 | 49 |

| Date | Time | Elsewhere | Casualties: Killed | Seriously Injured |
|---|---|---|---|---|
| **1944** | | | | |
| 6 Nov. | 0950 | Luton (Commer Works), Beds. | 19 | 23 |
| 16 Nov. | 0740 | Colliers Row, Essex | 12 | 32 |
| 19 Dec. | 0130 | Chelmsford, Essex | 39 | 35 |
| **1945** | | | | |
| 15 Jan. | 2310 | Rainham, Essex | 14 | 4 |
| 13 Feb. | 1847 | Harold Wood, Essex | 12 | 34 |

# Appendix XVI

## Effect of Flying Bombs on Civil Defence.
## Memorandum by Ministry of Home Security.

Confidential

Ministry of Home Security,
Whitehall,
London, S.W.1.

11th August, 1944.

Lessons From Recent Raids – Flying Bombs

1. Behaviour and Effects.
The Flying Bomb is designed for maximum blast effect and there is no fragmentation of the type with thick cased bombs. The blast effect is roughly equivalent to that of a thousand kilo parachute bomb. There is little or no crater, except occasionally in soft ground or when the bomb power-dives. Full descriptions of the bomb and its behaviour have already been circulated.

One of the principal causes of casualties is from broken glass, accentuated by the fact that much of the glass protection put up at the beginning of the war has been removed, or is no longer effective. Splintering of glass has often been saved by having the windows wide open and, in the case of sash windows, an aperture above and below the two panes of glass.

Frame buildings have again stood up well to blast effects. A direct hit on ordinary brick or stone buildings has generally caused complete collapse. When the bomb has fallen in a busy street in daytime, there have been a considerable number of glass casualties and many people

anxious to give them first aid, but not always competent to do so. Such action, however well meant, may not be very happy for the casualties.
2. Work of the Civil Defence Services.

All reports show that the work of the Services has never been better. They have been helped by the fact that incidents are single ones,[118] but it is only through long and intensive training that an almost clock-work precision has been reached. Many incidents have been cleared up within an hour.

The lessons which have been learnt so far are mainly a re-emphasis of old ones.

One important variation of normal practice has been introduced in London with success to meet this particular form of attack. Reporting of the fall of "fly" is carried out from N.F.S. Observation Posts or from posts established by local authorities on top of Control Centre buildings or individual depots or sometimes Wardens' Posts, the report being passed direct to the Control Centre. On receipt of a report of the fall of "fly" a flying squad is immediately ordered out, consisting of one or two heavy rescue parties, one or two light rescue parties,[119] one or two ambulances and sometimes a mobile first aid post. If the observation post is connected with a depot, Services are sent out direct and at the same time a report is made to the Controller of the action taken. On arrival at the incident any parties and vehicles found redundant are at once returned to their depots or, if additional parties are required, they can at once be requested in the normal way.

It has been found easier to spot the fall of "fly" than ordinary bombs and because, so far, no concentration of the attack has been effected it is safe to send out parties at once without waiting for details. The advantage of this procedure is the speed with which Services can arrive at the incident, probably in a matter of a few minutes only after the "fly" had fallen. In daylight, when crowds are likely quickly to congregate, the speedy arrival of Services is a great help; and most valuable in maintaining morale.

An Incident Officer is also at once ordered out. If he can accompany the flying column, so much the better. On the other hand, he may go straight out from the nearest Wardens' Post. In some cases, Incident Officers are being attached to fire stations from which observations are made. In this case he at once goes out with the first appliance sent. This practice has the advantage of providing a fully qualified Incident Officer immediately on the scene of the incident, which is an obvious advantage.

This adaption of normal procedure is very suitable for flying bomb tactics where the fall is spread. For a concentrated type of attack, it would be dangerous to disperse forces in this way without a clear picture of the whole situation.

Further, this procedure does not in any way affect the functions of Wardens as regards reporting, reconnaissance, etc. The observation post can spot the approximate location of the incident. Details as to damage and casualties can only be obtained on the spot in the normal way. It should be remembered also, that under foggy conditions the observation posts might be unable to function, in which case Wardens should immediately report the approximate location of the "fly" and should then proceed to make their normal reconnaissance and reports.

The quick adoption of this technique to meet the special conditions of "fly" attack is a good illustration of the flexibility of the Civil Defence organisation and emphasises the importance of tackling fresh problems on their merits.

It should be noted that, in country districts, the adoption of this technique may be impracticable, though the value of observation posts if they can be established remains high as difficulties have been experienced in locating "fly" in country districts, especially at night.

3. Help from other Services.

Valuable help has been received from British and Allied troops, Home Guard and the N.F.S. The flying bomb has so far caused few fires, the majority of which have been small, so that the N.F.S. have been free to assist Civil Defence. In London the N.F.S. have helped in reporting from their observation posts, and being very highly trained in quick turnout, are often able to arrive at the scene of the incident before the mobile Civil Defence Services. It is, of course, important that they work under the general direction of the Civil Defence Services, especially if rescue work is to be undertaken. Although the rescue services have never been stretched so far, the value of training in light rescue to Home Guard and N.F.S. has been well proved, especially in cases where they happen to arrive at the incident first. These two services have also given invaluable help in all sorts of other ways, especially the salving and removal of furniture.

4. Control of Public.

There has again been a tendency for sightseers to crowd round a daylight incident, especially in the early stages. The police have obtained valuable assistance from the N.F.S., troops and the Home Guard. It is vital to keep control of crowds if the work of the Civil Defence Services is not to be hampered, and the lives of casualties endangered.

5. Rescue and Casualty Services.

Rescue and first aid work have followed the normal lines. The value of mobile cranes to deal with heavy debris is again emphasised.

So far, the strength of these mobile services has been entirely adequate to deal with the situation. It is rare that up to 10% of the total resources of London Region have been engaged during any one period of 12 hours and more normally about 2%.

Valuable assistance has been given by the reinforcing groups from Mobile Regional Columns.

The following points have been noted as of general interest:

(a) Rescue of casualties from the top storeys of high buildings is quite often required, especially if a "fly" has exploded on the roof.

(b) All types of shelter have proved excellent against this form of attack and the public has again become highly shelter conscious. Rescue parties should bear this fact in mind at all incidents, even in the day time.

(c) Although flying bombs fall singly and do not, therefore, create the multiple incident of the type caused by a stick of ordinary bombs, the area of damage, especially in small domestic property may be large enough to necessitate the rescue work being divided up into sections as with a multiple incident.

(d) If a "fly" falls in a busy thoroughfare a number of people may be buried or trapped by debris in the street, or in shops. An extended and most careful search may be required and a great deal of debris may have to be turned over. Sometimes party walls have been left standing in a most precarious condition, and leaders may have some urgent and difficult decisions to take.

(e) The great importance of properly labelling casualties is again stressed.

(f) The importance of seeing that casualties are taken to the right hospitals, and especially are not sent to hospital unnecessarily, is again emphasised.

(g) The severely injured have been man-handled by persons who are untrained in first aid and in the gentle handling of casualties; pain and shock have thus been increased and the patient's chance of survival diminished.

(h) Severely injured casualties have been moved before the application of first aid (i.e. fractures have not been immobilised, etc.) thus increasing pain and shock and endangering the patient's life and limb.

(i) Severely injured persons have been carried for appreciable distances to hospitals, and to first aid posts, by unauthorised persons, although ambulances were present at their loading point at the incident. This untrained stretcher bearing was, in some instances, associated with imperfect and inadequate blanketing.

(j) Casualties have been whisked off on foot and by car from the incident by the public and unauthorised persons before the C.D. Services could reasonably be expected to arrive. The number, nature of injury, name and destination of these casualties are in such cases difficult if not impossible to ascertain until perhaps hours later. This has imposed an increased strain on the first aid post and hospital staffs and has also led to the distress of relatives and friends whose enquiries could not be answered as soon as they would have been in a controlled casualty evacuation.

(k) In the interest of the casualty it is very important that the leader or deputy leader of all Heavy Rescue Parties (in London) or Rescue parties should be skilled in first aid. In the absence of a doctor at the incident, the responsibility for the gentle handling and first aid treatment of all seriously injured persons will rest on him.

(l) Experience has shown that it is better, normally, to send a light mobile aid unit first to an incident and to hold the mobile first aid unit until the situation is clearer from the more detailed reports. It is also important to release any mobile aid units directly their work is finished. There has been a tendency, at times, to hold them too long.

(m) N.F.S. vehicles should not be used for the conveyance of seriously injured persons to hospital, save in the most exceptional cases. Slightly injured persons who cannot or should not walk, and who would otherwise require a sitting case car for transport to a first aid post, can be moved in such vehicles if they are available.

6. Reconnaissance.

(a) Rescue.

Reconnaissance of demolished property has, for the most part, been well carried out, with the result that rescue parties have been able to go straight for trapped people and get them out. It has not, of course, been so easy in places like churches, hotels, restaurants, shops, and Service hostels. Service Departments have been asked by Headquarters to try to ensure some system of registers in Service hostels available to the Wardens and this should be arranged between local authorities and local formations. One rescue party leader having just seen the "Reconnaissance" film, said that it enabled him to set about his reconnaissance in an ordered way.

(b) Search of less-damaged buildings.

The necessity for careful search of less heavily damaged buildings, i.e. those with roofs, windows and doors affected, has been brought out on a great many occasions. Casualties who have been injured by broken glass have been found inside houses, shops, etc., some distance from the scene of major damage. It is highly important for a thorough search to be made as quickly as possible of all property which has been affected even if only by the breaking of windows and that this search is carried out systematically.

It is equally important for a thorough search to be made at the same time for casualties outside buildings, especially if the incident occurs in daylight during working hours. The number of casualties from glass may be considerable and may be found over an appreciable area.

7. Incident Control.

Controllers, Heads of Services or A.R.P.O.s visiting incidents should be careful not to interfere with the work of the Incident Officer unless there is some excellent reason for such action.

Additional parking problems may arise from the presence of N.F.S. trailer pumps and towing vehicles and Service vehicles, particularly those belonging to the United States Forces. If hospitals or institutions have to be wholly or partially evacuated there may be a considerable number of single decker bus type ambulances. Marshalling and parking of these vehicles may present a special problem for the Incident Officer. Lorries engaged in debris clearance may also be present and will require to be fitted into the general arrangements so as to avoid interference with the work of the C.D. Services and their vehicles.

Incident Inquiry Points have again proved of the utmost value. The importance of clearly and conspicuously indicating their location is again emphasised as is the importance of easy access to inquirers.

There are a good many sources which the Incident Inquiry Point has to tap if it is to keep its information accurate and up-to-date, and it is not always easy for the Inquiry Point personnel to do this while at the same time competing with all their other work. In one Borough the Chief Warden has put into operation a plan under which his office obtains information from the police, hospitals, first aid posts and Rest Centres, sorts it out and supplies it to the appropriate Incident Inquiry Points. This action is taken as often as is necessary, which may be several times during the 24 hours. This system does not do away with the need for the Incident Inquiry Point tapping its own sources of information, but it may be found helpful in keeping a cross-check and it should save the Inquiry Points a certain amount of labour.

8. Checking of Information as to Missing Persons.

A system has been developed under which, as soon as known casualties have been dealt with, a complete list of the occupants of houses, flats, etc., affected by the incident is made out. Each person is then, so far as possible, accounted for, and when this check has been completed the list should contain only those who are missing. It does not, of course, follow that they are actually buried, but it means that for the time being at any rate they remain unaccounted for, and unless any further information is available, they may have to be assumed to be trapped. This list should also, as far as it is practicable, include names of persons known or thought to be involved in the incident in the street or in the vicinity. To obtain this latter information may be extremely difficult and sometimes impossible, but in a daylight incident, especially during working hours, efforts should be made to track down such persons because they may quite easily have become involved.

9. Wardens.

Since the bombing goes on throughout the 24 hours, continuous manning of Wardens' Posts has been necessary and the Service has been under considerable strain in consequence. Valuable help has been provided by reinforcements from Regions outside the present range of the flying bomb and the situation is satisfactory. The importance of working on a rota system in order to allow proper rest periods is again stressed.

Household registers have been invaluable and, for the most part, seem to have been well kept and effective, though evacuation makes the problem of keeping the registers accurate much harder. In this connection considerable help can often be obtained from local tradesmen, especially those dealing in rationed goods, since they are aware of prolonged absence from home through the ration book system. The need for service personnel in billets keeping proper registers is again stressed.

The standard of reporting has been good.

10. Supervisory Staff.

The continuity of the raiding has also caused considerable fatigue and, indeed, strain on Controllers and the more senior officials and technical supervisors, particularly if insufficient deputies have been available to establish a proper rota. Every effort must be made for a proper system of reliefs. Continued lack of sleep together with added strain will inevitably take its toll if care is not exercised.

11. Raid Spotters.

The value of raid spotters in this particular form of attack has proved high. They are an essential complement to the alarm within the alert system. Not only can the actual time which people may have to spend in a shelter be kept very low if an efficient raid spotter system is operating but the confidence felt by workers in the spotters helps greatly to reduce mental strain and to encourage people to concentrate on their jobs during alert periods.

12. Post Raid Services and work of W.V.S.

The post raid Services have worked smoothly, though the question of billeting and alternative accommodation has not always been easy to solve due to shortage of facilities.

One London borough has developed to a high pitch the principle of making Post Raid information available on the spot. Under present conditions, with raiding more or less continuous, this system has much to comment it, e.g.:

(a) Persons are able to retrieve their belongings, quickly without interruptions.

(b) Loss of time and possibly increased anxiety (due to frequent alerts and bombs) is avoided to some extent. Attendance at some central place, e.g. the Town Hall, however good the arrangements, cannot avoid these disadvantages save for those people living in the vicinity.

Meals have frequently been arranged at the Rest Centres, with the same object in view and mobile canteens have also been most useful on the spot. In wet weather, such as has predominated since "fly" attacks began, all these points help considerably to avoid further damage to personal belongings.

Another point of interest has been the display of a list of available billets in Rest Centres from which bombed out persons can select their billet and they are advised to go to friends as far as possible.

The W.V.S. have helped greatly in every variety of way and been a tower of strength. In this same borough they have been invaluable in canvassing houses to find out who is willing to take in bombed-out families, thus providing a thoroughly up-to-date register.

In addition to manning Incident Inquiry Points, they have also helped to staff Information Bureaux and have further visited each house in the area affected by a "fly" incident in order to find out if there is any service required by the occupiers. This particular form of help has been especially appreciated.

The whole of these arrangements, which have been worked admirably, have been developed with thought for the people as the first consideration. And with the idea of taking everything to them as far as it is possible.

It is realised that this is a counsel of perfection and may not always be practical. There is no doubt that where it can be done the extra trouble involved is well repaid. The psychological value is high.

13. General Work of the Civil Defence Services.

As has been indicated, the work of the Civil Defence Services has been of a very high order indeed. It is very clear that the lessons of the February and March raids have gone well home, particularly as regards incident control. The turnout of Services has been remarkably quick and, apart from fatigue due to the continuous nature of the attack, the work has proved well within the capacity of the establishments.

It is interesting to note that the general public have been universal in their praise and admiration for the work of the Civil Defence Services.

Probably the most difficult problem to be faced is that of competing with the first aid repairs to houses. This is, of course, an entirely disparate part of the work and urgent steps have been taken to increase the supply of labour in London. The blast damage from these bombs is extensive; one flying bomb may damage in one way or another 1,000 houses. The problem of first aid repairs is one of very considerable magnitude and the importance of executing repairs quickly remains as high as ever.

*O.C. Allen.*

*Inspector General's Department.*

# Appendix XVII

## Effect of Rockets on Civil Defence.
## Memorandum by Ministry of Home Security.

Ministry of Home Security,
Home Office,
Whitehall,
London, S.W.1.

8th January, 1945

Home Security Circular No. 3/1945
Lessons from Rocket Attacks.

1. Attacks by long range rockets have now been experienced for some weeks and it is possible to set out some points of interest about its effect on the operation of the Civil Defence Services.

Reporting of Location of Incidents.
2. Reporting the fall of a rocket presents more difficulties than the flying bomb and ordinary forms of attack, unless the flash or plume of smoke is seen. The noise of the explosion can be heard for considerable distances and is quite often less loud close to the incident than further away. It may be, in fact, a misleading guide.

3. Observation posts remain valuable with this form of attack, but the absence of warning and knowledge of the direction in which the missile may fall makes it difficult to focus attention on the correct area at the right time. The Wardens' express reports have, to some extent, resumed their importance as a first accurate location of an incident, especially at night. In any case they provide a check on any observation post reports.

4. Since there are, at times, smaller subsidiary craters caused by parts of the missile, care is needed that the real seat of damage is located.

These subsidiary craters have been reported as U.X. Bombs or shells.

5. In country districts, a form of cross checking between sub-controllers of neighbouring areas has been found helpful. Sub-controllers should investigate every possible source of information, and should remember the importance of speed in getting in an express report, in view of the time it may necessarily take services to arrive if the incident is "out in the country". Since the incident may be isolated time should not be spent in compiling a lot of details for the first report. They can be completed and despatched later. The urgent need is to get services to the incident with the least delay.

The Operation of Services.

6. The flying squad technique continues to work well. There have, however, been certain difficulties in country districts, again because of lack of warning when personnel are either sleeping at their depots or at home. And, on occasions, owing to considerable periods of inaction, cars, ambulances, etc., have not always started up very easily. In fact, the location of a rocket in a country district, unless falling in an urban area, may be a matter of considerable difficulty. There is no obvious solution to this problem, but all personnel on duty in areas where rockets are liable to fall should see that their transport is in order and will start.

7. If rocket attacks should be experienced in fog, additional difficulties will almost certainly be experienced in locating the site of the incident.

8. In built-up areas especially, very considerable numbers of Services are often required which throws an additional strain on the Incident Officers. Cases have occurred in which over 100 vehicles have been present including post-raid services. The parking situation therefore wants very careful watching.

The following two examples of bad incidents show the number of vehicles present in each case:

(a)
15 heavy rescue parties
6 light rescue parties
8 ambulances
10 N.F.S. pumps
3 mobile cranes
9 tipper lorries
1 mobile cleansing unit
1 mobile laundry
2 canteens plus a meals service vehicle.

(b)

17 heavy rescue parties

5 light rescue parties

15 ambulances

10 N.F.S. pumps

4 cranes

12 tipper lorries

9. In country districts the despatch of a flying squad on the express report being received has proved highly satisfactory. A typical flying squad may be composed of:

1 light mobile unit

1-2 rescue parties

2 ambulances

The size of the squad should be regarded as flexible and will be governed by the sub-controller's local knowledge. It should be remembered that rocket incidents may often produce, in built-up areas, more buried casualties than the flying bomb and also a considerable number of seriously injured i.e. hospital cases. This point is important in regard to the number of ambulances required and the distance to the nearest hospital. If the hospital is reasonably near, a shuttle service is the obvious answer. If there are a number of trapped casualties it may be important to get them away at once to hospital as soon as they are released. Such action adds to the strain on the ambulance service. It has been found that, on the whole, more ambulances are needed than with flying bomb incidents.

10. there have been occasions when incidents have occurred near Searchlight Companies. On request or their own initiative, they have floodlit the area surrounding the incident and have thus greatly facilitated the quick arrival of services. Such action is additional to the floodlighting of the incident to assist the work of rescue to which reference is also made in these notes.

Casualties.

11. The type of casualties experienced remains appreciably the same, though the proportion of seriously injured to killed, is, as with the flying bombs, greater than with ordinary types of bombs. Minor or major injuries from glass continue to be a considerable cause of casualties.

12. A few instances of burns, probably from the liquid oxygen or hydrogen peroxide as used in the propulsion of the rocket, have been experienced.

13. Some difficulties over records of casualties are still occurring, either because unofficial helpers or friends take them to their own

doctor or some local surgery, or sometimes because records have been duplicated due to a casualty being treated at both a first aid post and a mobile first aid unit, M.P.O.44 being completed at both.

14. It should be remembered that if a large incident in a busy thoroughfare is experienced in daylight, or at a time when there may be many people about, a considerable number of ambulances may be required at the outset to deal with surface casualties. Generally speaking, there has been a marked improvement in casualty handling.

Incident Control.
15. At larger incidents, it has again been necessary to have more than one Incident Officer, especially where the incident may be split by the crater. In such cases it is important to have a senior Incident Officer to co-ordinate the whole incident in accordance with the principles already laid down. In one case where only one Incident Officer was attempting to control a split incident, ambulances arrived and waited at one side while serious casualties were ready to be moved on the other.

16. The use of Incident Control vans, when available, has continued and they have been valuable.

17. Field telephones have been used with advantage, and on one occasion linked the incident to a nearby telephone point, thereby greatly assisting the Incident Officer's work.

18. The importance of industrial premises having their own trained Incident Officers has again been brought out. At a recent incident the local authority Incident Officer had to assume responsibility for an area covering both private and industrial premises, and was somewhat handicapped by lack of knowledge of the industrial premises and their P.A.D. organisation. The closest co-operation between local authority C.D. and industrial P.A.D. organisations is again emphasized.

Incident Inquiry Points.
19. These points have again proved their importance and value. Since there is no warning speed in setting up, the Point is very important to prevent the Incident Officer being swamped with enquires. No new problems have arisen, though the importance of providing cover, warmth and seating accommodation for enquirers is again emphasized. If the number of enquirers is large, or if the incident is split, more than one Point may be necessary. It is important to avoid queues and delays as far as possible; but, if they are unavoidable, everything should be done to look after the enquirers. A mobile canteen with cups of tea or chocolate is of especial value.

20. It must never be forgotten that the Inquiry Points are intended to be a source of information, in addition to their primary role of giving information. If there is more than one Point co-ordination must be arranged.

Rescue Work.

21. There are no outstanding new lessons so far. As the approach of the rocket cannot be heard, passers-by and others are taken unaware and are unable to take shelter. Sending a light rescue party (or outside London, a team of wardens trained in first aid) for a quick search of the surrounding area in the early stages of an incident has proved very helpful and enables lightly injured casualties to receive attention quickly. The team should if possible, have transport.

22. The use of cranes has again proved valuable and at times essential. They must, however, be used with discretion, and should not be regarded as a substitute for skilled rescue. Nor should rescue personnel be diverted from their primary task at the outset and turned on to filling skips.

23. Care is still needed in preventing unauthorised persons from walking about on debris. All debris should, at the start, be treated as if covering casualties, since, with the lack of warning, the number of passers-by is unlikely to be known. Loud speaker cars are of great value.

24. The importance of making a careful plan so that the searching of a site is systematic is again emphasized. Premises must be marked when they have been searched. A convenient method is to chalk a large S in a conspicuous place. Each house or building should be so marked.

25. Co-operation between the N.F.S. and rescue services where fire has occurred has been excellent. At one incident two people were rescued alive after 4 hours in a semi-basement under burning debris. The N.F.S. successfully kept the fire under control, avoided flooding the basement, and kept much of the heat and smoke from the trapped persons.

Lighting.

26. Lighting of incidents at night under this form of attack has been developed with great benefit to the general operations. Not only have a number of special lighting sets been made available on call, but the co-operation of anti-aircraft searchlight units has proved invaluable. When using searchlights, it has been found best to aim at a diffused glow produced by training the searchlight over the incident, preferably on to a wall or house, rather than throwing the beam direct onto the incident itself.

Tracing Casualties.
27. The tracing of casualties, especially in daytime, continues to prove a major difficulty. It has naturally been increased by lack of warning because more people may be in streets and buildings.

28. It is most important that householders' record cards are kept up-to-date. They have as usual proved quite invaluable.

General Points.
29. In addition a few points of general interest have been noted and are given below.
 (a) Use of Tipper Lorries.
   Tipper lorries have been employed with great advantage on the perimeter of incidents, working towards the centre shovelling up and removing light debris. This practice, provided it is not going to interfere in any way with the work of the rescue parties, is worth extension where suitable, particularly in helping to get roads cleared and to enable ambulances to get closer to the actual seat of damage.
 (b) Patrolling an area.
   This work is normally a police responsibility, but with their reduced numbers, sufficient are not always available. The absence of the Home Guard, now that they have been stood down, for assistance in patrolling at night has provided a problem especially where there has been a lot of damaged property and salvage and furniture removal has not yet been possible. The Fire Guards have voluntarily done admirable work in patrolling at night. With the numbers of wardens now available it may not always be possible for them to do this work as well as their own, although reinforcements from other parts of the district may be able to help. The point is of importance however and wants watching. In one area an experiment is being undertaken in forming squads of five wardens, each provided with motor transport, despatched from a central point to the incident, and having been given definite instructions as to their task beforehand.
 (c) House to House Visits.
   Members of the W.V.S. have again made a practice of visiting each house in the area affected to see if any help was required. This is proving a most excellent practice and has led to the discovery of unrecorded casualties and is greatly appreciated by the householders. The Housewives Section have also set up a Headquarters near an incident and organized parties to help

householders clear up their homes. Such parties should bring brooms, brushes and dustpans.

(d) Post Raid Services.

The taking of post raid services to the householders, as was often done during the flying bomb attack, has again proved valuable where it is practicable.

(e) Trapped Casualties Liable to Suffocation.

Cases do occur sometimes when casualties are trapped and may take some time to release, and in the meantime may be exposed to escaping gas fumes or in any case dust, and sometimes fire and smoke. There might be occasions when it is possible to get to such casualties remote breathing apparatus. This point is worth bearing in mind as it might be the means of saving their life. Circumstances, of course, will entirely dictate whether this course of action is possible.

(f) Survey of Scene of Damage.

In country districts especially, it is important for a responsible officer to carry out an early survey of the damage so that the requirements in tarpaulins, additional feeding facilities, etc., can be appreciated and demands passed to higher authority. The facilities available locally may be inadequate and the sooner reinforcements can be arranged the better, especially if appreciable distances have to be covered.

(g) Post Raid Requirements.

In country districts again, experience has shown the advantage of having a rest centre officer always on duty at Main County Control, who is at once informed of the character of the incident. He can then check up with his local officers as to the needs of the situation and take any appropriate action. Close liaison is equally important with the representatives of other Government Departments who may be involved, e.g. Ministry of Food, Assistance Board. These contacts are essential also at sub-control level. It is interesting to note that sub-controllers have had to make as many as 23 telephone calls on these different requirements, quite apart from messages ordering out services. The point to remember in country districts is that mutual assistance may be required and may take time to arrange and get to the spot.

(h) Rest Centre Service.

Owing to lack of warning it may very easily happen that, in country districts especially, by the time the incident has been located and reported, there will be a number of homeless to whom a rest centre is not at once available. It is clearly important to reduce this time lag as much as possible, especially in rural areas, where the rest centre officer may have some distance to travel to reach the incident. Sub-controllers should pass an immediate report to the rest centre officer, so that he can take immediate action and also go himself to the incident. In addition, it is a useful safeguard for the Main County Control, on receipt of the express report, to warn the rest centre officer on duty, so that he can check up the position and ensure that the necessary action is being taken.

(i)   Mobile Canteens.

Householders are still showing the same reluctance to leave their homes before their belongings have been salvaged. The provision, urgently, of a mobile canteen is a great help. It serves as a rallying point to the people and often helps the officer making the reconnaissance, to check up on the feeding and other facilities required.

The comfort and accommodation of workmen brought in to carry out first aid repairs is a matter of importance and is not always easy in a rural district. Feeding may have to be arranged, but at the contractor's expense.

Work of this kind often forms an extension of the rest centre service and all emphasises the importance of rapidly getting a proper picture of the whole situation.

30. It is possible that every now and again a really bad incident will be experienced in daytime and it has to be remembered also that, with the rocket, damage to services, i.e. water, gas, electricity, telephone, etc., is much more likely than was the case with the flying bomb. With the winter also, when people have fires, the risk of fire breaking out as a result of damage must be increased to some extent. So long as the scale of attack remains the same and no real concentration is achieved, the Services available should prove adequate, even though a bad incident may call for the full resources of a number of neighbouring areas. The general lessons, as has been shown, vary little from those of the flying bomb. Perhaps one of the most important points to watch is the location of the spot at which the missile has fallen. In country districts, especially, this is not easy, and it is therefore highly important that Services are at all time ready to turn out with all possible speed and that their vehicles are ready and can be started up and got away with the minimum of delay.

31. It may be said with confidence that, despite reductions, the work of all Services has been maintained at a very high level and there have

not normally been any undue delays in reaching the incident and starting operations. It should be remembered, however, that while speed in clearing up an incident is of the highest importance, it is equally essential to exercise care and thoroughness before deciding that the task is completed.

32. This circular is issued by direction of the Ministry of Home Security.

*W.B. Brown*

Issued to all local authorities and Chief Officers of Police in England, Wales and Scotland.

# Appendix XVIII

# Location of Fall of "Big Ben" Incidents

| No. | Date | Time | Location | Launching Area |
|---|---|---|---|---|

**1944**

*1st Week*

**September**

| No. | Date | Time | Location | |
|---|---|---|---|---|
| 1. | 8th | 1843 | Chiswick | |
| 2. | 8th | 1843 | Parn Wood, Nr. Epping | |
| 3. | 10th | 2130 | Frambridge, Nr. Southend | |
| 4. | 11th | 0907 | Lullingstone, Nr. Dartford | |
| 5. | 11th | 0930 | Magdelan Laver | |
| 6. | 12th | 0615 | Kew Gardens | |
| 7. | 12th | 0819 | Dagenham | |
| 8. | 12th | 0852 | Biggin Hill | |
| 9. | 12th | 1755 | Paglesham, Nr. Rochford | |
| 10. | 13th | 1105 | In the sea off Coln Point | |
| 11. | 13th | 0453 | Walthamstow | |
| 12. | 14th | 0725 | Woolwich | |
| 13. | 14th | 1316 | Rotherfield | |
| 14. | 15th | 0409 | Sunbury | |
| 15. | 15th | 1420 | River North of All Hallows | |

*2nd Week*

| No. | Date | Time | Location | |
|---|---|---|---|---|
| 16. | 16th | 0733 | Southgate | |
| 17. | 16th | 0828 | Wembley | |
| 18. | 16th | 1028 | Yiewsley | |
| 19. | 16th | 1520 | Willingdon, Nr. Eastbourne | |
| 20. | 16th | 2238 | Noak Hill, Nr. Romford | |

| | | | |
|---|---|---|---|
| 21. | 17th | 0511 | Knockholt, Nr. Westerham |
| 22. | 17th | 0604 | East Ham |
| 23. | 17th | 1205 | Hockley, Nr. Southend |
| 24. | 17th | 1311 | Coulsdon |
| 25. | 17th | 1856 | Lewisham |
| 26. | 18th | 1902 | Lambeth |

*3rd Week*

| | | | |
|---|---|---|---|
| 27. | 25th | 1905 | Hoxne |
| 28. | 26th | 1630 | Ranworth |
| 29. | 27th | 1047 | Newton Street, Faith, NW Norwich |
| 30. | 27th | 1625 | Whitlington Farm, ENE Norwich |
| 31. | 27th | 1750 | Beighton, ESE Norwich |
| 32. | 28th | 1420 | 8 miles NE Happisburg |
| 33. | 29th | 1312 | Hemsby, Nr. Yarmouth |
| 34. | 29th | 1945 | Coltishall |
| 35. | 29th | 2042 | Thorpe, Nr. Norwich |

*4th Week*

| | | | |
|---|---|---|---|
| 36. | 30th | 1214 | Damgate, E Norwich |

**October**

| | | | |
|---|---|---|---|
| 37. | 1st | 1755 | Bedingham, NW Bungay |
| 38. | 2nd | 0932 | St. Lawrence Hall, NW Ludham |
| 39. | 3rd | 1441 | Hopton, NW Lowestoft |
| 40. | 3rd | 1655 | Mill Farm, Gt. Witchingham |
| 41. | 3rd | 1949 | 2 miles N of Norwich |
| 42. | 3rd | 2010 | West of Bungay |
| 43. | 3rd | 2305 | Leytonstone |
| 44. | 4th | 0815 | Eastchurch, Isle of Sheppey |
| 45. | 4th | 1222 | In the sea, 10 miles off Yarmouth |
| 46. | 4th | 1340 | Rocland St. Mary, SE Norwich |
| 47. | 4th | 1647 | Crostwick, Nr. Norwich |
| 48. | 4th | 1726 | Yewing Farm, Rackheath |
| 49. | 5th | 0422 | Hoddesden |
| 50. | 5th | 0736 | In the sea off Gt. Yarmouth |
| 51. | 5th | 0904 | Taversham Hall Farm, Norwich |
| 52. | 5th | 1138 | Peasenhall |
| 53. | 5th | 1328 | 2 miles NE Brundall, Nr. Norwich |
| 54. | 5th | 1609 | Tunstall |
| 55. | 5th | 1744 | Little Plumstead |
| 56. | 6th | 0925 | Glebe Farm, Shotesham All Saints |

*5th Week*

| | | | |
|---|---|---|---|
| 57. | 7th | 0853 | Pitsea, Nr. Southend |
| 58. | 8th | 0903 | Tilbury |
| 59. | 9th | 0552 | Wanstead Flats |
| 60. | 9th | 0950 | Havengore Island |
| 61. | 9th | 1045 | Langley, SE Norwich |
| 62. | 9th | 1050 | Hillside Farm, SE Norwich |
| 63. | 9th | 1350 | Hyde Marsh, Nr. Frambridge |
| 64. | 9th | 1830 | In the sea off Suffolk |
| 65. | 10th | 0719 | In the sea off Clacton |
| 66. | 10th | 1025 | Navestock, NW Brentwood |
| 67. | 10th | 1600 | In the sea off Harwich |
| 68. | 10th | 1735 | Bramton, SE Norwich |
| 69. | 11th | 0045 | Rawreth, NW Southend |
| 70. | 11th | 0520 | North of Ockenden |
| 71. | 11th | 0650 | Southend |
| 72. | 11th | 0810 | Haddiscoe Hall, Nr. Beccles |
| 73. | 11th | 1051 | Rockland St. Mary, Nr. Norwich |
| 74. | 11th | 1421 | Playford, NE Ipswich |
| 75. | 12th | 0012 | Walthamstow |
| 76. | 12th | 0253 | In the sea off Southend |
| 77. | 12th | 0740 | Ingworth, N of Aylsham |
| 78. | 12th | 1058 | Rawreth, NW Southend |
| 79. | 13th | 0648 | Great Burtsead, E of Brentwood |
| 80. | 13th | 0724 | Little Wakering, ENE Southend |

*6th Week*

| | | | |
|---|---|---|---|
| 81. | 14th | 0222 | 1 mile E of Northaw, Nr. Cuffley |
| 82. | 14th | 2350 | Nr. Fairlop A/F |
| 83. | 15th | 0505 | Rettendon, SE Chelmsford |
| 84. | 17th | 1550 | Little Baddow, NE Chelmsford |
| 85. | 18th | 0632 | Chislet, NE Canterbury |
| 86. | 19th | 0717 | Borough Green, Nr Sevenoaks |
| 87. | 20th | 2015 | South Norwood |

*7th Week*

| | | | | |
|---|---|---|---|---|
| 88. | 21st | 0115 | Hayes | |
| 89. | 23rd | 0344 | 1 mile SW of Clacton (In sea) | C |
| 90. | 23rd | 1410 | Felmore Farm, Billericay | |
| 91. | 23rd | 1653 | St. Mary's at Hoo, Nr. Chatham | |
| 92. | 23rd | 1918 | Navestock Heath. | |
| 93. | 24th | 0028 | Langdon Hill, Nr. Tilbury | |
| 94. | 24th | 0207 | In sea Nr. Queenborough, Isle of Sheppey | |

| 95. | 24th | 0502 | Rushmere St. Andrew, Nr. Ipswich |
| 96. | 24th | 2044 | Wickford, Essex |
| 97. | 24th | 2047 | Fobbing, Essex |
| 98. | 24th | 2227 | Nr. Southminster |
| 99. | 25th | 1240 | Rawreth, Essex |
| 100. | 26th | 0810 | Walthamstow |
| 101. | 26th | 0840 | Bermondsey |
| 102. | 26th | 0900 | Barley, 3 miles SE Royston |
| 103. | 26th | 1014 | Welborn, 10 miles W Norwich |
| 104. | 26th | 1135 | Sheering |
| 105. | 26th | 1341 | In sea off Clacton |
| 106. | 26th | 1845 | Palmers Green |
| 107. | 26th | 2250 | Ilford |
| 108. | 27th | 0655 | Nr. Slough |
| 109. | 27th | 1015 | In field Nr. Swanley |
| 110. | 27th | 1121 | Wanstead |
| 111. | 27th | 1205 | Chingford, Forest Land |
| 112. | 27th | 1854 | Wanstead |
| 113. | 27th | 2325 | West Ham |
| 114. | 27th | 2347 | Lewisham |

*8th Week*

| 115. | 28th | 0459 | Ashford (Nr. Staines) |
| 116. | 28th | 1107 | Deptford (Burst in Mid-Air) |
| 117. | 28th | 1815 | Shalford (Nr. Braintree) |
| 118. | 28th | 1820 | Camberwell |
| 119. | 29th | 2357 | Shenfield, Essex |
| 120. | 30th | 0515 | Beckton, Nr. Barking |
| 121. | 30th | 1230 | West Ham, Victoria Dock |
| 122. | 30th | 1231 | West Ham, Forest Lane |
| 123. | 30th | 1623 | Woolwich |
| 124. | 30th | 1847 | Wapping, Hermitage Warf |
| 125. | 30th | 2038 | Elstree, Ridge Hill |
| 126. | 31st | 0256 | Hanwell Golf Course |
| 127. | 31st | 0740 | Surrey Commercial Docks |
| 128. | 31st | 1811 | Bexley Heath |
| 129. | 31st | 1836 | NE Woolwich |
| 130. | 31st | 2103 | Hendon, Kingsbury area |
| 131. | 31st | 2340 | Orpington |

**November**
| 132. | 1st | 0215 | Woolwich |

| | | | |
|---|---|---|---|
| 133. | 1st | 0513 | Dulwich |
| 134. | 1st | 1832 | Wanstead Flats |
| 135. | 1st | 1832 | New Cross |
| 136. | 1st | 2245 | Dartford |
| 137. | 2nd | 0330 | Ditton |
| 138. | 2nd | 1005 | Lewisham |
| 139. | 2nd | 1700 | Banstead |
| 140. | 2nd | 2058 | Long Reach |
| 141. | 3rd | 0058 | Hornchurch |
| 142. | 3rd | 0438 | Lewisham |
| 143. | 3rd | 1045 | Barking, Creekmouth |

*9th Week*

| | | | |
|---|---|---|---|
| 144. | 4th | 1056 | Ilford |
| 145. | 4th | 1725 | Sutton-at-Hone |
| 146. | 4th | 1805 | Wakering Stairs, ENE Southend |
| 147. | 4th | 2147 | N of Romford |
| 148. | 5th | 0036½ | Romford |
| 149. | 5th | 0130 | Penshurst |
| 150. | 5th | 0745 | Wandsworth |
| 151. | 5th | 1055 | Bermondsey |
| 152. | 5th | 1245 | Rainham, Nr. Barking |
| 153. | 5th | 1641 | Dagenham |
| 154. | 5th | 1712 | Islington |
| 155. | 6th | 0945 | Luton |
| 156. | 6th | 1051 | Yalding, SW Maidstone |
| 157. | 6th | 1458 | Bexley Heath |
| 158. | 6th | 1750 | Little Warley, Nr. Brentwood |
| 159. | 7th | 0108 | Weeley, Nr. Clacton |
| 160. | 7th | 0904 | Canvey Island area |
| 161. | 10th | 0645 | In the sea off Shoeburyness |
| 162. | 10th | 0815 | Hornsey |
| 163. | 10th | 1150 | Belvedere |
| 164. | 10th | 1451 | Aldgate High Street |
| 165. | 10th | 1510 | Fulbourne, Nr. Cambridge |

*10th Week*

| | | | |
|---|---|---|---|
| 166. | 11th | 1540 | Cliffe-at-Hooe, (In woods) |
| 167. | 11th | 1837 | Brook Hotel, Shooter's Hill Road, Greenwich. Casualties feared heavy |
| 168. | 11th | 1909 | S of Birchington, Kent |

| 169. | 11th | 2344 | Brook Place, 3 miles SW Sevenoaks | |
|---|---|---|---|---|
| 170. | 12th | 0008 | Rochester Gardens, Ilford | |
| 171. | 12th | 0229 | Noak Hill, NE of Romford | |
| 172. | 12th | 1135½ | Nazeing, Essex | |
| 173. | 12th | 1730 | Stone, Nr. Dartford | |
| 174. | 12th | 2053 | Westminster | |
| 175. | 12th | 2156 | West Ham | |
| 176. | 12th | 2343 | Swanscombe | |
| 177. | 13th | 0432 | Ockenden | |
| 178. | 13th | 0508 | West Ham | |
| 179. | 13th | 0812 | In the sea, NE Clacton | |
| 180. | 13th | 1249 | Erith | |
| 181. | 13th | 1638 | Graves End | |
| 182. | 13th | 2217 | Langdon Hills, Brentwood | |
| 183. | 13th | 2247 | Southborough, Nr. Tunbridge Wells | |
| 184. | 14th | 0621 | Orpington | |
| 185. | 14th | 0938 | Eltham | |
| 186. | 14th | 0940 | Greenwich | |
| 187. | 14th | 2137 | Tifford area | |
| 188. | 14th | 2216 | Rayleigh | |
| 189. | 14th | 2225 | Bermondsey | |
| 190. | 15th | 0008 | Stratford, Leytonstone Road | |
| 191. | 15th | 0206 | Southgate | |
| 192. | 15th | 0512 | Romford | |
| 193. | 15th | 0550 | Between Hertford and Harlow | |
| 194. | 15th | 0919 | In the sea off Southend | |
| 195. | 15th | 1250 | Lewisham | |
| 196. | 15th | 1643 | High Ongar | |
| 197. | 15th | 1718 | Finchley | |
| 198. | 16th | 0245 | Islington | |
| 199. | 16th | 0740 | NW Romford | |
| 200. | 17th | 0240 | Barking | |
| 201. | 17th | 0327 | North of Dartford | |
| 202. | 17th | 0450 | West Ham | |
| 203. | 17th | 0915 | Poplar, burst in the air | |
| 204. | 17th | 1056 | In the sea off Clacton | |
| 205. | 17th | 2145 | Rainham | |

*11th Week*

| 206. | 18th | 1113 | Stanford Rivers | The Hague/Leiden area |
| 207. | 18th | 1116 | Aldeburgh Road, Chadwell Heath | The Hague/Leiden area |

289

| | | | | |
|---|---|---|---|---|
| 208. | 18th | 1128 | Woolwich Possibly | Monster area |
| 209. | 18th | 1607 | Theydon Mount, SE Epping | Possibly The Hague area |
| 210. | 18th | 1608 | Erith, N Belvedere Road | Not known |
| 211. | 18th | 1948½ | East Ham | Possibly The Hague area |
| 212. | 18th | 2232 | Dagenham | Monster area |
| 213. | 19th | 0210 | Walthamstow | Monster area |
| 214. | 19th | 0705 | Peckham | Monster area |
| 215. | 19th | 0831 | Wandsworth | Monster area |
| 216. | 19th | 1058 | Hackney | |
| 217. | 19th | 1625 | Warren Hill, Chigwell | East of The Hague |
| 218. | 19th | 1922 | Welling | The Hague area |
| 219. | 19th | 2118 | Bickley | Monster area |
| 220. | 20th | 0102 | Pinner | SW of The Hague |
| 221. | 20th | 1000 | East Ham Possibly | The Hague area |
| 222. | 20th | 1315 | Abridge, Nr. Epping | Possibly The Hague area |
| 223. | 20th | 1852 | Believed in Plumstead Marches | The Hague area |
| 224. | 20th | 2054 | Woodford Bridge | The Hague area |
| 225. | 21st | 0252 | Tilbury area | Monster area |
| 226. | 21st | 0537½ | Erith Marshes | East of The Hague |
| 227. | 21st | 1200 | Walthamstow | The Hague area |
| 228. | 21st | 1203 | Little Waltham | East of The Hague |
| 229. | 21st | 1320 | Erith | |
| 230. | 21st | 1517½ | Laindon | Possibly Monster area |
| 231. | 21st | 1802 | Orpington | NE of The Hague |
| 232. | 21st | 2314 | Battersea | South of The Hague |
| 233. | 22nd | 1327 | Bradwell Marshes | Monster area |
| 234. | 22nd | 1504 | All Hallows | The Hague area |
| 235. | 22nd | 1602 | Great Wakering | Probably E Monster area |
| 236. | 22nd | 1940 | Bethnal Green | The Hague area |
| 237. | 22nd | 2034 | Welling | East of The Hague |
| 238. | 22nd | 2107 | Ilford | Monster area |
| 239. | 22nd | 2315 | Dagenham Marshes | Just E of The Hague |
| 240. | 23rd | 0155 | Silvertown | |
| 241. | 23rd | 1932 | West Wick | East of Monster area |
| 242. | 23rd | 2013 | Finsbury | The Hague |
| 243. | 23rd | 2015 | Bowers Gifford | The Hague |
| 244. | 24th | 0337 | West Ham | |

### 12th Week

| | | | | |
|---|---|---|---|---|
| 245. | 24th | 0800 | Waltham Cross | Monster area |
| 246. | 24th | 1045 | Braughing, Herts | Not known |

| | | | | |
|---|---|---|---|---|
| 247. | 24th | 1052 | Ilford | Between Hook of Holland and Delft |
| 248. | 24th | 1202 | West Ham | East of The Hague |
| 249. | 24th | 1207 | Tillingham | SE of The Hague |
| 250. | 24th | 2032½ | Poplar | East of Hook of Holland |
| 251. | 25th | 0925 | Wanstead | Hague area |
| 252. | 25th | 1035 | Chislehurst. Air burst | Hague area |
| 253. | 25th | 1116 | High Holborn | Monster area |
| 254. | 25th | 1130 | Great Warley | Probably Monster area |
| 255. | 25th | 1226 | Deptford | The Hague area |
| 256. | 26th | 0225 | 9 miles SE of Clacton | |
| 257. | 26th | 0540 | Ilford | Monster area |
| 258. | 26th | 0810 | Orfordness, in the sea | East of The Hague |
| 259. | 26th | 1101 | Rainham Possibly | Monster area |
| 260. | 26th | 1134 | Chigwell | Monster area |
| 261. | 26th | 1251 | Walthamstow | East of Monster area |
| 262. | 26th | 1345 | Poplar Possibly | Monster area |
| 263. | 26th | 1355 | Billericay | |
| 264. | 26th | 1743 | Cranham, 4 miles SE Romford | Monster area |
| 265. | 26th | 2006 | Horndon, 5 miles NE Tilbury | Monster area |
| 266. | 26th | 2107 | Hertford | The Hague area |
| 267. | 26th | 2325 | Canvey Island | The Hague area |
| 268. | 27th | 1616 | Sidcup | East of Delft |
| 269. | 27th | 2205½ | Woolwich | The Hague |
| 270. | 27th | 2313½ | Chingford | Between Hook of Holland and Delft |
| 271. | 28th | 1620 | 8 miles S Foulness Point, in sea | East of The Hague |
| 272. | 28th | 2015½ | Stepney. Air burst | The Hague |
| 273. | 28th | 2203 | East Newlands | Leiden area |
| 274. | 28th | 2335 | Burwash | East of The Hague |
| 275. | 29th | 0313 | Barling | |
| 276. | 29th | 1055½ | Sandon | SE of The Hague |
| 277. | 29th | 1514 | Bradwell | The Hague area |
| 278. | 29th | 1950 | Polsingford | East of The Hague |
| 279. | 29th | 2020½ | Woolwich | North of The Hague |
| 280. | 29th | 2111 | Bexley | West of Leiden |
| 281. | 29th | 2338½ | Gravesend | West of Leiden |
| 282. | 29th | 2355½ | Edmonton | Just East of The Hague |
| 283. | 30th | 0009 | Leytonstone | Hague area |
| 284. | 30th | 0110 | Greenwich | Monster area |

## December

| | | | | |
|---|---|---|---|---|
| 285. | 1st | 0803 | Enfield | Wassenaar area |
| 286. | 1st | 0803 | Eltham | The Hague area |
| 287. | 1st | 0900 | Barking Marshes | West of Leiden |
| 288. | 1st | 0931 | Lapwater Hall, Nr. Brentwood | East of The Hague |
| 289. | 1st | 1024 | Barking | The Hague area |
| 290. | 1st | 1024 | Leyton | The Hague area |
| 291. | 1st | 1301 | Hornchurch | The Hague area |
| 292. | 1st | 1308 | Great Burstead | Wassenaar area |
| 293. | 1st | 1825 | Muswell Hill | Katwijk area |
| 294. | 1st | 2112 | Pagelsham, Southend | Monster area |
| 295. | 1st | 2147 | Walthamstow | NE of The Hague |

*13th Week*

| | | | | |
|---|---|---|---|---|
| 296. | 2nd | 0735 | Ramsholt | The Hague area |
| 297. | 2nd | 0820 | Clacton, in the sea | East of The Hague |
| 298. | 2nd | 0831 | Benfleet | The Hague/Leiden area |
| 299. | 2nd | 1108½ | Dagenham | Just East of The Hague |
| 300. | 2nd | 2029 | Lambeth | Monster area |
| 301. | 2nd | 2134 | Grays Thurrock | Wassenaar area |
| 302. | 3rd | 0613 | Rainham | East of The Hague |
| 303. | 3rd | 0741 | Wennington, SE Rainham | Just East of The Hague |
| 304. | 3rd | 0929 | Burnham on Crouch | East of The Hague |
| 305. | 3rd | 0946 | Greenwich. Air burst | NE of The Hague |
| 306. | 3rd | 1030 | Herongate, SE Brentwood | East of The Hague |
| 307. | 3rd | 1231 | Wickford | East of The Hague |
| 308. | 3rd | 1451 | In River Thames, Erith Rds. | NE of The Hague |
| 309. | 3rd | 1708 | Grays Thurrock | East of The Hague |
| 310. | 3rd | 2109 | Bexley | The Hague |
| 311. | 4th | 0231½ | Tilbury | The Hague |
| 312. | 4th | 0936 | Canewdon, | N of Rochford |
| 313. | 5th | 2138½ | Dagenham | Wassenaar area |
| 314. | 5th | 2230½ | Woodham Ferrers | Probably The Hague |
| 315. | 6th | 0231½ | Great Burstead | |
| 316. | 6th | 0233½ | Camberwell | |
| 317. | 6th | 0446 | Nr. Woodham Ferrers | East of The Hague |
| 318. | 6th | 0547 | 25 miles East of Foulness | East of The Hague |
| 319. | 6th | 0715 | Crayford | East of The Hague |
| 320. | 6th | 1004 | Approx. 15 miles East of Naze | East of The Hague |
| 321. | 6th | 2307 | Marylebone | Possibly The Hague |
| 322. | 7th | 0123 | Hackney | East of Monster |
| 323. | 7th | 0203 | Braintree | Just East of The Hague |

| | | | | |
|---|---|---|---|---|
| 324. | 7th | 2008 | Hayes | East of The Hague |
| 325. | 7th | 0324 | Woodford Approx. | The Hague |
| 326. | 8th | 1245 | Canewdon | Leiden/Noordwijk area |
| 327. | 8th | 2211 | ½ mile South of Brentwood | Voorburg, E of The Hague |
| 328. | 8th | 2351 | East of Tiptree | Maassluis area |

*14th Week*

| | | | | |
|---|---|---|---|---|
| 329. | 9th | 0449 | Hornchurch | East of The Hague |
| 330. | 9th | 0524 | Canvey Island | East of The Hook |
| 331. | 9th | 0745 | Enfield | East of The Hague |
| 332. | 9th | 2236 | Bowers Gifford | The Hague area |
| 333. | 10th | 0038½ | Erith | East of The Hague |
| 334. | 10th | 0450 | Lewisham | East of The Hague |
| 335. | 10th | 2050 | 20 miles N of North Foreland | East of The Hague |
| 336. | 12th | 0121 | Approx. 10 miles SW Clacton | South of Leiden |
| 337. | 12th | 0424 | Southwark | SW of Delft |
| 338. | 12th | 0515 | Greenwich | East of The Hague |
| 339. | 12th | 0623 | Burnham-on-Crouch | South of Leiden |
| 340. | 12th | 1758½ | Sidcup | East of The Hague |
| 341. | 12th | 2034 | Creeksea | South of Monster |
| 342. | 12th | 2242 | Notting Hill | East of The Hague |
| 343. | 13th | 0018 | In sea SW Clacton | SE of Monster |
| 344. | 13th | 0323½ | Little Warley | East of The Hague |
| 345. | 13th | 0721 | Woolwich | SE of The Hague |
| 346. | 13th | 2205 | 2 miles N Foulness Point | East of The Hague |
| 347. | 13th | 2233 | Pitsea Marshes | SE of Monster |
| 348. | 14th | 0109 | Mouth of River Roach | SE of The Hague |
| 349. | 14th | 0216 | Bowes Park | SE of Monster |
| 350. | 14th | 0501 | Nuthampstead, Herts | East of The Hague |
| 351. | 14th | 1717 | Southwark | East of The Hague |
| 352. | 14th | 2042½ | 4 miles E Foulness Point | East of The Hague |
| 353. | 14th | 2106 | Great Stanbridge | Monster area |
| 354. | 14th | 2339½ | High Wood, Nr. Chelmsford | East of The Hague |
| 355. | 15th | 0014 | In River Crouch (Rayleigh) | Monster area |
| 356. | 15th | 0203 | High Ongar | NE of The Hague |
| 357. | 15th | 0250 | 9 miles E Shoeburyness | NE of The Hague |
| 358. | 15th | 0405 | Mottingham, Sidcup | SE of Monster |
| 359. | 15th | 2148 | 3 miles E Clacton | East of Monster |

*15th Week*

| | | | | |
|---|---|---|---|---|
| 360. | 16th | 1043 | In sea, 9 miles SW Clacton | Probably The Hague area |
| 361. | 16th | 2013 | 7 miles SE Foulness Point | East of The Hague |

| | | | | |
|---|---|---|---|---|
| 362. | 17th | 1602 | Leyton | East of The Hague |
| 363. | 17th | 1854 | Camberwell | East of The Hague |
| 364. | 18th | 0057 | Tillingham Marshes | Monster area |
| 365. | 18th | 1629 | Clacton foreshore | East of The Hague |
| 366. | 19th | 0047 | Hazeleigh Lodge, 2 miles S Maldon | SW of The Hague |
| 367. | 19th | 0125 | 1 mile N Chelmsford | Probably The Hague |
| 368. | 19th | 0605 | Ilford | SW of The Hague |
| 369. | 19th | 1131 | Bradwell Marshes | NE of The Hague |
| 370. | 19th | 2325 | Lewisham | East of The Hague |
| 371. | 20th | 0259 | Crayford | Monster area |
| 372. | 20th | 1208 | Brentwood | The Hague area? |
| 373. | 20th | 1415½ | Little Berkhamsted Hill | East of The Hague |
| 374. | 20th | 1700 | Cuffley | NE of The Hague |
| 375. | 20th | 1920 | Foulness Point. In sea | NE of The Hague |
| 376. | 20th | 2001 | Nevendon | NE of The Hague |
| 377. | 21st | 0144 | Noak Hill area | The Hague |
| 378. | 21st | 0434 | Brentwood | |
| 379. | 21st | 0440½ | Rayleigh | SE of The Hague |
| 380. | 21st | 0942½ | Bradwell-on-Sea | SE of The Hague |
| 381. | 21st | 1043½ | Firstead | SE of The Hague |
| 382. | 21st | | Barking | |

*16th Week*

| | | | | |
|---|---|---|---|---|
| 383. | 23rd | 1849 | Bexley | Voorburg area |
| 384. | 23rd | 1940 | Hackney. Air burst | Voorburg area |
| 385. | 23rd | 2028 | 20 miles E Shoeburyness | West of Maasdijk |
| 386. | 23rd | 2346 | Mildenhall area | SW of The Hague |
| 387. | 24th | 0737½ | Wanstead | The Hague/Hoorn area |
| 388. | 24th | 0937½ | Eastwood | The Hague/Delft area |
| 389. | 24th | 2323½ | 4 miles SW Epping | SSW The Hague |
| 390. | 26th | 2105 | Nazeing | Monster area |
| 391. | 26th | 2105 | Islington | Wassenaar/Voorburg |
| 392. | 26th | 2145 | Pitsea | East of The Hague |
| 393. | 26th | 2156 | Dartford Marshes | Maasdijk area |
| 394. | 27th | 0119 | Navestock | The Hague area |
| 395. | 27th | 0248 | Downham area | Monster area |
| 396. | 27th | 0456 | Waltham Holy Cross | SW of The Hague |
| 397. | 29th | 0614 | 1 mile S Southminster | SE of Monster |
| 398. | 29th | 0906 | 1 mile NE Mundon | The Hague area |
| 399. | 29th | 0916 | 1 mile NE Burnham-on-Crouch | The Hague area |
| 400. | 29th | 1931 | Tillingham | Monster area |

| 401. | 29th | 1954 | 3 miles E Brentwood | Monster area |
|---|---|---|---|---|
| 402. | 29th | 2006 | Barking | The Hague area |
| 403. | 29th | 2238½ | Croydon Monster area | |
| 404. | 29th | 2320 | Shotgate, 2 miles E Wickford | The Hague area |

*17th Week*

| 405. | 30th | 0859 | West Ham | The Hague/Delft area |
|---|---|---|---|---|
| 406. | 30th | 2058 | Ilford | The Hague area |
| 407. | 30th | 2134 | Northfleet | Possibly The Hague |
| 408. | 30th | 2234 | Sutton-at-Hone | The Hague/Leiden area |
| 409. | 30th | 2247 | Stansgate Abbey | The Hague area |
| 410. | 30th | 2249 | Orsett | Delft area |
| 411. | 31st | 0035½ | Ramsden Heath | The Hague area |
| 412. | 31st | 0209 | Enfield | The Hague area |
| 413. | 31st | 0255 | Romford | Wassenaar area |
| 414. | 31st | 0340 | Noak Hill | East of The Hague |
| 415. | 31st | 1912 | Stow Maries | East of The Hague |
| 416. | 31st | 1946 | 19 miles E Shoeburyness | Believed The Hague area |
| 417. | 31st | 2041 | Canvey Island | Wassenaar area |
| 418. | 31st | 2340 | Islington | SE of The Hague |

**1945**
*1st Week*

**January**

| 419. | 1st | 0155 | Laindon | Monster area |
|---|---|---|---|---|
| 420. | 1st | 0458 | Leyton | SW of The Hague |
| 421. | 1st | 0525 | Halstead | East of The Hague |
| 422. | 1st | 0622½ | Sandon | East of Delft |
| 423. | 1st | 0852 | Off Foulness | Point Maasdijk area |
| 424. | 1st | 2040 | 30 miles E Bradwell | SE of The Hague |
| 425. | 2nd | 0335½ | Barnes | NE of The Hague |
| 426. | 2nd | 0920 | Waltham Cross | Probably The Hague |
| 427. | 2nd | 1215 | Beckenham | Not known |
| 428. | 2nd | 1535 | Greenwich | The Hague |
| 429. | 2nd | 1546 | Doddinghurst | The Hague |
| 430. | 2nd | 1819½ | Stapleford | South of The Hague |
| 431. | 2nd | 1851 | Ramsden Heath | East of The Hague |
| 432. | 2nd | 2142 | Greenwich | The Hague/Leiden |
| 433. | 3rd | 0332 | Billericay area | The Hague |
| 434. | 3rd | 0839 | Edmonton P | robably The Hague |
| 435. | 3rd | 0850 | Chelsea | North of Delft |
| 436. | 3rd | 1305 | Southminster | Probably The Hague |

| | | | | |
|---|---|---|---|---|
| 437. | 3rd | 1851 | Harlow/Sheering | South of The Hague |
| 438. | 3rd | 2003 | Tonbridge | Wassenaar area |
| 439. | 3rd | 2350 | Hornsey | Probably The Hague |
| 440. | 4th | 0419 | Hoddesdon | WSW of The Hague |
| 441. | 4th | 1230 | West Ham | SSW of The Hague |
| 442. | 4th | 1236 | Titsey Hill | NE of The Hague |
| 443. | 4th | 1256 | Rayleigh | The Hague/Monster |
| 444. | 4th | 1543 | Runwell | WSW of The Hague |
| 445. | 4th | 1613 | Hackney | SW of The Hague |
| 446. | 4th | 1613 | Little Thurrock | East of The Hague |
| 447. | 4th | 1835½ | Clothall | Monster |
| 448. | 4th | 1932½ | Ilford | East of The Hague |
| 449. | 4th | 2029 | Lambeth | East of The Hague |
| 450. | 4th | 2106 | Stepney | Monster/Maasdijk |
| 451. | 4th | 2121 | In sea, Southwold | SW of The Hague |
| 452. | 4th | 2254½ | Dulwich | East of The Hague |
| 453. | 5th | 0012 | Bromley | SE of Hook of Holland |
| 454. | 5th | 0043 | Navestock Side | The Hague/Monster |
| 455. | 5th | 0336 | Wanstead | Monster/Naaldwijk |
| 456. | 5th | 0927½ | Raydon area | Delft |
| 457. | 5th | 1412 | East of Billericay | Monster |
| 458. | 5th | 1525 | Tolleshunt D'Arcy | East of The Hague |
| 459. | 5th | 2245 | Addington | NE of The Hague |
| 460. | 6th | 0215 | Dartford area | NE of The Hague |
| 461. | 6th | 0749 | SE Hatfield | The Hague |
| 462. | 6th | 0832 | Ongar Park Wood | The Hague |
| 463. | 6th | 1343 | Deptford | Delft |
| 464. | 6th | 1628½ | Northaw | Wassenaar |
| 465. | 6th | 1646 | West Ham | Wassenaar |
| 466. | 6th | 1706 | Dulwich | Monster/Naaldwijk |
| 467. | 6th | 1946 | Erith | SW of The Hague |
| 468. | 6th | 2201 | Beazley End | East of The Hague |
| 469. | 6th | 2246 | Camberwell | Monster/Naaldwijk |
| 470. | 7th | 0145 | Dagenham | The Hague |
| 471. | 7th | 0216 | Teddington | East of Delft |
| 472. | 7th | 0456 | Tottenham | S of The Hague |
| 473. | 7th | 0525 | Guildford, Hogs Back | SW of The Hague |
| 474. | 7th | 0612 | Great Baddow | SSW of The Hague |
| 475. | 7th | 1214 | Leytonstone | Possibly The Hague |
| 476. | 7th | 1540 | Cheshunt | SSW of The Hague |
| 477. | 7th | 1648 | Ilford | SSW of Leiden |
| 478. | 7th | 1715 | Islington | ENE of The Hague |

| 479. | 7th | 1736 | Hutton | SSE of The Hague |
| 480. | 7th | 1813 | Brightlingsea | The Hague |

*2nd Week*

| 481. | 8th | 1043½ | High Beech | Wassenaar/Voorburg |
| 482. | 8th | 1123½ | Islington | The Hague |
| 483. | 8th | 1213 | Sydenham | Wassenaar/Voorburg |
| 484. | 8th | 1237 | Hornsey | SW of The Hague |
| 485. | 8th | 1314½ | Wilmington | Wassenaar/Katwijk |
| 486. | 8th | 1413 | Barking Marshes | The Hague/Scheveningen |
| 487. | 8th | 1518 | Barking | The Hague/Scheveningen |
| 488. | 8th | 1602 | Datchworth | Wassenaar |
| 489. | 8th | 1633 | West Hampstead | The Hague/Leiden |
| 490. | 8th | 1822 | Clapham Common | The Hague/Naaldwijk |
| 491. | 8th | 1944 | Sidcup | Wassenaar/Voorburg |
| 492. | 8th | 2229 | Stoke Newington | Monster/Loosduinen |
| 493. | 9th | 1050 | Beckenham | Wassenaar |
| 494. | 9th | 1405 | South Ockendon | The Hague |
| 495. | 9th | 1716 | E Sawbridgeworth | The Hague/Loosduinen |
| 496. | 9th | 1802 | Basildon | Wassenaar/Voorburg |
| 497. | 9th | 1928 | Deptford | ENE of The Hague |
| 498. | 9th | 2215 | Great Warley Street | ENE of The Hague |
| 499. | 10th | 0027 | Edmonton | Monster/Naaldwijk |
| 500. | 10th | 1100 | Great Totham | Possibly The Hague |
| 501. | 10th | 1114 | Stoke Newington | Possibly Hook of Holland |
| 502. | 10th | 1420 | Henlow/Arlsley | Possibly The Hague |
| 503. | 10th | 1431 | Broomfield | Not known |
| 504. | 11th | 1025 | Battlesbridge | NE of The Hague |
| 505. | 12th | 1104 | South Green | Wassenaar/Voorburg |
| 506. | 12th | 1738½ | Marden Ash | Loosduinen |
| 507. | 12th | 1739 | Trimley | Wassenaar/Leidschendam |
| 508. | 12th | 1755 | Writtle | The Hague |
| 509. | 12th | 1935 | Boreham | The Hague |
| 510. | 12th | 1946 | Off Clacton | Monster/Maasdijk |
| 511. | 12th | 2045 | Ilford | Wassenaar/Voorburg |
| 512. | 12th | 2216 | Biddlestead | Wassenaar/Voorburg |
| 513. | 13th | 0059 | Toot Hill | East of The Hague |
| 514. | 13th | 0231 | Wood Green | East Hook of Holland |
| 515. | 13th | 0600 | Islington | The Hague/Scheveningen |
| 516. | 13th | 0708 | Poplar | Monster/Naaldwijk |
| 517. | 13th | 0749 | Watton-at-Stone | Loosduinen/Naaldwijk |
| 518. | 13th | 0857 | Broadoak End | The Hague |

| 519. | 13th | 1130 | Chigwell | The Hague/Loosduinen |
|---|---|---|---|---|
| 520. | 13th | 1153½ | Enfield | Probably East Monster |
| 521. | 13th | 1258½ | West Ham | Wassenaar |
| 522. | 13th | 1411 | South Hornchurch | Wassenaar/Voorburg |
| 523. | 13th | 1635 | West Tilbury | The Hague/Loosduinen |
| 524. | 13th | 1643 | East Foulness | The Hague/Voorburg |
| 525. | 13th | 1758 | Hockley | Voorburg |
| 526. | 14th | 1056 | Foulness Island | The Hague/Loosduinen |
| 527. | 14th | 1135 | Abbess Roding | Probably The Hague |
| 528. | 14th | 1212½ | Barking | The Hague/Loosduinen |
| 529. | 14th | 1347½ | Beaumont | Probably The Hague |
| 530. | 14th | 1529 | Cheshunt | Monster |
| 531. | 14th | 1550 | Ilford | East of Monster |
| 532. | 14th | 1613 | Lewisham | Wassenaar/Voorburg |
| 533. | 14th | 1738½ | Shoreditch | The Hague/Voorburg |
| 534. | 14th | 2059 | Barking | The Hague/Voorburg |

*3rd Week*

| 535. | 15th | 0518 | Off Shoeburyness | Monster/Naaldwijk |
|---|---|---|---|---|
| 536. | 15th | 0907 | Chingford | Naaldwijk/Maasdijk |
| 537. | 15th | 1113 | Near Whitstable | Not known |
| 538. | 15th | 1717 | Off Polling | The Hague/Delft |
| 539. | 15th | 1854 | Hackney | Monster |
| 540. | 15th | 2312½ | Rainham | Naaldwijk/Maasdijk |
| 541. | 16th | 0300 | Noak Hill | Monster/Naaldwijk |
| 542. | 16th | 0909 | Nr. Herne Bay | North of Voorburg |
| 543. | 16th | 1059½ | Chigwell | SSE of Voorburg |
| 544. | 16th | 1500 | Goldhanger | East of The Hague |
| 545. | 16th | 1910 | Sidcup | Voorburg/Delft |
| 546. | 16th | 2032 | Cock Clarks | South of The Hague |
| 547. | 16th | 2101 | Harlow | SW of The Hague |
| 548. | 16th | 2154 | Nr. Banstead | Hook of Holland |
| 549. | 17th | 0818 | Mayland | Wassenaar |
| 550. | 17th | 1142 | Bengeo | Not known |
| 551. | 17th | 1217½ | Essendon | Not known |
| 552. | 17th | 1417 | Corrington Marshes | Loosduinen/Scheveningen |
| 553. | 17th | 1642½ | East Hordon | The Hague/Monster |
| 554. | 17th | 1659 | Hatfield Broadoak | Loosduinen/Scheveningen |
| 555. | 17th | 1834 | Much Hadham | The Hague/Loosduinen |
| 556. | 17th | 1937½ | Chingford | The Hague/Loosduinen |
| 557. | 19th | 2309 | Barking | SW of The Hague |
| 558. | 19th | 2310 | Wanstead/Woodford | Wassenaar/Voorburg |

| | | | | |
|---|---|---|---|---|
| 559. | 19th | 2341 | Great Perndon | SW of The Hague |
| 560. | 20th | 0116 | Upminster | North of Voorburg |
| 561. | 20th | 0257½ | Canewdon | SW of The Hague |
| 562. | 20th | 0500½ | Walthamstow | Wassenaar / Voorburg |
| 563. | 20th | 0639 | East Ham | Loosduinen / Naaldwijk |
| 564. | 20th | 0855½ | Takeley | SW of Leiden |
| 565. | 20th | 1006 | Bishops Stortford | Not known |
| 566. | 20th | 1052½ | Potters Bar | The Hague / Loosduinen |
| 567. | 20th | 1121 | Barking | Not known |
| 568. | 20th | 1315 | East Barnet | The Hague / Wassenaar |
| 569. | 20th | 1609 | East Horndon | Scheveningen / Loosduinen |
| 570. | 20th | 1610 | Navestock | Wassenaar / Voorburg |
| 571. | 20th | 1637 | Riverhead | Wassenaar / Voorburg |
| 572. | 20th | 1808 | Broxbourne | Wassenaar / Voorburg |
| 573. | 20th | 1923½ | Greenwich | Monster / Naaldwijk |
| 574. | 20th | 1952 | Tottenham | Wassenaar / Voorburg |
| 575. | 20th | 2249½ | Wanstead / Woodford | Monster / Naaldwijk |
| 576. | 21st | 0205 | Plaxtol | Wassenaar / Voorburg |
| 577. | 21st | 1211½ | Hendon | SSW of The Hague |
| 578. | 21st | 1443 | Laindon | The Hague / Hoorn |
| 579. | 21st | 1546½ | Noak Hill | The Hague / Hoorn |
| 580. | 21st | 1650 | Greenwich | Monster |
| 581. | 21st | 1852 | Rainham | The Hague / Loosduinen |
| 582. | 21st | 1857 | Woolwich | SSW of Naaldwijk |
| 583. | 21st | 1912 | South Ockendon | The Hague / Rijswijk |

*4th Week*

| | | | | |
|---|---|---|---|---|
| 584. | 22nd | 1012 | West Thurrock | The Hague / Hoorn |
| 585. | 22nd | 1215 | Friern Barnet | Probably The Hague |
| 586. | 22nd | 1437 | Kingston-upon-Thames | Probably The Hague |
| 587. | 22nd | 1714 | Southwark | The Hague / Leiden |
| 588. | 23rd | 0837 | Hither Green | The Hague |
| 589. | 23rd | 0926 | Waltham Cross | Loosduinen |
| 590. | 23rd | 1050 | Mayland | Not known |
| 591. | 23rd | 1145 | Edmonton | Scheveningen / Loosduinen |
| 592. | 23rd | 1551 | Nr. Stapleford Abbots | Katwijk / Wassenaar |
| 593. | 23rd | 1914 | Dagenham | SW of Leiden |
| 594. | 23rd | 2152 | Horton Kirby | Voorburg |
| 595. | 24th | 0907 | Waltham Cross | Possibly The Hague |
| 596. | 24th | 1050 | Enfield | SSW of The Hague |
| 597. | 24th | 1143½ | Enfield | SSW of The Hague |
| 598. | 24th | 1619 | Greenwich | Wassenaar |

| | | | | |
|---|---|---|---|---|
| 599. | 24th | 2005 | Navestock | Monster / Naaldwijk |
| 600. | 25th | 0712 | Enfield | The Hague |
| 601. | 25th | 0819 | Willesden | SSW of The Hague |
| 602. | 25th | 0833 | Langdon Hills | Wassenaar / Voorburg |
| 603. | 25th | 1201 | Hatfield Heath | NE of The Hague |
| 604. | 25th | 1918 | Off Clacton | The Hague |
| 605. | 25th | 2145 | Greenwich | Monster / Naaldwijk |
| 606. | 26th | 0611 | Shenley | The Hague / Hoorn |
| 607. | 26th | 0624 | Wanstead / Woodford | Probably The Hague |
| 608. | 26th | 0632 | Woolwich | Wassenaar / Voorburg |
| 609. | 26th | 0905 | Leyton | Believed to be The Hague |
| 610. | 26th | 0940½ | Ardleigh Green | Not known |
| 611. | 26th | 0954 | Aveley | ENE of The Hague |
| 612. | 26th | 1040 | Clapham | Not known |
| 613. | 26th | 1210 | Dagenham | The Hague |
| 614. | 26th | 1443½ | Ilford | The Hague |
| 615. | 26th | 1817 | Croydon | Wassenaar / Stomowijk |
| 616. | 26th | 2301 | Woolwich | Wassenaar / Voorburg |
| 617. | 27th | 0004½ | East Ham | The Hague / Hoorn |
| 618. | 27th | 0214½ | Wickford | NE of The Hague |
| 619. | 27th | 0340 | Latchington area | ENE of The Hague |
| 620. | 27th | 0345 | East Ham | Voorburg |
| 621. | 27th | 0355 | Stanmore | The Hague |
| 622. | 27th | 0356½ | Wanstead / Woodford | Loosduinen |
| 623. | 27th | 0945 | Mount Nessing | Probably The Hague |
| 624. | 27th | 1226 | Tillingham | Voorburg / Delft |
| 625. | 27th | 1601 | Battersea | Loosduinen / Delft |
| 626. | 27th | 1625 | Datchworth Green | Loosduinen / Naaldwijk |
| 627. | 28th | 0019 | Forest Row | Scheveningen / Loosduinen |
| 628. | 28th | 0043 | West Ham | North of Voorburg |
| 629. | 28th | 0229 | Willesden | The Hague |
| 630. | 28th | 0330 | Benedon | Voorburg |
| 631. | 28th | 0507 | Bromley | SE of Naaldwijk |
| 632. | 28th | 0651 | Sidcup | Voorburg / Delft |
| 633. | 28th | 0730 | Kirby-le-Soken | South of Loosduinen |
| 634. | 28th | 1030 | East Ham | Probably The Hague |
| 635. | 29th | 0555 | Bradwell | The Hague |
| 636. | 29th | 0633½ | Waltham Cross | SW of The Hague |
| 637. | 29th | 0736½ | Great Amwell | The Hague / Leiden |
| 638. | 29th | 0852 | Darenth | The Hague |
| 639. | 29th | 0922 | Shotgate | Wassenaar |
| 640. | 29th | 0953½ | Bridge Marsh Island | Wassenaar / Voorburg |

| 641. | 29th | 1002 | Stoke Newington | Scheningen/The Hague |
| 642. | 29th | 1535 | Bradwell Bay A/F | The Hague/Loosduinen |

5th Week

**February**

| 643. | 1st | 0133½ | East of North Weald | East of Monster |
| 644. | 1st | 0208 | Althorn | Probably The Hague |
| 645. | 1st | 0303 | West Ham | Voorburg |
| 646. | 1st | 0403 | Harrow | The Hague/Loosduinen |
| 647. | 1st | 0519 | Chiddingstone | Wassenaar |
| 648. | 1st | 0611½ | Walthamstow | The Hague |
| 649. | 1st | 0731 | Walkern | Voorburg/Delft |
| 650. | 1st | 0746 | Chingford | Voorburg |
| 651 | 1st | 1010 | Chingford | SW of The Hague |
| 652. | 1st | 1400 | Hackney | Wassenaar/Voorburg |
| 653. | 1st | 1406 | Chingford | Loosduinen/Maasdijk |
| 654. | 2nd | 0613 | Woodham Mortimer | Loosduinen/Delft |
| 655. | 2nd | 0808 | Southminster | Wassenaar/Leidschendam |
| 656. | 2nd | 0822 | Deptford | Wassenaar/Leidschendam |
| 657. | 2nd | 1013 | Dagenham | NE of Voorburg |
| 658. | 2nd | 1041 | East Ham | Possibly The Hague |
| 659. | 2nd | 1243 | East Ham | Wassenaar |
| 660. | 2nd | 1255 | Walthamstow | Wassenaar/Voorburg |
| 661. | 3rd | 1125 | Epping Forest | Probably The Hague |
| 662. | 3rd | 1316 | Barking | Possibly The Hague |
| 663. | 3rd | 1515 | Ilford | The Hague/Loosduinen |
| 664. | 4th | 1448½ | Near Danebury | Possibly Monster |
| 665. | 4th | 1505 | Ilford | East of Wassenaar |
| 666. | 4th | 1506 | Dagenham | East of The Hague |
| 667. | 4th | 1726 | West Ham | Not known |
| 668. | 4th | 1731 | Ilford | Wassenaar |
| 669. | 4th | 1737 | Theydon Gernon | Loosduinen |
| 670. | 4th | 1813 | Doddinghurst | East of Monster |
| 671. | 4th | 1815 | Hackney | NNE of The Hague |
| 672. | 4th | 2221 | Wanstead/Woodford | Loosduinen |
| 673. | 4th | 2351 | Nr. Hornchurch | East of Voorburg/Delft |
| 674. | 4th | 2357 | Rettenden | NE Voorburg |

6th Week

| 675. | 5th | 0159½ | Chingford | The Hague |
| 676. | 5th | 0239 | Hackney | Wassenaar |
| 677. | 5th | 0535 | Epping Upland | SW of The Hague |

| 678. | 5th | 0814 | Willingale | The Hague/Poeldijk |
|---|---|---|---|---|
| 679. | 5th | 0941½ | Watton-at-Stone | Not known |
| 680. | 5th | 2109 | Waltham Holy Cross | The Hague |
| 681. | 6th | 0458 | Paglesham | Poeldijk area |
| 682. | 6th | 0638 | Essendon | The Hague/Loosduinen Area |
| 683. | 6th | 0734 | Tottenham | The Hague/Poeldijk area |
| 684. | 6th | 0948 | St. Mary Cray | Not known |
| 685. | 6th | 0951 | Ramsden Heath | The Hague area |
| 686. | 6th | 1256½ | Bradwell Bay | Probably The Hague area |
| 687. | 6th | 1805 | Crockenhill | Probably The Hague area |
| 688. | 6th | 1916 | Wanstead Flats | Voorburg/Delft area |
| 689. | 6th | 2146 | Woolwich | Wassenaar/Voorburg area |
| 690. | 7th | 1152½ | Ilford | Delft/Voorburg |
| 691. | 7th | 1210 | Barking | Probably The Hague |
| 692. | 7th | 1559 | Waltham Abbey | The Hague |
| 693. | 8th | 0032 | Bacton | Loosduinen/Maasdijk |
| 694. | 8th | 0108 | Walthamstow | Voorburg/Voorschoten |
| 695. | 8th | 0218 | In sea, Sherringham | Voorburg/Delft (Off Map) |
| 696. | 8th | 0303 | Chislehurst | Wassenaar/Voorburg |
| 697. | 8th | 0918 | Fobbing | Wassenaar/Voorburg |
| 698. | 8th | 1057 | Bethnal Green | SE of Voorburg |
| 699. | 8th | 1206 | Erith | Loosduinen/Hoorn |
| 700. | 8th | 1235 | Ilford | The Hague |
| 701. | 8th | 1543 | Rettendon | Wassenaar/Voorburg |
| 702. | 8th | 1743½ | Chislehurst/Sidcup | Hoorn |
| 703. | 8th | 1750½ | Greenwich | Voorburg |
| 704. | 8th | 2012 | Cock Clarks | NE of The Hague |
| 705. | 8th | 2238 | Dagenham | Voorburg/Rijswijk |
| 706. | 9th | 0542 | Navestock | Probably the Monster area |
| 707. | 9th | 0726½ | Stow Maries | Voorburg/Delft area |
| 708. | 9th | 1408½ | Poplar | The Hague/Voorburg area |
| 709. | 9th | 1608 | St. Pancras | East of Delft |
| 710. | 9th | 1725 | Hayes, Nr. Bromley | The Hague/Rijswijk area |
| 711. | 9th | 1903 | South of Clacton. In sea | East of Voorburg |
| 712. | 9th | 2134 | Chislehurst | Rijnsburg area |
| 713. | 10th | 0033 | Basildon | Rijswijk/Delft area |
| 714. | 10th | 0459 | Welling, Bexley | Not available |
| 715. | 10th | 0634 | Radley Green | Maasdijk/Maasluis |
| 716. | 10th | 0828 | Leyton | The Hague |
| 717. | 10th | 0924 | In sea, Bradwell | Monster/Maasdijk |
| 718. | 10th | 1058 | Woolwich | The Hague |

| | | | | |
|---|---|---|---|---|
| 719. | 10th | 1127 | Rawreth | Not known |
| 720. | 10th | 1247 | Purleigh | Wassenaar / Voorburg |
| 721. | 10th | 1503 | In sea, Clacton | The Hague / Hoorn |
| 722. | 10th | 1529 | Margaretting | The Hague |
| 723. | 10th | 1601 | Purfleet | Voorburg |
| 724. | 10th | 1914½ | Oxted | The Hague / Wassenaar |
| 725. | 10th | 2001 | Widford | Voorburg |
| 726. | 11th | 0103 | Romford | Naaldwijk |
| 727. | 11th | 0150 | Chertsey Mead | The Hague / Scipluiden |
| 728. | 11th | 0440 | Stoke Common | Naaldwijk / Maasdijk (Off Map) |
| 729. | 11th | 1231½ | Stratford | The Haue / Wassenaar |
| 730. | 11th | 1331 | Bromley | The Hague / Rijswijk |
| 731. | 11th | 1451½ | Walthamstow | Katwijk / Westeing |
| 732. | 11th | 1607 | Romford | Wassenaar / Voorburg |
| 733. | 11th | 1816½ | East Ham | Wassenaar / Voorburg |
| 734. | 11th | 2200 | Lewisham | Wassenaar / Voorburg |

*7th Week*

| | | | | |
|---|---|---|---|---|
| 735. | 12th | 0515 | Leatherhead | East of The Hague |
| 736. | 12th | 0716 | In sea, Clacton | Naaldwijk / Maasdijk |
| 737. | 12th | 0722 | Beauchamp Roding | NE of The Hague |
| 738. | 12th | 1030 | Bayford | The Hague |
| 739. | 12th | 1346 | Mountnessing | Voorburg / Wassenaar |
| 740. | 12th | 1604 | Great Warley | SW of Leiden |
| 741. | 12th | 1845 | Great Totham | East of The Hague |
| 742. | 12th | 1846 | Dengie | Wassenaar |
| 743. | 12th | 2028 | Walthamstow | East of Delft |
| 744. | 12th | 2305 | Hackney | Wassenaar / Voorburg |
| 745. | 13th | 0224 | In sea, Orfordness | Monster (Off Map) |
| 746. | 13th | 0342 | West of Halstead | Wassenaar / Voorburg |
| 747. | 13th | 0617 | Cheshunt | Voorburg |
| 748. | 13th | 1549 | High Laver | The Hague / Voorburg |
| 749. | 13th | 1553 | Thames Haven | Delft |
| 750. | 13th | 1615 | Braxted Park | Wassenaar / Voorburg |
| 751. | 13th | 1633½ | Erith | Wassenaar / Voorburg |
| 752. | 13th | 1639 | Depden | Maassluis |
| 753. | 13th | 1644 | Wood Green | Wassenaar / Voorburg |
| 754. | 13th | 1845½ | Harold Wood | Poeldijk / Naaldwijk |
| 755. | 13th | 1852 | West Ham | The Hague |
| 756. | 13th | 1915 | Bexley | The Hague / Rijswijk |
| 757. | 13th | 2258 | Ilford | Voorburg |

| 758. | 13th | 2347 | Horndon-on-the-Hill | The Hague |
|------|------|------|---------------------|-----------|
| 759. | 14th | 0032½ | Platt | Kerkehout / Voorburg |
| 760. | 14th | 0221 | Farningham | The Hague |
| 761. | 14th | 0302 | Cranham | Voorburg |
| 762. | 14th | 0503 | Rawreth | Wassenaar / Leidschendam |
| 763. | 14th | 0536 | Canvey Island | The Hague / Delft |
| 764. | 14th | 0955 | Camberwell | Not known |
| 765. | 14th | 1441½ | Chislehurst / Sidcup | Wassenaar / Kerkehout |
| 766. | 14th | 1455 | Havering | Kerkehout / Voorburg |
| 767. | 14th | 1700 | Havering | Wassenaar / Westeing |
| 768. | 14th | 1711½ | Finsbury | East of The Hague |
| 769. | 14th | 1712 | Mountnessing | The Hague |
| 770. | 14th | 2023 | South Green | Wassenaar / Leidschendam |
| 771. | 14th | 2158 | Hammersmith | Monster / Naaldwijk |
| 772. | 14th | 2231 | Hackney | NE of The Hague |
| 773. | 14th | 2357 | Latchingdon / Snoreham | The Hague / Leiden |
| 774. | 15th | 0055 | Erith | Monster / Naaldwijk |
| 775. | 15th | 0704 | Crayford | Loosduinen / Naaldwijk |
| 776. | 15th | 0930 | Iver Heath | Wassenaar / Kerkehout |
| 777. | 15th | 1122 | Shoreham | East of The Hague |
| 778. | 15th | 1136 | Corringham Marshes | Probably The Hague |
| 779. | 15th | 1447 | In Sea, SE Foulness | Not known |
| 780. | 16th | 1610 | North of Shenfield | Wassenaar / Voorburg area |
| 781. | 16th | 2124 | Nr. West Hanningfield | E of The Hague / Voorburg |
| 782. | 16th | 2134½ | West Hanningfield | Wassenaar / Voorburg area |
| 783. | 16th | 2154 | Woolwich | The Hague / Wassenaar area |
| 784. | 16th | 2344 | Leyton | The Hague / Delft |
| 785. | 17th | 0041 | Nr. Steeple | Wassenaar / Voorburg |
| 786. | 17th | 0049½ | Upper Kirby | Monster area |
| 787. | 17th | 0054 | Dunton | Wassenaar / Voorburg |
| 788. | 17th | 0332 | Aylesford | East of The Hague |
| 789. | 17th | 0341½ | Althorne | Wassenaar / Voorburg |
| 790. | 17th | 0428 | Garston Park | Maasdijk / Zwartewaal |
| 791. | 17th | 0542 | Ilford | The Hague / Rijswijk |
| 792. | 17th | 0533 | Poplar | Kerkehout / Voorburg |
| 793. | 17th | 0622 | Rawreth | Wassenaar / Voorburg |
| 794. | 17th | 0810 | Lynsted | The Hague / Rijswijk |
| 795. | 17th | 0849 | Brentwood | Leidschendam |
| 796. | 17th | 1132 | Willingale | Not known |
| 797. | 17th | 1422 | St. Marys Hoo | Not known |
| 798. | 18th | 0055 | Chingford | Wassenaar |

| 799. | 18th | 0116 | Canvey Island area | Wassenaar |
|---|---|---|---|---|
| 800. | 18th | 0425 | Ilford | Wassenaar |
| 801. | 18th | 0732 | Woodham Ferrers | Wassenaar / The Hague |
| 802. | 18th | 0810 | Wickford Ramsden | Wassenaar / Voorburg |
| 803. | 18th | 0817 | Nr. Pitsea | The Hague |
| 804. | 18th | 0940 | Aveley | Wassenaar / Valkenburg |
| 805. | 18th | 1015 | Dartford Heath | The Hague / Rijksdorp |
| 806. | 18th | 1201 | Rochester | The Hague / Rijswijk |
| 807. | 18th | 1218 | Bexley | The Hague |
| 808. | 18th | 1441 | Poplar | The Hague / Wassenaar |
| 809. | 18th | 1521 | Canewdon | The Hague / Rijksdorp |
| 810. | 18th | 1806 | In Sea, Clacton | Wassenaar |
| 811. | 18th | 1944 | Erith | Wassenaar / Voorburg |
| 812. | 18th | 1952½ | Woolwich | Wassenaar |
| *813* | | | *Not listed or allocated* | |

*8th Week*

| 814. | 19th | 0446 | Off East Anglian Coast | Voorburg / Westeing |
|---|---|---|---|---|
| 815. | 19th | 0456 | Abbess Roding | Rijswijk / Kerthout |
| 816. | 19th | 0719½ | Epping Forest | Rijsdorp / The Hague |
| 817. | 19th | 0727 | Wanstead / Woodford | Voorburg / Den Deil |
| 818. | 19th | 0742 | Crayford | Leidschendam / den Deil |
| 819. | 19th | 1106 | Woolwich | Wassenaar / Kerkehout |
| 820. | 19th | 1144 | Greenwich | The Hague / Delft |
| 821. | 19th | 1357 | Off Clacton | Westeing / Nootdorp |
| 822. | 19th | 1419½ | Walthamstow | Wassenaar / Kerkehout |
| 823. | 19th | 2221½ | Stoke | Loosduinen / Naaldwijk / Hook |
| 824. | 19th | 2255 | Laindon | Wassenaar / Westeing |
| 825. | 20th | 0116 | Greenwich | Wassenaar / Westeing |
| 826. | 20th | 0432 | Poplar | Wassenaar / Voorburg |
| 827. | 20th | 0844 | Mundon | Monster |
| 828. | 20th | 0957 | Earl Stoneham | Probably The Hague |
| 829. | 20th | 1121 | Upminster | |
| 830. | 20th | 1137 | Ilford | Probably The Hague |
| 831. | 20th | 1323 | Rainham | East of The Hague |
| 832. | 20th | 1337 | Waltham Holy Cross | Probably The Hague |
| 833. | 20th | 1538 | Highwood | Probably The Hague |
| 834. | 20th | 1756 | Woolwich | East of The Hague |
| 835. | 20th | 2035 | Romford | NE of The Hague |
| 836. | 20th | 2047 | Chingford | The Hague / Rijswijk |
| 837. | 20th | 2255 | Foulness Island | The Hague / Poeldijk |
| 838. | 20th | 2329 | Barking | Valkenburg / Kerkehout |

| 839. | 21st | 0917 | Sidcup | NE of The Hague |
|------|------|------|--------|-----------------|
| 840. | 21st | 1121½ | Beckenham | Wassenaar/Leidschendam |
| 841. | 21st | 1258 | Ilford | NE of The Hague |
| 842. | 21st | 1617 | South Ockendon | The Hague area |
| 843. | 21st | 2218 | Ilford | Loosduinen/Monster area |
| 844. | 22nd | 0921½ | Epping | Wassenaar/Voorburg |
| 845. | 22nd | 1446 | Eynsford | Wassenaar area |
| 846. | 22nd | 1753 | Heston | The Hague/Wassenaar area |
| 847. | 22nd | 2011 | Off Clacton, in sea | Rijksdorf/Leidschendam area |
| 848. | 22nd | 2102 | West Romford | Wassenaar/Voorburg area |
| 849. | 22nd | 2148½ | Althorne | The Hague area |
| 850. | 22nd | 2248 | Warley | Loosduinen/Naaldwijk/Hook |
| 851. | 22nd | 2251 | Greenwich | Wassenaar/Voorburg |
| 852. | 23rd | 0004 | East Ham | The Hague area |
| 853. | 23rd | 0103½ | Waltham Holy Cross | Rijksdorf/Westeing area |
| 854. | 23rd | 0437 | Chigwell | Monster area |
| 855. | 23rd | 0746 | Dagenham | Naaldwijk/Massdijk area |
| 856. | 23rd | 0908 | Chigwell | The Hague area |
| 857. | 23rd | 0945 | Sevenoaks | Probably Monster area |
| 858. | 23rd | 1124½ | Cheshunt | The Hague area |
| 859. | 23rd | 1242 | Off Folkestone | The Hague/Hoorn area |
| 860. | 23rd | 1339 | 1 mile NW of Epping | Voorburg/Wassenaar area |
| 861. | 23rd | 1425 | Blackmore | Probably The Hague area |
| 862. | 23rd | 1643 | Cold Norton | East of The Hague |
| 863. | 23rd | 1659 | Chelmsford | East of The Hague |
| 864. | 24th | 0740 | Dagenham | East of The Hague |

*9th Week*

| 865. | 26th | 0910 | Woolwich | Wassenaar/Voorburg area |
|------|------|------|----------|-------------------------|
| 866. | 26th | 0911 | Bobbingworth | Not ascertainable |
| 867. | 26th | 0922 | 8 miles SE of Clacton, in sea | East of The Hague |
| 868. | 26th | 0935½ | Ilford | East of The Hague |
| 869. | 26th | 1127 | Belvedere, Erith | The Hague area |
| 870. | 26th | 1611½ | SW of Clacton, in sea | Wassenaar/Voorburg area |
| 871. | 26th | 1826½ | Leyton | Wassenaar/Voorburg area |
| 872. | 26th | 2025 | West Ham | Wassenaar/Voorburg area |
| 873. | 26th | 2305 | Pitsea Marshes | Wassenaar/Kerkehout area |
| 874. | 27th | 0123 | West Thurrock Marshes | Wassenaar/Voorburg |

| 875. | 27th | 0125 | Dagenham | Wassenaar/Kerkehout area |
|---|---|---|---|---|
| 876. | 27th | 0224 | Kelvedon Hatch | Probably The Hague area |
| 877. | 27th | 0229 | Ilford | The Hague/Rijswijk area |
| 878. | 27th | 0443 | Chevening | Wassenaar area |
| 879. | 27th | 0533 | Theydon Garnon | Monster area |
| 880. | 27th | 0745 | North Stifford | The Hague area |
| 881. | 27th | 0921½ | Swanscombe | NE of The Hague |
| 882. | 27th | 1051 | Ingatestone | NE of The Hague |
| 883. | 28th | 0022½ | New Hall Green | The Hague area |
| 884. | 28th | 0121 | Enfield | The Hague area |
| 885. | 28th | 0314 | East Ham | The Hague area |
| 886. | 28th | 0507 | Erith | The Hague area |

**March**

| 887. | 1st | 0108½ | Billericay | NE of The Hague |
|---|---|---|---|---|
| 888. | 1st | 0234½ | Little Leighs | Voorburg/Kerkehout |
| 889. | 1st | 0507½ | Barnet | NE of Delft |
| 890. | 1st | 0509 | Stapleford Tawney | Wassenaar/Voorburg area |
| 891. | 1st | 0546 | Woolwich | NE of The Hague |
| 892. | 1st | 0732 | Woolwich | Voorburg/Kerkehout area |
| 893. | 1st | 0806½ | Shoreditch | Wassenaar area |
| 894. | 1st | 0823 | Orpington | NE of The Hague |
| 895. | 1st | 1527½ | Walthamstow | The Hague area |
| 896. | 1st | 1610½ | Wickford | Wassenaar/Voorburg area |
| 897. | 1st | 1728 | Horndon on the Hill | NE of The Hague |
| 898. | 1st | 2313 | West Ham | East of Voorburg |
| 899. | 2nd | 0102 | Ashington | The Hague/Loosduinen |
| 900. | 2nd | 0219 | Havering | Monster/Hoorn |
| 901. | 2nd | 0449 | Greenwich | Kerkehout/Voorburg |
| 902. | 2nd | 0452 | Orpington | East of The Hague area |
| 903. | 2nd | 0541 | Chigwell | Monster area |
| 904. | 2nd | 0548 | Chigwell | Wassenaar/Leidschendam |
| 905. | 2nd | 0551 | 1 mile N of North Fambridge | The Hague area |
| 906. | 2nd | 0739 | Herongate | Kerkehout/Leidschendam |
| 907. | 2nd | 0750 | Egypt Bay | East of The Hague |
| 908. | 2nd | 0818 | Off Southend | Rijswijk/Delft |
| 909. | 2nd | 0922 | Brentwood | Possibly The Hague area |
| 910. | 2nd | 1106 | Greenwich | The Hague area |
| 911. | 2nd | 1221½ | Orpington | Leidschendam area |
| 912. | 2nd | 2303½ | Chigwell | Naaldwijk/Maasdijk area |
| 913. | 2nd | 2311 | Bermondsey | NE of The Hague |

| 914. | 2nd | 2315½ | Woking | The Hague/Delft area |
|---|---|---|---|---|
| 915. | 3rd | 0114 | Foulness Island | Voorburg area |
| 916. | 3rd | 0232 | Edmonton | East of The Hague |
| 917. | 3rd | 0335 | Theydon Bois | Poeldijk/Naaldwijk area |
| 918. | 3rd | 0347 | Woolwich & Sidcup area, air burst | The Hague area |
| 919. | 3rd | 0439 | Woolwich, air burst | Wassenaar area |
| 920. | 3rd | 0449 | Sevenoaks | Waalsdorperlaan area |
| 921. | 3rd | 0601 | Ilford | Hook of Holland area |
| 922. | 3rd | 0614½ | In sea, off Clacton | The Hague |
| 923. | 3rd | 1217½ | Deptford | The Hague |
| 924. | 4th | 0135 | Havering atte Bower | Monster/Naaldwijk area |
| 925. | 4th | 0452 | Penshurst | The Hague area |
| 926. | 4th | 0538 | Bermondsey, air burst | The Hague area |
| 927. | 4th | 0820 | Chingford | Wassenaar/Voorburg area |
| 928. | 4th | 0908 | Mouth of The Thames | The Hague area |

*10th Week*

| 929. | 5th | 2007 | Woolwich | 1½ miles west of Waalsdorperlaan |
|---|---|---|---|---|
| 930. | 5th | 2232 | Rainham | Waalsdorperlaan |
| 931. | 6th | 0057 | Bexley | Waalsdorperlaan |
| 932. | 6th | 0307 | Rainham | East of The Hook |
| 933. | 6th | 0309½ | West Ham | The Hague |
| 934. | 6th | 0435 | Sidcup | Wassenaar/Voorburg |
| 935. | 6th | 0618½ | Barking | Naaldwijk |
| 936. | 6th | 0835 | Woolwich | The Hague |
| 937. | 6th | 1233 | Bowers Marshes | The Hague |
| 938. | 6th | 1257 | Wandsworth | The Hague |
| 939. | 6th | 1658 | Walthamstow | Waalsdorperlaan, Duindicht |
| 940. | 6th | 1938 | Wandsworth | Waalsdorperlaan |
| 941. | 6th | 1938½ | West Ham | Waalsdorperlaan |
| 942. | 6th | 2144 | Woolwich | Leidschendam |
| 943. | 6th | 2324 | Ilford | The Hook |
| 944. | 6th | 2326 | Chigwell | 1 mile SW Waalsdorperlaan |
| 945. | 7th | 0159 | Near Navestock | The Hague |
| 946. | 7th | 0313 | Stanford Rivers | The Hook/Buiten |
| 947. | 7th | 0320 | Deptford | Leidschendam |
| 948. | 7th | 0603 | Edmonton | The Hague/Zorgvleit |
| 949. | 7th | 0837 | Greenwich | The Hague/Zorgvleit |
| 950. | 7th | 1033 | Sidcup area | East side of Afvoet Canal |
| 951. | 7th | 1257 | Poplar | Kerkehout/Rijswijk |

| | | | | |
|---|---|---|---|---|
| 952. | 7th | 1455 | Brundish (Norfolk) | NE of The Hague |
| 953. | 7th | 1700 | Waltham Holy Cross | The Hague/Duindigt |
| 954. | 7th | 2159½ | Ilford | Monster area |
| 955. | 7th | 2332 | Dagenham | The Hague/Houtrust |
| 956. | 8th | 0049 | Chigwell | Monster area |
| 957. | 8th | 0137½ | Woolwich | NE of The Hague |
| 958. | 8th | 0152 | Woolwich | The Hague/Duindigt racetrack |
| 959. | 8th | 0324 | Writtle | The Hook |
| 960. | 8th | 0421 | 12 miles ESE of Clacton | Ganzenhoek/Langenhorst |
| 961. | 8th | 0436½ | St. Mary Cray | NE of The Hague |
| 962. | 8th | 0504 | Ilford | The Hague |
| 963. | 8th | 0912 | West Ham | Wassenaar/Leidschendam |
| 964. | 8th | 1102½ | Finsbury | Ganzenhoek/Langenhorst |
| 965. | 8th | 1206 | Blackheath | Probably The Hague |
| 966. | 8th | 1455 | Sidcup | Zorgvliet |
| 967. | 8th | 1953 | Horton Kirby | East Hague |
| 968. | 8th | 2017 | Dunton | The Hague/Loosduinen |
| 969. | 8th | 2146 | Bennington | NE of The Hague |
| 970. | 8th | 2151½ | Harold Park | The Hook |
| 971. | 8th | 2303 | Off Canvey Island | The Hague/Scheveningen |
| 972. | 9th | 0040 | Kenton | 's-Gravenzande |
| 973. | 9th | 0218½ | Marden | The Hague |
| 974. | 9th | 0406 | Pitsea | Waalsdorperlaan |
| 975. | 9th | 0427 | Greenwich | Waalsdorperlaan |
| 976. | 9th | 0829 | Greenwich | South of The Hague |
| 977. | 9th | 0838 | 3 miles SSW of Southend | Monster area |
| 978. | 9th | 1106 | In The Thames | Probably The Hague area |
| 979. | 9th | 1351 | Waltham Holy Cross | Zorgvliet |
| 980. | 9th | 2259 | South Ockenden | East of The Hook |
| 981. | 10th | 0001 | Beckenham | North of Duindicht |
| 982. | 10th | 0016½ | Biggin Hill | The Hague |
| 983. | 10th | 0126½ | Pilgrims Hatch | The Hook/Monster |
| 984. | 10th | 0150 | Enfield | The Hague/Houtrust |
| 985. | 10th | 0422 | 1 mile SSW of Rawreth | The Hague/Houtrust |
| 986. | 10th | 0957 | West Mill | The Hague/Houtrust |
| 987. | 10th | 1001 | Bexley | The Hague/Houtrust |
| 988. | 11th | 0709 | Near mouth of River Crouch | The Hague/Houtrust |
| 989. | 11th | 0740 | West Ham | South of The Hague/ Houtrust |
| 990. | 11th | 1002 | Westerham | North of The Hague |
| 991. | 11th | 2004 | Deptford | North of The Hague |

| | | | | |
|---|---|---|---|---|
| 992. | 11th | 2040 | Canvey Island | Hook of Holland |
| 993. | 11th | 2151 | Bulphan | The Hague/Duindigt |

*11th week*

| | | | | |
|---|---|---|---|---|
| 994. | 12th | 0011 | Ilford | The Hague/Duindigt |
| 995. | 12th | 0026 | Upminster | The Hague/Duindigt |
| 996. | 12th | 0129 | Greensted | s-Gravenzande |
| 997. | 12th | 0205 | 6-7 miles SE of Clacton | The Hague/Haagsche Bosch |
| 998. | 12th | 0233½ | Sidcup | South of The Hague |
| 999. | 12th | 0240 | Sidcup | Haagsche Bosch |
| 1000. | 12th | 0445 | Little Warley | Westvliet |
| 1001. | 12th | 0447 | Hainault Forest | Hook of Holland |
| 1002. | 12th | 0505 | NW of Hornchurch | The Hague area |
| 1003. | 12th | 0701 | Woolwich | Duindigt area |
| 1004. | 12th | 0718 | Althorne | Duindigt area |
| 1005. | 12th | 0903 | Thames Estuary | The Hague/Zorvgliet |
| 1006. | 12th | 1117 | Lower Kirby | Bloemdaal |
| 1007. | 12th | 2119½ | Epping | Hook of Holland |
| 1008. | 12th | 2346 | Nazeing | Hook of Holland |
| 1009. | 13th | 0327 | Tillingham Marshes | Hook of Holland |
| 1010. | 13th | 0629 | 1¾ miles NE of Brentwood | The Hague |
| 1011. | 13th | 0830½ | Erith | The Hague/Zorgvliet |
| 1012. | 14th | 0039 | Havering | Hook of Holland |
| 1013. | 14th | 2122 | Rainham | Monster area |
| 1014. | 14th | 2327 | Sutton at Hone | The Hague area |
| 1015. | 15th | 0016 | Near Erith, in Thames | Hook of Holland |
| 1016. | 15th | 0101 | Beckenham | The Hague area |
| 1017. | 15th | 0242 | Dagenham, in Thames | The Hague area |
| 1018. | 15th | 0333 | Woolwich, in Thames | Monster area |
| 1019. | 15th | 0624 | Rayleigh | South of Haagsche Bosch |
| 1020. | 15th | 0911 | Richmond | South of The Hague |
| 1021. | 15th | 1327 | Tottenham | The Hague/Houtrust |
| 1022. | 15th | 2226½ | Hornchurch | Hook of Holland |
| 1023. | 15th | 2257 | Neasden | S of The Hague/Houtrust |
| 1024. | 15th | 2345 | Near Maldon | The Hague/Houtrust |
| 1025. | 16th | 0234 | Willesden | NE of The Hague/Houtrust |
| 1026. | 16th | 0254 | In sea, 15-20 miles N of North Foreland | E of The Hague/Houtrust |
| 1027. | 16th | 0634 | Leyton | The Hague/Haagsche Bosch |

| | | | | |
|---|---|---|---|---|
| 1028. | 16th | 0651 | Stock | The Hague |
| 1029. | 16th | 0853 | East Ham | The Hague / W of Zorgvliet |
| 1030. | 16th | 0937½ | Dengie | The Hague / Zorgvliet |
| 1031. | 16th | 2306 | Basildon | The Hague |
| 1032. | 17th | 0009½ | 3 miles South of Upminster | The Hague / Haagsche Bosch |
| 1033. | 17th | 0055 | Near Hornchurch | Hook of Holland |
| 1034. | 17th | 0334½ | Wennington Marshes | Hook of Holland |
| 1035. | 17th | 0516 | Hampstead | The Hague / Haagsche Bosch |
| 1036. | 17th | 0736½ | Dartford | NE of The Hague |
| 1037. | 17th | 0811 | Woolwich | The Hague / Westbroek Park |
| 1038. | 17th | 1245 | Greenwich | The Hague / Zorgvliet |
| 1039. | 17th | 1320 | Stepney | S of The Hague / Houtrust |
| 1040. | 17th | 2226½ | Barking | Monster area |
| 1041. | 18th | 0038½ | West Ham | The Hague / Westbroek Area |
| 1042. | 18th | 0133½ | Cranham | 's-Gravenzande |
| 1043. | 18th | 0141½ | Battlesbridge | North of The Hague |
| 1044. | 18th | 0203 | Epping | The Hague area |
| 1045. | 18th | 0340 | Ightham | N of the Hook of Holland |
| 1046. | 18th | 0630 | Aylesford | NE of The Hague / Zorgvliet |
| 1047. | 18th | 0640½ | Hutton | Haagsche Bosch |
| 1048. | 18th | 0646½ | Barking | The Hague / Zorgvliet |
| 1049. | 18th | 0934 | Marble Arch | North of Loosduinen |

*12th Week*

| | | | | |
|---|---|---|---|---|
| 1050. | 19th | 0004 | Theydon Garnon (Epping) | Haagsche Bosch |
| 1051. | 19th | 0006 | 2 miles South of Harlow | Groot Hazebroek |
| 1052. | 19th | 0133 | South Hornchurch | The Hague / Houtrust |
| 1053. | 19th | 0137 | Nutfield | Central Hague |
| 1054. | 19th | 1008 | Wargrave (Off Map) | Scheveningen |
| 1055. | 19th | 1031 | Erith | Probably The Hague |
| 1056. | 19th | 1555 | Woolwich | Northern Hague |
| 1057. | 19th | 2220½ | Theydon Bois | South of Hook of Holland |
| 1058. | 19th | 2245½ | Hatfield Broad Oak | The Hague / Haagsche Bosch |
| 1059. | 20th | 0128 | Little Warley | The Hague / Haagsche Bosch |

| | | | | |
|---|---|---|---|---|
| 1060. | 20th | 0410 | West Hanningfield | The Hague/Haagsche Bosch |
| 1061. | 20th | 0537 | Hornchurch | The Hague/Zorgvliet |
| 1062. | 20th | 0703 | Parslow Common | The Hague |
| 1063. | 20th | 0820 | Sidcup | The Hague/Zorgvliet |
| 1064. | 20th | 0953 | Mayland | N of The Hague/ Loosduinen |
| 1065. | 21st | 0040 | Wanstead/Woodford | The Hague/Zorgvliet |
| 1066. | 21st | 0936 | Heston & Isleworth | The Hague/West Broek Park |
| 1067. | 21st | 1139 | Hampstead | SW of The Hague |
| 1068. | 21st | 1343½ | Ruislip | The Hague/Zorgvliet |
| 1069. | 21st | 1844 | NE Romford | The Hague/Zorgvliet |
| 1070. | 21st | 2133 | 6 miles NW Braintree | The Hague/Marlot |
| 1071. | 21st | 2240 | Woodham Ferrers | The Hague/Haagsche Bosch |
| 1072. | 21st | 2355 | 4 miles E Bishop's Stortford | The Hague/Haagsche Bosch |
| 1073. | 22nd | 0206 | Off Blackwater River | The Hague/Houtrust |
| 1074. | 22nd | 0236½ | Near Carnewdon | The Hague/Haagsche Bosch |
| 1075. | 22nd | 0243½ | Epping, Fairfield | The Hague/Houtrust |
| 1076. | 22nd | 0335 | Harrow | The Hague/Houtrust |
| 1077. | 22nd | 0357 | Hoo, near Strood | N of Haagsche Bosch |
| 1078. | 22nd | 0522 | Stock | Hook of Holland |
| 1079. | 22nd | 0547 | Boreham, NNE Chelmsford | N of The Hague |
| 1080. | 22nd | 0602 | Leyton | The Hague/Haagsche Bosch |
| 1081. | 22nd | 0702 | Brightlingsea | S of Duinguit |
| 1082. | 22nd | 0744 | 5 miles off Bradwell | The Hague/Zorgvliet |
| 1083. | 22nd | 0813 | Dagenham | The Hague/Zorgvliet |
| 1084. | 22nd | 0952 | South Woodham | The Hague/Zorgvliet |
| 1085. | 22nd | 1030 | Dagenham | N of The Hague |
| 1086. | 22nd | 2145 | 20 miles SE Yarmouth (Off Map) | N of Haagsche Bosch |
| 1087. | 22nd | 2321 | Dartford | Hook of Holland |
| 1088. | 22nd | 2342 | Southminster | NW of Haagsche Bosch |
| 1089. | 23rd | 0140 | Greenwich | The Hague/Haagsche Bosch |
| 1090. | 23rd | 0315 | Off Clacton | The Hague/Houtrust |
| 1091. | 23rd | 0430 | Stepney | N of Monster |
| 1092. | 23rd | 0626 | North Weald | The Hague |
| 1093. | 23rd | 0649 | Little Gaddesden | Northern Hague |

| | | | | |
|---|---|---|---|---|
| 1094. | 23rd | 0941 | West of Althorne | The Hague / Zorgvliet |
| 1095. | 23rd | 1232 | Stapleford | The Hague / Houtrust |
| 1096. | 23rd | 2316½ | Waltham Holy Cross | The Hague / Zorgvliet |
| 1097. | 24th | 0131 | Poplar | The Hague / Haagsche Bosch |
| 1098. | 25th | 2233½ | St. Pancras | The Hague / Alexanderveld |
| 1099. | 25th | 2300 | Enfield | The Hague / Haagsche Bosch |
| 1100. | 25th | 2344 | Stepney | The Hague / Bosches van Poot |

*13th Week*

| | | | | |
|---|---|---|---|---|
| 1101 | 26th | 0005 | Lambourne | Hook of Holland |
| 1102 | 26th | 0404 | Cheshunt | The Hague / Houtrust |
| 1103. | 26th | 0420½ | Bermondsey | The Hague / Haagsche Bosch |
| 1104. | 26th | 0442 | Hornchurch | Hook of Holland |
| 1105. | 26th | 0903½ | Navestock | The Hague / Zorgvliet |
| 1106. | 26th | 1443½ | Ilford | The Hague / Houtrust |
| 1107. | 26th | 1522 | Bromley | The Hague / Houtrust |
| 1108. | 26th | 1908 | Romford | The Hague / Zorgvliet |
| 1109. | 26th | 2230½ | Noak Hill | The Hague / Haagsche Bosch |
| 1110. | 27th | 0022 | Edmonton | The Hague / Haagsche Bosch |
| 1111. | 27th | 0302 | Cheshunt | The Hague / Houtrust |
| 1112. | 27th | 0330½ | Ilford | Haagsche Bosch |
| 1113. | 27th | 0404 | Hutton Park | The Hague / Haagsche Bosch |
| 1114. | 27th | 0721 | Stepney | The Hague / Haagsche Bosch |
| 1115. | 27th | 1654 | Orpington | The Hague / Zorgvliet |

# Notes and Sources

1    In conversation with the Senior Narrator, Air Historical Branch, Generalfeld Marschal Milch has stated that the flying bomb was conceived in February 1942. He also said that he knew nothing about the rocket and was not interested in it. It is known, however, that the A.4 rocket is based on rockets made in the early thirties by the Berlin Cosmonautical Society whose principal engineers were absorbed into the research organisation of the German Army between 1932 and 1934 (Air Ministry Weekly Intelligence Summary, No.293, 14th April 1945).

2    This was an important argument that was used in 1943 against those who attempted to discredit the evidence in favour of the rocket, on the grounds that the Germans were attempting an elaborate hoax. It was pointed out that no hoax was likely to be so elaborate as to have misled an obviously well-informed agent more than three years before further evidence of development began to accumulate.

3    This was a much more accurate assessment than most that were to be made during the next twelve months. But Dr. Crow was right for the wrong reason, as his estimate was based on the assumption that the Germans were using a more primitive form of propulsion than was actually the case.

4    The same information was available in the Air Intelligence Department of the Air Ministry, where it came within the province of the Assistant Director of Intelligence (Science), Dr. R.V. Jones. He has stated in an interview with the narrator that he did not consider that sufficient was known to warrant informing the operational staff.

5    This was the date on which the Prime Minister gave his approval. It seems fairly clear, however, that the Vice-Chiefs of Staff had at first not visualised this method of a special investigation, though they had obviously not been sure what was the right method to adopt. According to the records of the Chiefs of Staff Committee, the suggestion that they might consider putting the matter in the hands of a single individual came to them from the Secretary of the Committee (C.O.S. (43)189(O)). They approved the suggestion and forwarded the name of Mr. Sandys to the Prime Minister.

6    For his exact terms of reference see Appendix 2.

7    It may be that the Germans considered workers from these countries more tractable than others and therefore more suitable for the highly secret constructions on which they were employed. We received, however, numerous valuable reports, first-hand as well as second-hand, from these men.

8    Even at the lowest figure of 50,000 killed and seriously injured the casualties would be more than five times as big as those of September 1940. The basis on which the Ministry's

calculations rested was an incident at Hendon on the night of 13th February 1941 when a 2,5000 kg. bomb, falling in an area whose population density was 150 to the acre, killed eighty people, seriously injured one hundred and forty-eight and slightly injured three hundred. This original estimate was, however, considerably scaled down before the end of 1943.

9   In reply it was pointed out that certain areas of the Baltic were known to be closed to shipping.

10   The term 'flying bomb' is preferred throughout the narrative to 'pilotless aircraft' though it was not until June 1944 that the former became the official description.

11   The estimate was prepared by A.D.I. (Science) at the Air Ministry and was completed by the end of December 1943. It is compared below with figures complied after operations began in June 1944.

|  | Estimate of Dec. 1943 | Actual |
|---|---|---|
| Operational Range | 120-140 miles | Normally 120-140 miles |
| Speed | 300-400 m.p.h. | Varying up to 400 m.p.h. |
| Warhead | 1-2 tons | Approx. 1 ton |
| Operational Height | Generally about 6,500 ft. but as low as 1,500 ft. | 1,000-4,000 ft. but some very low |
| Control | Magnetic | Magnetic |
| Wing Span | 19-22 feet | 17 ft. 6 ins. |
| Length | 17½ -20 feet | 25 ft. 4½ ins. |
| Root Chord | 4-5½ feet | 4 feet |

12   The reason why Bomber Command were prepared to attack a small and isolated target such as a ski site but not an equally isolated target deep in Germany, such as the Fürstenwalde factory, was that the blind bombing equipment which made the first possible could not be used for the second. "Oboe" entailed special ground stations in the United Kingdom which could only control aircraft up to a limited range, approximately two hundred and fifty miles. 3cm. "H2S", the equipment which Bomber Command thought they might eventually use to attack small and distant targets by night, was carried in the aircraft and could therefore be used anywhere within the range of the aircraft. But it was a less accurate aid than "Oboe"; hence the Command's unwillingness to attack targets such as Fürstenwalde until sufficient aircraft had been fitted with H2S to counterbalance the inherent inaccuracies of the equipment.

13   The resources available in December 1943 were as follows:

|  | No. of Squadrons. | Aircraft. |
|---|---|---|
| 9th Bomber Command | 32 | 288 |
| Light Bombers   } 2nd T.A.F. | 12 | 192 |
| Fighter-Bombers} | 12 | 192 |
|  | 56 | 672 |

14   The Marauders of Ninth Bomber Command were equipped with the Norden Mk. XIV bombsight, with which excellent results had been achieved in the Mediterranean area, where visibility was generally much better than in north-west Europe. The Mitchells of the Tactical Air Force were equipped with the same sight less the computer box, and whatever the conditions could not be expected to achieve such good results as the Marauders.

15   Results were reported in four categories: Category A – concentrated groups of hits in target area with one or more direct hits on essential buildings; Category B – hit within target area near enough to cause probable damage to essential buildings; Category C –

some hits in target area but none near essential buildings; Category D – no hits in target area.

16  This was a curious phrase that gives the impression that the Air C.-in-C., A.E.A.F., – Air Chief Marshal Leigh-Mallory – was the officer responsible for the air defence of the country and that G.O.C.-in-C. Anti-Aircraft Command – General Pile – was his chief consultant. The first was true in the sense that the defensive part of the old Fighter Command, under the name of Air Defence of Great Britain, was one of the forces under the command of Air Chief Marshal Leigh-Mallory who was nominally responsible to the Chiefs of Staff for the air defence of the country. Nevertheless, the operational control of all the air defences of the United Kingdom, including Anti-Aircraft Command, remained the responsibility under Air C.-in-C., A.E.A.F., of the Air Marshal Commanding, A.D.G.B. But even supposing that the latter organisation had not been in being and that Air Chief Marshal Leigh-Mallory had directly controlled the air defences it is rather surprising that he should be instructed to consult the anti-aircraft commander. He would do that as a matter of course but he would do it also as a matter of grace on the part of a commanding officer.

17  It will perhaps assist the reader if he is reminded of the code words for a number of operations, which are used in the narrative where convenient: 'Crossbow' – German long-range attack in general; 'Diver' – attack by flying bombs; "Big Ben" – attack by rockets; 'Overlord' – the operation for the invasion of France.

18  See Appendix 4.

19  At some indeterminable date prior to 6th June this was amended to 192 light guns.

20  The channels whereby the plan was approved are significant of the unusual division of responsibilities for air defence. It was nominally prepared by Air C.-in-C., A.E.A.F. at the "invitation" of the British Chiefs of Staff, and was in fact the work of the Air Marshal Commanding, A.D.G.B. Having been approved by Air Chief Marshal Leigh-Mallory, it was approved in turn by General Eisenhower, the British Chiefs of Staff and, lastly, by the Prime Minister. The Air Ministry appears to have had no status in the matter.

21  General Doolittle succeeded General Eaker in January 1944.

22  Experiments carried out by the Proving Ground Command of the U.S. Army Air Forces at Eglin Field, Florida, during February 1944 indicated that the most satisfactory weapon to employ against ski sites was the 2,000 lb. bomb, which was not confirmed in actual operations. The explanation appears to be that the replicas of ski sites which were constructed for the trails were based on inaccurate specifications. It is clear from the American report that the roofs and walls of the various buildings were constructed of reinforced concrete, which was not the case in the German originals. How this error, which nullified a careful and elaborate experiment, arose is difficult to say. A British report of late December 1943 on the constructional details of the sites (J.I.C. (43) 523 (0) Appendix C) stated emphatically that the walls of the main buildings were not reinforced, and the roofs only lightly reinforced at the side angles. Whether or not the Americans were able to make use of the British note is not known. Their report says only that "plans were obtained from British and American Intelligence officers".

23  This was prepared by the Operational Research Centre at Air Ministry.

24  There was intelligence evidence at the time that this was what the Germans planned; but no more than ninety-six ski sites were built in the area Cherbourg – Pas de Calais.

25  Up to 11th March 1944 it was believed that only six sites had been repaired. Between that date and 8th April twelve were repaired. Progress was maintained and a further eleven had been repaired by the end of the month.

26     It had been laid down in a directive dated 27th March 1944 from the Combined Chiefs of Staff to General Eisenhower that the control of the Allied Air Forces by the latter "would naturally be subject to Intervention …. by the British Chiefs of Staff should their requirements for the security of the British Isles not be fully met."

27     The whole question is very confused. On 3rd May Air Chief Marshal Tedder is recorded as saying at a meeting at which A.E.A.F., Bomber Command and the U.S. Strategical Air Forces were represented that 'Crossbow' targets "should continue to have overriding priority for the present." Yet three days later Lieut.-General Spaatz informed a meeting at which Air Chief Marshal Tedder was present that "Pointblank" was the chief operation of the 8th Air Force to which 'Crossbow' was secondary. Moreover, the arrangements whereby fighters of the 9th Air Force could be called on for "Pointblank" operations, irrespective of their other commitments, were not rescinded until 26th June.

28     The Ministry of Economic Warfare tentatively advanced the estimate that the effort in man-hours required to produce a flying bomb was one-eighth that for a complete fighter aircraft. Air Intelligence no less diffidently suggested a somewhat higher figure, one sixth. Lord Cherwell considered that the proportionate effort would be more like two-fifths.

29     From information which was not received until April 1945 it appears that the first attacks on ski sites in December 1943 had sharply revealed to the Germans how vulnerable was this type of site; and from January 1944 onwards work on designing, and later building a new type of site, smaller than the ski site and more effectively concealed and camouflaged, was pushed forward energetically. (Air Ministry Weekly Intelligence Summary, 19th May 1945).

30     All figures of flying bombs reported by the defences, all those that fell on land and all claims for the various sorts of defence are taken from an analysis carried out by the Air Warfare Analysis Section of Air Ministry during the autumn of 1944 and afterwards.

31     According to the prisoner mentioned above and, independently, Generalfeldmarschall Milch, orders to commence the attack, were given on 10th June, by Hitler himself. Also, according to Milch, those responsible for launching had always estimated that it would take ten days from the receipt of orders to fire, to the beginning of heavy sustained attacks. It was, therefore, reckoned something of a feat to have begun the offensive proper on 15th June.

32     It is interesting that just after midnight the Germans also carried out a long-range artillery bombardment of Folkstone and Maidstone spread over a period of nearly four hours from 0010 hours to 0400 hours. Folkstone received twenty-four rounds and Maidstone, which was not shelled at any other time during the war, received eight. One further shell fell at Otham, two and a half miles south-east of Maidstone.

33     In a minute dated 13th June, Air Commodore Pelly, Chief Intelligence Officer at A.E.A.F. Headquarters, informed Air Chief Marshal Leigh-Mallory: "The Chiefs of Staff are not unduly worried about 'Crossbow'. They do not wish air support to be diverted to it from 'Overlord', but would like A.E.A.F. to do what they reasonably can about it …… The Home Secretary is going to make a fuss at the War Cabinet meeting this evening; but the Chiefs of Staff are determined that you should not be made to divert effort from 'Overlord'."

      The conclusions of the War Cabinet meeting that same day included the following: "He (the Home Secretary) would be grateful if as much effort as could be spared from the battle fronts could be diverted to attacks on the pilotless aircraft sites and their supply sites."

34     The total number launched by the Germans was over two hundred. It is believed that for the whole of the attack from northern France a factor of 25 per cent should be added to

the number reported by the defences to give the approximate total number that the Germans fired against us.

35    The wording of this decision is important in connection with the redeployment of the defences during July..

36    On 18th June, General Eisenhower minuted Air Chief Marshal Tedder as follows: "In order that my desires, expressed verbally at the meeting this morning, may be perfectly clear and of record, with the respect of 'Crossbow' targets, these targets are to take first priority over everything except the urgent requirements of the battle; this priority to obtain until we can be certain that we have definitely gotten the upper hand of this particular menace."

37    During bad weather Liberators of the 8th Air Force, using the 'G-H' technique of radio-aided bombing, accounted for most of the effort of this force against 'Crossbow' targets. This technique allowed blind bombing up to a range of approximately 250 miles from the controlling ground stations. Stations had been erected on the South coast early in 1944 for the particular purpose of controlling attacks against flying bomb sites, and Mitchells of No. 2 Group as well as Liberators had been equipped for purpose. The average bombing accuracy was of the order of 500 yards; and while good results were occasionally achieved, on the whole the technique was not sufficiently accurate for the unseen attack of such small targets as most of the 'Crossbow' sites. Lieut.-General Doolittle held a particularly poor opinion of its effectiveness.

38    It is difficult to see how such an attack could be a contribution to defence against flying bombs except as a mere reprisal. It was in fact only partly carried out. On 21st June the 8th Air Force went to Berlin, but not Bomber Command.

39    They were usually referred to as 'supply depots'. The term 'storage depots' is here preferred in order to avoid any confusion with 'supply site'.

40    It was later reported that only flying bombs with the larger wing span had been positively identified. The earlier confusion most probably arose from the fact that the flying bomb which had fallen in Sweden in May, and which British intelligence officers had had an opportunity to examine, had a wing span of 16 feet. During July it was also established that a proportion of flying bombs was fitted with warheads containing a more powerful explosive filling than the majority.

41    It is fairly well established that most flying bombs started at about 200 m.p.h. and increased in speed throughout their flight, crossing the coast at about 340 m.p.h. and attaining as much as 400 m.p.h. by the time London was reached.

42    These figures were reported on 15th July (C.B.C. (44) 22, Annex) and as such are not fully reliable.

43    What was in fact the German aiming point is still not certain. All the evidence available at the time of writing comes from a prisoner captured in April 1945, who stated that Tower Bridge was the chief aiming point but that there were a dozen others, the exact location of which he could not remember, but which were all centred on Tower Bridge. Even so, the fall of shot was further south than the Germans intended.

44    That the bombing policy which the Deputy Supreme Commander was anxious to pursue was not expressed in any formal directive may be some explanation; but there is good evidence that the commander of the 8th Air Force did much as he wished on some occasions. On 17th August, for example, Air Chief Marshal Tedder asked Lieut.-General Doolittle why the 8th Air Force was only carrying out two light attacks against storage depots that day and was reserving its main effort for the attack on some thirteen bridges. Lieut.-General Doolittle said that he thought the latter were the more important targets;

to which the Deputy Supreme Commander replied that 'Crossbow' must come first. The Historical Officer at A.E.A.F. Headquarters, who attended this and all other important meetings, has commented: "This is a symptom of General Doolittle's reluctance to bomb targets outside Germany, or to bomb targets that he has not chosen himself". There was never such a marked clash on the question of 'Crossbow' targets between Air Chief Marshal Harris and Air Chief Marshal Tedder. But the former held the same view as Lieut.-General Doolittle, namely, that the only effective answer to the flying bomb, as indeed to every aspect of the German war effort, was to shatter the economy of Germany and deny the enemy the means of making war. Thus, both officers were unsympathetic to any policy that diverted their forces from the main objective, the attack of German industry.

45   A signal despatched by the commandant of St. Leu d'Esserent on the morning after the attack of 7th July stated that all roads and approaches to the depot were completely destroyed; there were many subsidences over the underground workings; and the presence of many delayed-action bombs made it too dangerous for work to be continued, although much of the plant had not been affected. This document was captured in the autumn of 1944.

46   The first was at the Royal Military Chapel, Wellington Barracks, which was hit and demolished at twenty minutes past eleven on Sunday morning, 18th June, whilst a service was in progress. 121 people were killed and 68 seriously injured, including 58 civilians killed and 20 seriously injured. The second was at Turks Row, Chelsea, at 0747 hours on 3rd July, when 64 soldiers, mostly Americans, were killed and fifty seriously injured. In addition, 10 civilians were killed.

47   The Germans appear to have made up their minds before the attack about the best height, speed and range for the bombs to be despatched; and there were no major alterations in these respects throughout the attack from the sites in northern France. What seems to have been their consistently short shooting may indicate that no modifications to increase the range of the bomb was practicable at the time; on the other hand, it may be that they knew very little about the fall of shot in London.

On this latter point it is noteworthy that early in the attack it was discovered that the collation of the obituary notices published in 'The Times' and 'Daily Telegraph' of people who had been killed by "enemy action" gave a mean point of impact that corresponded closely to the true one. Accordingly, in July, newspaper editors were given instructions that denied this potential source of intelligence to the enemy. And it has in fact emerged since May 1945 that the Germans were attempting to exploit information of this sort. A map attached to a G.A.F. Intelligence Report of late July 1944 (A.I. 12/E. 1430) shows 75 plots of the fall of flying bombs in the London area obtained from obituary notices in 'The Times' and 'Daily Telegraph', the period covered being 21st June – 6th July. The mean point of impact of the plots is at Brixton Church, only one and a half miles west of the true M.P.I. for the same period. The same report includes another map giving 63 plots obtained from German intelligence sources in England. The M.P.I. of these is just east of Waterloo Bridge, about four miles N.N.W. of the true position. Obituary notices were, therefore, a more reliable guide to the fall of shot than the report of agents; but the Germans appear not to have realised it.

British counter-Intelligence at this time was in fact attempting to conceal the true M.P.I. by 'feeding' to German sources plots of the fall of bombs which together would give an M.P.I. in central London, north of the true position and where the Germans doubtless hoped it would be. These measures appear to have been very effective.

[48] Token barrages were retained at London, Plymouth, Southampton, Portsmouth, Dover and the Thames, containing 169 balloons compared to 531 before the 'Diver' deployment.

[49] One effect of this was to necessitate the redeployment of a number of L.A.A. units.

[50] e.g. on 26th/27th June, out of 670 balloons that could have been flown, only 271 were flown, and these for only two hours of the twenty-four. On the following day half of the available balloons flew for six hours. On the 28th/29th, 320 balloons flew for seven hours. Altogether, the barrage was grounded for approximately one-third of the period 15th June- 15th July; when in action, an average of 742 balloons, out of an average operational strength of 852 balloons, were flown.

[51] In an interview with the narrator Air Marshal Hill said that on 20th June he began to carry out flying bomb patrols himself, partly so that he could better appreciate the practical difficulties, but partly also to improve the team spirit of the common enterprise. He carried out 62 patrols, using each type of single-seater fighter, with the exception of the Meteor, that was being employed in the battle.

[52] This was quite unavoidable in the circumstances; and it only added to the difficulties of the defences when requests came in that fighters should take care not to shoot down bombs on a stated property, however important that property might be. Where the chances of this could be reduced by making some alteration in the static defences, A.D.G.B. Headquarters did their best to oblige, and small adjustments were made, particularly to the balloon barrage. But to ask pilots travelling at up to 400 m.p.h., and intent on their quarry, to pay scrupulous regard to the landscape below them, was to ask too much.

[53] Cf. a signal from the G.O.C., No. 2 A.A. Group to all his units: "As from 17th July it has been arranged that there will be practically no restrictions of fire in the 'Diver' Belt ..........The fighter will enter the gun belt at his peril. This concession has not been won without considerable misgivings on the part of the R.A.F., in consequence of which the obligation has been placed in us to bring down the flying bombs in numbers sufficient to more than cover those which have fallen to the fighters as a result of chases over the gun belt."

[54] The steps that were taken between 10th and 13th July preliminary to this decision have little or no official record. What happened, however, has been established through the co-operation of Air Marshal Hill, Sir Robert Watson-Watt and Air Vice-Marshal G.H. Ambler, Deputy Senior Air Staff Officer at A.D.G.B. Headquarters at the time. After the decision of the 10th to give the guns freedom of action in their inland positions even when fighters were operating, Air Marshal Hill instructed Air Vice-Marshal Ambler to prepare an explanation of the intention behind the move for the benefit of subordinate formations of A.D.G.B. Air Vice-Marshal Ambler was not convinced that the decision was well made, and decided to prepare a full appreciation of the situation. In his own words, "In order to keep my reasoning impartial, I prepared this appreciation strictly in accordance with the recommended method contained in the War Manual." It was finished during the night of 12th July and showed, in Air Vice-Marshal Ambler's view, that to maintain the guns inland, south of London, was wrong; they ought to be redeployed on the coast, which implied action diametrically opposed to that decided upon three days earlier. However, Sir Robert Watson-Watt had also been studying the problem and had independently arrived at the same conclusion as Air Vice-Marshal Ambler; and on the morning of 13th July he arrived at A.D.G.B. Headquarters at a most opportune time to confirm the plan that Air Vice-Marshal Ambler, who had so far consulted nobody, had formulated.

The two men immediately put the case to Air Marshal Hill and the Senior Air Staff Officer, Air Vice-Marshal W.B. Callaway, who were convinced by it. The next step was to consult General Pile. Sir Robert Watson-Watt therefore walked over to the neighbouring Anti-Aircraft Command Headquarters and returned "within half an hour" with the information that General Pile was in entire agreement with the proposed redeployment. The actual decision was taken by Air Marshal Hill at a conference held at 5.30 p.m. the same day.

Air Vice-Marshal Ambler's appreciation was still in draft form but had now served its purpose. However, for record purposes he had a number of copies typed on the 14th (see Appendix 8).

55    i.e. the Chief of Staff Committee.

56    Air Marshal Hill was, in fact, not only convinced that the new plan offered the only hope of materially increasing the success of the defences but that if he waited for Air Ministry approval it might be a matter of days, if not weeks, before he could move. That there would certainly have been some delay is clear enough from the debate that actually took place on the wisdom as well as the propriety of the decision.

57    See minute, A.C.A.S. (Ops.) – C.A.S., 17th July, in A.D. of Ops. (S.C.) 104/5, and also Conclusion (c) of the Chiefs of Staff Meeting of 18th July: "Agreed that the constitutional responsibility of the Air Ministry for the Air Defence of Great Britain, and the responsibility of the Chiefs of Staff Committee for advising the Government on the military aspects of defence measures, remained unchanged by any of the special machinery set up to deal with 'Crossbow'."

58    This was a belief widely held by ordinary people, whose views were reflected in a minute, dated 13th July, from Mr. Churchill to the Secretary of State for Air, in which he asked why it was that such a small weight in flying bombs caused damage that seemed to be eight to ten times greater than that caused by an equal tonnage of British bombs on a German city. The answer of the experts was that this was simply untrue: that far from being more effective the flying bomb was markedly inferior to a British bomb containing a comparable weight of high explosive.

59    Eight storage depots were known or suspected at the time, but five were temporarily not listed for attack either because of damage already inflicted or because of insufficient evidence that they were yet in full use. The three selected were Rilly la Montagne, St. Leu d'Esserent and Bois de Cassan.

60    In order of priority, these were:

| | |
|---|---|
| Ober Raderach | Hydrogen Peroxide Plant |
| Peenemünde and Zinnowitz | Hydrogen Peroxide Plant and Experimental Station |
| Rheinfelden | Hydrogen Peroxide Plant |
| Düsseldorf | Hydrogen Peroxide Plant |
| Hollriegelskreuth | Hydrogen Peroxide Plant |
| Klausthal | Hydrogen Peroxide Plant and Explosive Factory |
| Fallersleben | Hydrogen Peroxide Plant and Assembly Factory |

61    One attack, that is, against a German target known, or strongly suspected, to be a 'Crossbow' target. The Opel motor works at Rüsselsheim was also attacked, on 20th July by the 8th Air Force. But this was not listed as a 'Crossbow' target until early in August.

62    Evidence had been accumulating that there was a storage depot in the Forêt de Nieppe, fifteen miles south-east of St. Omer, and, as we have seen, it was heavily attacked during

the week 2nd-9th August. But there was not the same concrete evidence as in the case of the depots in the Oise valley that it was used for flying bomb storage; and in fact, it was proved later to have been used only for rocket storage. There was also evidence that the Germans had organised, for the whole of the belt of modified sites, a chain of supply points, intermediate to the storage depots and the sites, which could perhaps serve as alternative, though less capacious, storage depots to the main depots such as St. Leu d'Esserent and Rilly la Montagne. By the beginning of August, thirteen such points had been identified between Rouen and St. Omer, all of them in or near the launching site area; they were underground and had rail facilities. They continued to be studied, and on 17th August it was reported that the work was still going on at some of them, but that on the whole, evidence pointed to their use as storage depots for rockets rather than flying bombs, though this did not mean that the latter could not be stored there. On 26th August nine were recommended for attack as rocket targets.

63 The airfields were at Venlo, Gilze Rijon, Brussels-Melsbroke, Le Culot, Eindhoven, Soesterberg and Deelen.

64 The exact figures were 786 compared to 356.

65 About the middle of August an attempt was made in the Deputy Directorate of Science at the Air Ministry to express graphically the effect of the bombing of launching sites on the scale of enemy activity. The results indicated that the average activity in any zone where a number of sites had been destroyed, fell within four days to 18 per cent of that previously achieved. No firm conclusions could be drawn, however, as in no single zone of the launching site organisation had all the sites been attacked; and only if this had been done could the value of this type of attack have been measured with any accuracy.

66 A similar assessment was also attempted for the bombing of storage depots. In this case, the officers of the Directorate were more certain of the validity of their conclusions, which were that after 1,000 tons of bombs had been dropped on a depot the scale of attack decreased for a week until it reached about half that obtaining before the bombing. Thereafter it increased steadily.

67 It involved the laying of no less than 3,000 miles of cable for inter-battery lines alone. 30,000 tons of stores and 30,000 tons of heavy gun ammunition were also moved into the coastal belt. In the first week of the move the vehicles of Anti-Aircraft Command travelled 2¾ million miles.

68 Some 1,250 sites were reconnoitred, which represented the maximum number of balloons that Balloon Command could have flown in addition to the 1,750 already deployed in the main barrage south of the river.

69 By this time the main barrage was absorbing all supplies of L.Z. balloons and the extension could only be supplied with MK.VI balloons, which were less robust and were flown from lighter cables than the L.Z. type.

70 General Pile's aim was not to reinforce the gun belt at this stage but to provide reliefs for the overworked batteries that had been in action there since the beginning of the attack. He wanted also to provide against the replacement for the twelve batteries of 21st Army group which were deployed in the belt, but which were liable to be withdrawn at short notice. In addition, he was shortly to lose ten mixed H.A.A. batteries, which were to be disbanded owing to the shortage of A.T.S.

71 Excluding guns of less than 40 mm. calibre.

72 During July the possibility of using radar-equipped naval ships as fighter control stations was examined, the advantage being that they could, in theory, detect a flying bomb earlier than a coastal radar station. The Admiralty were unable to provide a suitable ship,

however, until after the main attack on London was over. During August other measures were introduced to assist interception over the sea. A chain of buoys was moored fifteen miles out to sea, with an interval of six miles between each buoy, to warn pilots when they were approaching the gun belt and also help them pinpoint their position; at night, six slowly revolving searchlight beams served the same purpose. Also, during daylight, white rockets were fired from launches patrolling in the Le Treport – Dungeness – Dover – Calais area, to mark the passage of flying bombs.

[73]   27 per cent of the targets presented to fighters overland during the period 17th July-15th August, were destroyed, compared to 34 per cent over the much larger patrol area that was available to fighters in the first five weeks of the attack. It should not be forgotten, however, that those shot down over the sea represented clear victories, whereas many of the bombs destroyed overland frequently caused damage and casualties in the districts south and south-east of London.

[74]   These were Nos. 422 and 425 U.S.A.A.F. Squadrons, which were armed with the P.61A ("Black Widow") fighter. They carried out regular patrols, usually four a night, from 16th July-10th August.

[75]   The success of the four squadrons was almost entirely due to their specialisation in night patrols, and in particular to the skill of their pilots in overcoming the difficulty of estimating range at night. Various methods were tried at various times. Aircraft occasionally patrolled in pairs  so that the pilot of one could fly to one side of the bomb, estimate the range between it and the other aircraft, which would be flying behind the bomb and pass the information by R/T. 'Monica' radar, a set used by Bomber Command to give warnings of the approach of hostile night fighters, was also used by a few Mosquitos to give range. Better known still – or at any rate, more publicised – was Sir Thomas Merton's Grating Range Finder, which did not, however, come into service, and then only in small numbers, until the last fortnight of the attack.

[76]   This was most unsatisfactory, and soon after the formation of the Joint Crossbow Committee an attempt was made to remedy the position, despite the lack of accurate information, by a new method of approach. At the beginning of August, the list of 'Crossbow' industrial targets was divided into two parts. The first of these, 'A' targets, contained only factories which were known to be engaged on the assembly of flying bombs or rockets, or on the manufacture of an essential component, such as the gyro unit, provided that in the latter case the whole system of production of the particular component could be identified by intelligence. The list of 'A' targets was very limited, and most of the suspected factories went into the 'B' list, for which the criterion was either that they should have some connection with 'Crossbow' and also be of general importance to the German war potential (such as the Opel works at Rüsselsheim), or that they should have an important secondary connexion with 'Crossbow' production. Factories on the 'A' list merited attack on high priority; the remainder were assigned to the bomber forces to fill out missions in particular areas. Nine factories were at one time or another placed on the 'A' list. Of these four were attacked – Fallersleben, Peenemünde, Ober Raderach and Weimar. The second and third were attacked as hydrogen peroxide plants, the fourth solely in connection with rocket production. Altogether nineteen factories were included in the 'B' list, of which only one, the Opel works at Rüsselsheim was attacked.

[77]   Air Marshal Hill, in conversation with the narrator, has said that the difference in 'atmosphere' prior to and after the redeployment was remarkable. The recriminations which had been an unhappy feature of the earlier period largely disappeared.

[78]  At the daily conference at A.E.A.F. Headquarters on 15th August Air Chief Marshal Tedder directed the 8th Air Force to attack 'Crossbow' targets on the following day. At the next day's conference, however, General Doolittle announced that his forces were that day attacking industrial targets in the Leipzig area; and when Air Chief Marshal Tedder asked why, in view of his instructions, 'Crossbow' targets were not being attacked, he returned the question-begging answer that there were none in the Leipzig area. It was too late to alter the programme for the day, but it was agreed that on the 17th the 8th would attack 'Crossbow' targets and fuel dumps in northern France and Belgium. Weather on the 17th forbad the plan; but it was carried out on the 18th to the extent that the 8th dropped 100 tons on two airfields in France and Holland which were being used by flying bomb launching aircraft and 88 tons on the fuel depot at Pacy-sur-Armançon. In addition, they dropped nearly thirteen hundred tons of bombs on railway bridges in Belgium, airfields in eastern France and an aircraft factory at Weippy near Metz.

[79]  Our intelligence also knew by the third week in August that in the middle of July the Germans had been considering a new programme of site construction. Sixty to seventy new sites were to be built between the Seine and St. Omer and a second firing regiment was to be formed to operate them. This plan was modified (probably early in August), confining construction to the area north of the Somme. It was never carried out (C.O.S. (44) 750 (O)).

[80]  The attack was primarily planned not so much against flying bombs as to hasten the disintegration of the retreating German armies in northern France. Nevertheless, first priority for air support was claimed for it on the grounds that it was a 'Crossbow' counter-measure.

[81]  On the night of 1st/2nd September two composite aircraft (Me.109/Ju.88) operated over the North Sea. In one case the explosive filled Ju.88 fell at Hothfield in Kent, in the other at Warsop in Nottinghamshire. No casualties were caused and only slight damage.

[82]  The heavy and 40mm. guns were manned by the following formations:

| Belt | | Heavy Guns | 40 mm. Guns |
| --- | --- | --- | --- |
| Anti-Aircraft Command | | 448 | 478 |
| U.S. Army | | 80 | - |
| 21st Army Group | | 48 | 216 |
| R.A. Training Establishments | 16 | 36 | |
| R.A.F. Regiment | | - | 192 |
| Box | | | |
| Anti-Aircraft Command | | 136 | 78 |
| 21st Army Group | | 72 | - |
| R.A.F. Regiment | | - | 100 |

These numbers fell slightly during the rest of the month. The mobile 3.7″ guns of 21st Army Group were withdrawn between 20th and 27th August for employment in Europe. The light guns of the R.A.F. Regiment were also largely withdrawn from the coastal belt towards the end of August. None of these guns, however, were equipped with the latest types of fire-control instruments, and the barrage was little affected by their withdrawal.

[83]  It is noteworthy that when the question of giving the guns complete freedom of action had been under discussion in July, the scientific staff of Anti-Aircraft Command had calculated that the guns should succeed in shooting down 60 per cent of the bombs that entered the barrage.

[84]  This was the number of squadrons that Air Marshal Hill had intimated on 22nd August his willingness to release in order to provide escort for daylight attacks by Bomber

Command against oil targets in the Ruhr. (A.E.A.F. Cdrs. Conferences, Mtg. 22nd August 1944).

[85] He could not carry much, for the good reason that he had to cycle two hundred miles from the Blizna area to the landing ground where he was picked up. This landing ground was in German hands by day, but was taken over by the partisans at night. The Dakota became bogged and only got off the ground at the fifth attempt. It was typical of the rigid discipline of the Polish movement that to the mortification of the Intelligence officers in this country who were eagerly awaiting his arrival the Polish leader refused to divulge any information until he had reported to his Polish superior in London.

[86] A.C.A.S. (1) informed the Chiefs of Staff on 28th April that Blizna was under suspicion. They were also kept fully informed of the constructional advances at the large sites.

[87] Professor Ellis actually arrived at this conclusion by hypothesis – one of the few instances where the scientific approach arrived at exactly the same result as Intelligence.

[88] This was putting the position at its worst. The report of A.D.I. (Science) (C.B.C. (44)24) on which Mr. Morrison based this figure, said, "the warhead is probably between 3 and 7 tons". Moreover, this was not an estimate for which A.D.I. (Science) who had compiled the report reluctantly, had much evidence. In general, A.D.I. (Science) was unwilling to transmit information that might be made the basis for elaborate counter-measures until he was reasonably sure that it was well-founded. To the criticism that information might not be discovered until it was too late for effective counter-measures to be planned, he could, in the particular instance of the rocket, reply that in fact the rocket was not the menace it was made out to be, and that unnecessary alarm was caused by requiring Air Intelligence to provide, before evidence was sufficiently conclusive, estimates of explosive capacity that proved to be exaggerated.

[89] The discussion is recorded in the Secretary's Standard File of War Cabinet Conclusions.

[90] "As long ago as 22nd February I warned the House that Hitler was preparing to attack this country by new methods, and it is quite possible that attempts will be made with long range rockets containing a heavier explosive charge than the flying bomb, and intended to produce a great deal more mischief. London, we may expect, will be the primary target on account of the probable inaccuracy of the new weapon. We therefore advise the classes for whom evacuation facilities have been provided by the Government, and others with no war duties here who can make their own arrangements, to take the opportunity of leaving the capital in a timely, orderly and gradual manner. It is by no means certain that the enemy has solved the difficult technical problems connected with the aiming of the rockets, but nonetheless I do not wish to minimise the ordeal to which we may be subjected, except to say that I am sure it is not one we will not be able to bear." (Hansard, vol. 402, 2nd August, 1944, col. 477-8).

[91] This was much less than what had been feared from a thousand rockets with 7-ton warheads, but it would have been far from negligible. It represented some 80 tons of high explosive compared to a daily average of 48 tons during the worst weeks of flying bomb attacks.

[92] Wizernes and perhaps Watten, were the only ones that were connected with A.4 rockets; but this was not learned until the autumn of 1944.

[93] These special projects were controlled by the American 8th Air Force. The intention was to attack the sites with war-worn aircraft filled with explosives or jellied gasoline. A crew of two took the aircraft off the ground, the automatic pilot was set and the explosives armed and the crew then baled out. An accompanying aircraft specially equipped, took over control, guided the aircraft to the target and attempted to bring it down on the site.

all told, seven attempts were made against the four sites between 4th and 12th August; six times the load consisted of 11 tons of nitro-starch, once of 4,000 gallons of jellied gasoline. On three occasions pilotless aircraft – Fortresses – were brought near the target; and once one was crashed within half a mile of the site at Siracourt. On the other occasions, either control difficulties developed and the aircraft had to be dumped in the Channel, or the aircraft exploded in mid-air, killing the crew. The experiments, therefore, failed to do any damage to the sites. But much was learned from them and eventually the technique was used successfully against Heligoland.

[94] On 11th July the Chiefs of Staff approached the Prime Minister to ask for his personal intervention with Stalin to safeguard what might be found at Blizna when it was occupied. On 22nd July Stalin gave his approval and a mission of technical experts who were chosen from the Ministry of Supply, the War Office and the Air Ministry was despatched. The mission reached Teheran on the last day of July; but there it was held up and it was not until 11th August that it left for Moscow. Fighting in the Blizna area was still going on and the mission was not allowed to proceed there until 3rd September. They stayed in the area nearly three weeks and brought back some useful information, most of it confirming what had been learned from the Swedish rocket.

[95] There were twelve in all.

[96] There was a slight difference of emphasis between the view taken by A.D.I. (Science) in his report of 27th August and that of Mr. Sandys' committee in a report of 28th August. The former concluded that the Germans would be driven by the Allied advance to launch the rocket as soon as they could; whereas Mr. Sandys concluded that the advance, the bombing of storage depots, and transport difficulties, might well force the enemy to abandon their plans for bombardment. The difference is insignificant and would hardly be worth noting except that it appears to have been the cause for the withdrawal, at Mr. Sandys' request, of the report of A.D.I. (Science). (C.O.S. (44) 290th Meeting, 29th August 1944).

[97] That part of Holland and Belgium west of a line Texel – Amsterdam – Tilburg – Antwerp – Terneuzen was placed on the photographic reconnaissance programme on 1st September. By 16th September 95 per cent of the area had been covered, mostly in the week following the first rocket attacks.

[98] So far, it has not been established whether these were the only rockets fired against London on 8th September. Two were also fired against Paris on the morning of the 8th, of which one fell in the city: they were fired from a point on the Houffalize – St. Vith road. The battery responsible was transferred to Holland the next day for the attack of London. These were not the first A-4 rockets to be fired by the Germans against an enemy. According to a well-informed prisoner, a number were fired against Leningrad in 1943 at a range of just over 100 miles. Many of them burst in the air prematurely, a fault which had not been entirely overcome before the attack on London began. The Russian government never informed the western Allies of the attacks: probably they were unaware that the weapon was being used. (A.D.I.K. 364/1945).

[99] The Directorate of Operations (Special Operations), which had been specially formed for controlling and co-ordinating 'Crossbow' counter-measures and intelligence, was abolished in October and a proportion of its staff transferred to the Directorate of Operations (Air Defence) for 'Crossbow' duties.

[100] Nos. 214 and 223 Squadrons were maintaining almost continuous patrols over the launching areas at this time and were jamming suspicious signals. No. 192 Squadron was also patrolling purely to listen for suspicious signals.

101   Precisely how many flying bombs were launched against England from the air during the main attack is difficult to say. It was probably about four hundred.

102   This Gruppe was known to Air Intelligence at the time as III/K.G.3. The unit appears to have been renumbered about this time, however, to I/K.G.53 – 'Legion Kondor'.

103   A number of captured German documents give the total German effort over much of this period. They show that between 21st October and 10th/11th November 865 flying bombs were launched against Brussels and Antwerp, 733 against Antwerp.

They also show that 1176 flying bombs were launched against London by aircraft of I/K.G.53 between 7th/8th July and 10th/11th November. This is a far higher number than that reported by the British defence, which was 514. Part of the discrepancy can be explained by the difficulty of distinguishing between air-launched bombs and those fired from sites, a difficulty which applied between 8th July and 2nd September. But it is also clear that a good proportion of air-launched bombs failed to reach England. One German document gives the night by night launchings over the period 28th/29th October to 10th/11th November as 201 flying bombs. But only 120 of them came near enough to the coast to be reported, which represents a failure of forty per cent. Assuming a similar percentage of failures for the whole period 21st October to 25th November the Germans then launched about 425 bombs against London compared to well over twice that number against Antwerp.

On the same assumption, about 780 flying bombs were air-launched against London between 16th September and 25th November and about four hundred during the main attack from northern France in June – September.

The German documents also record an attack on Paris on the night of 1st/2nd September with twenty-three air-launched flying bombs. So far as is known, none of these fell anywhere near the target.

104   Hydrous Calcium Sulphate, from which Plaster of Paris is made.

105   A list of the most serious rocket incidents is given at Appendix 15.

106   Bombing sorties were mostly flown by Spitfire XVI aircraft; occasionally the Spitfire XIV and Spitfire IX were employed. Each type usually carried two 250 lb. bombs in wing racks and a jettisonable petrol tank under the fuselage to increase its range. This bomb load was eventually increased on occasion by 1 x 500 lb. bomb when arrangements were made for aircraft operating from the United Kingdom to refuel in Belgium.

107   At the end of January 1945, the positions of 105 light anti-aircraft guns and 44 heavy had been identified in the area Hook of Holland – Leiden.

108   The weekly casualty figures of the Ministry of Home Security which are used throughout the narrative actually relate to the period 3rd January – 15th February.

109   There is no record from German sources of the total number of flying bombs launched from the air after 11th November 1944. The number of launching failures is not likely to have been less than before that date, when it was approximately forty per cent. This factor should be added, therefore, to the number of bombs reported by the defences between 11th November and 14th January to arrive at approximately the total number launched.

110   It fell at Hornsey at 0213 hours on the morning of the 14th.

111   According to the Anti-Aircraft Command historian, permission to deploy was not granted "in spite of repeated requests."

112   This reasoning was not unopposed. According to the officer in charge at this time of Intelligence 3F at Fighter Command, the section responsible for the recommending of targets, officers of the Allied Central Interpretation Unit at Medmenham, which was responsible for the study of reconnaissance photographs, protested against the continued

attack of the Haagsche Bosch on the grounds that photographs showed no rockets there after 24th February.

[113] The details, which are interesting as indicative of how a public warning system would have worked with the equipment available at the time, were as follows:

| No. of incidents in UK. | No. of incidents in London. | Warnings given. | False warnings. | Incidents in London without warning. |
|---|---|---|---|---|
| 243 | 123 | 228 | 8 | 3 |

[114] It should again be noted that the number of flying bombs reported by the defences is smaller than that launched by the Germans. No precise figure for the latter is available at the time of writing but the addition of a factor of twenty-five per cent to the number reported gives a figure that is unlikely to be far from the truth.

[115] Leiden main station is flanked on one side by a hospital and on the other by houses.

[116] General Pile cited the unaccountable inconsistency between a British analysis which proved that the surface temperature of the rocket reached 1200° C and the fact that an unexploded rocket which had fallen in England had a warhead casing covered in paint which showed no signs of scorching. There was also no satisfactory explanation of how it happened that a number of rockets exploded in the air.

[117] The crossing of the Rhine at Remagen by the U.S. Army was the occasion for the most accurate rocket firing of which there is any record. Between dawn on 17th March and on the 18th eleven rockets fell in the bridgehead, seven within five miles of the bridge. If one wild shot is excluded, the mean point of impact was less than two miles due west of the bridge.

[118] Instances have occurred of bombs falling very close to, or even on, the site of a previous incident, but with a considerable time interval.

[119] Organisation peculiar to London Region: the equivalent would be 1 or 2 rescue parties.